GOGOL

A Life

by

DAVID
MAGARSHACK

GROVE PRESS, INC.

New York

CONTENTS

INTRODUCTORY

It is difficult to convey Gogol's unique position in Russian life and literature to anyone outside Russia. 'You can have no idea what this immense and cruel loss means to us,' Turgenev wrote shortly after Gogol's death on the 21st of February 1852 (O.S.), to his friends in France. 'Gogol was more than a writer to us: he revealed us to ourselves. . . . Perhaps my words, written under the stress of grief, will strike you as exaggerated. But you don't know him; you only know the less significant of his works; but even if you knew them all, you would find it difficult to understand what he meant to us. One has to be a Russian to feel it. Even the most acute minds among the foreigners saw Gogol only as a humorist in the English manner. They failed to see his historic significance. I repeat, one has to be a Russian to realize what we have lost.'

Vissarion Belinsky, the great Russian critic, proclaimed Gogol to be one of the leading Russian writers of the day as soon as he appeared on the Russian literary scene. A characteristic feature of Gogol's genius, Belinsky declared, was that no one could be indifferent to it. 'Gogol', he wrote, 'was either passionately loved or bitterly hated.' What struck Belinsky as well as many other Russian contemporary critics, who did not share Belinsky's radical views, was that everything in Gogol's writings was simple and ordinary, natural and true, and yet at the same time new and original. 'In Gogol's works,' Belinsky wrote, 'fidelity to nature is the result of his great creative powers and shows his deep insight into the essence of life, his unerring tact and all-embracing feeling for reality.'

Gogol's influence during the ten short years of his literary activity was so great that, according to Belinsky, 'it killed two spurious movements in Russian literature: affected and stilted idealism, waving a cardboard sword about like some painted actor, and—later—satiric didacticism.' Unlike Pushkin, who saw in Gogol's writings only a merciless exposure of the gross vulgarity of Russian life, Belinsky was struck by the remarkable

13

ability of his genius to penetrate into the very heart and soul of the ordinary events of life. 'By his nature,' Belinsky wrote, 'Gogol is not inclined to idealize life. Any kind of idealization seems an abstraction and not real life to him; in real life good and evil, triviality and greatness are to him not separate entities but human qualities that are evenly divided. What he excels in portraying is not trivial man but man in general, man as he is, plain and unvarnished.' And in his famous letter to Gogol, in which he condemned Gogol's ill-conceived attempt in his *Selected Passages from Correspondence with my Friends* to turn Russia into a happy and contented land of masters and slaves, Belinsky none the less described Gogol as 'the great writer who by his profoundly true works has helped Russia to regain her awareness of herself by providing her with the opportunity of looking at herself as in a mirror'.

Nikolai Chernyshevsky, a critic no less opposed to Gogol's reactionary views than Belinsky, likewise claimed Gogol to be 'incomparably the most significant Russian writer'.

Alexander Herzen summed up Gogol's achievement in a single phrase: 'Has anyone', he wrote, 'raised higher than he the pillory to which he nailed Russian life?'

Russian critics have always laid great stress on the 'denunciatory' character of Gogol's writings. Gogol himself is more often than not regarded as the not altogether willing founder of a school of writers whose chief aim was to expose the vices and abuses of the autocratic régime of the Tsars. But at the beginning of the present century a scholarly critic like N. A. Kotlyarevsky could survey Gogol's influence on Russian life in a more dispassionate spirit. He made no bones about Gogol's political views. Unlike Chernyshevsky, who declared that the trouble with Gogol was that he read the wrong kind of books, or the modern Russian critics, who contend that it was Gogol's aristocratic friends who were responsible for his reactionary views, Kotlyarevsky points out that Gogol had always been a die-hard conservative. 'Gogol', he declares, 'never wished for a better régime for Russia than the one under which he lived: a firmly based autocracy, recognized by everyone, established by God and placed above all the authorities in the land, subject to no control and all-powerful so far as human conditions are concerned; an orthodox faith, jealous and placed under the special protection of God; noblemen—the Tsar's lieutenants, the heads of their numerous serf families, their instructors in matters of religion and duty to their Tsar and their country; finally, the lower orders, who because of their Slav nature were God-fearing, loyal, good-natured and quick-witted, realizing that all power came from God and meekly satisfied with their lot as tillers of the soil—these were the basic principles of the social and political faith in which Gogol believed from the days of his childhood and which he never renounced. . . . It is obvious', Kotlyarevsky goes on, 'that all those who were dissatisfied with the way of life which made such characters as those which appeared in Gogol's works possible, could find support for their beliefs in such a novel as *Dead Souls*, and its author had unwillingly to reconcile himself to the fact that the admirers of his genius had gone much further than he in their condemnation of the negative aspects of Russian life and proposed remedies for them other than those in which he believed. For Gogol', Kotlyarevsky emphasizes, 'was the only writer for his time: no one's eye penetrated more deeply into the hidden depths of Russian life, no one was able to make his characters so typical and, if in evaluating a work of art, we are to regard as of primary importance the ability of its writer to reveal the hidden springs of contemporary life, to show the general trend of the thoughts, feelings, aspirations and habits not only of one particular person, but of whole groups of people of which the entire social organism is composed —if this ability is to be prized above everything else in a writer, then the history of the Russian realistic novel undoubtedly starts with Gogol, in whose works the truth of life corresponds entirely to the truth of creative art.'

But it was not Gogol's ability 'to reveal the hidden springs of life', nor his ability, as Turgenev put it, to reveal the Russians to themselves, nor what another Russian critic called 'the destructive power of his laughter' that explains his unique influence upon his contemporaries. It was his style, his manner of writing, the way in which he created his remarkable gallery of human types rather than the fact of their creation that was finally instrumental in destroying the respect of the Russian people for their rulers. In his monograph on *How Gogol Worked* the well-known Russian writer, Vikenty Veresayev, draws this interesting comparison between Gogol's style and the style of the other great Russian writers of the nineteenth century: 'The literary style,' he writes, 'the remoteness from living speech is one of the greatest faults as well as the greatest tragedy of our writers. Leo Tolstoy dreamed in his old age of "translating his works into the Russian language". An unprepared reader has to get used to the language of Pushkin, Tyutchev, Turgenev, Dostoevsky and Chekhov. Only Gogol, whose knowledge of Russian was poorer than that of any of them, was able to become accessible to the uneducated man without lowering the supreme qualities of his creative work. In this respect', Veresayev concludes, 'Gogol is the most democratic of our writers.'

It is, indeed, this direct impact on the 'uneducated man' that made Gogol into such a powerful social force in Russia. He alone seemed to possess the secret of insinuating himself into the minds of his readers and, as Ogaryov, the revolutionary poet and Herzen's closest friend, put it, 'irrevocably undermining' the Russian people's respect for the Tsarist government. V. Rozanov, a conservative critic generally hostile to Gogol, summed up this aspect of Gogol's influence in an even more striking manner. 'The heart of the matter', he wrote, 'and the main point about Gogol's "advent into Russia" is that Russia was, or at least appeared to be, a "monumental", "majestic" and "great" power; yet Gogol walked over these real or imaginary "monuments" with his thin, weak feet and crushed them all, so that not a trace of them remained.'

This extraordinary power of a creative artist to bring about what amounted to a revolution in the minds of his countrymen becomes even more extraordinary when one considers that it was wielded by an entirely unknown man, the son of an obscure and comparatively poor Ukrainian landowner, a man whose social position, at a time when good birth and wealth meant everything, was utterly insignificant. What sort of man, then, was Gogol? What strange destiny brought him out of his obscurity and hurled him into the great world of art? What was the nature of the influence he exercised over the literary worlds of Moscow and Petersburg? What is the explanation of his firm belief in his 'mission' to reform mankind? And why did his life end so tragically? At school he was nicknamed 'the mysterious dwarf' and an air of mystery clung to him all through his life. It is perhaps only now, over a hundred years after his death, that a careful study of all the available material of his life may provide a solution to this fascinating literary and human problem.

Part One

THE MYSTERIOUS DWARF

¶ I

There was a blot on Gogol's escutcheon. Ostap Gogol, one of his ancestors in the seventeenth century, a colonel of a Cossack regiment, is known to have served under the Polish King Jan Casimir and to have adopted the Catholic faith, though later on he is said to have recanted and returned to the bosom of the true Orthodox Church. He was rewarded for his services to the Polish king with an estate in the Kiev province. Gogol's great-grandfather, Jan Gogol, acquired the Gogol family estate in Poltava province, named Janovshchina after him and afterwards renamed Vassilevka after Gogol's father Vassily. Gogol's grandfather Afanasy, in his petition to the authorities to be put on the noblemen's register, claimed that his ancestors 'by the name of Gogol were of Polish nationality'. To Gogol this undeniable link with the Polish nation and the Catholic Church was extremely distasteful and, indeed, though inordinately proud of being a nobleman, he was never very anxious to discuss his ancestry. Shortly after his arrival in Petersburg he dropped his Polish-sounding name of Janovsky (his family was known as Gogol-Janovsky) on the pretext that he did not know where it came from and that 'the Poles invented it'.

Vassily Gogol, who like his father had received his education in a divinity school, was a fairly successful farmer. His estate comprised about three thousand acres and he owned a total of three hundred and eighty-four serfs. His distillery (every Ukrainian landowner seems to have owned a distillery as well as one or two public houses) brought him in a few thousand roubles a year. The fair he started in Vassilevka was another source of income. It took place four times a year and undoubtedly supplied Gogol with a great deal of local colour for his Ukrainian tales. Vassily seems to have been a very mild, good-natured person. His health had always been rather delicate and he was subject to fits of black melancholy which Gogol inherited from him. At the age of twenty-five he fell violently in love with a thirteen-year-old girl, Maria Ivanovna Kosyarovsky, the daughter of a neighbouring landowner, and he conducted his courtship in accordance with the best precepts of the sentimental school which was then in vogue. 'My darling Masha,' he wrote to Maria Ivanovna, 'many obstacles have deprived me of the happiness of visiting you today. The feebleness of my health conjures up all sorts of dreadful visions in my mind and fierce despair lacerates my soul. I assure you that no one in the world can love anyone so much as your unhappy Vassily, your ever faithful friend, loves and respects you. Please do not show these unhappy outpourings of passion to your parents.' The young girl, however, did not dare to read her lover's letters, but always handed them to her father who would open them with a solemnity appropriate to the occasion and then read them aloud to the whole family. But letter-writing did not satisfy the love-sick young wooer. 'Every time I went for a walk with some village girls along the bank of the river Psyol,' Maria Ivanovna recalled many years later, 'I would hear beautiful music coming from across the river. It was not difficult to guess who was playing it, and the music followed me all the way home.' After their wedding the bride, being only a girl of fourteen, returned to her father's house, but six months later her husband claimed her. During the fourteen years of their married life they had twelve children, of whom only five survived. Gogol was their third child, the first two having died soon after birth. Maria Ivanovna, who was only eighteen when Gogol was born, had offered up special prayers before the wonder-working icon of Saint Nicholas in the nearby village of Dikanka, promising to name her child Nikolai if it should be a boy. She took the further precaution of having it delivered by a well-known doctor in Sorochintsy, where Gogol was born on the 19th of March 1809 (O.S.). He was christened on May the 9th, his patron saint's day.

Maria Ivanovna was, according to her biographer, a deeply religious woman who was particularly fond of the ritual side of the Greek Orthodox faith. She believed in premonitions and dreams. 'Sometimes', she wrote in one of her letters to a relative, 'I am overcome by gloomy thoughts. I have premonitions of disaster and I believe in dreams.' Her simple faith expressed itself best in what Gogol called her favourite Pangloss system: 'Everything is for the best in the best of all possible worlds.' When one of her daughters fell ill, she wrote to a relative: 'My darling Masha was terribly ill and you can't imagine what I felt at the time, but God arranges everything for the best, sometimes to make us more than ever aware of His mercy.' And in another letter she wrote: 'Remember that God never abandons those who put their trust in Him, and I am absolutely certain that He will help me in my present straits and sooner or later set my mind at rest, or else it is necessary that I should be constantly worried here so that He shall reward me in my future life. And what greater happiness can one expect!' Gogol himself, in a letter to his school friend Alexander Danilevsky, on the 29th of December 1839, rather wryly summed up his mother's character in these words: 'You know that my mother looks but does not see, that she does things she never intended doing and, thinking of her children's happiness, makes them unhappy and then puts the whole blame on God, saying that it was God's will that this should happen.'

Vassily Gogol's influence on his son was very slight, although he undoubtedly possessed some literary gifts. He was a facile versifier (he even used to write some of his letters in verse) and was the author of two Ukrainian comedies, *The Simpleton* and *Dog-Sheep*, written in a light, jocular vein which was very popular at the time, with a comic devil, a deacon in a long coat, and a sly country wench as its chief characters. He produced his comedies at Kibintsy, the estate of a local magnate, Dmitry Troshchinsky, a distant relative of his, whose general factotum he had been after retiring from the civil service (he had a job at the Poltava post office). He and his wife acted in several plays he had produced at the Troshchinsky country house. He was also a great gardener (Gogol undoubtedly got his love for gardening from him). He liked to build little grottoes and summer-houses in his garden and give poetic names to every avenue in it. A clearing in the little wood near his house he named 'The Vale of Peace'. He would not allow anyone to make a noise near the large pond in the garden for fear of frightening away the nightingales. He was essentially a sociable person, which Gogol never was. He knew how to amuse and entertain his guests and was consequently a very popular figure in the neighbourhood. He was too busy with his own and other people's affairs to pay much attention to his son. He died at the early age of forty-five when Gogol was only a boy of sixteen.

It was his mother who exerted the greatest influence on Gogol during his childhood. She pampered him as a child and was mainly responsible for his becoming a capricious egoist. It was his mother's naïve piety that sowed the first seeds of his fanatical faith, and it was she who instilled in him the fear of the devil and hell-fire. We have Gogol's own testimony for the source of his religious feelings which, dormant during the creative years of his life, came to the surface with irresistible force whenever his creative powers began to weaken. He went through such a period at the very beginning of his literary career in the autumn of 1833. And it was on October the 2nd of that year that he wrote a furious letter to his mother with instructions on how to bring up his little sister Olga to be a religious woman by describing to her 'in the colours that are most pleasing to children' the delights that await the righteous in the after-life' and 'the terrible and cruel agonies' that await the sinners. In this letter Gogol gives a remarkable picture of his own religious education. 'I remember very well how I was educated,' he wrote. 'You did your best to give me the best possible education but, unfortunately, parents are very rarely good educators of their children. You were still very young then. It was your first experience of children and you could not be expected to know how to deal with them. I remember: I never felt anything strongly, I looked upon everything as on something that had been created for my pleasure. I did not love anyone in particular, except only you, and even then only because nature had breathed that feeling into me. I looked upon everything with indifferent eyes; I went to church because I was told to, or was taken there, but as I stood there I saw nothing except the chasuble of the priest, and heard nothing except the horrible howling of the deacon. I crossed myself because I saw that everyone was crossing himself. Only once—I remember this occasion very clearly—I asked you to tell me about the Last Judgement, and you told me, a child, so well, so intelligibly, so movingly about the bliss that awaits the people who lead virtuous lives, and you described so strikingly the eternal sufferings of sinners that it awakened all my sensibilities and afterwards aroused in me the most lofty thoughts.'

These 'lofty thoughts' aroused in him by his primitive fear of the devil and hell-fire were, fourteen years later, to be the cause of the greatest literary failure of his career, and were eventually to bring about his utter ruin.

This letter to his mother, written at a time of great mental distress, is remarkable also for a different reason. For it reveals an important aspect of his physical and mental make-up that has puzzled all his biographers. This aspect of his character concerns his attitude to women. In his letter he implored his mother to keep his sister Olga away from the serf-girls' room. As in all big or small country houses of Russian landowners, the serf-girls were usually kept in a special room where they did all sorts of housework for their mistress. The moral tone of this room was never very high, and it is obvious from the disgust with which Gogol speaks of his mother's serf-girls that his aversion to them was based on something more personal than his disapproval of their morals. Indeed, Gogol most probably had his first experience of sex with his mother's serf-girls. 'My morals here', he wrote to his mother from Petersburg, 'are incomparably purer than at home.' This experience must have filled him with a horror that was physical rather than moral. For Gogol realized even as a boy that he was, as he afterwards admitted, 'different' from others. 'As far as I am concerned', he wrote to his mother from Nezhin on the 10th of June 1825, that is, when he was only sixteen, 'I shall accomplish my task in this world, and if I cannot do so quite as any other man, I shall at least try to be like any other man.' What this difference was he never really understood. But there can be no doubt that it was in his attitude to women, in his physical aversion to them, that this difference lay. He admitted as much shortly before his death to his doctor, whom he told that he had never felt any need for intercourse with women, nor had he derived any particular pleasure from it.

¶ 2

Gogol was a very weak and delicate baby and for several weeks it was uncertain whether he would live. It was not until six weeks after his birth that it was considered safe to take him home to

Vassilevka. He never was a healthy child. He suffered from scrofula, an illness which afflicted all his brothers and sisters and which left him a little deaf in one ear. He was a precocious child. 'When he was three years old', his mother records, 'and had not yet begun to learn anything, his father would point out the different countries in an atlas, and he memorized each of them so well from the different colours that when asked to show them a short time later, he could name them all without mistake. We were surprised at his memory, then we gave him cards with the letters of the alphabet, and before he was five he would write out words with chalk on the table and put them together into sentences, so that we stopped paying any attention to it. It never occurred to us to find out what he was doing at the table, but when the late Vassily Vassilyevich Kapnist [author of the famous satiric play *Slander* and a neighbour of the Gogols] paid us a visit, he saw my five-year-old son bending over the table and writing something on a piece of paper. He took the paper from him and saw that my son was trying to write some poetry. He then told us that we ought to place him in the hands of a good teacher.'

Gogol's education was at first entrusted to a divinity student. In 1819, at the age of ten, he with his younger brother Ivan was sent to a school in Poltava, where they lived at the house of one of the schoolteachers. A few of Gogol's letters from Poltava have been preserved. They are not remarkable in any way, except, perhaps, as showing that Gogol was never a particularly keen scholar. Here is one of his letters from Poltava, written in the summer of 1820, in the formal and conventional style in which he always wrote home:

Dearest parents, I am very glad to hear that you are both well. I consider it my first duty and pleasure to pray to God to preserve your health which is so precious to me. The holidays are rapidly approaching, and I haven't yet had time to finish everything. I shall therefore have to work hard during my holidays to pass with honours into the second form. I badly need a teacher of mathematics. [Gogol was never good at mathematics.] If you come to Poltava soon I'm sure you will settle everything in the best possible way for me. Kissing your precious hands, I have the honour to be, with my deepest filial respect, your obedient son,

NIKOLAI GOGOL-JANOVSKY.

Gogol did not stay in Poltava long. During the holidays his younger brother fell ill and died. A year later, Gogol was placed in the newly-founded public school at Nezhin, about two hundred miles from Vassilevka, where he spent the next seven years from May 1821, to June 1828.

Gogol joined the public school at Nezhin as a paying scholar and after the first year he continued on a State scholarship which he seems to have obtained thanks to Troshchinsky's influence. Danilevsky, who had followed him from the Poltava school to the Nezhin high school, described him as 'a sickly child. His face', he declared, 'seemed to be transparent. He suffered from scrofula and there was a discharge from his ears.' His Latin master Ivan Kulzhinsky described him as 'a fair-haired boy in a grey cotton tunic [the uniform of the lower classes of the school]. He was always silent, as though hiding something in his soul, with an indolent look and a shuffling way of walking.'

Even as a boy Gogol was round-shouldered and near-sighted. The most characteristic feature of his face was his long, thin nose. 'My nose,' he was to describe it later in the album of one of his women friends, 'is most decidedly bird-like, pointed and long. However, in spite of its ridiculous appearance, it is a good beast: it has never been known to turn up, it has never sneezed to please my superiors or the authorities—in short, in spite of its excessive size, it has behaved itself with great moderation, for which, no doubt, it has got the reputation of a liberal.'

He was proud ('My pride', he confessed later in a letter to a friend, 'grew with me from my cradle'), secretive, insolent to his teachers, most of whom he despised, and contemptuous of the pedantic atmosphere that reigned in the school. 'I taught him for three years', Kulzhinsky records, 'and he learnt nothing except to translate the first paragraph from the Latin primer: *Universus mundus plerumque distribitur in duas partes, coelum et terram*, for which he was nicknamed "*universus mundus*". During his lessons Gogol always used to keep some book under his desk and paid no attention either to *coelum* or *terram*. It must be admitted that he learnt nothing either from me or from my colleagues. . . . Gogol was known at school as a lazy, though apparently not ungifted boy, who did not take the trouble even to learn how to spell.'

On the 1st of March 1828, a few months before leaving school, Gogol wrote to his mother that what really surprised him was that

23

he had learnt as much as he had at that 'stupid institution'. 'If I know something', he declared, 'I owe it entirely to myself.' As for his life at school, 'hardly anyone', he wrote in the same letter, 'has endured so much ingratitude, injustice, icy contempt, etc. I put up with it all without protest, and no one has heard any complaints from me. . . . Indeed, everyone regards me as an enigma; no one has found out what I am really like. At home I am considered to be wilful, a kind of intolerable pedant who thinks that he is cleverer than anybody else, that he is made differently from other people. . . . At school they call me a meek fellow, the ideal of simplicity and patience. In one place I am quiet, modest, polite, in another—sullen, dreamy, uncouth, and so on, in a third —loquacious and tiresome to the extreme; some think I am clever, others that I am stupid. Think what you like of me, but it is only from my true career that you will find out my true character. . . .'

Gogol's record at school shows that he could hardly have been considered meek, simple or patient. 'At school', he wrote to the poet Zhukovsky on the 10th of January 1848, 'I occasionally felt a disposition to merriment and annoyed my classmates by my ill-timed jokes. But those were only passing fits. Mostly, I was rather melancholy and given to meditation.' He was indeed well known for his childish, spiteful pranks and for his ability to make up biting epigrams upon his schoolmates and teachers.

In discussing the rumours spread about Chichikov by the provincial ladies in the ninth chapter of Dead Souls, Gogol gives this description of one of these pranks, known among the schoolchildren as 'the hussar'.

'Their position was at first similar to that of the schoolboy who woke to find that his classmates, who had risen earlier, had stuffed a *hussar*—a piece of paper filled with snuff—into his nose while he was asleep. Having inhaled the snuff with all the force of a sleeping person, he wakes up, jumps out of bed, looks round him like a fool with his eyes popping out of his head, and cannot understand where he is or what has happened to him, and only afterwards becomes aware of the room lit up by the oblique rays of the sun, of the laughter of his classmates hiding in the corners of the dormitory, and of the dawn peeping through the windows, with the awakened woods resounding with the songs of thousands of birds, and the flashing stream, twisting and turning among the thin rushes, covered densely with naked boys calling to their friends to come for a swim, and only then at last realizes that there is a *hussar* in his nose.'

In spite of his almost pathological reserve, Gogol soon made a number of friends, some of whom remained his closest friends during the rest of his life. 'I love my old friends more than ever,' he wrote to one of them in 1847, 'especially those whose friendship with me began from the days of the unforgettable Nezhin.' One of his closest friends at school was Gerasim Vysotsky. 'From the very first days of our life at school', Gogol wrote to Vysotsky, who had already obtained a post in one of the government departments in Petersburg, on the 17th of January 1827, 'we understood each other, and the stupidities of people brought us together, and together we derided them.' Vysotsky, like Gogol, had the utmost contempt for his teachers and he was particularly good at inventing sarcastic nicknames for them and his schoolmates. He suffered from some eye ailment and spent most of his time at the school sanatorium, which became a sort of club for some of the boys. He usually sat there all day long under an umbrella. He and Gogol had much in common, but Vysotsky was older and much more authoritative. Once Gogol, to escape punishment, pretended to be mad. His face, one of his school friends recalls, became distorted, his eyes blazed savagely, his hair seemed to stand on end, he gnashed his teeth, foamed at the mouth, threw himself down on the floor and began to smash the furniture. The headmaster was sent for. He approached Gogol cautiously and touched him on the shoulder, but Gogol seized a chair and drove him to cover. Gogol was eventually seized by the four school porters, who took him to the sanatorium where he spent two months in the company of Vysotsky, his attacks of simulated madness returning every time he had a visit from the school doctor.

Besides Vysotsky and Danilevsky, his closest friends at school were Nikolai Prokopovich, who was later to become the editor of the first collected edition of his works, and Konstantin Bazili, a native of Athens, whose family had fled from Greece after the Turkish massacre of the Greeks in 1821, and who was later to accompany Gogol on his journey to Jerusalem. Nestor Kukolnik, who was to become famous for his patriotic novel and pseudo-classical dramas, was closely associated with Gogol in editing several school magazines, though Gogol never really liked him and later nicknamed him 'the lofty one'. About his attitude to his schoolmates, Gogol left the following characteristic confession in a letter to Maria Balabin, a former pupil of his in Petersburg. 'When I was a boy at school,' he wrote from Rome on the 7th of November 1838, 'I was very vain; I wanted desperately to know what my schoolfellows thought of me. I could not help feeling that what they said to me was not what they thought of me. So I used to pick a quarrel with a schoolfriend who, in his anger, naturally told me everything that was bad about me. That was all I wanted: having found out all about myself, I was perfectly satisfied.'

But although Gogol learnt very little at school, his French and German being as bad as his Latin, and his mathematics even worse, he showed a great interest in contemporary Russian literature, and copied out all the latest poems, especially those by Pushkin. His letters home, too, are filled with requests to send him the Petersburg literary magazines. At the age of fourteen he became keenly interested in the theatre, and took an active part in all the school theatricals. His letters home are full of requests for plays, costumes and all sorts of props, including linen for the scenery. 'The first play we are performing', he wrote home on the 22nd of January 1824 (O.S.), 'is *Œdipus in Athens*, a tragedy by Ozerov. . . . I shall let you know how I perform my part.' He then added this characteristic note: 'I have just learnt of the death of Vassily Kapnist [the playwright], but you never told me anything about it, just as if I were still a child, and as if you could not rely on me for anything. I think, dear Father, that if you saw me now you would surely say that I have changed, both as regards my morals and my progress at school. If you could only see how well I have got on with my painting! (I can say this about myself without vanity.)'

He was so elated by his success as an actor (he was particularly good in women's parts) that in September of the same year he asked his father to give him a part in the play he usually produced at Kibintsy at Christmas. 'Be sure', he wrote, 'that I shall perform it very well.' But his father's illness prevented him from going home that Christmas, and in April of the next year his father died. 'Do not worry, dearest mother,' he wrote on the 23rd of April 1825 (O.S.), on receiving the news of his father's death, 'I have borne the blow with the steadfastness of a true Christian.

At first, it is true, I was terribly distressed by the news, but I did not let anyone see how grieved I was. When left alone, however, I gave way completely to insane despair. I even wanted to take my life, but God restrained me in time; and in the evening I was only aware of a feeling of sadness, which was in the end transformed into a slight and hardly perceptible feeling of melancholy, mixed with a feeling of reverence for the Almighty. I bless thee, holy faith! It is only in thee that I find consolation and an alleviation of my grief. And so, dearest mother, I am calm now, though I cannot be happy having lost the best of fathers, the truest friend, everything that was precious to my heart. . . . But I have you and I am not as yet crushed by fate. . . . To you I shall devote all my life. . . .' This not altogether genuine effusion was followed by a matter-of-fact postscript: 'If it is not too much trouble, and if you can possibly do so, please send me ten roubles for a book—the history of Russian literature. . . .'

Next day, in another letter to his mother, Gogol for the first time mentioned the fact that he had been doing some writing of his own. 'I had in mind', he wrote, 'to send father some of my writings as well as some pictures I had painted, but he did not seem interested. I don't know whether to send them to you, for you may not accept favourably these first fruits of your parental solicitude for me. . . .'

Gogol's juvenile writings, most of which have been lost, appeared in the school magazines which, Bazili records, 'our literary circle began to issue (in manuscript, of course) in 1825, 1826 and 1827. Together with Gogol, though not always without quarrels or fights, for both of us were quick-tempered, I published a monthly magazine of about fifty pages in a yellow cover with vignettes of our own design. It contained stories, criticisms of the best contemporary literary works, as well as topical articles in which Gogol mostly made fun of our teachers under fictitious names. . . . On Sundays our circle, consisting of about twenty boys, met to read and discuss our contributions.'

At one of these meetings Gogol's first prose work, *The Brothers Tverdoslavich, a historical tale*, was condemned unanimously, Bazili remarking to Gogol that one could see at once that he would never become a writer of fiction. Gogol immediately tore up his manuscript and threw it into the fire. It was the first of his works he burnt. Gogol's other juvenile works, of which only one or two poems are extant, included a satire on the people of Nezhin under the title *Something about Nezhin, or A Fool is a Law unto Himself*. Prokopovich records that Gogol read him a ballad entitled *Two Little Fishes*, in which he described his own fate and that of his deceased brother. He also wrote a tragedy *The Robbers*, in iambic pentameters, an epic poem, *Russia under the Tartar Yoke*, and a number of other poems 'in a lyrical and serious vein', as Gogol himself described them in his *Author's Confession*. The titles of the school magazines, too, show the great literary ambitions of the young contributors: 'The Meteor of Literature', 'The Northern Sunrise', 'The Literary Echo' (an almanack edited by Prokopovich), 'The Star', and a special magazine devoted entirely to verse, which Gogol entitled 'Parnassus' Dung'.

It was at this time, too, that Gogol, whose appearance was usually slovenly and untidy, acquired his taste for fine clothes. His letters home are full of requests for blue material for a waistcoat and for money to buy a dress-coat, a light summer-coat, cravats, and so on. 'Gogol', Kulzhinsky records, 'seems to have been the first to put on ordinary clothes [instead of his blue school uniform]. I can still see him in his light brown frock-coat, the tails of which were lined with some red check material. Such a lining was considered at the time the *ne plus ultra* for a young man, and Gogol, striding along at school, kept incessantly throwing up the tails of his frock-coat with both hands, as though unintentionally, so as to show the lining.'

¶ 3

The greatest event during Gogol's life at school, an event that made 'the hateful school' of which he was 'sick to death' (as he wrote to his mother), bearable to him, was the arrival in May 1825 of Nikolai Belousov, a new teacher who, unlike the other teachers, was not a pedant but a man of wide education and liberal views. Gogol described Belousov in the first chapter of the second part of *Dead Souls* as 'the idol of the schoolboys' and 'a rare person, who treated his pupils as friends'. He possessed, Gogol declared, the gift of 'divining the nature of man'. Belousov's influence on Gogol's development as a writer cannot be overestimated. Gogol himself declared that he had brought about 'a revolution' not only in his writings but in his whole outlook on life.

Belousov was first appointed junior master of political science, and later on, at the suggestion of the headmaster, he gave a whole course of lectures on 'natural rights' to his senior pupils. He arrived at the Nezhin high school seven months before the Decembrist insurrection, and was quite certainly in sympathy with the views of the members of the secret revolutionary societies which prepared it. His critical attitude towards the government, though never openly expressed, made a deep impression on his pupils, including Gogol himself. It was, for instance, established during the government inquiry into the 'subversive tendencies' at the Nezhin high school in 1830, that several schoolboys had been talking openly about impending political changes that would be 'worse than the French revolution'. Two of Gogol's closest friends, Danilevsky and Prokopovich, were said to have been heard singing a revolutionary song in which the members of the royal family were threatened with execution. It is not clear whether Gogol took part in these disloyal manifestations, but he certainly knew all about them, and in the quarrel that shortly developed between Belousov and Mikhail Bilevich, the second master, he was among the staunchest supporters of his favourite teacher.

On the 7th of May 1827, Bilevich submitted a report to the teachers' council in which he accused Belousov of spreading subversive and 'freethinking' ideas among his pupils that were not consistent 'with the Christian religion'. The report emphasized the slackening of discipline and morals among the schoolboys, who were accused of singing 'indecent' songs, indulging in merry-making and showing disrespect to their teachers. Gogol's name was mentioned among those who were consistently disrespectful to their masters. Bilevich further declared that he had noticed among some of the pupils certain signs of freethinking, which were a direct result of Belousov's lectures on natural rights. In view of the increasingly stringent reactionary régime following upon the suppression of the Decembrist insurrection, such an accusation was bound to have (and, in fact, did have) serious consequences for Belousov and those of the teachers who shared his views.

In his reply, Belousov contended that because certain writers on natural rights had been introducing political discussions into their books, the teaching of natural rights had become 'dangerous', and that was why Bilevich was trying to put the blame on him for the supposed prevalence of 'freethinking' ideas among some of his pupils.

A conspectus of these lectures, made by Gogol, has been preserved and it is thus possible to follow up the genesis of these ideas. Gogol's conspectus consists of two parts: the history of natural rights and the theory of natural rights. Belousov regarded the natural rights of man as the rational basis for the organization of society, and human reason as the 'purest source' of natural rights. Laws passed by the State were morally obligatory only in so far as they did not contradict the laws of nature. 'Man', Belousov claimed, 'has a right to his personality, that is to say, he has a right to be just as nature has formed him.' This led him to insist on 'the inviolability of personality', that is, the freedom and independence of a man's personality. Man's right to liberty, Belousov thought, was sacred and could not be impugned by anyone. 'Members of a civil society', he told his pupils, 'have the right to enjoy freedom under law, that is to say, everyone must have a special sphere of individual freedom which permits him to insist on his rights without any interference from anyone else.' To Gogol, who was extremely susceptible to the slightest affront to his vanity and always prone to exaggerate his physical as well as his mental sufferings, Belousov's teachings about personal 'injuries' must have been particularly welcome. Belousov regarded a personal injury as a violation of the 'elementary', that is, the natural and sovereign rights of man. An injured man, he claimed, had a sacred right to defend himself and others from an attack, for 'defence is the only way of making good an act of injury'. Every wrongdoer, he insisted, was legally obliged to compensate the man he had injured and, he added, the amount of compensation must be fixed by the injured person.

It is true that certain principles enunciated by Belousov, such as that every man enjoys certain inalienable rights from his birth which make him in every respect the equal of all other men, could hardly have appealed to Gogol, who never doubted the justice of serfdom. But on the whole, the rather circumspect generalities of his favourite teacher greatly appealed to Gogol, who all through his life avoided going too deeply into any social problem, preferring to concentrate on its moral rather than on its political aspects. Belousov, indeed, steered clear of any political implications of man's 'natural rights' and he went out of his way to stress 'the inviolability' and 'sanctity' of the person of the Tsar, which was in full accord with Gogol's own ideas about the monarchy.

The persecution of Belousov by Bilevich and his associates, including the Scripture master, Father Pavel Volynsky, one of Gogol's chief enemies at school, who kept punishing him for his 'insolent words' and 'bad behaviour', filled Gogol with a sense of injustice, which he gradually began to regard as the greatest evil that he was called upon to eradicate. The whole affair reached its climax during Gogol's schooldays in an interrogation, on the 3rd of November 1827, of nine schoolboys, including Gogol. The main accusation brought by Bilevich against Belousov was that instead of keeping to the textbook passed by the Ministry of Education, Belousov lectured to his pupils from his own notes. In his signed testimony Gogol, unlike his fellow-students, added that 'in explaining the differences between the rights of man and ethics Professor Belousov kept to the textbook'. Gogol's attempt to exonerate Belousov was unsuccessful. A year after Gogol had left school the Government took a hand in the investigation, and Belousov and his associates were dismissed and exiled to different parts of Russia and the school itself was closed down and turned into a technical college. Gogol learnt about Belousov's fate shortly after his arrival in Petersburg and four years later, in a letter to a friend on the 14th of August 1834, he put the chief blame for it on the Nezhin 'professors' who, he declared, were 'great rogues' and were responsible for 'inflicting suffering' on many people.

¶ 4

By the beginning of 1827 Gogol had made up his mind to go to Petersburg where, he felt, his ambitions would be realized and he would become, as he put it in his *Author's Confession*, 'a famous man'. But what exactly were his ambitions? Gogol explained

31

them at great length in the letters he wrote to his old school friend Vysotsky, his uncle Kosyarovsky and his mother. He talked of devoting himself to the cause of banishing injustice from the world, of doing something really useful for humanity, of his horror of wasting his life in obscurity and of his 'firm and unshakable determination' to serve his country by joining the civil service. But none of these reasons sounds convincing. At the age of eighteen, Gogol may have appeared a 'ridiculous dreamer' to his mother and relations, but he was neither ridiculous nor a dreamer. To discover Gogol's real intentions one has only to look at what he actually did after his arrival in Petersburg. He did not try to get a job in the civil service; instead, he spent the last penny he had on publishing the long narrative poem he had brought with him and whose failure was such a blow to him that he decided to leave Russia for good. His ambitions therefore were to win fame as a writer. That he failed to achieve recognition at once shows that he was mistaken in the literary medium he had chosen, but not in his feeling that literature alone would save him from being 'buried in obscurity', as he put it in one of his letters to Vysotsky.

He had written to Vysotsky to find out about the conditions of life in Petersburg, for he knew very well that it was only in Petersburg, the centre of the Russian literary world, that he could achieve his ambition. It is surely significant that in his first letter to Vysotsky on the 17th of January 1827 (O.S.), he should, after complaining of 'the bitterness of his imprisonment' at school, have inquired for news about the Petersburg theatre. 'You have told me so little about the theatre,' he wrote. 'What is it like? . . . I suppose you don't miss a single performance—you are there every evening!' In his second letter to Vysotsky on March the 19th, he again demanded to be told the smallest particulars about life in Petersburg. 'I'd like to know all about it,' he wrote, 'so as to be able to make my plans in good time.' In his last letter, of June the 26th, he brushed away Vysotsky's warnings of 'the monstrous difficulties' of life in Petersburg, though he admitted that 'the terribly high prices, especially of food', rather frightened him. But his mind was made up; nothing could stop him now. He would not 'be buried in obscurity' among creatures 'who have crushed the high destiny of man under the rubbish-heap of their ludicrous self-complacency'. Vysotsky had even hinted that he and a few of his friends might be forced to go abroad in search of a living. Little dreaming how soon his disappointment with Petersburg would drive him out of Russia, Gogol agreed to join them 'after a year', for he was determined to try his luck first. 'I am already', he wrote, 'imagining myself in Petersburg in a cheerful little room with its windows looking out on the Neva, for I have always dreamt of finding such a place for myself. I don't know whether my plans will ever materialize, whether I shall actually live in such a heavenly place, or whether the inexorable wheel of fortune will cast me, together with a crowd of the self-complacent rabble (horrible thought!), among nonentities into some God-forsaken hole, and allot me the dark abode of obscurity in the world.' And in preparation for his triumph in Petersburg, he requested Vysotsky to order him a dress-coat from one of the best tailors in town. He wanted to know how much 'such an excellent dress-coat of the latest fashion' would cost. He also wanted to know what were the fashionable materials for waistcoats and trousers, as well as the prices and the cost of making them. 'What', he asked, 'is the fashionable colour for dress-coats? I should very much like', he added, 'to get myself a blue one with metal buttons, for I am so tired of my black frock-coats that I can't bear to look at them any more.'

This was the last letter Gogol wrote to Vysotsky who, to Gogol's disgust, soon left Petersburg, accepting an insignificant post 'among nonentities' in 'some God-forsaken hole' in the Ukraine. But then no one, least of all his relations, took Gogol's ravings about Petersburg seriously. Sophia Skalon, the daughter of the playwright Kapnist, records that when Gogol came to take leave of her before his departure for Petersburg, he amazed her by saying, 'Good-bye, Sophia Vassilyevna. You will either hear nothing of me, or something very good.' These words, Sophia Skalon observes, provoked general surprise, 'for no one expected anything unusual from the young man'.

Gogol's consciousness of his latent creative powers was fully justified: within three years he did crash into the Petersburg literary world, becoming the intimate friend of its leading luminaries, including Pushkin.

It now became Gogol's task to convince his relatives, and especially his mother, of the importance of his journey to Petersburg. The 'mysterious dwarf' kept his secret, but he first tried to win over to his side his uncle Peter Kosyarovsky, a liberal-minded man who had great influence with his mother, by pretending that he wished to obtain a post at the Ministry of Justice in order to help to eradicate injustice—the greatest evil in the world—in Russia. (He was really telling only half a lie, since in his writings he consistently pursued the same aim.)

'Ever since the early days of my childhood [he wrote to his uncle on the 3rd of October 1827 (O.S.)], ever since the days when I could hardly understand anything, I have been consumed by an unquenchable desire to dedicate my life to the good of the State, and to be of some use to it, however small. The dreadful thought that I might not be able to do so, that my path might be barred, that I might not be allowed to be of the slightest use to my country, used to plunge me into the deepest melancholy. Cold sweat broke out on my face at the thought that I might turn to dust without having impressed my name on the world by a single great achievement—to live in the world without leaving a trace of one's existence—that was the most terrible thing to me. I carefully considered all the offices of State and I chose one: the Department of Justice. I realized that there would be more work for me there, that it was only there that my work would be of real benefit and real use to humanity. Injustice, the greatest evil in the world, lacerated my heart most of all. I vowed to dedicate every moment of my brief life to doing good. For two years I have been constantly occupied with the study of international and natural law, as fundamental to all laws, and now I'm studying the laws of our country. Will my ambitions ever be realized? Or will obscurity engulf them in its dark cloud? All during these years [Gogol went on] I have kept these long-cherished thoughts of mine hidden within me. Trusting no one, secretive, I did not confide my plans to anyone. . . . And who was there I could trust and for what reason should I have spoken my mind—so that people should laugh at my crazy ideas and think me a wild dreamer, a shallow character? . . . I don't know why I am telling you my secret now—perhaps it is because you have taken a greater interest in me than anyone else, or is it because of our close relationship? I am not sure what made me do it—something I do not understand myself set my pen in motion, a sort of in-visible power made me do it. I had a feeling that you would not think a person to be a ridiculous dreamer who for three years has kept steadfastly to one aim and whose determination to pursue the course he has mapped out for himself is merely strengthened by the jibes and hints he has received. But [he concluded] if you do not sympathize with my plans, you will, I hope, keep this letter secret. . . . Even my mother, who wanted to find out what I had in mind, cannot say for certain what I intend to do, though I cannot tell you now why.'

The reason was simple: his mother, naïve, silly and improvident woman though she was, realized much better than he how precarious were his chances of making a successful career in Petersburg, and it was she, no doubt, who had kept taunting him with being 'a wild dreamer'. She would have liked him to settle down in Vassilevka and become a landowner like his father. But Gogol, as he explained to her in a letter on the 12th of March 1839, was 'not born to be a farmer' and, in view 'of the existing order of things' in Russia, he could not take up farming 'without having first acquired a name, high rank and a position carrying some weight in society'. He therefore applied all his energies to bullying his mother into letting him go to Petersburg. On the 26th of February 1827 (O.S.), he wrote to her: 'All I am thinking of now is my future career. Awake or asleep, I dream of Petersburg and my service to the State.' A month later, having apparently received little encouragement from his mother, he tried to appeal to her feelings for his late father, and even went so far as to suggest that it was 'this pure and exalted being' who had inspired him to undertake his journey 'for the benefit of our country, for the happiness of our fellow-citizens and for the good of our fellow-men'. He assured his mother that he actually seemed to see 'this angel, pointing firmly and inflexibly towards the goal of my eager quest'.

In his next letter, of April the 6th, he renewed his attack on his still recalcitrant mother. This time he assured her that the plan of his life was remarkably precise and accurate in every detail and that every copeck was strictly accounted for. The only thing he could not deny himself, he added, betraying for once his real aims, was his passion '*to see and feel the Beautiful*'. He had therefore spent forty roubles ('a not inconsiderable sum in my present condition') on a miniature edition of Schiller's works, and was now spending several hours a day reading the German poet 'with the utmost pleasure', a bare-faced lie since, according to Prokopovich, he could hardly make out the meaning of a single line of Schiller's, and soon gave up trying. Nor, he further told his mother, did he neglect the Russian writers, though he could only afford to buy one book in six months. 'Sometimes', he wrote in the same letter, 'I read an announcement of the appearance of a new work of art in the world: my heart beats fast and—I let drop the newspaper with a deep sigh at the thought that I cannot afford it. My desire to get it interferes with my sleep and when, at such a time, I receive money, I am more overjoyed than any miser. . . . This', he concludes unblushingly, 'sweetens my separation from *you*.'

Towards the end of 1827, Gogol's pressure on his mother increased. On the one hand, he tried to convince her that he had turned over a new leaf so far as his studies were concerned. 'From morning till night', he wrote to her on December the 15th, 'not a single idle moment interrupts my profound studies.' By his 'perseverance and iron endurance' he hoped to lay 'the foundations of the great edifice' which he had designed for himself. On the other hand, to leave no doubt in his mother's mind about his firm decision not to become a landowner, he told her that he had made up his mind to give up his share of the estate. He would want some financial assistance from her only during the first two or three years in Petersburg, but the money she would be sending would be merely 'an investment at a high rate of interest' which would 'treble her capital'. 'All I want', he wrote, 'is just a little cottage where I could stay when visiting you.' And in reply to his mother's repeated assertions that he was a dreamer, he wrote on the 1st of March 1828: 'No, I know people too well to be a dreamer. The lessons they have taught me will remain for ever imprinted on my mind, and they are a guarantee of my happiness. . . . It is an absolute truth', he concluded with dogmatic assurance, 'that a man who has become thoroughly experienced in the ways of the world, a man who has repeatedly suffered all sorts of misfortunes, will eventually be the happiest man in the world.'

Gogol's subsequent career was to give the lie to this 'absolute truth', but this time he got what he wanted: faced with his 'iron determination', poor Maria Ivanovna had to yield in the end.

¶ 5

Gogol passed his final examinations in June 1828. His school certificate gives him good marks for practically every subject in the curriculum, but confers on him the lowest, that is, the fourteenth grade in the civil service. This rather belies the genuineness of his good marks, for the Nezhin public school was entitled to confer the twelfth grade on its good students. Considering the importance which rank played in the bureaucratic structure of the Russian Empire under Nicholas I, this setback boded ill for Gogol's professed desire for a civil service career. But it would seem that Gogol himself was beginning to have his doubts about Petersburg as the gateway to fame and success. 'I am leaving for Petersburg without fail at the beginning of winter,' he wrote to Peter Kosyarovsky from Vassilevka on the 28th of September 1828 (O.S.), 'and God only knows where I shall go from there; it is quite possible that I shall go abroad, that there will be no news of me for several years and, I confess, I am not particularly anxious to return home, especially as I have many times been a witness to the worries and struggles of this wonderful mother of ours and what a terrible effect they have on her health. . . . So far as I am concerned, I have done all I could. I am taking only a little money with me, just enough to defray my travelling expenses and to tide me over the first few months in Petersburg; to make sure that mother is well provided for,' he went on to outline a plan he never carried out, 'I am renouncing my claim on my inheritance and am now busy drawing up a deed of gift, according to which the part of the estate which was bequeathed to me, including the house, the garden, the woods and the ponds, becomes the property of my mother . . . I shall always be able to make a living . . . I know some trades: I am a good tailor, I am not bad at painting walls, and I know quite a bit about the art of cooking; if you think I am joking—ask mother and she will tell you. . . . And so', he concluded, 'I shall always be able to earn enough to keep myself.'

On the same day, Maria Ivanovna wrote to Peter Kosyarovsky: 'He [Gogol] behaves very sensibly for a boy of his age. . . . I don't know what God will be pleased to do in future, but I shall obey His sacred will. I wonder whether my Nikosha has written to you about the estate. He says he can't remember whether he has or not. Two months ago he surprised me by trying to persuade me to make over his part of the estate to me, assuring me that it would be helpful and even necessary for my peace of mind, in case my sons-in-law should not treat me kindly, while he, perhaps, would be far away from me, and he moved me to tears by this suggestion of his. . . . My Nikosha', she went on, 'has been given the rank of university student of the fourteenth grade. He should have been given the twelfth grade, but he does not bear them any grudge, particularly as his teachers said that he was worthy of being given even the tenth grade, though he had been bad at school, but they should have given him the twelfth grade, according to all the rules. He should have tried to curry favour with them, but he could not do so.'

Apart from Belousov's lectures, the Nezhin high school contributed very little to the store of knowledge a writer of his genius might have been expected to possess. Gogol, in fact, can be said to have been the least educated of all the great Russian writers of the nineteenth century. On the other hand, it would be false to assume that his schooldays were entirely wasted. Through the literary circles he gained a thorough knowledge of modern Russian literature, which was completely disregarded in the school curriculum, and the school magazines provided him with his first chance of trying his hand at original writing; it was at school, too, that he developed his aesthetic sense through his interest in painting and architecture and his love of the drama. A school essay of his which has been preserved and which he wrote in his last year at Nezhin deals with the aims of literary criticism. The only interesting point Gogol made in it was his characteristic assertion of the moral basis of literature. 'It is necessary', he wrote, 'that the pen of the reviewer or critic should be guided by a true desire for what is good and useful.'

A good idea of Gogol's interests during his last two years at school and the first years of his life in Petersburg can be gleaned from the scrapbook he compiled between 1826 and 1831. It is a veritable mine of all sorts of information from every imaginable field of knowledge. It includes notes about chemists' weights; pasted-in pictures of architectural designs; a table of weights and measures in different countries; a carefully copied out table of the heights of different 'remarkable monuments'; fifteen pictures illustrating various objects of ancient Greece and Rome, such as Agamemnon's helmet, Apollo's bow, ancient statues, etc.; a comparative table of the currency and coins of different nations; an extract about the distribution of trees and shrubs in Europe; two pen drawings of male and female figures; a drawing of different types of fences; an extract from a textbook on the history of art; extracts from Thierry's *Reflections on history in general*; a commercial dictionary; two drawings of bridges: one with an elegant railing, and a primitive one of a trunk thrown across a stream; linear measures; twenty-six pen drawings of ancient Greek musical instruments; an extract from a book about ancient Russian shrovetide customs; a fragment of a monograph on Russian customs and the home life of Tsar Fyodor Ioannovich; an extract from another book on Russian costumes and customs; an extract from Winckelmann's *Persian clothes*; carefully copied out graphs of the four planetary systems: the Ptolemaic system, the Tikhobragov system, the Egyptian system and the Copernican system; five pasted-in ornaments with Italian captions; a map made by Baron Herberstein during his sojourn in Russia (1549); an extract from Giles Fletcher's book about ancient Russian weddings; a key to Erdmann's shorthand; a comparison between the horticultural years in France and Russia; twelve drawings of different types of garden seats; a note on the architecture of theatres; a list of the names of the actors and actresses of the Petersburg theatre; a list of Scribe's plays; two pen drawings of the façades of houses; a table of Slavonic numerals; a description of the clock on the Spasskaya Tower in the Kremlin; a Ukrainian-Russian dictionary; and many notes on Ukrainian folklore, games, proverbs, sayings, etc., which he later used in his Ukrainian tales.

This unmethodical, haphazard and almost casual compilation is highly characteristic of Gogol's way of filling in the gaps in his education. His constant preoccupation with the significant, 'living' detail merely confirmed him in his contempt for the often unimaginative, though painstaking research carried out by scholars, with the result that, whether as a reader in history at Petersburg university or, towards the end of his life, as a compiler of a Russian dictionary, or textbooks of geography and Russian literature, he lacked the indispensable grounding in his subject and invariably failed in the task he set himself.

There was one habit he had acquired during his schooldays

that became an obsession with him—his passion for the open road. Most of his life he spent rushing from one place to another. Whenever he felt depressed, whenever his imaginary illnesses drove him to distraction, he took to the open road. 'Travelling and change of place', he wrote to a friend from Rome on the 28th of February 1843, 'are as necessary to me as my daily bread. My head is so strangely constructed that sometimes I suddenly have to career through a few hundred miles to exchange one impression for another, to clarify my inner vision, and to be in a condition to embrace and integrate what I want.' And three years later he wrote to Zhukovsky: 'The open road helps me more than anything. Such, it seems, is the will of God.'

At school, he went home only during the long summer holidays. The long journey between Nezhin and Vassilevka was usually made in a primitive carriage, more often than not in a cart, and took several days, and they were the happiest days of his life. In the sixth chapter of *Dead Souls*, Gogol describes these journeys from school, during which his extraordinary powers of observation absorbed and stored up every little detail and helped him to accumulate the material he used with such remarkable effect in his stories.

'Before, long, long ago, in the days of my youth [he writes], in the days of my childhood, which have passed away like a dream never to return, I felt happy whenever I happened to drive up for the first time to an unfamiliar place: it mattered not whether it was a little hamlet, or a poor little provincial town, or a large village or some suburb, the inquisitive eyes of youth found a great deal that was of interest there. Every building, everything that bore the mark of some noticeable peculiarity—everything made me pause in amazement. Whether it was a government building, constructed of stone and of an all too familiar architecture, with half its frontage covered with blind windows, standing up incongruously all alone from among a mass of rough-hewn, one-storied timbered artisan dwellings, or a round, regular cupola covered with white sheets of iron, rising above a new, snow-white church, or a market-place, or a provincial dandy who happened to take a stroll in the centre of the town—nothing escaped my fresh, sharp observation and, thrusting my nose out of my travelling cart, I gazed at the cut of some coat I had never seen before, at the wooden boxes of nails or sulphur, whose yellow colour I could discern from a distance, or raisins and soap, which caught my sight for a moment from the doors of some grocer's shop, together with the jars of dried-up Moscow sweets; I stared at an infantry officer, walking by himself, who had been cast into this dull provincial hole from goodness only knows what province, or at a merchant in a close-fitting, pleated Siberian coat, who drove past in a trap at a spanking pace, and I was carried away in my thoughts after them into their poor, wretched lives. If some district government clerk happened to pass by, I immediately wondered where he was going, was it to a party given by some colleague of his or straight home where, after sitting on the front steps of his house for half an hour till darkness had fallen, he sat down to an early supper with his mother, his wife, his wife's sister, and the rest of his family, and tried to imagine what they would be talking about while their serf-girl in her necklace or their serf-boy in his thick tunic brought in a tallow candle in an ancient candlestick after the soup. Every time I drove up to the village of some country squire I gazed curiously at the tall, narrow, wooden belfry or the wide, dark, old wooden church. From the distance, the red roof and the white chimneys of the manor house beckoned invitingly to me through the green foliage of the trees, and I waited impatiently for the orchards which surrounded it to fall back on either side so that it should appear with its, in those days, alas, far from vulgar exterior; and from its appearance I tried to guess what sort of a man the landowner himself might be, whether he was stout, whether he had any sons or a whole bevy of daughters, six in all with their loud, happy girlish laughter, their games, and his youngest daughter always the most beautiful of them all, and whether they had black eyes, and whether he himself was a merry fellow or as gloomy as the last days of September, looking perpetually at the calendar and talking everlastingly about his rye and wheat, a subject so boring to young people.'

But at the time when he was working on his last revision of the first part of *Dead Souls* he was already becoming increasingly absorbed in himself, and he could not help noticing a general slackening of interest in his surroundings, accompanied by an ominous weakening of his creative powers. 'Now', he concludes this autobiographical passage, 'it is with indifference that I drive up to every unknown village, and it is with indifference that I

41

gaze at its vulgar exterior; there is a cold and uncomfortable look in my eyes, I am not amused any more, and what in former years would have awakened a lively interest in my face, laughter and incessant speech, now slips by me without notice and my motionless lips keep an apathetic silence. Oh, my youth! Oh, my freshness!'

Gogol's amazing powers of observation and his ability, as he himself expressed it in his *Author's Confession*, 'not only to mimic but also to divine a man, that is to say, to divine what he would say in certain circumstances and the exact words in which he would put his thoughts', which manifested themselves very early in his life, were undoubtedly sharpened by what he had seen and heard during his school holidays at Kibintsy, the great mansion of Dmitry Troshchinsky, a former Minister of Justice, a man whose meteoric career in the reigns of Catherine the Great and Emperor Paul earned him the adulatory admiration of all his numerous relations and neighbours. Troshchinsky was the wealthiest landlord in the district. He owned over two hundred thousand acres of land and six thousand serfs. His mansion contained a magnificent library, rare pictures, priceless collections of armour, coins, medals, snuff-boxes and furniture, including a bureau, a porcelain clock and silver candlesticks owned by Marie Antoinette. He had his own serf orchestra and serf players, as well as two jesters; one of them, a defrocked priest, was the particular butt of Troshchinsky's guests, who used to glue his beard with sealing wax to a table and amuse themselves by watching the feebleminded old man trying to free himself. Gogol gives this description of Kibintsy in the sixth chapter of *Dead Souls*:

'A traveller would stop in amazement at the sight of his mansion, wondering what great prince took up his residence among those obscure, small landlords: his white stone buildings with their multitude of belvederes, chimneys and weathervanes look like palaces and are surrounded on all sides by numerous wings and all sorts of cottages for his guests. What does he not possess? Theatres, ballrooms, and all through the night his gardens are lit by lights and lampions and resound to the thunder of music. Half the province is there—all dressed up and promenading gaily beneath the trees, and nothing in this unnatural illumination strikes anyone as incongruous or menacing when a branch, bathed in artificial light and robbed of its natural bright colour, leaps out dramatically from the thicket of trees, and the night sky above appears darker, sterner and a hundred times more lowering because of it, and the stern tree-tops, rustling high up with their leaves and retreating deeper and deeper into the impenetrable darkness, express their indignation at this tawdry glare which lights up their roots underneath.'

Gogol had often visited Kibintsy with his parents and watched the great man appear among his guests, wearing his resplendent uniform and his numerous medals and decorations. At first he shared the general feeling of abject respect Troshchinsky inspired in everybody. He, too, regarded him as a statesman who had conferred a great honour on the Ukraine, and was proud of his benevolent attitude towards his family, regarding his father's obsequious grovelling before Troshchinsky as only natural. Indeed, the streak of obsequiousness Gogol himself manifested later on in the presence of important personages in Petersburg was something he had unconsciously acquired at Kibintsy. In his letters to his mother from Nezhin he often referred to Troshchinsky as their 'benefactor', an opinion shared by all his family. In one of these letters he wrote: 'I am impatient to know the opinion of the great man even about the least important matters.' But little by little he saw through that eighteenth-century grandee, and before he left his school at Nezhin he was already referring to Kibintsy as 'Sodom'. 'I expect', he wrote in one of his letters to his uncle, 'the gentlemen at Kibintsy are kicking up a hell of a row.'

But Kibintsy was undoubtedly important to Gogol as a writer, for it was there that, unobserved by anybody, he could study humanity in its less admirable aspects, and it was there that he must have found the prototypes of some of his most famous characters.

In September 1828 Troschchinsky promised Maria Ivanovna to honour her lowly homestead with a visit and Gogol was dispatched post-haste to different Ukrainian market towns to buy comestibles and wines to grace so great an occasion. Her 'benefactor' did not turn up after all, but Gogol enjoyed himself hugely. 'Although his excellency has not deigned to arrive', Gogol wrote to his uncle, 'we did not spend the time badly at all, going from one country fair to another and spending all the money we had. I alone squandered a couple of roubles, but our servants had the best of it, because all our purchases went to them. . . . Only a few days ago, I returned from Kremenchug, where there was also a fair and where I spent most of our money on wires and snacks; but our guests have not turned up and I daresay the provisions I bought will last us for a whole year.'

A few months later Gogol was on his way to Petersburg.

Part Two

FROM DEFEAT TO TRIUMPH

¶ I

Gogol left for Petersburg on the 13th of December 1828 (O.S.), together with his school friend Danilevsky and his twenty-five-year-old serf-servant Yakim Nimchenko. His excitement can be easily imagined. For years he had dreamed of that moment, and now it had come. The high road to Petersburg and success lay open to him. He had with him several letters of introduction, including one to a high official which his mother had obtained from her 'benefactor' Troshchinsky. But unknown to her and to anybody else, he had also taken with him the manuscript of *Hans Kuechelgarten*, the long narrative poem on which he chiefly relied to win him fame and success. He chose the longest route to Petersburg so as not to spoil, Danilevsky records, 'the first solemn moment of his entry into Petersburg' by taking the more usual and shorter route by way of Moscow. The two young travellers stopped for a few days in Nezhin to see some of their old school friends, particularly Prokopovich, who was to join them in Petersburg later. Nothing unusual happened on the way, but the nearer they got to Petersburg the stronger grew their excitement: they forgot about the frost and, like children, kept thrusting their heads out of the carriage windows, eager to catch a glimpse of the capital. Gogol seemed to be quite beside himself with excitement and had to pay dearly for it: he caught a cold and, what was much worse, his nose got frostbitten, so that he was compelled to spend his first days in Petersburg shut up in his room. The inevitable result of all this excitement was a period of disappointment and acute depression. 'I am sorry', he wrote to his mother on the 3rd of January 1829, 'not to have written to you at once on my arrival in Petersburg, but I am feeling terribly depressed and I have been sitting about for almost a week without doing anything.' Peters-

burg was quite different from what he had imagined it to be.
'I had imagined it', he wrote in the same letter, 'to be much more
beautiful and more magnificent, and the rumours spread about it
are just lies.' Life in the capital, too, as he had been warned, was
terribly expensive. 'To live here more or less decently', he writes,
'is incomparably dearer than we expected. We pay eighty roubles
a month for our flat, for bare walls, logs and water. It consists of
two small rooms with use of kitchen. . . . All this', he goes on
'makes me feel as though I lived in a desert; I must give up my
greatest pleasure—the theatre—for if I went there once, I'd go
there again and again, and that's very bad for me, I mean for my
meagre pocket. I have spent over three hundred roubles in travelling expenses alone, and the purchase of a dress-coat and trousers
cost me two hundred roubles, and I spent another hundred on a
hat, boots, cabs and other trashy but necessary trifles, and eighty
roubles on remaking my overcoat and on the collar I had to buy
for it. . . . I had great trouble with my letters of introduction,
too: not one of them had the addresses written on them. I had to
engage special commission agents to find the places for me and
the swindlers' fleeced me and were of no use at all. I'm sorry', he
concludes his first letter from Petersburg, 'but I can't write any
more. This is enough for the first time.'

Thus the period of his 'failures', which he afterwards regarded
as a special sign of grace, but of which he never tired of complaining at the time, set in immediately he set foot in Petersburg. He
was still pretending to his mother that he was doing his best to
obtain a job in the civil service, though most of the time he was
busy revising his poem. 'My Nikosha', Maria Ivanovna wrote to
Peter Kosyarovsky (who died soon after Gogol's departure for
Petersburg), 'had warned me not to worry if it took him some
time to get a job, because Kutuzov [a former Minister of Justice,
to whom Troshchinsky had given him a letter of introduction] is
trying to get him a good and profitable post, which is very difficult to obtain in the civil service now, because it is simply full of
people. I wrote to my Nikosha not to trouble Kutuzov and to rely
patiently on his efforts, but he replied: "You advise me not
to trouble Kutuzov: that would be excellent if I could carry
on without eating or renting a flat or wearing out my boots,
but as I do not possess such talents, that is, as I cannot live on air,
I cannot help being bored by my inactivity, sitting in a cold room

and having the great misfortune of asking you for money, knowing full well your present circumstances." So', poor Maria Ivanovna concludes, 'he comforted me a little by saying that he had some hope of something, but that he dared not count on it and that he was sorry not to have thought of it before, and I don't know what he means by that.'

What Gogol hoped for was certainly not a job in the civil service. He did, in fact, go to see Kutuzov immediately after recovering from his cold. According to Danilevsky, Kutuzov received him well, made him feel at home and invited him to come and see him again whenever he wished; but Gogol, young and inexperienced as he was, realized that he could not count on Kutuzov to obtain for him 'the good and profitable job' his mother was dreaming of for him. What he had in mind must have been a job on the stage for which he probably applied at the time.

His success as an actor at school must have encouraged him in the belief that he would be a success also on the professional stage. Many years later he wrote to Zhukovsky: 'If I had become an actor, I would have achieved a secure position in life: actors earn ten thousand roubles a year or more, and you know yourself that I would not have been a bad actor.' Gogol, indeed, was so sure of his acting abilities that early one morning he simply called at the office of Prince Sergey Gagarin, the director of the Imperial Theatres, and asked to join the company of the Alexandrinsky Theatre. The director had not got up yet, and he was received by Nikolai Mundt, the secretary of the Imperial Theatres. 'I saw before me', Mundt records, 'a young man of an extremely unprepossessing appearance, his face swathed in a black handkerchief, and whose clothes, though decent, were far from elegant. The young man', he continues, 'bowed rather stiffly and said rather shyly that he'd like to see the director of the Imperial Theatres.'

Asked to wait, Gogol sat down at the window and began looking at the Neva. He kept pulling faces, touching his cheek with his hand (the black handkerchief was merely a disguise for his shyness: he was, in fact, already acting a part), and drumming with his fingers on the window pane. At last he was shown into the director's office.

'What do you want?' Prince Gagarin, who had a rather forbidding appearance, asked sternly.

Gogol, who never could overcome his shyness in the presence of authority, stammered, twirling his hat nervously in his hands:

'I'd like to become an actor, sir.'

'What do you want to go on the stage for? As a nobleman you could join the civil service, couldn't you?'

By this time Gogol had recovered a little from his shyness and replied in a firmer voice:

'I am not a rich man, sir, and I don't think I will be able to obtain a decent living in the civil service. I'm afraid I'm not fit to be a civil servant. Besides, I feel a calling for the stage.'

'Have you acted before?'

'Never, sir,' Gogol replied, no doubt thinking that his success in the school theatricals would hardly impress the director.

'You mustn't think that everyone can become an actor,' said the prince. 'To be an actor one must have talent.'

'Perhaps I have some talent.'

'Perhaps! What kind of parts do you think you could take?'

'I'm afraid, sir, I don't know very well myself, but I'd rather like tragic parts.'

The prince looked him up and down and said with an ironic smile:

'Well, Mr. Gogol, I think comedy would be more in your line. However, that's your business!'

The prince gave Gogol a note requesting the manager of the Imperial Theatres to give him an audition. Soon after the interview, however, Gogol received the money his mother had borrowed, together with 'several pages of moral precepts' which Maria Ivanovna, as she confessed, never failed to include in every letter to her wayward son, and in his reply to her on April the 30th, he admitted that he had been very hard up. 'Still,' he went on, 'that's of no importance. What does it matter if I can't afford a dinner for a whole week? I expect I shall have to go through much worse times in my life. . . . The only thing I know is that if I had been three, four, or a hundred times worse off, it would not have shaken my determination to carry on.'

Ukrainian stories being very popular at the time, it occurred to him that he might be able to get some money by writing a few himself. He therefore asked his mother to send him any information she could collect about the habits and customs of the Ukrainians. 'I want it very badly', he wrote. 'In your next letter I expect a full description of the clothes of a village deacon, from his coat to his boots, with their proper names, as they are called by the most inveterate, the most ancient, the least changed Ukrainians; also what the dresses worn by our peasant girls, to the last ribbon, are called—as well as those of the peasants and their wives. Secondly, a detailed description of the dresses worn by them up to the time of the hetmans. You remember, we once saw a peasant girl dressed like that in our church. . . . Further, a circumstantial description of a wedding, without leaving out the smallest details; you can ask Demyan (I believe that is his name—I can't remember his surname) about it. He seems to know all sorts of customs and superstitious beliefs about weddings. Also a few words about Christmas carols, Saint John's Eve, and the water-nymphs. If, in addition, you know something about ghosts or house-demons, tell me all about them in detail, what they are called and what they do; there are lots of superstitions, terrible tales of ancient times, legends, etc., etc., etc., that are still current among the peasants. All this will be of the greatest interest to me.'

Finally, he asked his mother to send him his father's two Ukrainian comedies, as he would like to see if one of them could be performed on the Petersburg stage. 'I should at least get some royalties for it,' he wrote, 'for in my opinion nothing must be neglected—everything must be tried. If one thing doesn't come off, one must try another, if that fails—a third, and so on. Sometimes the smallest thing may be of great help. . . .'

Gogol, therefore, looked upon the Ukrainian stories he was about to write merely as a way of getting, as he put it to his mother, 'this damned, vile money to be without which there can be nothing worse in the world.' It never occurred to him that they would make him famous. All his hopes for fame were centred on the long 'serious' narrative poem he had been revising for publication all this time. He had been four months in Petersburg and all his enthusiasm had evaporated. At bottom, however fantastic his dreams, he was a realist, and nothing could be more realistic than the description of Petersburg in the late 'twenties he gave to his mother in the same letter.

'Petersburg [he wrote] is not at all like any other European capital or Moscow. Every capital bears the characteristics of its inhabitants, who leave the stamp of their nationality on it, but Petersburg has no character of its own: the foreigners who settled here have become acclimatized and are no longer like foreigners, and the Russians, for their part, have grown to look like foreigners and are neither the one nor the other. . . . Everyone here is either a civil servant or an official of some sort, everyone talks of his department or ministry, everything is suppressed, everyone is steeped in trivial, useless occupations, on which his life is hopelessly wasted. It is amusing to come across them in the streets, on the pavements; they are so absorbed in their own thoughts that you can hear them cursing and talking to themselves, some of them emphasizing their words by brandishing their arms or by other gestures. . . . The houses here are large, especially in the main part of the town, but they are not very tall, mostly of three or four stories, very rarely of five or six, perhaps only four or five in the whole city, and many of the houses display a great number of signboards. The house in which I live has two tailors, one *marchande-de-modes*, a bootmaker, a soap manufacturer, a mender of broken crockery, a decorator and housepainter, a pastrycook's shop, a grocery, a shop for keeping winter clothes, a tobacconist's, and, finally, a registered midwife. It is no wonder, therefore, that it is stuck all over with signboards. I live on the fifth floor, but I'm afraid I can't afford to live even here. . . . There are many promenades in Petersburg. In winter, people who have nothing to do go for a walk on Nevsky Avenue from twelve to two o'clock (the civil servants are busy at that time). In spring, if this season can be called spring, for the trees are still bare, people go for a promenade to Yekaterinhof, the Summer Gardens or the Admiralty Boulevard. All these promenades, however, especially the Yekaterinhof one on the first of May, are quite deplorable affairs: the whole pleasure consists in getting into your carriage and driving to Yekaterinhof and back again. A whole line of these carriages stretches for almost ten miles and so close to one another are they that the horses' muzzles of the carriage behind exchange friendly kisses with the gorgeously apparelled tall footmen of the carriage in front. . . . I, too, directed my humble footsteps thither, but, enclosed in a cloud of dust and unable to breathe in the crush, I turned back. At this time [he concludes], Petersburg is becoming deserted, everybody is leaving for the country. . . . The nights don't last longer than an hour now; in summer there won't be any at all—just the short interval between sunset and sunrise, which is neither like an evening nor a morning. . . .'

¶ 2

Gogol's audition at the Bolshoy Theatre was a complete failure. The producer of the company belonged to the old school of acting. He was convinced that a true tragic actor must be able to read verse in a drawling, howling and sobbing voice, professionally known as 'dramatic hiccoughing'. Gogol was asked to read monologues from the works of the Russian pseudo-classical dramatists who were very fashionable at the time. He read them without any attempt at declamation, but the presence of other actors (a rehearsal had been going on at the time) made him nervous, and he kept stopping in the middle of a line, stammering, and was obviously quite unable to grasp the meaning of the involved, high-sounding phrases. It was a humiliating experience, and Gogol never forgot it. He never bothered to inquire about the result of his audition, and when, years later, he met Mundt at a literary gathering, he pretended not to know him.

'My hopes,' he wrote to his mother on the 23rd of May 1829 (O.S.), 'that is to say, a small part of them, have not been realized, and it is a good thing I did not really count on them, it is a good thing I possess a sufficient reserve of doubt about anything that might happen.' He then proceeded to prepare his mother for the possibility of his going abroad by inventing the story of a rich man who was interested in him and who was ready to finance such a journey. Unhappily, he went on, his 'generous friend' had suddenly died and all his plans had fallen through. He made it quite clear to his mother that he did not intend to get a job in the civil service. 'I have been offered a job for a thousand roubles a year,' he wrote, 'but am I to sell my health and my precious time for a price that could scarcely pay for the yearly rent of a flat and my dinners? And . . . to have no more than two hours of free time a day and be chained to an office desk for the rest of the time, copying out the stupid nonsense of the heads of departments, etc. . . . .' Quite possibly, he went on, he might be offered a better job, but if it meant spending a great deal of his time on 'stupid occupations', he would not hesitate to refuse it. In the meantime, he simply had to have three hundred roubles, and though he knew his mother would find it almost impossible to send them to him, he hoped that in a short time he would be really 'settled', and then he would no longer worry her with requests for money. He had, in fact, already published *Hans Kuechelgarten* at his own expense under the pseudonym of V. Alov, and was about to distribute copies of his 'idyll in scenes' among the Petersburg booksellers. He had also sent off the review copies as well as one or two inscribed copies to well-known literary figures, including Peter Pletnyov, professor and later rector of Petersburg University, who was to become within a short time his most influential patron and one of his closest friends.

Gogol's introduction to his poem is very revealing. Its pompous tone barely conceals his anxiety to anticipate criticism by playing down the importance of the poem, and at the same time confidently assumes that it is a masterpiece. As for his naïve attempt at mystification, it would not deceive a child, let alone an experienced critic.

'This poem', Gogol declares in his introduction, 'would never have been published had not circumstances, important to the author alone, compelled him to do so. It is the work of an eighteen-year-old boy. Without attempting to judge its merits or demerits, and leaving that to the enlightened public, we can only say that many scenes of this idyll have unfortunately not been preserved; they would probably have served as a connecting link for the now disjointed fragments of the poem and helped to complete the characterization of its hero. We, at any rate, are proud to have been instrumental in acquainting the world with the creative work of a young man of talent.'

The action of the poem takes place during Greece's struggle for her independence. In the sixth scene the inhabitants of Hans Kuechelgarten's German village are discussing the political news of the day, the Greeks and the Turks, Missolonghi, the Greek leader Kolokotroni, Canning and the English Parliament, and the disasters and rebellions in Madrid, all events that occurred between 1823 and 1826. Hans Kuechelgarten himself visits Athens after its capture by the Turks, the Acropolis having surrendered on the 5th of June 1827. In scene thirteen, Gogol describes 'the destruction and dishonour' that met his hero's 'confused gaze' as he wandered sadly round the Acropolis and, catching sight of the turban of a Turkish soldier, mused forlornly on the glories of ancient Greece, 'the land of beautiful classical creations and noble deeds, the land of freedom . . .' The sixteenth scene (scenes fourteen and fifteen are 'missing') takes place two years later, that is, in 1829, the year of the publication of the poem, when Gogol was twenty and not eighteen years old. This internal evidence, therefore, proves conclusively that, having started his poem at school, Gogol revised and finished it during the first five months of his sojourn in Petersburg.

There is further evidence which shows that while the poem reflects faithfully Gogol's views and feelings between 1826 and 1829, it is biographical in a much wider sense than is generally accepted by his biographers and critics. Kotlyarevsky, for instance, takes Hans to be 'a portrait of Gogol himself, an idealized portrait, no doubt, but a true one all the same'. Gogol's earlier biographer and critic, V. E. Shenrok, points out that Gogol described in it his own 'vague yearnings for foreign countries, which lured him by their supposedly ample scope for disinterested service to humanity and the abundance of aesthetic pleasures'. As has been repeatedly pointed out, certain lines in Hans's song in the eighth scene are simply repetitions of passages from Gogol's letters to Vysotsky and Peter Kosyarovsky. Such lines, for instance, as

> *Shall I inglorious to my grave be sped,*
> *And e'en while living to the world be dead?*

or

> *Am I, who in love with fame have fallen,*
> *To be doomed to obscurity all my life?*

or

> *I'm yours! I'm yours! From this bleak desert*
> *An entrance into the heav'nly places I'll gain . . .*

And even more characteristic of the young Gogol is the passage at the end of the poem in which he makes Hans laugh sarcastically at himself for having confided his dreams to 'an odious and feeble-minded world', for having thrown himself into the arms of people who could not understand him, for having believed in their 'wicked undertakings', for not having realized that they were 'as cold as the grave' and 'as low as the most contemptible creatures', that 'cupidity and honours' were the only things that preoccupied them, that they 'disgraced the divine gifts, trampled inspiration under their feet and despised revelation', that their 'simulated ardour' was 'cold' and 'their awakening fatal'.

But the identification of Hans Kuechelgarten with Gogol does not explain his curious choice of a German for the hero of his poem. *Hans Kuechelgarten*, in fact, is autobiographical in quite a different sense from what Gogol's biographers have taken it to be. In Hans Gogol depicted the sort of dreamer his mother and friends had accused him of being. A typically German dreamer like Hans would necessarily be disappointed when faced with reality. He would be satisfied to spend the rest of his days in 'quiet seclusion', to find happiness 'in the bosom of his family', and refuse 'to listen to the turmoil of the world'. Not so Gogol. Not so the man who, as he explains in the 'meditation' at the end of the seventeenth scene, was 'heaven's favourite', and who blessed 'the wondrous moment of self-knowledge and the realization of his great powers' and understood 'the highest purpose of existence'. Such a man was not troubled by 'the vain shadow of dreams' or by 'the tawdry brilliance of glory'. He remains firm 'amid the living fragments' and all he hears are 'the blessings of posterity'. The trouble with Hans, Gogol is at pains to explain, is that his soul lacks 'a will of iron', and that he does not possess 'the powers to withstand the vanities of the world'. But so far as Gogol was concerned, he refused to contemplate the ideal his mother held out before him, the ideal of family happiness, to which Hans in the end succumbs. Instead, he chose the difficult path of fighting for the ideals of 'goodness and humanity'.

This idea of self-dedication is the only original idea in Gogol's poem, but it was expressed in terms that could be easily misinterpreted as the empty vapourings of a vain and inexperienced youth (as Gogol's letters to his uncle and his mother were misinterpreted). It is no wonder, then, that it did not impress the critics, particularly as the poem itself is unmistakably derivative, the influence of Zhukovsky's idylls and ballads being especially noticeable, and certain parts of it, such as, for instance, the passage describing Luise's father, the old pastor in Hans's village, having been quite obviously lifted from Johann Heinrich Voss's idyll *Luise*, which Gogol had read in a Russian translation and which had given him the idea for his poem.

The only two reviews of *Hans Kuechelgarten*, which appeared in *The Northern Bee*, edited by the reactionary critic and novelist Faddey Bulgarin, and *The Moscow Telegraph*, edited by the 'liberal' critic and novelist Nikolai Polevoy, had nothing good to say of the poem or its author. It was the review by Polevoy, one of the most distinguished critics of the day, in which he openly made fun of the poem and its author, that hurt and upset Gogol most. His great hopes of breaking out of the 'dark abode of obscurity' had been shattered, and there was only one thing left for him to do before he shook the hateful dust of Petersburg from his feet: accompanied by his servant Yakim, he collected all the copies of his poem from the bookshops, took a room in a hotel and burnt them. It was the second work of his he had burnt. He was to burn many more: the burning of his works was to become an act of self-inflicted punishment for his own shortcomings as a writer, an act almost of self-immolation. But at the age of twenty, it was an angry protest against the blindness of people who had failed to recognize his genius.

By burning his book, Gogol had burnt his boats: he decided to carry out his plan—which now seemed to him to be divinely sanctioned—to leave Russia for 'some ideal country of happiness and rational productive labour,' by which, according to Danilevsky, he meant the United States of America, where, he wrote to his mother, he hoped 'to become a new man' and 'blossom out by the strength of my soul in perpetual work and activity'. There was one snag, though: he had no money. But here a lucky chance came to his rescue. His mother sent him one thousand four hundred and fifty roubles to pay the interest on their mortgaged estate and, as he wrote to her on July the 24th, 'everything was settled in the best possible way'. He went to the bank, inquired how much time they allowed a mortgagee before foreclosing on his estate, was told that they were ready to wait for four months provided an additional payment of five roubles per thousand a month was made, and decided to use the money his mother had raised with so much trouble for his journey. 'A mad, reckless action,' he wrote his mother, 'but what else could I do?' He promised not to ask her for money again and, as a compensation for the money he had appropriated, again gave her permission to sell his part of the estate.

But he still had to find some valid reason for so drastic a step as emigrating from his country for the purpose, as he explained to his mother, of reforming his 'spoilt and corrupt' character. He found two: an unhappy love affair and the will of God.

¶ 3

Gogol's unhappy love affair is usually dismissed by his bio-graphers as pure invention. The whole episode is treated as a mere excuse for misappropriating the money his mother had en-trusted to him and without which he could not go abroad. But it is doubtful whether Gogol, who was the sort of person who never learns the value of money, ever realized that what he did was in any way discreditable or dishonest. The hysterical tone of the letter announcing his intention to leave Russia, which he wrote on the 24th of July 1829 (O.S.), was not due to a guilty conscience but to his own feeling of uneasiness at the drastic action he was taking. Gogol, of course, was well known among his friends for inventing the most fantastic excuses in order to get out of an awkward situation. Sergey Aksakov, the author of *A Family Chronicle*, who had known Gogol intimately for twenty years, explains in his *Story of my Acquaintance with Gogol* that the white lies Gogol told 'were due to his natural secretiveness and reti-cence as well as to the rule he had made in his childhood that in certain circumstances it was not only a mistake to tell the truth, but absolutely necessary to tell some cock-and-bull story to conceal it'. Gogol certainly told a great number of cock-and-bull stories to his mother, but there is something in his exaggerated account (Gogol always dramatized anything unpleasant that happened to him) of his falling in love with 'a divinity who was slightly tainted with human passions', as he quaintly put it in his letter to his mother, that rings true. Besides, when, two years later, he wrote the first draft of his famous story *Nevsky Avenue* (he revised it for publication in October 1834), he included this incident as the main episode in the painter Piscaryov's tragic life. A comparison between Gogol's account of it in his mother's letter and the artistically transmuted version of it in the final draft of the story shows so striking a similarity between the description of the girl in *Nevsky Avenue* and Piscaryov's feelings and Gogol's own des-cription of the girl and his feelings that he could not possibly have just invented the whole episode. Moreover, when one compares the two love affairs in *Nevsky Avenue*, that of Piscaryov and the young prostitute and that of Pirogov and the wife of the German tinsmith, one is immediately struck by the difference in the manner in which the two incidents are recounted: Pirogov's affair is described objectively, while Piscaryov's fatal infatuation is described subjectively, and so deep a subjective penetration into the heart of an unworldly dreamer like Piscaryov could hardly have been possible if Gogol himself had not experienced an infatuation of a similar kind. Gogol himself admits that he was unable to fall in love with a woman. 'If', he wrote to his mother, 'she had been a woman, she would never have made such an inexpressibly terrible impression on me, even if she had exerted all the powers of her charm. She was a divinity.' But to find that this 'divinity' was a prostitute must have had as shattering an effect on Gogol as on Piscaryov. Indeed, it led Gogol to the conclusion that the whole thing must have been a punishment inflicted upon him by God for resisting His will.

'Darling mother [Gogol begins his letter of July the 24th], I don't know what your feelings will be when you read this letter . . . but I must reveal to you the full agony of my lacerated soul. I feel the heavy hand of God meting out just punishment to me. Madman! I wanted to resist the incessant promptings of my heart, which God alone has implanted in me. . . . It was He who pointed the way to a foreign land to me so that I may rise a few rungs at a time to the highest rung of the ladder, from which I will be in a position to broadcast happiness and work for the benefit of the world. And I dared to reject these divine intentions and crawl about in this city among these civil servants who lead such fruitless lives . . . to spend all my life in a place where I can see no future for myself, where all the years spent in worthless occupations would haunt me with awful reproaches—what a horrible prospect! What good is it to be promoted after fifty years of service to the rank of some State Councillor and have scarcely enough money to live decently on your salary, if you have not the power to contribute a farthing's worth of good to humanity?

'. . . Everywhere [Gogol went on] I keep meeting with failure and, what is so strange, where I could least have expected it. Utterly incapable people, who have no one to put in a good word for them, easily obtain what I could not obtain with the aid of my patrons. Is not that a clear indication of God's will? Are not all my failures meant as a punishment to lead me on to the right path? Well, I still persisted, waiting for months in the hope of getting something. At last, what a terrible punishment! Nothing in the world could have been more bitter and more cruel for me! I cannot, I have not the strength to describe it. Mother, dear mother, I know you are my only true friend. . . . To you alone I can tell it. . . . You know I have been endowed with resolution and firmness which are rare in a young man. . . . Who could have expected such weakness from me? But I saw her—no, I won't tell you her name—she is too high for any man, let alone for me. I would have called her an angel, but such an expression does not suit her. She is a divinity who is only slightly tainted with human passions. [This is certainly a curiously involved, roundabout way of describing a prostitute but, as will be seen, his mother was not deceived by it.] A face whose expressive splendour is at once engraved upon one's heart, eyes which instantaneously pierce one's soul, but whose radiance, burning and penetrating everything, no man could endure. Oh, if you could have seen me then! . . . It is true I could conceal it from everybody, but could I conceal it from myself? A fiendish anguish with all sorts of agonies was seething in my breast. Oh, what a cruel state to be in! I cannot help feeling that if hell awaits the sinners, it is not so agonizing. No, it was not love—at least I have never heard of such a love. In this transport of madness and of the most terrible mental agonies, all I longed for was just to look at her, all I craved for was just to look at her once. To look at her once again—that was my sole desire, which grew stronger and stronger, accompanied by a corrosive feeling of anguish. I looked upon my terrible state with horror. I lost interest in everything in the world, life and death were both insupportable, and my soul could give no account of what was taking place inside it. I saw that I had to run from my own self if I wished to preserve my life and preserve at least the shadow of peace in my lacerated soul. With deep emotion I recognized the Invisible Hand taking care of me and blessing the journey so wondrously assigned to me. No, the being which He sent me to rob me of my peace of mind and to undermine my precariously constructed world was not a woman. . . . It was a divinity created by Himself, a part of Himself. But for heaven's sake don't ask me for her name. She is too high, too high! . . .

All Gogol's beautiful girls were, in fact, 'too high' for his heroes. His young heroines were quite rightly described by a Russian critic as 'a collection of chocolate-box beauties'. They were not women but 'divinities'. He could never experience the ordinary love of a man for a woman. 'You are lucky,' he wrote on the 20th of December 1832, to Danilevsky, who was spending a short time in the Caucasus where he had fallen in love with a local beauty, 'it is your destiny to enjoy the greatest happiness on earth—love; but I——' Unable to enjoy the ordinary relationship between men and women, he was determined, he wrote to his mother in the same letter, 'at least to dedicate my whole life to the happiness of my fellow-men'.

In conclusion, Gogol promised his mother to return to Vassilevka in a year or two and asked her again to send him any material she could gather about Ukrainian customs, etc., for he hoped to publish a book of short stories, which, he added, revealing his intention of never returning to Russia, 'if it ever appears, will be in a foreign tongue'.

Gogol carefully concealed from his mother the real reason for his flight from Russia, and in his posthumously published *Author's Confession*, he again attempted to find a reason for it that concealed the truth and that accorded more closely with his views during the last years of his life. 'I have never had any craving or passion for foreign countries', he wrote. 'I did not even possess that insatiable curiosity with which a young man, eager for impressions, is obsessed. But, strange to say, even in my childhood, even at school . . . I could not help feeling that in the future I should have to commit some great act of self-sacrifice and that it was just for the sake of my service to my country that I would have to educate myself somewhere far away from her. I did not know how it would be or why it ought to be so; I did not even bother to think about it, but I imagined myself so vividly in some foreign country longing for my motherland; this image pursued me so often that it made me feel sad. Perhaps, it was simply the romantic craving which sometimes worried even Pushkin—to go abroad solely in order, as he expressed it—

> *Beneath the sky of my Africa*
> *To sigh for dark and gloomy Russia.*

Be that as it may, but this craving, which I felt in spite of myself, was so strong that five months had not passed since my arrival in Petersburg when I boarded a ship, unable to resist a feeling I did not myself understand. The purpose and aim of my journey were not clear to me. All I knew was that I was not going away to enjoy a trip abroad, but rather to endure a great deal of suffering —as though I foresaw that I should be able to gain a full appreciation of Russia only outside Russia and should acquire a love for her far away from her. But the moment I found myself at sea, on a foreign ship, among foreigners (the steamer was English and there was not a single Russian on board), I felt sad; I was so sorry to have left behind me the friends and comrades of my childhood whom I had always loved that even before I stepped on firm land I was thinking of returning. I spent only three days abroad and, in spite of the fact that the novelty of things began to arouse my interest, I hastened to return on the same steamer, afraid that otherwise I should not be able to return. . . .'

Gogol spent six weeks and not three days abroad, but the remarkable thing about this account is his ability to reshape his life in accordance with the views he held at the time, and apparently persuade himself that the important thing is not what has happened, but what ought to have happened.

¶ 4

Gogol arrived in Lübeck on August the 13th after a journey of six days by sea. 'I am writing to you at night', he wrote to his mother shortly after his arrival. 'The window of my room is open, the moon is shining, and the city looks enchanted. . . . The courtesy and a sort of charm of address of the local inhabitants please me very much. . . . After spending several days on the steamship, and surrounded by Englishmen whose manners and education are far from perfect or even decent (which is the general rule with all seamen), I was a little comforted by Lübeck. . . .' It was only now, he went on, that he realized the grief he had caused her, and, he added, 'it was in vain that I tried to persuade myself that I had been forced to obey the will of Him who rules us from above. . . . Often I think to myself: Why has God, having created a heart which is, perhaps, unique, or at least uncommon, in the world, an honest soul which is burning with ardent love for everything that is exalted and beautiful, why has He given him such a crude exterior? Why has He clothed it all in such a terrible mixture of contradictions, stubbornness, arrogant self-confidence and the most abject humility? But my mortal reason is powerless to grasp the great designs of Providence.'

After this revealing self-analysis, Gogol went on to give his mother another and even less credible reason for his journey. 'The chief reason for my journey', he wrote, 'was that all during the spring and summer in Petersburg I had been ill; now, though recovered, my face and arms are covered by a rash. The doctor told me that this was the result of scrofula, that my blood is poisoned, that I would have to take a blood-cleansing decoction, and advised me to take the waters at Trawemuende, where I shall have to spend a fortnight. If you wish', he concluded, 'you have only to tell me, and I will leave Lübeck.'

Maria Ivanovna, naturally, took the hint and at once wrote back telling him to return to Petersburg and take a job in the civil service. But Gogol's 'chief reason' for leaving Petersburg had a most unfortunate sequel. Maria Ivanovna, remembering her son's hysterical description of his unhappy love affair and little impressed by the lady's divine attributes, at once assumed that the real reason for his flight from Petersburg was that he had contracted syphilis. Gogol was horrified by the way his inventive imagination (according to Danilevsky, the story of the rash was a pure invention) had played him false. On his return to Petersburg he wrote to his mother (on September the 24th): 'I expected everything from you, but this I did not expect. How could you think that I was the victim of lechery, that I had reached the last stage of human degradation? So at last you have decided to saddle me with an illness the very thought of which has always made me tremble with horror. . . . Here is my true confession: it was only the proud ambitions of youth, which, however, sprang from a pure source, from a burning desire, unrestrained by common sense, to be useful that enticed me so far. But I am ready to answer to God if I have been guilty of an immoral act, and indeed my morals here have been incomparably purer than they ever were at school or at home.'

It was at best a feeble excuse, and 'the proud ambitions of youth' must have very soon made him realize the fantastic nature of his adventure. But he travelled as far as Sweden, where he found the women particularly good-looking, then turned back and sailed for the island of Bornholm, which he thought charming with its 'wild, bare cliffs, green valleys and red houses', and from there to Denmark and Hamburg. After a short stay in Hamburg, he returned by sea to Petersburg. All his money was gone, his literary career seemed to have been stifled at birth, and all that lay before him was the hateful prospect of a job in the civil service. No wonder Prokopovich, with whom he shared his Petersburg flat, found him sitting dejectedly at the table with his head buried in his hands. . . .

'It is only two days since I arrived in Petersburg from Hamburg', he wrote to his mother on September the 24th. 'God has humbled my pride—it is His sacred will.'

The breath-taking leap which carried Gogol in the next sixteen months from 'insignificance' to fame, from literary 'obscurity' to friendship with the most famous writers of the age, was certainly one of the most dramatic incidents in his life. But before that he had to go through a period of deep humiliation and pain. Left without any means of subsistence, he had to approach his mother's cousin, Andrey Troshchinsky, a nephew of his family's 'benefactor' Dmitry Troshchinsky, who luckily lived in Petersburg at the time. It was through Andrey Troshchinsky that he obtained his first job at the Ministry of the Interior in the Department of Public Works, where he served for only three months, from the 15th of November 1829 to the 25th of February 1830 (O.S.), transferring to the Court Ministry in the Department of Royal Estates where he served for eleven months, from the 10th of April 1830 to the 9th of March 1831 (O.S.). Andrey Troshchinsky also advanced him money (his mother being unable to support him any longer), and he did so rather grudgingly. 'I recently handed Andrey Andreyevich, at his request, one of my letters home', Gogol wrote to his mother on the 12th of November 1829 (O.S.), 'for him to read. You will, therefore, not be surprised if I flattered him a little in it. Still, he did do a lot for me: it is thanks to him that I have warm winter clothing, and he also paid the rent of my flat.' A few months later Gogol told his mother that Andrey Troshchinsky had made it clear to him that 'he is helping me only so long as your financial position warrants it, that he has a family to support, that his affairs, too, are not always in a good state. And', Gogol added, 'you can't imagine what it costs me now to mention my straitened circumstances to him.' The

New Year of 1830 he met 'coldly and lifelessly' although, as he wrote to his mother, 'the coming of a new year has always been a solemn occasion for me'. What, he asked himself, would the new year bring him?

It brought him, to begin with, the first publication of one of his Ukrainian stories in a Petersburg journal. The failure of *Hans Kuechelgarten* had made him realize that he would never become a successful poet, and he now turned to prose. He spent all his spare time in writing his Ukrainian stories, and one of them, *St. John's Eve*, was published anonymously in the February and March issues of *Home Annals* under the title: *Bisavryuk or St. John's Eve, a Ukrainian Story (based on a popular legend) told by the Deacon of a Village Parish Church*. It was based, as Gogol noted in his scrapbook, on the popular belief that 'a fern (bilix) bursts into flame at midnight on Saint John's Eve, and that any-one who succeeds in plucking it and is brave enough not to be frightened by any phantoms that may appear to him, will find a buried treasure'. The editor and founder of the journal, which was soon to become Belinsky's mouthpiece under another editor, had so mutilated the style of the story by 'cleaning up' its collo-quialisms and Ukrainianisms that Gogol, always extremely touchy about his style, never sent him any more of his works, and when he published it in his first volume of *Evenings on a Farm near Dikanka*, added a short introduction in which he made the 'deacon' indignantly deny that the story published in the Petersburg journal had ever been told by him.

'All my income now', Gogol wrote to his mother on the 2nd of February 1830 (O.S.), 'is derived from an occasional article or story for the journals, and therefore do not be angry if I trouble you so often with requests to send me any information about the Ukraine. This supplies me with my bread and butter. Now, too, I'd like to ask you to send me such information, whenever you happen to hear of some amusing incident among the peasants or among landowners. . . . Please', he pleaded not for the first time, 'describe to me also their habits, customs and beliefs. Ask my aunts about the clothes that were common in their time and what materials they were made of, and everything in the greatest detail; also what incidents happened in their time, amusing, comical, sad and terrible. Do not omit anything, everything is of value to me.' His salary of six hundred roubles a year, he pointed out in another letter to his mother, who, as he observed in a letter to Danilevsky, expected him to become a Cabinet Minister, was insufficient to provide even a bare existence for him, since the minimum he could live on was a hundred roubles a month. 'I am still walking about in the same clothes in which I arrived in Petersburg', he wrote on the 2nd of April 1830 (O.S.). 'My frock-coat is worn out and I had to make do with my summer overcoat all winter.' And to convince his mother that he was not being extravagant, he sent her an account of his income and expenses for January 1830. His income consisted of his salary of fifty roubles, thirty roubles he received from Andrey Troshchinsky, and twenty roubles received for a translation from the French of an article 'On the Russian trade at the end of the sixteenth and beginning of the seventeenth centuries', published in the *Northern Archives*—a total of one hundred roubles. In the same month he spent twenty-five roubles on rent, twenty-five roubles on dinners, seven roubles on firewood, twenty roubles on sugar, tea and bread, three roubles on candles, two roubles for the water-carrier, three roubles on gloves, five roubles on his laundry, ten roubles on his servant, two roubles fifty copecks on two handkerchiefs, five roubles on sundries, four roubles on braces, and one rouble fifty copecks on a bath, a total of one hundred and thirteen roubles. As for his mother's naïve idea about making a fortune in the civil service by taking bribes, he pointed out to her that times were different, that 'the possibilities of receiving bribes' were limited, and that it took years and years before one could hope to get a decent salary. He, for instance, could not afford to take a cottage in the country, although everyone in town seemed to have left for it. 'Fate', he wrote to his mother on June the 3rd (O.S.), 'seems to have decreed that I should remain on the fifth floor this summer.' He then proceeded to give the following account of how he spent his day. 'At nine o'clock in the morning I leave for the office and stay there till three o'clock in the afternoon; at half-past three I have dinner; after dinner, at five o'clock, I go to an art class at the Academy of Arts, where I study painting, which I am quite unable to give up. . . . I spend two hours three times a week in the class. At seven I go home or spend the evening with some of my friends—and I have got not a few of these. Indeed, there are no less than twenty-five of my Nezhin schoolfriends living in Petersburg now. . . . Each of us eats at home and our friends are quite

satisfied to be regaled with talk only. . . . Three times a week I
visit friends who have families of their own. I have tea and spend
the evening with them. At nine in the evening I go for a walk in
the country. At eleven I return home, have tea if I have not had
any elsewhere (you must not think this is late: I have no supper),
and sometimes I don't come home before twelve or one o'clock,
and there are still lots of people out in the streets at that hour. As
you know, we have no nights here; it is light all through the night,
except that there is no sun. . . . I have not given up my literary
work', he concludes, 'but as I do not intend to publish my stories
in a journal, they will not appear for some time yet.'

Pavel Annenkov, the Russian critic and literary historian, who
knew Gogol for twenty years, having first met him in 1832,
has left a full description of these meetings of friends at Gogol's
flat. Gogol, he records, often left his work to be among his friends,
chiefly to talk about the problems of art, which alone interested
him. He never discussed his own work and plans with them because he wished to remain as they had known him at first. He
lived in a flat looking out on to a courtyard, in two small rooms.
'I vividly remember the dark stairs leading up to his flat,' Annenkov writes, 'the small entrance hall with its partition, the small
bedroom where he slept and poured out tea for his guests, and the
other room—a larger one—with a plain sofa by the wall, a large
table at the window piled high with books, and a writing bureau
next to it. The first time I happened to go to one of his tea parties,
he was standing by the *samovar* and all he said to me was: "You've
come just in time." Among his visitors was a middle-aged man
who was talking to him about the habits of madmen and the strict,
almost logical consistency which could be observed in the development of their ideas. When one of his friends began calling them
all to go home, Gogol remarked, alluding to his visitor: "You go,
he knows when it's time for him to leave." The greater part of the
material which he gathered from the stories of the middle-aged
man he later used in his *Diary of a Madman*.'

Gogol was at the time collecting English keepsakes with views
of Greece, India, Persia, and other countries, in which the main
effect was produced by the remarkable fineness of the etching and
the sharp contrasts of light and shade. He liked to show his expensive almanacs from which, incidentally, he obtained his romantic
ideas of the architecture of different peoples and their views on

art. The staid, always serious Yakim was Gogol's valet at the time. Gogol treated him in a rather patriarchal manner, sometimes saying to him, 'I'll slap your ugly mug', which did not prevent Yakim from being rude to his master, nor his master from taking care of Yakim's daily needs.

Gogol's friends, Annenkov further records, used to entertain each other at tea parties, and the one whose turn it was to act as host did his best to outdo everyone else by the choice, variety and elegance of the knot-shaped biscuits, always remarking that they were worth *their weight in gold*. In all such cases Gogol acted as the stern and impartial judge and valuer. Those meetings were notable for their gaiety and ridicule of the baseness and hypocrisy of certain literary and journalistic figures. But what Gogol liked most of all was to make up epigrams and songs about their common friends and acquaintances. Some of these, with the help of Prokopovich and Danilevsky, turned out to be extremely neat and humorous. The same thing happened at the dinners, to which everyone was expected to contribute his share and at which Gogol himself prepared the curd and boiled dumplings and other Ukrainian dishes. The most important dinner, to which again everyone contributed, was the one Gogol gave on his name-day, May the 9th, at which he appeared dressed in a fantastic costume of his own invention. He donned a very short, loose white coat with a high waist and padded shoulders and a dazzlingly bright tie, and fluffed up his curled quiff, which, as one of his friends expressed it, made him really look like a cockerel.

During the animated and heated debates which took place at these meetings, his powers of observation never relaxed. They seemed to be part of his very nature. He could be said, Annenkov observes, never to undress and it was impossible to catch him off his guard. His keen eyes were always on the look-out for any idiosyncrasies that he might discover in people: he seemed anxious to see even the most obvious things. Nothing escaped him. He listened carefully to any remarks, descriptions, stories and observations of his friends, and quite often made use of them in his writings. In this, and in the free expression of their views and ideas, his friends did his work for him. The poetic outlook was so natural and seemed such an ordinary matter to him that the theory of creative art which he expounded at the time was remarkable for its extraordinary simplicity. He used to say that for a story to be successful it was sufficient if its author described his own room or a familiar street. 'He who possesses the ability to give a vivid description of his flat', Gogol used to say, 'could with time become a very remarkable author.' But if his theory was a little too simple and made no mention of many qualities a writer has to possess, his criticism was remarkable for its diversity, its depth and the extraordinary complexity of its demands. He guessed by instinct any character that was invented and not living. Such a character, he used to declare, aroused in him the same kind of disgust as a corpse or a skeleton. He hated every kind of idealization in art. He could never get used to the high-flown dramas of Kukolnik, which were at the time praised in Petersburg, nor to the sentimental novels of Polevoy, which were highly praised in Moscow. The kind of poetry which one obtains from the contemplation of living, existing, real things was so deeply felt by him that, while constantly and persistently avoiding the clever fellows who have ready definitions of every imaginable subject, and constantly and stubbornly laughing at them, he could spend hours talking to any stable or factory owner or work-man or any specialist who knew nothing except his own particular trade. He collected the information he received from these people in his little notebooks. In choosing a man to talk to, he never hesi-tated between a clever judge of literature and the first expert of some trade he came across.

Such was Gogol as Annenkov knew him in the early 'thirties.

¶ 5

By the end of 1830 Gogol had already written a number of articles and stories, some of which were published in the annual almanac *Northern Flowers* and the *Literary Gazette*, both edited by the poet Anton Delvig, who was a close friend of Pushkin's. It was probably Delvig who gave Gogol a letter of introduction to Zhukovsky, the forty-seven-year-old romantic poet who was at the time tutor to the future Alexander II. Four years before his death, Gogol recalled his first meeting with Zhukovsky in a letter he wrote to him on the 10th of January 1848. 'I, a young man who had scarcely entered the world,' Gogol wrote, 'came for the first time to see you, who had already completed half of your literary career. That was at the Shepelevsky Palace. That room exists no longer. But I can still see it as it was then to the last piece of furniture and to the last thing in it. You gave me your hand as to a fellow-writer! How lovingly and with what benevolence you looked at me! What brought us together, you and me, who were so unequal in years, was Art. We felt an affinity which was stronger than any relationship. Why? Because we both felt the sanctity of Art.' Zhukovsky introduced him to Pletnyov, who was at the time one of the supervisors of the Patriotic Institute for Young Ladies, a boarding-school for the daughters of the Russian nobility. Impressed by Gogol's literary abilities and his apparent enthusiasm for education, Pletnyov procured for him the post of history teacher in the lower forms of the Institute. In addition, Pletnyov obtained for him private lessons and, what was more important, was instrumental in introducing him to Pushkin. 'I must introduce you to a young writer who shows great promise', Pletnyov wrote to Pushkin on the 22nd of February 1831 (O.S.). 'You have probably noticed in *Northern Flowers* a fragment from an historical novel signed OOOO [*Hetman*, Gogol's first unfinished historical novel which he signed OOOO because of the four O's in his name and double-barrelled surname], as well as another article under the title of *Woman* and a chapter from a Ukrainian story, *The Teacher*, in the *Literary Gazette*. They were written by Gogol-Janovsky. He was educated at the Nezhin high school. At first he thought of becoming a civil servant, but his passion for pedagogy has brought him under my wing. Zhukovsky is in raptures over him. I am impatient to introduce him to you.' The introduction did not take place until three months later, on the 20th of May 1831 (O.S.), at a literary party at Pletnyov's. By that time Gogol had already resigned from the civil service (he left the Ministry on March the 9th), and had been teaching at the Patriotic Institute since the 10th of March 1831 (O.S.).

His success in placing his articles and stories in Delvig's journals and, particularly, his introduction to two such influential persons as Zhukovsky and Pletnyov naturally raised Gogol's spirits considerably and, in writing to his mother in February, he expressed the hope of being able to provide for himself by his own work. 'Believe me,' he exclaimed fervently and, as it soon proved, a little prematurely, 'God has nothing but happiness in store for us in future. . . . How I thank the Supreme Hand', he went on, giving expression to a theme that was to recur again and again in his correspondence, 'for those failures and troubles which I had to experience. I would not have exchanged them for any treasures in the world. It was the best education I have ever had. But then what wonderful peace reigns in my heart now! . . .' It was not until April the 16th that he told his mother of his resignation from the civil service, and the reason he gave for it is characteristic. 'I fell ill with haemorrhoids', he wrote, 'and at first I thought it was a terribly dangerous illness. But later I discovered that there is not a single man in Petersburg who does not suffer from it. The doctors advised me not to lead a sedentary life and that was why I was glad to give up my stupid work at the Ministry. . . .' And to make his new job more palatable to his mother, who had been dreaming of a splendid career for him in the civil service, he went on: 'The Empress has commanded me to lecture at the Institute of Young Ladies, which is under her personal patronage. Still,' he hastened to add, 'you mustn't think that this means a great deal, but instead of sitting at a desk in agony forty-two hours a week, I am now busy for only six hours and I am even getting a little bigger salary, and instead of wasting my time on stupid and senseless work, I am doing something which gives me great pleasure. . . . Meanwhile, I am quietly carrying on at home with my work, which will make me famous: I have plenty of time for it now.' He had, in fact, already finished the stories of the first volume of *Evenings on a Farm near Dikanka* and was busy writing the stories of the second volume.

The only good thing he got out of the civil service, Gogol used to say afterwards, was his skill in sewing loose pages into books. 'I don't think our families will be greatly pleased with either of us,' he wrote to Danilevsky, who had just resigned from the army with the rank of cadet; 'with me for becoming a teacher instead of a Cabinet Minister and with you for being a cadet instead of a field-marshal.'

Gogol took up his teaching work with great enthusiasm. For a time, indeed, he regarded it as his vocation in life. He gave private lessons in three aristocratic houses: at Nikolai Longinov's, where he taught three small boys, at the retired General Peter Balabin's, where he taught the general's little daughter Maria, who was to become a great friend of his afterwards, and, in the summer of 1831, at the Pavlovsk country house of Prince Alexey Vassilchikov, whose mentally deficient son he tried to teach to talk. According to Longinov's youngest son Mikhail, the future bibliographer, historian, provincial governor and head of the Board of Censors, Gogol was an extremely good teacher of children. 'The first impression Gogol made on us, boys from nine to thirteen years', Longinov writes in his reminiscences, 'was a very favourable one, because in the good-humoured face of our teacher we could find no trace of pedantry, moroseness, or severity, which are often thought to be inseparable from the calling of tutor. On the other hand, it is fair to say that it was only our feeling of decorum that prevented us from bursting out laughing at Gogol's comic figure. His small stature, his thin and bent nose, his bowed legs, the curly quiff on his head, his abrupt speech, which was continually interrupted by slight nasal sounds, his twitching face —all this caught one's eye first of all. Add to this his clothes, which presented a strange contrast of foppery and slovenliness, and you get a picture of what Gogol looked like as a young man.' Gogol was supposed to be teaching the boys Russian, but instead, being at the time in the first flush of his ill-starred career as a historian, he prepared to teach them history. 'You can't teach anyone to write fluently and interestingly', he told them. 'That ability is given by nature and not by teaching.' The children also liked Gogol's lessons because, Longinov writes, 'he used to tell us a great number of funny stories, and always laughed goodhumouredly together with us. . . . On the day he gave us a lesson', Longinov goes on, 'he often dined with us, usually choosing a place at the table nearest to us, enjoying our chatter, and himself full of high spirits. His stories were extremely funny. I still remember the comic way in which he told us of the rumours, which were just then current in town, about some dancing chairs in a room over the royal stables [the incident of the 'dancing chairs' occurred in December 1833]. This story seems to have amused him particularly because a few years later he included it in his story *The Nose*.' Longinov also noticed Gogol's profound diffidence in the presence of his superiors. While he was on the best of terms with his mother, Longinov records, discussing his literary plans with her and reading his published stories to her ('I was most of all surprised', Gogol wrote to his mother at the time, 'by the intelligence of the high society ladies here and flattered by the friendly attitude of some of them towards me'), he seemed to be strangely tongue-tied in the presence of Longinov's father, who was one of the trustees of the girls' school where Gogol taught.

Count Vladimir Sollogub, a writer of some distinction and a notorious man-about-town, met Gogol for the first time at the house of his aunt, Princess Vassilchikov, in Pavlovsk. Sollogub, who was only seventeen at the time, entered the nursery and found his cousin's teacher sitting at the writing-desk, showing his mentally deficient pupil pictures of farm animals and imitating their bleating, bellowing, grunting, and so on. 'This, my dear,' Gogol was saying, 'is a ram. Understand? A ram—baa, baa. . . . And this is a cow—moo, moo. . . .' The young teacher, Sollogub thought, seemed to derive a peculiar pleasure from imitating animal sounds. 'I must confess', Sollogub writes in his reminiscences, 'this scene made me feel sad and I was sorry to see a man reduced to such a pitiable state as to consent to do this sort of work for his daily bread.' The young count felt so upset that he left the room hurriedly without listening to his aunt and just catching the teacher's name: Nikolai Vassilyevich Gogol. But Sollogub need not have been so upset: besides being moved by pity for his unhappy pupil, Gogol obviously enjoyed imitating animal sounds. Sollogub was also present that summer at a reading which Gogol gave at his aunt's house of *A May Night or A Drowned Woman*. Like everyone else who heard Gogol's readings, he was amazed at the masterly way in which every shade of feeling, every impression was evoked. 'He who has not heard Gogol read his works', Sollogub writes, 'cannot claim to know them completely. He invested them with a special quality by his calmness, his pronunciation, by all sorts of elusive shades of irony and humour, which vibrated in his voice and passed quickly across his odd face with its pointed nose, while his little grey eyes smiled good-humouredly, and he kept tossing up the hair which always fell over his forehead. . . . I frankly confess', Sollogub concludes, 'I was amazed, I was carried away; I felt like taking him in my arms and carrying him out into the open air, the place where he belonged. *A May Night* remains my favourite Gogol story, perhaps because I am indebted to it for my being one of the first in Russia to appreciate this man of genius.'

71

¶ 6

Gogol's meeting with Pushkin was of crucial importance to his development as a writer. 'Pushkin', Gogol wrote in his *Author's Confession*, 'made me take a serious view of my writing. He had long been trying to persuade me to undertake a big work and, at last, one day after I had read him a short description of a small scene, which struck him more forcibly than anything else I had read, he said to me: "How can you, with this ability to divine a man's character and display him as if he were alive—how can you possibly, with this ability of yours, fail to write a big work? It's simply scandalous!" After that, he began talking to me about my weak constitution and my illnesses, which might put an early end to my life; brought forward as an example Cervantes, who, though he had written several very remarkable and excellent stories, would not have occupied the place he now occupies in world literature if he had not set about writing *Don Quixote*, and, in conclusion, he presented me with his own subject, which he wished to make into some sort of a poem and which, according to his own words, he would not have given to anyone else. This was the subject of *Dead Souls*. (The idea of the *Government Inspector* also belonged to him.)'

Gogol wrote two essays on Pushkin, in both of which he expressed his unbounded admiration for his works. The first, on *Boris Godunov*, he wrote about five months before his meeting with Pushkin, and a few weeks after the publication of Pushkin's historical drama. He dedicated it to Pletnyov, but he did not finish it, and it was published posthumously in January 1881. It is written in the dithyrambic style affected by Gogol in those days. But the feelings he expressed were genuine enough, and his appreciation of *Boris Godunov* as 'a great' and 'wonderful' play shows that he was not influenced by the majority of the critics, who almost unanimously condemned it. He ends his essay with a vow never to prostitute his own genius.

His second essay, *A Few Words about Pushkin*, which he began in 1832 and published two years later in his volume of stories and essays entitled *Arabesques*, is written in a much simpler style and still remains one of the finest critical appreciations of Pushkin's genius. Gogol stressed the fact that Pushkin was above all a

72

Russian national poet, a poet, he explained, whose true national qualities did not lie in 'the description of a *sarafan,* but in the spirit of the nation itself'. In Pushkin, he was the first to point out, Russian nature, the Russian spirit, the Russian language and the Russian character were reflected with such purity, 'with such cleansed purity', as 'a landscape is reflected in the convex surface of an optical glass'. With great acuteness, he observed the chief merit of Pushkin's poetry, which distinguishes it from the writings of other poets, to consist in 'his extraordinary skill in bringing out the essential character of a thing with a few touches. His epithets', he goes on, 'are so precise and daring that sometimes they take the place of a whole description. . . . A few lines of his are always worth a whole poem. It is hardly possible to say of any other poet's short piece that it contains as much grandeur, simplicity and power as any short piece of Pushkin's.'

When Gogol was writing this essay, Pushkin's reputation had slumped considerably. His admirers had abandoned him and had begun hinting that he had disappointed everyone's expectations. The so-called 'pseudo-sublime school' of writers, with their inflated sentiments and high-sounding phrases, was enjoying its short-lived popularity. The most successful dramatist of that school was Gogol's school friend Kukolnik, whose tragedy *Torquato Tasso* was one of the great theatrical successes of the season. The tragedy was based on the romantic idea that there was no place for a genius in the prosaic world, that he had to hide away from it in the desert, for life on earth was just 'an insomnia of passions'. 'In *Tasso*', Gogol wrote to Danilevsky on the 30th of March 1832 (O.S.), 'all the characters are extraordinarily noble and full of self-sacrifice and, in addition, include a thirteen-year-old boy, a poet who is head over ears in love with Tasso. The "lofty one" plays about with similes as with a ball; he shakes earth, heaven and hell like a feather.' In view of such an aberration of public taste, Gogol tried to defend Pushkin and himself by claiming that the ordinary life of ordinary people was also full of poetry. 'The more ordinary a thing is,' he wrote in his essay on Pushkin, 'the greater must the poet be to be able to extract from it the extraordinary, and to make sure that this extraordinary is true to life.' The true poet, Gogol pointed out, was faced with two alternatives: he had either to pitch his style as high as possible and win the acclaim of the public, or he had to remain faith-

ful to truth alone: be lofty where his subject was lofty, be shrill
and bold when shrillness and boldness were in place, and keep
calm where things were not at boiling point. But in that case 'good-
bye to popularity! . . .' The true poet did not choose the first
alternative, because he wanted to remain a poet and because
everyone who felt that there was a spark of the sacred vocation in
him possessed an acute sense of what was right or wrong. 'No one
will deny', Gogol declares, 'that a wild mountaineer, who is his
own judge and his own master, is much more interesting a figure
than some country judge and, though he has killed his enemy or
burnt down a whole village, he appeals to our imagination and
arouses our sympathies more powerfully than our own judges in
their worn-out frock-coats covered with tobacco stains, who have
ruined hundreds of people, freeborn as well as serfs. But the one
and the other belong to our world: both have the right to our
attention, though the things we see less frequently strike our
imagination more powerfully.'

Gogol concludes his article with a reflection that is as true today
as it was at the time he wrote it: 'Alas, it is an undeniable fact that
the more a poet becomes a poet, the more he expresses feelings
that are only known to poets, the more does the crowd round him
dwindle and at last becomes so small that he can count his true
admirers on the fingers of his hand.'

At the end of 1846 Gogol wrote his article *On the Contemporary
Review* in which he again discussed his relations with Pushkin and
gave an account of Pushkin's aims in publishing his quarterly and
of the part he himself played in it. 'Pushkin', Gogol wrote,
'wanted to make *The Contemporary Review* into a quarterly like
the English quarterlies and publish articles in them that were
more comprehensive and more weighty than the articles published in the monthlies and weeklies. He was not, however, very
anxious to publish the journal, as he did not expect it to have
much popular appeal. But I prevailed on him to carry on with its
publication and promised him to be a loyal contributor. In my
articles he found a great deal that could impart liveliness to his
journal, a liveliness that he knew he lacked himself. But I was
then still young in spirit; I could take more quickly to heart the
things in which he had already lost interest. My arguments and
my promise to write for his journal persuaded him; but I should
not have been able to keep my promise even if he had been alive.'

It was, in fact, their work on *The Contemporary Review* that nearly put an end to their close friendship, for Gogol was getting more and more annoyed with Pushkin for the arbitrary way in which he treated his articles. Gogol, who had always strongly resented any changes made by editors in his articles, could not forgive Pushkin for unceremoniously correcting, cutting, and even refusing to publish some of them. This made their close collaboration impossible, and was one of the reasons that led Gogol, who never wavered in his admiration of Pushkin's genius, to leave Russia in 1836. 'I had no time and I could not take leave even of Pushkin', he wrote to Zhukovsky from Hamburg on the 28th of June 1836. 'However, that was his own fault.'

But in 1831, and in the following four years, nothing occurred to cloud their friendship. Pushkin, Gogol's servant Yakim records, used to spend whole nights at Gogol's flat, listening to Gogol read his works to him, or reading his own poems to Gogol. When Gogol was out, Pushkin would rummage about in his papers in his anxiety to find out what new story Gogol had written. He followed Gogol's progress lovingly and kept telling him constantly: 'Write, write!' and, Yakim adds, laughed a lot at Gogol's stories and always left in a cheerful mood.

In the summer of 1831, Gogol and Pushkin met almost daily. 'All summer', Gogol wrote to Danilevsky from Petersburg on the 2nd of November 1831 (O.S.), 'I lived in Pavlovsk and Tsarskoye Selo.... Almost every evening we met: Zhukovsky, Pushkin and I. Oh, if only you knew the delightful things that have appeared from the pens of these two great men. Pushkin—a poem written in octaves, *The Little House in Kolomna,* in which the whole of Kolomna and Petersburg come alive. In addition, Russian fairy tales—not like *Russlan and Ludmila,* but absolutely Russian.... Zhukovsky, too, has written Russian fairy-tales and—strange to say, you won't be able to recognize Zhukovsky. It is as though quite a new poet had appeared, and a purely Russian one, too—nothing of the old German influence.'

Pushkin had also finished his *Belkin Stories,* and he sent them by Gogol, who left Pavlovsk for Petersburg on August the 15th, to Pletnyov. The first volume of Gogol's *Evenings on a Farm near Dikanka* was being printed at the time, and in his letter to Pushkin on August the 31st, Gogol described the effect his stories had had on the compositors. 'My visit to the printers was most interesting', he wrote. 'As soon as I thrust my head in at the door the compositors, catching sight of me, burst out laughing and, snorting and sniggering into their hands, turned to the wall. I went at once to the foreman, who with some reluctance said to me: "The stuff you were good enough to send us from Pavlovsk for printing is very comical, indeed, Sir, and has greatly amused the compositors."' In his reply, Pushkin congratulated Gogol on his 'first triumph'.

The book was published at the beginning of September 1831, and indeed proved a triumph for Gogol. Pushkin wrote a short review of it in the form of a letter to the editor of the *Literary Supplement to the Russian Pensioner*, in which he told the story of the amusement of the compositors when setting up the book. 'Molière and Fielding', Pushkin wrote, 'would probably have been glad to set their compositors roaring with laughter. . . . These stories', Pushkin went on, 'amazed me. This is real gaiety, straightforward, unforced, without affectation and without prudishness. And in places, what poetry! What sensitivity! All this is so unusual in our literature that I still cannot come to my senses. . . . I congratulate the public on a diverting book, and I wish its author many more successes. Please take his side if our journalists, as is their custom, should attack the *indecency* of his expressions, his bad taste, etc. It is high time we had a good laugh at the "*précieuses ridicules*" of our literature, the gentlemen who talk incessantly of their beautiful lady readers, whom they have not got, high society, to which they are not admitted, and all in the style of the valet of Professor Tredyakovsky [a minor poet and philologist of the eighteenth century].'

Pushkin's fears were not unfounded. In spite of the great success of the book, a number of prominent critics attacked it, particularly Polevoy, who criticized Gogol for his supposed 'spurious Ukrainianisms', his 'poor invention', his 'deviation from the accepted forms of good taste and the laws of elegance', and, finally, for his 'mistakes in grammar and spelling'.

In the copy of the book Gogol sent to his mother, he wrote that 'everyone liked it, beginning with the Empress'. He sent another copy, 'with a sentimental inscription', as he wrote to Zhukovsky, to Alexandra Rosset, a twenty-two-year-old lady-in-waiting to the Empress, to whom Pushkin had introduced him in Pavlovsk, and who was later to become one of his closest friends. Alexandra

Rosset, whom Gogol nicknamed 'the swallow' (she married Nikolai Smirnov, a rich landowner, in January 1832), was an intelligent and sharp-tongued young woman, a famous court beauty to whom Pushkin wrote two poems, in one of which he praised her black eyes and in the other, her 'goodness', her 'free mind' and her love of truth. She often approached the Emperor when some of her literary friends experienced difficulties with the censors, and was nicknamed by them *notre dame aux bons secours de la littérature russe en détresse.*

Gogol was so elated by the success of his book that he expressed the hope to his mother (prematurely, as it turned out) that she would not have 'to suffer' very much longer. 'I repeat,' he wrote on the 9th of October 1831 (O.S.), 'do not worry about anything, do not take anything to heart, and try to be more cheerful. One fine lad you have already provided for. He won't cost you any more now, and next year you will perhaps get the interest on the money you have spent on him.' He even sent presents home: a reticule and gloves for his mother, and bracelets and clasps for his sisters. In March 1832, the second volume of *Evenings on a Farm near Dikanka* was published and at the age of twenty-three Gogol became one of the most famous writers in Russia. 'The devil take me if I am not now in the seventh heaven,' he wrote to Danilevsky on the 10th of March 1832 (O.S.), 'but I take the same sardonic view as you of fame and everything else, though my mistress is much sterner than yours!' His eldest sister, Maria, was getting married, and he sent her five hundred roubles as a wedding present. 'When I get rich', he wrote to his mother on the 10th of March 1832 (O.S.), 'I shall send more.' But his hopes of riches were soon dispelled. 'I have no money at all now', he wrote to Danilevsky on April the 26th, 'and I don't know if I shall have enough to send you your parcel.'

In the middle of June 1832, Gogol left for Vassilevka to fetch his two younger sisters, Anna and Yelisaveta, for whom he had obtained scholarships to the Patriotic Institute after assuring his mother, a stickler for social etiquette, that no children of merchants and artisans were admitted there. On the way he stopped for a week in Moscow, where he met the local literary and theatrical celebrities, some of whom were to remain his close friends to the end of his life.

¶ 7

Among Gogol's works published between 1830 and 1832, two in particular, *Woman* and *Ivan Fyodorovich Shponka and his Aunt*, stand out as giving an insight into the 'riddle of his existence', to which Gogol referred again and again, and which seems to have puzzled most of his biographers. It was the critic Rozanov who was the first to refer in cautious but unmistakable terms to some 'defect in Gogol's nature', which he defined as 'a lack of something that everyone has, that no one is deprived of'. Of all Gogol's intimate friends, it was only Sergey Aksakov who had been forcibly struck by this curious 'defect'. 'I don't know a single person', he wrote to his younger son Ivan, 'who loved Gogol as a friend, irrespective of his talent. People laughed at me when I used to say that Gogol did not exist for me as a personality, that I looked with veneration and love upon this precious vessel in which the great gift of creative art was enclosed, though I disliked the form of this vessel.' Still more outspoken is Aksakov's remark in his reminiscences about Gogol's enigmatic nature. 'To such an extent was Gogol not a man to me', he wrote, 'that I, who in my youth was terribly afraid of corpses, could not arouse in myself this feeling of natural dread in the presence of his dead body.'

In his essay *Woman*, Gogol quite unconsciously presents us with a solution to this fundamental problem of his personality. 'We grow mature and improve ourselves,' he writes, 'but when? When we comprehend woman more deeply and more perfectly. What is woman? The language of the gods! She is poetry, she is thought, and we are only her embodiment in reality. We are constantly fired by her impulses, and the longer and the stronger their influence upon us, the higher and more beautiful we become. While his idea is still in the head of the artist, while it is being created and has not yet assumed its corporeal form—it is woman; when it materializes and becomes tangible—it is man. . . . Why, then, is the artist so anxious to transform his immortal idea into crude matter, moulding it by our ordinary feelings? Because he is swayed by the one high feeling of giving expression to the divine in the matter itself, to make accessible to people just a small fraction of the infinite world of his soul—to embody woman in man.'

This transcendental idea of woman made man lies at the core of Gogol's conception of sex and his disgust with its ordinary manifestations, and that is why every time Gogol depicts a beautiful and sexually desirable young woman, he either makes her into an insipid 'chocolate-box beauty', as in his *Evenings on a Farm near Dikanka*, or endows her with demonic powers which lead to the utter ruin of her lover, as, for example, in *Viy, Nevsky Avenue, Taras Bulba*, or even in *Dead Souls*, where Chichikov's downfall is brought about by the sexually desirable young daughter of the Governor.

In *Shponka*, Gogol expresses his dread of natural sex relations in the dream of his hero, who tells his aunt that he does not know what to do with a wife, and has a nightmare when he realizes that he will have to marry his neighbour's daughter.

'He went to bed earlier than usual [Gogol writes] but, in spite of all his efforts, could not fall asleep. At last longed-for sleep, that universal bearer of peace, came; but what a sleep! He had never had such incoherent dreams. First, he dreamed that everything was whirling noisily around him, and he was running, running as fast as his legs would carry him—now he was at his last gasp. . . . Suddenly someone caught him by the ear. "Hey, who is it?" "It's me, your wife!" a voice shouted in his ear. And he woke up. Then he imagined that he was already married, that everything in their home was so queer, so strange: a double-bed stood in his room instead of a single one. His wife was sitting on a chair. He felt strange; he did not know how to approach her, what to say to her, and then he noticed that she had the face of a goose. Turning away, he saw another wife, also with the face of a goose. He turned in another direction, and there was a third wife. Behind—still another wife. He was seized with panic and rushed into the garden; but there it was hot. He took off his hat—and saw a wife sitting in his hat. His face was covered with perspiration. He put his hand in his pocket for his handkerchief—and there was a wife in his pocket, too; he took some cottonwool out of his ear—and there, too, sat a wife. . . . Then he suddenly began hopping on one leg, and his Aunt, looking at him, said with a dignified air: "Yes, you must hop on one leg now because you are a married man." He went towards her—but his Aunt was no longer his Aunt but a belfry. And he felt that someone was dragging him by a rope on the belfry. "Who's dragging me?" he asked plaintively. "It's me, your wife. I'm pulling you because you are a bell!" "No, I'm not a bell, I'm Ivan Fyodorovich," he screamed. "Yes, you are," said the colonel of his regiment, who was passing by. Then he dreamed that his wife was not a human being at all but a sort of woollen material; that he went into a shop in Mogilyov. "What sort of material would you like?" said the shopkeeper. "You'd better take a wife, it's the most fashionable material, sir, very good quality material, indeed, sir, everyone is having frock-coats made of it now." The shopkeeper measured and cut out his wife. Ivan Fyodorovich took her under his arm and went off to a Jewish tailor. "No," said the Jew, "that's bad material, no one has frock-coats made of it now. . . ." Ivan Fyodorovich kept waking up in terror and in an almost fainting condition. Cold sweat poured from his brow.'

It was, however, only when Gogol was emotionally involved (as he was when writing his stories) that this hidden inner conflict came to the surface. The nearest Gogol himself came to acknowledging the existence in his early stories of carefully concealed autobiographical details was in a letter to Alexandra Smirnov on the 24th of December 1844. 'It is quite true', he wrote, 'that you will find in them little bits of my mental and psychical state in those days, but without my personal confession no one will ever notice or see them.'

But he gave himself away more than he knew or, indeed, more than he could have suspected.

¶ 8

In his 'candid account' of the history of his authorship in *An Author's Confession*, Gogol purposely played down the literary merits of his early stories, since their gay humour did not accord with his austere and, as it proved, disastrous attitude towards literature as a service to the State. 'The gaiety which people noticed in my first works to appear in print', he wrote, 'was caused by the need to satisfy the peculiar state of my mind at the time. I was subject to fits of melancholia, which I could not explain myself, and which were, perhaps, caused by the state of my health.

To divert myself I used to imagine all sorts of funny things. I invented funny characters, placed them mentally in the funniest situations I could think of, without worrying my head about why I did so, what it was for, or whether any of my readers would benefit from it. Youth, during which no important questions occur to one, spurred me on. This is the origin of those of my first works which made some people laugh as light-heartedly and unconsciously as myself, while others seemed at a loss to decide how an intelligent man could have thought of such nonsense.' Six months later, on the 10th of January 1848, he wrote to Zhukovsky that he had never thought that he would become 'a satiric writer' and would 'amuse' his readers. . . . 'I was always of a melancholy disposition', he went on, 'and given to brooding. Later on, illness and hypochondria were added to it. And this illness and hypochondria were the cause of the gaiety which appeared in my first works: to divert myself I invented, without rhyme or reason, my heroes, put them into funny situations—that is the origin of my stories.'

Now, it is quite true that like most humorous writers Gogol was given to fits of melancholy ('the great melancholic', Pushkin had nicknamed him) and hypochondria, but, as his letters and the reminiscences of his friends show, it is not true that he wrote his first 'gay and light-hearted' stories as an escape from illness and his fits of melancholia. He wrote them not to amuse himself, but to obtain renown and—money. In the last years of his life renown and money were of no account to him, but at the beginning of his literary career it was fame that he yearned for most.

Neither is Gogol's assertion, in *An Author's Confession*, that he had never invented anything in his imagination, and did not possess the ability to do so, as important as some of his critics seem to think. It is quite true that, for instance, in his *Evenings on a Farm near Dikanka* Gogol made full use of the material his mother had sent him, of similar themes in the stories of his contemporaries, and, above all, of the folk-songs, folk-ballads and the characters of the Ukrainian puppet theatre, such as the comic devil, the wicked old woman, the boastful Pole, the brave Cossack, the cunning gypsy, the simple-minded peasant, and the deacon with his high-flown speech, all of whom appear in one guise or another in his Ukrainian stories. But then, it is not the plot or even the theme of a story that matters, but its treatment and, in a writer of genius, the ability to integrate idea and character. Gogol's assertion that he never 'painted a portrait in the sense of a simple copy', but 'created' it, is an exact and unobjectionable description of the process familiar to every creative writer; but when he goes on to assert that he created it as a result of 'deliberation' rather than 'imagination' he is merely justifying the requests to his friends and readers to send him all sorts of facts of Russian life at a time when his imaginative powers were beginning to fail. The criticism that Gogol was never able to invent the plots of his stories (based on his own admission), can equally be brought against Shakespeare.

Gogol was much fairer to himself when he wrote in his introduction to the collected edition of his works in 1842: 'In undertaking this edition of my works, hitherto published separately, I examined them anew: there is a great deal in them that is immature, a great deal that has not been thought out, and a great deal that is childish and imperfect. What could be corrected, has been corrected, and what could not, has been left as it was. The whole of the first part [i.e. *The Evenings on a Farm near Dikanka*] ought to have been left out completely: it represents my first immature experiments which are unworthy of the critical attention of the reader; but they contain the first sweet moments of my youthful inspiration, and I was loath to exclude them as one is loath to wrench from one's memory the first games of one's irrecoverable childhood. The indulgent reader may skip the whole of the first volume and start with the second.'

The 'indulgent reader' did nothing of the sort. *Evenings on a Farm near Dikanka* remains one of the most enjoyable and least dated works of pure imagination in Russian literature, least dated, perhaps, just because Gogol, in recreating the customs and popular beliefs of Ukrainian country people, did not attempt to paint a true picture of their lives, but mingled realism with fantasy. Indeed, he often ignored reality for the sake of greater artistic effect. Thus, as one Russian critic points out, the *Evenings* abound in 'realistic inexactitudes', such as match-making during a fair and at harvest time, a wedding in May without the traditional marriage ceremonies, young boys' and girls' merrymaking during weekdays, etc.

The remarkable feature of most of these stories—*The Sorochinsky Fair, St. John's Eve, A May Night, The Lost Letter* of the first part, and *Christmas Eve* and *The Bewitched Spot* of the second part, is its peculiar humour, so different from the rather mechanical humour of Gogol's earlier story *The Teacher*. It is, Belinsky defined it, 'a quiet, good-natured humour, in which the author pretends to be a simpleton'. In fact, by the pretence that the stories are told by a simple-minded bee-keeper, the red-haired Panko, Gogol invented a narrative style which, while seemingly good-natured and innocent, concealed a most deadly sting. This narrative style, too, enabled him to act as the ironic commentator on the embarrassing situations in which his heroes found themselves and to indulge in the asides and digressions which are such a characteristic feature of his style. This method—so typical of Gogol—of projecting his own personality into the story, of superimposing his own emotional life upon it and conducting the narrative on two parallel plains—subjective and objective—thus sharing with his readers his most cherished thoughts and feelings, this way of seeing life, as he put it in the famous phrase in the seventh chapter of *Dead Souls*, 'through the laughter visible to the world and the tears unknown to it', can already be seen in its rudimentary form in his earliest stories.

Another important characteristic of Gogol's narrative style finds expression for the first time in *The Terrible Vengeance* and *Ivan Fyodorovich Shponka and his Aunt*, the two remarkable and so dissimilar stories in the second volume of *Evenings on a Farm near Dikanka*, namely, the curious ambiguity of Gogol's approach to his reader: the hidden meaning tucked away, consciously or unconsciously, in the narrative, which, though the reader may be only dimly aware of it, burns itself into his mind or, as Gogol put it in his *Author's Confession*, makes him accept suggestions no arguments or sermons could suggest.

Outwardly, *The Terrible Vengeance*, first published with the sub-title *An Old Legend*, deals with the historic theme of the Ukrainian wars of independence, which Gogol had already attempted in his first historical novel *Hetman*, and which he was successfully to attempt again in *Taras Bulba*. But the historic element in the story is completely overshadowed by its universal theme of the conflict of good and evil, placed against an archetypal background of supernatural forces and told in a style perfectly modelled on the Ukrainian folk-songs and historical ballads yet so original that it is unique in Russian poetic prose.

83

The Terrible Vengeance is the only story in the *Evenings* from which the comic element is entirely absent: its tragic theme is unrelieved by any ray of hope. It is a tale of predestined doom, and it is, perhaps, not surprising that some of Gogol's biographers should have remarked on the curious coincidence between the sorcerer's vain attempts to obtain absolution for his terrible sins in the scene with the hermit, and Gogol's own obsession with his 'sins' during the last few years of his life.

Ivan Fyodorovich Shponka and his Aunt is Gogol's first successful attempt at social criticism by the method which he defined as 'extracting the extraordinary from the ordinary'. Here, too, for the first time, Gogol perfected his typical method of creating a character by collecting, as he expressed it many years later in his *Author's Confession*, 'all the rags to the last pin of the daily round of a man's life'. Every character of the story comes to life because Gogol had by then learnt the secret of making the most effective use of the most *insignificant* detail, and squeezing the last ounce of humour out of the most ordinary situation with the help of his extraordinary genius for observation.

Part Three

HISTORIAN AND ESSAYIST

¶ 1

Gogol had two reasons for stopping in Moscow on his way to Vassilevka at the end of June 1832: first, since he was becoming more and more interested in history and was even seriously thinking of devoting his life to its study, he was anxious to meet so eminent an historian as Mikhail Pogodin, who was also a well-known literary figure; secondly, he had an idea for a play and wished to establish theatrical connexions in Moscow by meeting Mikhail Shchepkin, the famous Moscow actor and producer, as well as Mikhail Zagoskin, the director of the Moscow Imperial Theatres and a popular novelist and playwright.

In 1832, Pogodin published a collected edition of his short stories dealing with the life of the lower classes (Pogodin himself was the son of a serf-valet) and written in a realistic style, though tinged with German romanticism, so popular at Moscow University at the time. He was also the author of several historical plays. 'I made the acquaintance of Gogol', Pogodin wrote in his diary at the end of June, 'and had the opportunity of doing him a favour.' The favour was an introduction to Sergey Aksakov, a close friend of Zagoskin's, through whom Gogol wished to effect his introduction to the director of the Moscow Imperial Theatres. This was the beginning of Gogol's lasting and curiously one-sided friendship with the Aksakov family.

Writing to Alexandra Smirnov from Genoa on the 20th of May 1847, Gogol characterized his relationship with the Aksakovs in these words: 'Though I greatly respected the old man [Sergey Aksakov] and his kind wife for their kindness, and loved their son Konstantin [the leading spirit among the Moscow Slavophils] for his youthful enthusiasm, arising out of a pure source in spite of its

85

immoderation and its excessive expression, I always kept at a distance from them. When I visited them I almost never spoke to them about myself; I even tried to speak as little as possible to them, and I did nothing to make them like me. I saw from the very beginning that they were capable of worshipping one to quite an unreasonable degree.'

It was, indeed, the excessive kindness and admiration of the Aksakovs, who were deeply devoted to one another, Sergey Aksakov being always referred to by his children as 'daddikins', that made Gogol withdraw into himself when at their house: he liked to be mastered, and never took kindly to people who went out of their way to express their admiration for him. In his *Story of My Acquaintance with Gogol*, Sergey Aksakov gives a detailed description of his first meeting with Gogol and the unfortunate impression he made. It was a Saturday evening. Sergey Aksakov, who was forty at the time, and three of his friends were playing cards when Pogodin suddenly entered the room with 'a very young man', went up to Aksakov and said: 'Here is Nikolai Vassilyevich Gogol!' Aksakov was overwhelmed with confusion at this unexpected meeting with the young Petersburg celebrity and rushed to put on his coat, muttering 'meaningless and trite expressions of welcome'. It was, according to Aksakov, 'not so much a cold as a confused' reception. Nor was Gogol's appearance especially prepossessing. The quiff on his head, the carefully trimmed side-burns, clean-shaven lips and chin, and high, stiffly starched collar produced a most unfortunate impression on the patriarchal Aksakov. His clothes, furthermore, showed a marked tendency to dandyism, particularly his brightly-coloured waistcoat with its big watch-chain. There was, Aksakov thought, something typically Ukrainian and disingenuous about Gogol. Soon Konstantin, who was then a boy of fifteen, appeared and engaged Gogol in a 'spirited' conversation. On Konstantin, too, Gogol made a very 'unsympathetic' impression. He seems to have behaved very discourteously and haughtily, and all he said was that he had been rather fat before but was very thin now. He left an hour later, telling Aksakov that he would like to be introduced to Zagoskin and would call again in the morning for that purpose.

'A few days later', Aksakov writes, 'Gogol called rather early and I told him how much I admired his *Dikanka*, but apparently my remark sounded like an ordinary compliment to him and he accepted it very drily. On the whole, there was something forbidding about him, something that prevented me from expressing my sincere enthusiasm and deep feelings, of which I am capable to excess. On the way [to Zagoskin's] he surprised me by his complaints about his illnesses (I did not know at the time that he had already mentioned it to Konstantin), and he even said that he suffered from an incurable disease. I looked at him with surprised and incredulous eyes, for he seemed to be in perfect health. I asked him what was wrong with him, but he replied rather vaguely that it was his bowels.' They went on to discuss Zagoskin's plays, and Gogol did not think they were the sort of thing one should write for the stage. Aksakov replied that there was nothing to write about, everything in society being so dull, decorous and empty. 'Gogol', Aksakov goes on, 'looked at me rather significantly, and said that it was not true, that one could find real humour everywhere and that it was only because we lived in the midst of it that we did not see it; but that if a playwright put it into a dramatic work of art, we would split our sides laughing at ourselves and be surprised at not having noticed it before.' Aksakov was rather taken aback, for, as he confesses, he never expected to hear such things from Gogol.

Zagoskin welcomed Gogol with rather exaggerated expressions of admiration. He rushed up to kiss him several times, then began embracing Aksakov, slapping him on the back, calling him endearing names, in short, Aksakov declares, he was perfectly nice in his own way. He then began speaking about himself, his numerous occupations, his wide reading, his archaeological works, his travels abroad (he had never been farther than Danzig), etc., etc. Everyone, Aksakov remarks, knew that it was all nonsense, and that the only man who really believed it was Zagoskin. 'Gogol', he writes, 'realized it at once, and talked to Zagoskin as though he had known him for years.' Zagoskin began showing Gogol his books and boasting about them; then he showed Gogol his collection of snuff-boxes and caskets. But Gogol was soon tired of it: he suddenly took out his watch, said he was sorry he had another appointment and, promising to call again, took his leave. Except for a few ordinary and trivial remarks, he had said nothing at all during his visit.

Quite different was Gogol's behaviour during his visit to

Shchepkin. With true artists, especially if they were fellow-Ukrainians, there was no sign of his habitual reserve. He was his natural self: gay, humorous and full of fun. He did not even bother to get an introduction to the famous actor. He went to see him and, finding him at lunch with his numerous family and friends (there were twenty-five people at table), stopped at the door of the dining-room, cocked his head a little to one side and recited a humorous Ukrainian folk-song. At first they stared at him in bewilderment, then they realized who he was. Shchepkin rose from the table to embrace him and after dinner they spent a few hours talking together.

The other acquaintances Gogol made during his first visit to Moscow included Ivan Kireyevsky, the critic and future theoretician of the Slavophil movement, Mikhail Maximovich, an outstanding ethnographer and historian who was at the time professor of history at Moscow University, and seventy-two-year-old Ivan Dmitriyev, eighteenth-century poet and fable-writer, 'the patriarch of Russian poetry', as Gogol called him.

Gogol left Moscow on July the 7th and, on arriving in Vassilevka, found the family estate almost completely ruined. 'Lots of unpaid debts', he wrote to Pogodin, his 'soul-mate', as he had called his new friend in an earlier letter, 'creditors pressing us on all sides and we find it absolutely impossible to pay them now.' In desperation, he asked Pogodin to find out whether the Moscow booksellers would be interested in another edition of his *Evenings on a Farm near Dikanka*. 'What fools these booksellers are!' he voiced the sentiment of many another author in distress. 'Don't they realize the book is in great demand? Turning away profits! I'm ready to sell them the whole edition for three thousand roubles if they will not give me more. Why, this means less than three roubles a copy and they will sell it for fifteen—a net profit of twelve roubles per book!' He was even willing to accept one thousand five hundred roubles in advance, but nothing came of it: he was too new a writer for the booksellers to take the risk.

The position of the other landowners in the Ukraine, it appears from Gogol's letter to the poet Dmitriyev from Vassilevka on July the 20th, was not very much better. 'Now I live in the country', he wrote. 'What, one cannot help asking oneself, hasn't this region got? A wonderful, glorious summer! Corn, all sorts of fruits, plenty of everything! And yet the people are poor, the

estates are ruined, and the landowners in debt. . . . The landowners realize themselves that they cannot increase their income
by growing corn or distilling spirits. They are beginning to realize
that it is time to start manufactures and factories, but they lack
the capital with which to do it; the happy idea is allowed to
slumber and then to die, while they try to forget their misfortunes
by chasing after hares. I must confess I felt very sad to see the
ruined estate of my mother; if only we could spend another thousand roubles on it, it would increase its income six times over in
three years. But money is absolutely unobtainable here.'

But the general atmosphere of the 'vegetative existence', which
had so outraged Gogol while he was at school, cast a spell on him,
too, during the summer and autumn of 1832. It was, indeed, so
irresistible that, as Gogol put it in his *Old-World Landowners*,
'you cannot help giving up, at least for a short time, all your pre-
sumptuous dreams, and sliding imperceptibly with all your senses
into the lowly bucolic life'. He spent his days lying on a rug under
an apple-tree, with a bucket of iced water beside him, or going to
watch the haymakers and reapers in the fields, or visiting his
friends and relations at their country houses with their 'singing'
doors and the portrait of Peter III adorning the dingy walls of
their dining-rooms. (Peter III was a great favourite of the Russian
landowners, for he had freed them by his decree of 1762 from
compulsory military service.) And all the time he did nothing but
eat and eat and eat the luscious Ukrainian dishes and the fruits of
the earth. 'I think', he wrote to Pogodin on September the 2nd,
'my health has improved a little, though I still feel a slight pain
in my chest and a heaviness in my stomach, but that is perhaps
because I cannot possibly diet here. As though on purpose, the
cursed fruitfulness of the Ukraine this year is continually seducing
me, and my poor stomach is incessantly occupied with the digestion of apples and pears.' To Dmitriyev he wrote at the same
time in a more poetic vein: 'The whole of August was lovely
here, and the beginning of September is like summer—and I am
enjoying myself thoroughly. Perhaps there is no one in the world
who is so fiercely in love with nature as I. I am afraid to let go of
her for a moment, I catch at her every movement, and as time
goes on I discover more and more of her elusive charms. . . .'

But while he ate and watched others eating, his old disgust with
this sort of life arose in him and—mellowed by the beautiful

89

autumn and the blue skies of his native land—he jotted down the first drafts of one of his finest stories, *The Old-World Landowners*, taking his grandfather and grandmother, Afanasy Demyanovich and Tatyana Semyonovna Gogol-Janovsky, as the models for his two gentle heroes, Afanasy Ivanovich and Pulcheria Ivanovna, and introducing some of his family superstitions—the mysterious voices his father was said to have heard before his death—into his story with the following autobiographical note:

'You have, no doubt, happened sometimes to hear a voice calling you by name, which the common people explain by saying that a soul is pining away with grief for a man and is calling him, after which his death follows inevitably. I must confess this mysterious call always filled me with dread. I remember hearing it often as a child: sometimes someone clearly pronounced my name behind me. It usually happened on very clear and sunny days; not a single leaf stirred on a tree in the garden, everything around was dead-still, even the grasshopper stopped its chirping at that time; there was not a soul in the garden; but, I confess, if I were overtaken in the middle of an impenetrable wood on a wild, stormy night, with the elements raging furiously above and around me, I should not be so frightened as I was of that terrifying stillness on a cloudless day. Every time I heard those voices I used to run from the garden breathlessly and in terror, and only quieted down when I ran across some man, the sight of whom banished the terrible emptiness from my heart.'

So seductive was the air and the food of his native land that Gogol forgot, or was too lazy to remember, the beginning of the autumn term at the Patriotic Institute. His two young sisters, too, fell ill with measles, and that delayed his return to Petersburg for several more weeks. 'Gogol', Pletnyov wrote to Zhukovsky, 'spent the summer on his estate. You know that he is a teacher at the Patriotic Institute and has to account for himself. But what did he do? For four months we haven't had any news of him. A funny fellow!' But Gogol did not seem to care very much about his duties as a teacher, though he was annoyed when the headmistress deducted three hundred roubles from his salary, and moved heaven and earth to have them restored to him. In this he was successful.

Before he left Vassilevka for Petersburg there was another delay: suddenly he realized that it was impossible to go on so long a journey with two young girls without a maid to look after them. But this difficulty was soon overcome in a truly patriarchal fashion: three days before their departure it was decided that the best way to solve the problem was to marry off Gogol's servant Yakim to one of their domestic girl-serfs, Yakim's or the girl's consent to the marriage being considered superfluous. This settled, Gogol, his two sisters and the newly-weds (poor Yakim took to drink after their arrival in Petersburg, for which Gogol gave him a good hiding!) set out for Moscow. But on the way another mishap occurred: their ramshackle family carriage broke down in Kursk, and Gogol was obliged to spend a whole week in that 'dull and dumb town', as he described it in a letter to Pletnyov.

Gogol's short stay in Kursk was the only occasion on which he could actually have studied life in a Russian provincial town, the scene of two of his most famous works, *The Government Inspector* and *Dead Souls*. He had travelled three times from home to Petersburg and twice from Petersburg home, making altogether twenty-seven days of travel, and spent seven days in Kursk, before the publication of *The Government Inspector*, and twenty days of non-stop travel between the publication of his play and his departure in 1836 abroad, where he wrote *Dead Souls*. 'Gogol', a Russian critic observes, 'has never paid a visit to a Russian landowner, he has never had dinner with any Manilov, has never seen Sobakevich dispatch a whole side of mutton, has never spent the night at Korobochka's, has never attended a provincial ball, so unconvincingly described by him, and so on and so forth. Nothing of all this, which is generally considered so typical of Russian life, did Gogol actually see or observe.' Which, of course, is quite true, but proves very little since Gogol had had ample opportunity of observing 'typical Russian life' in Moscow and Petersburg, and a week in a provincial town was quite enough for him to get a clear idea of what life was like there.

Back in Moscow, where he again stayed for four days, he paid another visit to Zagoskin with Sergey Aksakov. Like Nozdryov in *Dead Souls*, Zagoskin kept showing Gogol all the remarkable things in his house. He was particularly proud of his folding chairs, and while displaying them to Gogol he accidentally caught Aksakov's hand in the springs, causing him to cry out with pain. Gogol, Aksakov records, did not even smile, but afterwards he often recalled this incident and, without laughing himself, told it 'in so masterly a fashion' that he made everybody roar with laughter. 'Gogol', Aksakov writes, 'had many original ways of telling his jokes, and in telling them he used such original expressions that it is quite impossible to reproduce them. Afterwards', Aksakov concludes, 'I became convinced after many experiments that the repetition of Gogol's expressions, which made his listeners split their sides with laughter when he used them himself, produced no effect whatever when I or someone else repeated them.'

Gogol was very pleased with his reception in Moscow. It had welcomed him, he wrote to his mother, with the same cordiality as before, and his new friends implored him to stay longer.

'In Moscow [his sister Yelisaveta records], our brother took us to see the sights and to the theatre. . . . In Petersburg, too, he tried to entertain us by taking us several times to the theatre, the zoo and other places. . . . While we were staying with him, he changed his flat twice and saw to everything himself, except the curtains, which a woman sewed but which he himself always cut out and even showed the woman how to sew. In the evenings he usually had visitors, but we never came out to see them; sometimes he gave big parties, and then again he looked after everything himself, and even prepared some sort of biscuits, dipping them in chocolate—he was very fond of them. . . . Sometimes our brother went to see someone in the evening and then we went to bed earlier. . . . After his lessons at the Institute [his sister concludes], he always used to bring us sweets. But he had a sweet tooth himself, and sometimes consumed a whole jar of jam alone, and if I happened to ask him for some he used to say, "Wait, I'd better show you how a friend of mine eats it—look, like this, and another friend of mine eats it like that," and so on. And while I laughed at his imitations, he'd finish the whole jar.'

By the time Gogol had settled in his new and, as it soon appeared, very cold flat in Petersburg, he had completed the plots of a short story (*The Old-World Landowners*) and a play (*Vladimir Third Class*), not to mention a new design for a rug he sent to his mother from Petersburg. Before starting on his comedy, he jotted down in his notebook the following 'old rule' for writing plays: 'He [the hero] is already about to get what he wants and to seize it in his hand, when suddenly something happens to stop him and his desired object is removed to an enormous distance. It is just like a game of chance. A sudden and unexpected discovery which all at once gives a new turn to the action and puts it in an entirely new light.' But in spite of this excellent rule, designed to keep the interest of the audience alive, he did not seem able to start writing his play.

'I don't think I wrote to you that I have gone crazy over a comedy [he told Pogodin in his letter of the 20th of February 1833 (O.S.)]. While in Moscow, on the road and now here it has never been out of my mind for a moment. But so far I haven't written anything. I have already begun working out its plot, I have already written its title at the top of the first page of a thick notebook—and how much malice, laughter, wit! But I stopped suddenly, realizing that my pen keeps writing things the censorship will never pass. And what is the use of writing a play if it is never going to be performed? Drama comes to life only on the stage. Without it, a play is like a soul without a body. And what master will display before the public an unfinished work? All that remains for me to do is to think of a subject so innocent that it would not even hurt the feelings of a policeman. But what sort of comedy is it if it has no truth and no malice? And so I just cannot possibly sit down and write a comedy. But the moment I settle down to write history—the stage comes floating into my mind, I can hear the audience applauding, faces are thrust out of the boxes, the stalls, the gallery, I can see them grinning—and to the devil with history! And that is why [Gogol concludes] my mind seems to be paralysed.'

And yet, he told Pogodin in the same letter, never before had he yearned for fame as much as he did now that he had tasted it.

Gogol never did finish his comedy and only four scenes of it have been preserved. One of them he published under the title *A Morning of a Businessman* (originally a civil servant) in Pushkin's *Contemporary Review* in 1836, and the second, third and fourth he published under the titles *A Lawsuit, The Servants' Hall,* and *A Fragment* in his first collected works in 1842. The protagonist of the comedy, a civil servant by the name of Ivan Barsukov, is a gambler and a typical bureaucrat. He treats his subordinates with undisguised contempt and his only ambition in life is to receive the order of Vladimir Third Class. He forges a will disinheriting his brother in his own favour. But he is unmasked in the end and, failing to get his order, goes mad and imagines himself to be the order of Vladimir Third Class. One of the lost scenes, which is said to have been the best in the play, shows Barsukov before a looking-glass trying on the imaginary order.

During the last years of his life Gogol always pretended that his views had never changed, but his conviction that a good comedy must have 'malice, laughter, and wit' shows how radically different his outlook on life and literature was in the early 'thirties. This becomes even clearer from the advice he gave Pogodin on how he should treat the aristocracy in one of his historical plays. 'For God's sake', he wrote, 'see that the *boyars* are stupid men. This is necessary, as well as that they should be ridiculous. For the more noble and the higher a class, the more stupid it is. That is an axiom. And if you want proof, you have only to look round you. It is because of this that even a person of little intelligence among them towers above the rest, and he is talked of as a person of great erudition. This is always so in any country. And in your play, if you don't mind my saying so, the *boyars* are sometimes more intelligent than our aristocratic statesmen of today.'

This, undoubtedly, was Gogol's opinion of the aristocracy during the most active period of his life, in the decade between 1832 and 1842, when all his important works were written, though at the very end of this decade a change-over to his more rigid and reactionary outlook can be observed. What led him to write his greatest works was anger with the prevailing order in Russia. If he had been in Russia, he wrote to his former pupil Maria Balabin from Rome on the 7th of November 1838, he would have got angry again, and furiously too, with his beloved Russia. 'And without anger,' he added, 'you know, one can't say very much: only when one is angry does one tell the truth.' It was, indeed, the absence of social criticism in the *Evenings on a Farm near Dikanka* that explains the contempt with which he refers to his first stories in the letter to Pogodin from Petersburg on the 1st of February 1833 (O.S.). 'You ask me about my *Evenings*?' he wrote. 'The devil take them! I am not issuing a new edition of them, although a little more money would come in very handy to me just now; but to write for it, adding more fairy-tales, I simply cannot. . . . I have even forgotten that I am the creator of those *Evenings*.

. . . May they be doomed to oblivion till I produce something weighty, great and artistic!'

And since at the beginning of 1833 he had not yet learnt how to escape the sharp claws of the censorship, he could not write anything 'weighty, great and artistic'. Instead, he turned to history.

¶ 2

Gogol's interest in history dates from 1831 when, as Longinov relates in his reminiscences, he was busy compiling 'synchronistic tables' for the teaching of history according to a new method. His experience as a teacher of history at the Patriotic Institute must have confirmed him in his belief that he had an important contribution to make as a historian, and he was intending to use the notes for his lectures to his pupils as a basis for writing, as he told Pogodin, 'a general history and general geography' in two or three volumes under the title of 'The World and Its Peoples'. But his 'cursed desire to be original' seems to have interfered with the progress of his work. 'Somehow', he wrote to Pogodin on the 20th of February 1833 (O.S.), 'I can't get on with my work. It is not with inspiration and joy that my pen scratches the paper. As soon as I start writing I see my own shortcomings: one moment I am sorry I haven't planned it on a larger scale, and the next a new system suddenly rears its head and demolishes the old one. In vain do I assure myself that it is only a sketch, that it won't injure my reputation and that I shall have only one judge, and he a friend of mine. But I just can't go on.'

Pushkin had in the meantime finished his *History of Pugachov* ('So interesting that it is a perfect novel', Gogol wrote to Pogodin) and this spurred on Gogol's efforts to write a great historical treatise. 'If only you knew what a terrible time I've been through', he wrote to Maximovich on November the 9th, 'and how everything within me is torn to pieces. How much I have suffered! But now I hope that everything will be well, and I shall again be able to do something. Now I have begun writing the history of our poor, beloved Ukraine. Nothing calms one so much as history. My thoughts begin to flow more quietly and calmly. I can't help feeling that I shall write it and that I shall say many things that have not been said before me.' Two months later, on the 11th of January 1834 (O.S.), he wrote to Pogodin that he was completely absorbed in writing a history of the Ukraine as well as a general history. 'Both', he declared, 'are already progressing, which fills me with calm and indifference to worldly cares. Oh, my dear fellow,' he goes on, 'how many ideas come into my head now! It seems to me I shall do something not usually done in my general history. My Ukrainian history is also extremely tempestuous, but then it could not be anything else. I am criticized for its style, which is too volcanic and not interesting and alive historically; but what kind of history is it if it is dull!'

No doubt it was as a result of this criticism by his Petersburg friends that a fortnight earlier Gogol had published an announcement in a newspaper, in which he declared that half of his history of the Ukraine was ready, but that he was delaying its publication because he suspected the existence of sources unknown to him and therefore asked anyone possessing any materials relating to the Ukraine to send them to him. On February the 12th he informed Maximovich that his history of the Ukraine would be in six small or four large volumes. If he had really written two volumes of it, as he suggested in his announcement, it certainly seems strange that only a short introduction to it, first published at the beginning of 1834 in the *Journal of the Ministry of Public Education*, and republished in the first part of *Arabesques*, should have been preserved. Gogol's grandiose plans, in fact, never came to anything, though at the time he had no doubt that he would carry them out. Basically, his passion for originality and for saying something no one had ever said before, blinded him to the fact that he did not possess sufficient knowledge of history, nor training as a historian, to be able to say anything new. Besides, what mattered to him was not the dry analysis of historical events, but their artistic reconstruction: the appeal to the emotions rather than to reason. 'I do not like arguments when they only remain arguments,' he remarks in his *Old-World Landowners*, after discussing the curious historical fact that 'trivial causes sometimes lead to great events' and 'great undertakings sometimes lead to trivial conclusions.' That was why his passion for Ukrainian folk-songs had led him to assume that it was in them and not in the old chronicles that the key to the history of his native country was to be found. 'Every sound of a song', he wrote to Izmail Sreznevsky, editor of Ukrainian folk-lore materials, on the 6th of March 1834 (O.S.), 'tells me more vividly of our past than our dull and brief chronicles. . . . These chronicles are like the man who locked his stable after his horses had been stolen. . . . If our country had not such a rich store of folk-songs, I should never have been writing her history, for I should never have had any idea of her past; and my history would have been quite different from what I propose to make it now.' And in his article *On Ukrainian Folk-songs*, published by the Ministry of Public Education in April 1834, and republished in the second part of *Arabesques*, Gogol elaborated his idea of folk-songs as an historical source. 'Folk-songs', he wrote, 'are a living and vivid history of the people. . . . The historian must not search in them for any indications of the date of a battle, nor for any exact account of it. . . . But if he wants to learn about the everyday life of the people, the elements of its character, the subtle shades of its feelings, its emotions, sufferings and amusements, if he wants to inquire into the spirit of a past age, the general character of the people as a whole, and of each individual separately, then he will be fully satisfied: the history of the people will be revealed to him in all its grandeur.' Gogol also regarded geography as a vital element in the study of history. In his introduction to the history of the Ukraine he wrote: 'A great many problems in history are solved by geography, for upon the nature of the land depends the way of life and even the character of its people.'

Gogol was not only intending to write voluminous works on the history of the world and of the Ukraine, he was also applying for the post of professor of world history at the newly-founded University of Kiev. He therefore decided, as he wrote to Pushkin on the 23rd of December 1833 (O.S.), not to waste time and, instead of explaining his views to Count Sergey Uvarov, the Minister of Education, submit his ideas to him in writing. When eventually he obtained the post, not of professor, but of reader of history at Petersburg University, his colleagues assumed that he owed it to his influential friends, namely, Pletnyov and Zhukovsky. An examination of the 'plan' he submitted to Uvarov, however, shows that he owed it principally to his 'serpent-like wisdom', for in it he pointed out that his chief aim as a professor of history would be to make his students into 'meek, obedient, grateful and indispensable champions of the Great Emperor so that neither in prosperity nor in adversity should they betray their duty, their faith, their honour and their oath to be loyal to their country and to their Emperor'. He also promised to make them 'firm and steadfast in their rules so that no thoughtless fanatic and no momentary disturbance' should shake their loyalty to the throne.

The last assurance must have appealed particularly to the authorities, who anticipated trouble at the universities and did their best to make sure that no 'dangerous thoughts' spread among the students.

As for the 'plan' proper (which Gogol afterwards published in *Arabesques*), it mapped out a programme of tuition that only a genius could have carried out, but then Gogol, as Professor Nikitenko observes in his diary, 'imagined that his genius justified him in putting forward big claims. I confess', Nikitenko went on, 'that I, too, thought that a man who was so sure of himself would not make a mess of things.'

Gogol began the outline of his plan with a series of general remarks such as that 'world history must embrace, all at once and fully, the entire human race. . . . The world . . . must be presented in the colossal grandeur in which it has appeared to mankind, inspired by the mysterious ways of Providence which so inscrutably find expression in it. . . . The professor's style must be exciting and fiery . . . for if he follows dead scholastic rules, even his most just remarks will provoke suppressed laughter and a desire to act and reason in defiance of his teaching, and then the most sacred words he utters, such as devotion to one's religion and loyalty to one's motherland and the Emperor will be treated with contempt by his students. . . . His words must be simple and easily comprehensible, but at times they must be lofty and inspire lofty thoughts. . . . Each lecture must be complete in itself, so that in the minds of the students it should appear as a well-balanced poem. . . .'

Having thus outlined the general system of lecturing he proposed to follow, Gogol summarized what should have been the essential part of his 'plan' in a few sentences. This plan, which, he explained, was drawn up 'after many observations and experiments', consisted first of all of a brief sketch of the history of mankind 'in few but powerful words', showing how the history of mankind began in the East 'with its ancient patriarchal rulers and religions, invested with profound mystery', secondly, 'of an analysis of the history of all States and nations', and thirdly, 'a comparative survey of each part of the world'. No more, no less.

At the end of 1833, Gogol's hopes of obtaining the chair of world history at Kiev University seemed about to be realized. Uvarov, he wrote to Maximovich, who had already been appointed to the Chair of Russian Literature, had promised him the post and even asked him to send in an application for it. 'To Kiev, to the ancient and beautiful Kiev', he wrote to Maximovich in December, overflowing with Ukrainian patriotism. 'It is ours, not theirs —isn't that so?' And it was in this state of elation and anticipation of the great literary and historical works that he would accomplish in the following year that Gogol on New Year's Eve wrote the following invocation to his genius, which was published four years after his death:

'A great and solemn moment. Lord, how the waves of different emotions have mingled with and crowded round it! No, it is not a dream. It is that fateful and irresistible borderline between memory and hope. . . . Already there is no memory, it has flown away, it is already supplanted by hope. My past echoes at my heels; the mist above me is pierced by the light of my still-unpredictable future. I implore you, life of my soul, my genius, oh, do not conceal yourself from me! Keep watch over me at this moment and do not depart from me during the whole of this coming year which dawns so invitingly upon me. What will you be like, my future? Brilliant, far-flung? Will you brim over with my great exploits, or . . . Oh, be brilliant! be active and wholly devoted to work and quiet repose! Why do you stand so mysteriously before me—1834? May you, too, be my guardian angel. If sloth and insensibility dare come near me even for a short while—oh, wake me then! Do not let them take hold of me! Let your eloquent numerals stand before me like a never-silent clock, like my conscience: so that each numeral should resound in my ears louder than a tocsin! So that like a galvanic rod, it should produce a convulsive shock all through my body.

'Mysterious, inscrutable 1834! Where shall I leave my mark upon you with my great works? Amid this huddle of houses, these thunderous streets, these seething thoroughfares—this hideous agglomeration of fashions, parades, civil servants, wild northern lights, splendour and drab meanness? Or in my beautiful, ancient, longed-for Kiev, blest with orchards, rich in fruits of all kinds, encircled by my lovely and wonderful sky, full of ravishing nights, where the hills are covered with shrubs, interspersed with seemingly harmonious ravines, and watered by my pure and swift Dnieper. Will it be there? . . . Oh, I do not know what to call you, my genius! You, who flew past my ears with your harmonious songs even when I lay in my cradle, awakening in me thoughts too deep for my understanding and fostering in me such vast and delightful dreams! Oh, look at me! I am on my knees. I am at your feet! Oh, do not part from me! Dwell on earth with me, if only for two hours a day, like a dear brother! I shall achieve. . . . I shall achieve. Life is seething within me. My labours will be inspired. A divinity, inaccessible on earth, will hover over them. . . . I shall achieve. . . . Oh, kiss and bless me!'

¶ 3

The new year, however, began with a great disappointment for Gogol. Uvarov would not hear of giving him the chair of history at Kiev. All he promised him was a readership in history, and even that was not certain. 'Uvarov', Gogol wrote to Maximovich on May the 28th, 'keeps me here—I don't know why. . . . I shall go off my head if they offer me the Chair of Russian History. If they keep me dangling any longer I shall throw everything up and go to the Caucasus, for I am not feeling at all well.' A week earlier he had enlisted the aid of Pushkin. 'If', he wrote to the poet, 'Uvarov mentions me to you, tell him that you have been to see me and found me barely alive; you can also make use of this opportunity to abuse me thoroughly for living here; tell him that the doctors have ordered me to leave town at once, and after saying that if I stay here another month I will most probably die, change the subject and talk about the weather or something else. I can't help thinking that it might be of some use. . . .'

But it wasn't. Fate itself, as he wrote to Maximovich, was against him: he did not get his job in Kiev; instead, he was offered the post of reader in medieval history at Petersburg University. Gogol delivered his first lecture to the second-year students of the philosophical faculty on July the 24th. (For his lectures he used Henry Hallam's *View of the State of Europe during the Middle Ages*, which he read in a French translation and from which he made detailed notes.) A description of Gogol's inaugural lecture was left by one of his students. Gogol appeared in the lecture room at two o'clock in the company of the dean of the faculty. He was very nervous. He twisted his hat, crumpled his gloves and eyed the students suspiciously. He began with a brief explanation of what his lecture would be about and, as he talked, slowly mounted the rostrum. As he ascended the steps, his face grew paler and paler. When he was about to start his lecture, the rector of the university walked in and he had to descend again to greet him. A dead silence followed. Gogol grew pale again, but he mounted the rostrum and began his lecture on the Nature of Medieval History, first published in the official organ of the Ministry of Education under the title *About the Middle Ages: an Introductory Lecture read at Petersburg University by the Reader in History, N. V. Gogol,* and republished minus its subtitle in the first part of *Arabesques.* Gogol had prepared the lecture beforehand and learnt it by heart, so that he had no difficulty in delivering it. After the lecture he told his students: 'To begin with, gentlemen, I have tried to show you only the main features of the Middle Ages; next time we shall turn to the facts themselves, and to do that we shall have to arm ourselves with a dissecting knife.'

But, alas, where historical facts were concerned, a dissecting knife did not seem to be of much use. Gogol's second lecture was a failure. He arrived late and began it with a sentence that was 'fiery' enough: 'Asia has always been a people-erupting volcano.' Then he said a few words about the great transmigration of peoples but so tamely, lifelessly and incoherently that the students were bored and could hardly believe that it was the same Gogol who had read them such a brilliant lecture the week before. This time his lecture lasted only twenty minutes and, after telling his students what books to read on the subject, he left. The students soon lost interest in Gogol's lectures and his audience dwindled.

Turgenev, who was one of his students in 1835, described his lectures as rather 'original'. To begin with, Gogol missed two lectures out of three, and even when he did lecture, he merely whispered something incoherently and showed his students some engravings of views of Palestine and other Near Eastern countries.

All the time he looked terribly shy. 'We were all convinced', Turgenev writes, '(and we were hardly mistaken), that he had no idea of history, and that Mr. Gogol-Janovsky (as he was called on the time-table of the lectures), our professor, had nothing in common with Gogol the writer, already famous as the author of *Evenings on a Farm near Dikanka.*'

Professor Nikitenko noted in his diary: 'Gogol reads his university lectures so badly that his students treat him with derision. The university authorities are afraid they might play some trick on him which may have unpleasant consequences.' Another of Gogol's colleagues, Professor Vassilyev, wrote afterwards: 'Everyone at once recognized Gogol's incompetence. . . . There was only one thing left for him to do: to startle his audience by fine phrases. . . . Gogol lost interest in his work and just managed to carry on till the end of the academic year, occasionally turning up at lectures with his cheek tied round with a black handkerchief, as a sign that he had toothache, and mostly missing them out for the same reason. . . . At the annual examination he also appeared with his face swathed in a black handkerchief. . . . Knowing how shaky he was in his subject, the students explained his silence by his fear of showing his ignorance.'

Gogol himself blamed the students for the failure of his lectures, though he very soon seems to have realized that his university career was a great mistake. 'Every day', he wrote to Pogodin on the 14th of December 1834 (O.S.), 'I see something new and I realize my mistakes. Don't think that I was merely trying to awaken [my students'] feelings and imagination. I swear I had a much higher aim. Perhaps I am still inexperienced. I may be young in my ideas, but I shall grow old one day. Why, then, do I see my mistakes within one week? . . . Do you realize what it means not to meet with sympathy, what it means not to meet with any response? In this university I feel myself alone, absolutely alone. No one comes to hear me, not once have I observed any student struck by the light of truth. And that is why I have now completely given up any artistic finish [to my lectures] and, most of all, any desire to wake my sleepy students. . . . Oh, if only one student understood me! It's a colourless crowd, just like Petersburg.'

Worse than the indifference of the students was the hostility of his fellow-lecturers. One of them, Fyodor Chizhov, observes in his reminiscences that the professors of the university met Gogol coldly. 'The majority of us', he writes, 'hardly knew him as a creative writer and did not properly appreciate his *Evenings on a Farm near Dikanka*; besides, his very entry into the university by means of backstairs influence kept us away from him as a man.' Gogol, of course, repaid his colleagues in the same coin. 'For a moment', Professor Nikitenko wrote in his diary, 'pride gave place to the bitter realization of his inexperience and helplessness, but in the end it did not shake Gogol's faith in his all-round genius. Though after a reprimand from the provost he had to change his supercilious tone to the rector, dean and other members of the university, he still remained in the circle of his friends the same omniscient, profound genius as he had been before.'

It is a miracle Gogol was allowed to carry on with this farce. But the educational authorities seemed still impressed by his promise to publish volumes of historical works. The official report for 1835 of the Petersburg Educational District contained the following notice: 'The reader in history at Petersburg University, Mr. Gogol-Janovsky, has undertaken, in addition to his regular university duties, to write a History of the Middle Ages which will consist of eight or nine volumes. He also intends to issue an abbreviated edition of this history in one volume.'

The summer of 1835 Gogol again spent at Vassilevka and later he paid a visit to Kiev where, according to Maximovich, with whom he stayed, he was profoundly impressed by the holy places. In July, he was dismissed by the Patriotic Institute. He had been very slack in attendance and, according to his sister Yelisaveta, often did not turn up at his lessons 'sometimes because he was ill, but more often because he was lazy'. And at the end of 1835 he resigned from his university post. His position had become intolerable, but he hung on because his salary was his only regular income. Only three months before his resignation he wrote to Pushkin: 'Except for my rotten university salary of six hundred roubles [a year], I have no other source of income.' But the university authorities, too, were only too anxious to get rid of him. They did it by demanding that he should pass his doctoral examination, a feat that was quite beyond him. 'I have turned my back on the university', he wrote to Pogodin on the 6th of December 1835 (O.S.), 'and in a month's time I shall again be a free Cossack. Unrecognized I mounted the rostrum and unrecognized

103

I descended. But during these sixteen inglorious months of my humiliation—because it is the general opinion that it is not the right job for me—during these sixteen months I have profited greatly and added a great deal to the treasury of my soul. It was not childish thoughts, nor the limited scope of my knowledge, but lofty ideas full of truth and terrifying grandeur, that agitated me. . . . Peace to you, my heavenly visitors, which bestowed heavenly moments upon me in my little flat beneath the garret! No one knows about you, I drop you again to the bottom of my soul till a new awakening; for then you will come up again with renewed strength, and the shameless insolence of a learned ignoramus, the learned and illiterate mob, the crowd which always agrees with anything, etc., etc., will not dare to resist you. I am telling this only to you; I would not tell it to anyone else: for I would be called a boaster and nothing more. Away, away from all this!' Having bidden farewell in this typical dithyrambic manner to the academic world of learned ignoramuses, Gogol concluded: 'Now I have emerged into the open air. Fresh air is necessary to life, as rain to a flower, and a walk to a man who has been sitting in his study for hours on end. Let us laugh, laugh now as much as we can. Long live comedy!'

He had, in fact, not wasted those 'inglorious' sixteen months. It was not toothache that kept him away from the lecture room, but hard work. 'I am working like a horse', he wrote to Maximovich as early as the 23rd of August 1834 (O.S.), 'but on my own things and not on my lectures.' During those months he had published two volumes of articles and short stories under the titles respectively of *Arabesques* and *Mirgorod*, had written two plays, *Marriage* and his great dramatic masterpiece *The Government Inspector*, and had begun writing *Dead Souls*.

¶ 4

Gogol made his first appearance as an essayist in a hotch-potch of articles and stories which he published in 1835 under the general title of *Arabesques*. 'I am sending you', he wrote to Maximovich on the 22nd of January 1835 (O.S.), 'a scramble, a mishmash, a porridge, and I leave it to you to decide whether there is any butter in it. . . .' 'In it', he wrote to Pogodin on the same day, 'there is a great deal that is childish, and I cast it into the world so as to cast everything old out of my room and at the same time pull myself together and start a new life. . . .' The same not altogether sincere apologetic tone marks Gogol's introduction to *Arabesques*. 'I confess', he writes, 'that if I had published this collection a year ago, when I was a little more severe on my own works, I should, perhaps, not have included some of the articles in it. But instead of judging one's *past* severely, it is much better to be implacable towards one's *present* work. To destroy what we have written before seems as unjust as to forget the past days of our youth. Besides, if a work contains two or three new truths, an author has no right to conceal them from his readers, and for two or three true ideas one can forgive the imperfection of the whole.'

Gogol was thinking of his historical articles, rather than of his stories. In the same letter he asked Pogodin to tell him what he thought of the historical articles, because the opinion of a well-known historian like Pogodin would be of great help to him, as he had got some 'learned enemies' at the University. It was this fear of his 'learned enemies' that made Gogol antedate some of these articles. The whole collection was divided into two parts. The first part included seven articles (*Sculpture, Painting and Music, About the Middle Ages, On the Teaching of World History, A Glance at the Composition of the Ukraine, A Few Words about Pushkin, On Modern Architecture,* and *Al Mamun (an historical portrait),* and two stories (*A Chapter from an Historical Novel* and *The Portrait*). The second part included six articles (*Life, Schloezer, Muller and Herder, On Ukrainian Folk-songs, Thoughts on Geography (for children), The Last Day of Pompeii (a painting by Bryulov),* and *On the Migrations of Peoples at the End of the Fifth Century),* and three stories (*Nevsky Avenue, The Prisoner (a fragment from an Historical Novel),* and *The Diary of a Madman*).

Gogol's conception of art as the most important moral factor in life appears as early as in his first article in *Arabesques—Sculpture, Painting and Music*—which he dated 1831, though he most certainly revised it thoroughly in 1834. Gogol had no ear for music and that was, no doubt, why he placed it above sculpture and painting and charged it with the arduous task of saving mankind from the temptations to which the industrial revolution had exposed it. 'We yearn to save our poor souls,' he writes, 'to escape from these terrible seducers and—fling ourselves into music. Oh, music, be our custodian, our saviour! Do not leave us! Arouse more often our mercantile souls! Strike more sharply upon our slumbering feelings! Excite, tear them, and drive away if only for one moment this terrible, cold selfishness which is trying to take possession of our world!'

Of the historical articles in *Arabesques*, *About the Middle Ages* and *Al Mamun* are the most interesting. Both were lectures he read at Petersburg University. The first was the introductory lecture to his course on medieval history, and the second he read in the presence of Pushkin and Zhukovsky in October 1834, at a time when he still had great hopes of making his mark as an historian. Both lectures fully conformed to Gogol's idea that 'a professor's style must be exciting and fiery and must hold the attention of the audience'. They were, in fact, imaginative reconstructions of certain historical events and persons, and relied for their effect on 'inspiration' rather than learning. 'Involuntarily', he exclaims in the first, 'one falls on one's knees as one follows the wondrous ways of Providence: the Popes, as though on purpose, were invested with power in order to give the young States time to get stronger and grow to maturity, in order to make them learn to obey before they were ready to give orders to others, in order to provide them with the energy without which the life of nations is colourless and powerless.' The Crusades were 'an event which towers like a giant over the other events, which, too, were extraordinary and wonderful . . .'. The Arabs were 'the glory of eastern nations . . . but after a century this extraordinary people has already vanished, so that you can't help asking yourself whether it ever existed, or was merely a figment of your imagination. . . .' Woman in the Middle Ages was 'a goddess'. Attila was 'a little man, almost a dwarf, with an enormous head, with small Kalmuk eyes, so piercing that none of his subjects could bear to look at them without an involuntary shudder. By the look in his eyes alone he ruled all his tribes'—they were, in fact, the same eyes as those which Gogol gave to Petromikhail, the usurer in the first version of *The Portrait*.

Al Mamun was another of Gogol's attempts to convey historical events in the heightened, emotional narrative style that was so characteristic of him at the time. He saw the cause of the decay of the Arab empire in Al Mamun's attempt to introduce Greek philosophy to a nation 'whose imagination swamped the emasculated deductions of cold reasoning. . . . Al Mamun', he writes, 'left out of account the great truth that culture is drawn from the people itself, that if it is to be introduced from outside at all, it must never exceed the capacity of the people to absorb it, for a people can only develop out of its own national elements.' He saw Al Mamun's chief mistake as putting 'theoretical philosophers and poets' in responsible positions in the State. 'Their sphere is quite different', he writes. 'They should be granted the patronage of the ruler of a State and allowed to go their own way.' But even as early as that Gogol reserved for himself a special role in influencing the policies of his country by making an exception in favour of 'those great poets who combine in themselves the philosopher, the poet, and the historian, who have gained a deep insight into man and nature, fathomed the past and foreseen the future, whose voice is heard by the entire people. . . . Wise potentates honour them with their conversation, guard their precious lives and are careful not to crush them by the manifold activities of a ruler. They are summoned only to important Councils of State as experts on the human heart.'

It was characteristic of Gogol that in his essay on the three German historians, Schloezer, Muller and Herder, he should single out the first for his 'happy moments of sudden inspiration' and the last for looking at history 'with spiritual eyes', though he criticized him for being 'a wise man in his knowledge of the ideal man and mankind, but a baby in his knowledge of man'.

The short essay on *Life* which introduces the second part of *Arabesques* is a frankly lyrical and wholly unscientific attempt to summarize the essence of the ancient religions of Greece and Rome culminating in Christianity.

In his essay *On Modern Architecture*, which he wrote during the second half of 1833 (he himself dated it 1831), Gogol expresses his preference for Gothic architecture as the creation of the purely European spirit, the taste for which, he writes, had spread quickly all over Europe, 'thanks to Walter Scott's mighty word', Walter Scott being, in his opinion, the first 'to shake off the dust from Gothic architecture and show its merits to the whole world. . . . In England', Gogol continues, 'all the new churches are built in the Gothic style. They are very charming and pleasant to look at, but, alas, they lack the true grandeur of the great buildings of the past.' His predilection for grandeur and originality leads him again into all sorts of exaggerations such as the suggestion that every city should consist of various architectural styles, 'gloomy Gothic, heavily decorated Eastern, colossal Egyptian, and classical Greek' buildings standing side by side in the same street. Architecture, he points out, is also the chronicle of the world, and he confesses that as a boy he thought that every city should have a street whose buildings should represent the history of architecture throughout the ages, so that by walking through it one could learn everything there was to know about architecture.

During his life in Petersburg, Gogol never figured as a prophet (he grew fond of that thankless role later on), but in his essay on Bryulov's painting of *The Last Day of Pompeii*, written in 1834 when it was exhibited at the Hermitage, he uttered a prophecy on the future of Russian literature of the nineteenth century which shows how remarkable his literary intuition was at a time when, except in poetry, that literature showed no real signs of greatness. 'I don't remember', he wrote, 'who it was who said that the appearance of a great genius who would embrace the whole life of the nineteenth century was impossible. This is absolutely unjust, and such an idea reveals a feeling of hopelessness and smacks of pusillanimity. On the contrary, never will the flight of genius be so striking as in our own times; never have the materials been so well prepared for him as in the nineteenth century. And his steps will assuredly be the steps of a giant and will be apparent to everyone. . . .' This is true of himself as well as of the other great Russian writers of the nineteenth century who followed him.

Of the two articles Gogol contributed to Pushkin's *Contemporary*, the first, published in April 1836, under the title *On the Condition of Journalistic Literature in 1834 and 1835*, is remarkable chiefly for Gogol's criticism of two of the most popular Petersburg journals: *The Library for Reading*, founded in 1834 by the Petersburg bookseller Alexander Smirdin and edited by Osip Senkovsky, a professor of Oriental languages at Petersburg University, and *The Northern Bee*, edited by the redoubtable Faddey Bulgarin, both of them unprincipled time-servers and rabid supporters of the reactionary régime of Nicholas I. The article appeared at a time when the authorities were bent on eradicating every vestige of 'liberal' thought in the periodical journals (*The Moscow Telegraph*, edited by Nikolai Polevoy, 'a fanatical liberal', as the Minister of Education, Count Uvarov, called him, had been closed down in 1834 for criticizing Kukolnik's ultra-patriotic play *The Hand of the Almighty Saved the Motherland*, and *The Telescope*, the other progressive monthly, in which Belinsky began his career as critic, was closed down in 1836 for publishing Peter Chaadayev's famous *Philosophic Letter* attacking 'the dead stagnation' of Russian society). Gogol's attack on the two most 'patriotic' editors of the day created a sensation and led Pushkin, who was anxious for the fate of his quarterly, to publish a guarded recantation of Gogol's views.

The chief brunt of his attack Gogol directed against Senkovsky, whom he criticized for the complete absence of literary taste in his articles. 'What he likes today', Gogol writes, 'he ridicules to-morrow. He was the first to put Kukolnik on a level with Goethe, declaring that he did so only because he wished to do so. Walter Scott,' Gogol goes on, 'that great genius whose immortal works embrace life with such fullness, Walter Scott he described as a charlatan. And this was said to educated people who had read Walter Scott. We can be sure that Mr. Senkovsky said it without thinking because he never cares what he says and never remembers in one article what he has written in another.' What Gogol, characteristically, disliked most about Senkovsky was his 'unheard-of' habit of revising almost all the stories that appeared in his journal. 'It is interesting', Gogol writes, 'that he himself freely admits it. "In our journal we do things quite differently", he writes. "We never publish a story in the form in which we get it. We revise them all. Sometimes we make up one story out of two or three, and it is considerably improved by our revision." Such a strange tutelage', Gogol declares, 'has never before been known in Russia.'

As for the 'official' *Northern Bee*, Gogol dismissed it in one sentence. 'It is', he writes, 'a sort of wastepaper basket into which everyone throws anything he likes.'

In 1835, a group of Moscow writers, including Pogodin and Stepan Shevyryov, Professor of Russian Literature at Moscow University, began publishing *The Moscow Observer* in an attempt to break the monopoly of the two popular Petersburg periodicals.

Shevyryov wrote an article for it in which he attacked the 'mercenary spirit' of the Russian writers and editors, which, he claimed, explained the decay of Russian literature in the 'thirties. Such attacks, Gogol declared, were unjustified since literature had become a trade because of the greater demand for it. 'That a writer buys a house and a carriage and pair', Gogol writes, 'is no great tragedy; what is bad is that people should buy bad merchandise and be proud of their purchase.'

In general, Gogol criticized the Russian periodical press for its narrowness of outlook and its failure to comment on the important events in the literary world. 'Did our journals', Gogol writes, 'explain to their readers who Walter Scott [who died in 1832] was, and what his influence amounted to, or what is the significance of the modern French romantic literature, why it has arisen, what is the cause of the aberration of its taste and what is its character? Why prose has taken the place of poetry in our country? What is the level of education of the Russian public? What is the nature of the originality of our writers? In vain', Gogol goes on, 'will a reader try to find in them any new ideas or any trace of a profound and conscientious study of these problems. Walter Scott was dismissed in a few abusive sentences. French literature they accepted with childish enthusiasm, asserting that the French fashionable writers have fathomed the secrets of the human heart which had remained a mystery to Cervantes and Shakespeare . . . others denounced it, and yet themselves wrote in the same vein with even greater absurdities. . . .'

Turning, finally, to the Russian book reviewers, Gogol criticized them for their lack of personal opinions. They never wrote that a certain book was good and deserved attention for certain specific reasons. 'This book', the reviewers, according to Gogol, wrote, 'is a great masterpiece, and its author is greater than Walter Scott, Humboldt, Goethe and Byron. Take it, rebind it, and put it in your library, buy its second edition and put that in your library too: why not have two copies of a good book?' Gogol further objected to 'the literary ignorance' of the Russian reviewers. He accused them of playing about with the names of established writers and of those who were just embarking on their literary career. 'One reviewer abuses those whom his opponent has praised', he writes, 'and all this is done without analysis and without thought. Some writers even owe their fame to the quarrel between two reviewers. Without mentioning any of our native writers, a reviewer, discussing some stupid book, will invariably drag in Shakespeare, whom he has never read. But then, it is the fashion now to talk about Shakespeare—so let's have Shakespeare! "Let us see", he writes, "how our author compares with Shakespeare," and yet the reviewed book is pure nonsense, written without any pretensions to rivalling Shakespeare, and comparing favourably only with the spirit and mode of expression of the reviewer himself!'

Lack of aesthetic taste, self-conceit and pettiness of mind were the principal sins of the Russian reviewer that Gogol condemned in his article. 'And yet', he concludes, 'criticism based on true taste and true intelligence, criticism by a man of great talent, ought to be considered of equal literary merit with any other creative writing: in it is seen the writer whose work is being analysed, and even more so the critic who analyses it. Criticism written by a man of talent survives the ephemerality of journalism. It is invaluable for the history of literature. Our literature is young, we have only a few great writers, but to a thoughtful reviewer it represents a whole field of study, work for several years. Our writers are cast in quite a special mould, and notwithstanding their general feature, namely that of imitation, they exhibit purely Russian elements; and our imitation, too, bears quite a northern character and represents a phenomenon which is of great interest even to European literature.'

In his second article, *Petersburg Notes for 1836*, published in *The Contemporary* in 1837, Gogol draws a light-hearted parallel between Petersburg and Moscow—'the fat old fishwife from whom you won't hear anything but bad language', as he wrote to Maximovich on the 12th of March 1834 (O.S.). Gogol must have written the first part of this article in 1835, for Pushkin refers to it in the second chapter of his *Journey from Moscow to Petersburg*. 'Incidentally', Pushkin writes, 'I have found among my papers an interesting comparison between our two capitals. It was written by one of my friends, a great melancholic, who occasionally has his lighter moments.' The second part of the article deals with the Petersburg theatre and was written after the production of *The Government Inspector*. It is a revised version of Gogol's unpublished article *The Petersburg Stage in 1835–'36*. He concludes it with a description of Petersburg in early spring, ending on an autobiographical note, in which he describes his feelings on Easter morning in 1836, when he was already planning to go abroad.

'I love spring intensely [he writes]. Even here, in this wild North, she is mine. It seems to me that no one loves her as much as I. With her, my youth comes back to me; with her, my past is more than a memory: it is before my eyes and is ready to well out of them in a flood of tears. I was so enraptured by the bright, clear days of Easter that I had not noticed the great fair in Admiralty Square. Only from a distance did I see how the swings carried into the air some smart young gentleman sitting close beside some lady in a fashionable hat; I caught a glimpse of a signboard on a corner booth on which was painted a red-haired devil with an axe in his hand. I saw nothing more. . . . The city has dried up after the rain; the pavements are dry. The Petersburg gentlemen stroll along the streets in short coats and with all sorts of walking sticks; instead of the cumbrous carriages, flies and phaetons bowl along the parqueted roads. Books are not read with the same zest. Instead of woollen stockings the shop-windows display summer caps and riding crops. . . . It is wonderful to be able to turn one's back on sedentary life, to think of a long journey to new countries beneath different skies and amid green southern groves. It is wonderful to imagine at the end of some Petersburg street the snow-capped mountains of the Caucasus, or the lakes of Switzerland or Italy crowned with laurels and anemones, or Greece, lovely in its emptiness. . . . But wait! the houses of Petersburg are still piled-up on either side of me. . . .'

Part Four

THE MATURE ARTIST

¶ I

'In Russian society', Ivan Panayev, poet, novelist, and memoirist writes in his *Literary Reminiscences*, 'there was a vague feeling of the need of a new direction in Russian literature, and a desire that it should come down to earth from its isolated artistic heights and take an active part in social problems. We were all bored to tears by artists and heroes spouting rhetorical phrases. What we wanted to see was a living man and, especially, a Russian. And at that moment Gogol suddenly made his appearance.'

Panayev had in mind the 'artists and heroes' of the 'problem' novels in which, as Belinsky observed, there was 'more intellect and education than talent'. These novels were full of high-sounding sentiments and melodramatic situations, lacking the sense of reality to be found even in Gogol's most fantastic stories. The only story in which Gogol approached the 'rhetorical' school of Russian writers is the first version of *The Portrait*, a 'problem' story published in Part I of *Arabesques*, whose main theme is the corrupting influence of money on art. (In the revised version of the story, completed in 1842, Gogol's exaggerated ideas of art as a means for man's salvation can already be plainly discerned.) It resembles *The Terrible Vengeance* in that it is shorn of the comic element, but it completely lacks the poetic intensity of Gogol's earlier tale. The main fault of the first version of *The Portrait*, however, is that its fantastic elements are not leavened by those brilliant touches of realism which make the most incredible situations in Gogol's stories acceptable to the reader. A comparison between the same scene in the first and second versions will show how Gogol corrected this serious defect. (In the first version the artist's name is Chertkov, and in the second Chartkov, a change by which Gogol wished to emphasize the fact that his second version was, as he said, 'a completely new story'.) The scene describes the visit of his landlord and a police officer to the artist's studio at the beginning of the first part of the story:

'You can see for yourself, sir,' said the landlord, to the police officer, spreading out his arms, 'he just doesn't pay his rent. Just doesn't pay.'

'I must warn you, sir,' said the police officer, pushing a finger between the buttons of his uniform, 'that you have to pay the three months' rent you owe to your landlord.'

'I'd be glad to pay,' Chertkov replied calmly, 'but what can I do if I haven't got the money?'

'In that case, sir, the landlord will have to take all your movable property to the value of the rent you owe him, and you must vacate your flat immediately.'

'Take what you want,' Chertkov replied almost impassively.

'Your pictures, sir,' said the police officer, examining some of them, 'have been painted not without skill. A pity, though, they're not finished and the colours, too, don't seem to be quite vivid. I don't suppose, sir, you could afford to buy paints. And what picture is this? I mean the one wrapped in a cloth.'

The police officer walked up unceremoniously to the picture and pulled down the sheet, for these gentry allow themselves no little liberty when face to face with poverty and helplessness. The portrait seemed to surprise him, but the extraordinary liveliness of the eyes produced the same effect on everyone. Examining the picture, he must have grasped the frame a little too firmly between his fingers, policemen's hands being made in a somewhat clumsy fashion, for it suddenly broke; a small piece of wood dropped on to the floor together with a jingling roll of gold, and a few shining coins rolled all over the floor. Chertkov rushed eagerly to pick them up and snatched several sovereigns out of the hands of the policeman, who had picked them up.

'Why do you say you can't pay your rent?' the police officer observed with a pleasant smile. 'You have plenty of gold coins, haven't you?'

'These coins are sacred to me!' cried Chertkov, afraid of the policeman's experienced hands. 'They were entrusted to me by my late father. However,' he added, flinging a few gold coins to his landlord, 'here's your rent.'

The landlord's face and manners changed at once, and so did the face and manners of the worthy custodian of drunken cabmen.

The police officer started apologizing. He assured Chertkov that he was only doing his duty, but had no authority to make him pay his rent; to convince Chertkov of his good intentions, he offered him a pinch of snuff as a consolation prize. The landlord declared that he was only joking, and he did so with the same shamelessness and protestations with which the merchants in the Arcade address their customers.

But Chertkov rushed out of the room and made up his mind not to stay in his old flat a day longer. . . .

And here is the second version of the same scene, from which the clumsy characterization of the three men and the 'rhetorical' explanations of the artist have been removed and the whole incident made much more realistic and credible.

'You can see for yourself, sir,' said the landlord to the police officer with a deprecatory wave of the hands. 'He just doesn't pay his rent. Just doesn't pay!'

'What do you expect me to do if I have no money,' said Chartkov. 'Can't you wait a little longer? I'll pay you.'

'I'm afraid, sir, I can't wait,' said the landlord crossly, waving the key in his hand. 'I'm used to decent tenants, sir. Lieutenant-Colonel Potogonkin has been living in my house for seven years; Anna Petrovna Bukhmisterova has rented the coach-house and the stables with two stalls, keeps three servants—that's the kind of tenants I have. I am not in the habit, sir, of having trouble with my tenants about the rent, and that's the truth. Will you please be so good as to pay at once or look for another place!'

'Well, sir, if you've undertaken to pay, you have to pay,' said the police inspector with a slight shake of the head, pushing a finger between the buttons of his uniform.

'But what am I to pay him with? That's the question. You see, I haven't got a penny.'

'In that case, sir, you'd better satisfy Ivan Ivanovich by giving him some of your pictures,' said the police officer. 'He might agree to be paid in pictures.'

'No, sir, thank you very much! No pictures for me. I might have considered it if this gentleman's pictures were anything decent, something you could hang on a wall, such as a general with a star, or a portrait of Prince Kutuzov, but look at those pictures of his! There, if you please, is a portrait of a peasant, a peasant in a shirt, a portrait of his servant, the young fellow who grinds his colours for him. Now fancy painting a portrait of that oaf! I shall give him a good thrashing one day; he's been removing all the nails from the bolts on the doors, the rascal! . . . Look at the kind of things he paints. There's a picture of his room. Now what I'd like to know, sir, is why, if he must paint his room, he doesn't tidy it up first. Look at that! Painted it with all the filth and rubbish on the floor! See what a mess he's made of my flat? I tell you, sir, some of my tenants have been living in my house for over seven years! Gentlemen, sir, colonels! Anna Petrovna Bukhmisterova. . . . No, sir, there's no worse tenant in the world than an artist. Lives like a pig and doesn't pay his rent! It's an absolute scandal, sir!'

And the poor artist had to listen patiently to all this. Meanwhile, the police inspector amused himself by an examination of the pictures and sketches, showing at once that he had a much more sensitive imagination than the landlord and that his soul was not altogether impervious to artistic impressions.

'Ah,' he said, poking a finger into a picture of a nude, 'nice bit of goods, that. . . . And what's that black mark doing under the nose of this fellow here? Been taking too much snuff, or what?'

'Shadow,' Chartkov muttered gruffly, without looking at the policeman.

'But you should have put it somewhere else, sir,' said the police officer. 'Shows up too much under the nose. And whose portrait is that?' he went on, going up to the portrait of the old man. 'Looks a bit of a horror, don't he? Wonder if he really did look so terrifying. Bless my soul, seems to look through you, don't he? Makes your flesh creep. Ugh, what a Gromoboy [the hero of Zhukovsky's ballad, *The Twelve Sleeping Maidens*, who sold his soul to the devil]. Who was your model?'

'Oh, some man . . .' said Chartkov.

He stopped short without finishing the sentence, for at that moment there was a loud crack. The police inspector must have grasped the frame of the portrait too firmly between his fingers and, a policeman's grip being notoriously clumsy, he broke the moulding at the side, which fell into the hollow frame, with the exception of one piece which dropped out together with a packet wrapped in blue paper, which fell with a heavy thud on to the floor. Chartkov's eyes immediately caught the inscription on the roll: one thousand sovereigns, and he flew like mad to pick it up. Seizing it, he clasped it convulsively in his hand, which sank with the weight.

'I could have sworn I heard the jingling of money,' said the police officer, who had heard the noise of something falling on the floor, but was not quick enough to see what it was, owing to the lightning rapidity with which Chartkov had picked up the roll of gold coins.

'What has it got to do with you whether I have anything or not?'

'All it's got to do with me, sir, is that you have to pay your landlord at once the rent you owe him. You seem to have the money, but you don't want to pay him. Isn't that so?'

'All right, I'll pay him today.'

'But why didn't you pay him before, sir? Why give your landlord all this trouble? Why waste the time of the police, sir?'

'I didn't want to touch that money. I shall pay him in full this evening and I'm leaving his flat tomorrow. I don't want to stay with such a landlord!'

'Well, it seems he'll pay you all right, sir,' said the police officer, turning to the landlord. 'But if he doesn't satisfy you in full this evening, he'll have to take the consequences, artist or no artist.'

Having delivered this warning, the police inspector put on his three-cornered hat and walked out into the passage, followed by the landlord, whose head was lowered as though he were sunk in deep thought.

'Thank God they've gone at last,' said Chartkov as he heard the front door closing behind his visitors.

The demonic element in the story, too, is very crudely handled in the first version, especially in the second part of it. In the first version, the main emphasis is on the intrusion of mysterious demonic powers into the life and work of an artist, while in the second, it is on the retribution suffered by an artist who regards his art mainly as a money-making trade. Again, in the second part of the second version of *The Portrait*, Gogol removed all the crudely fantastic effects of the portrait on its owners and concentrated its main interest on the need for the religious dedication of the artist to his art, with which, at the time of his revision of the story in 1841–2, he was becoming more and more preoccupied. For the mysterious usurer of the two versions, Gogol used for his prototype an Indian usurer whose main practice was among Petersburg actors. The actor Karatygin described him in his memoirs as having 'a bronze face tattooed in many colours, in which his black pupils glowed like coals from the yellowish whites of his red-rimmed eyes'.

A remarkable anticipation of modern methods of psychiatric treatment is to be found in both versions of the story. 'The doctor', Gogol writes, 'who attended him [Chartkov] and who had heard something of the strange story of his life, tried his utmost to find the secret relationship between the phantoms he saw in his dreams and the events of his life, but had no time to do so.'

Nevsky Avenue, the first story in Part II of *Arabesques*, like *The Portrait*, consists of two separate stories, but it differs from *The Portrait* in that it completely dispenses with the fantastic element. Only in the first story, which deals with the artist Piscaryov's unhappy love affair, does the fantastic element intrude, but it is wholly confined to the realm of dreams (as in the revised version of *The Portrait*). This love affair is told with so deep an insight into the secret places of the young artist's mind that, as has been suggested earlier, it seems likely that a similar incident took place in Gogol's life, too. The theme of Piscaryov's tragic involvement with reality is wonderfully integrated with the two main characters—the artist and the young prostitute whom he meets on Nevsky Avenue, and who appears to him in his dreams as the direct opposite of what she is; and there can be no doubt that Gogol had met both of them in life and studied them in their natural surroundings.

The tragedy of Piscaryov, a character endowed with the sensibilities of a poet, is beautifully contrasted in *Nevsky Avenue* with the comedy, almost the farce, of the unhappy adventure of Lieutenant Pirogov, an all-too-common type of army officer, a philistine *par excellence*, whose 'naïve impudence and self-conceit', as Dostoevsky described it, is a faithful reflection of the shallowness of his mind.

Gogol wrote *The Diary of a Madman*, the last story in his miscellany *Arabesques*, in 1833-4. His first intention seems to have been to make his hero a musician, for he had entitled the story *The Diary of a Mad Musician*, but finding it impossible to write his play *Vladimir Third Class*, he incorporated its main theme into his story, making its hero, Poprishchin, a low-grade civil servant, and giving his chief the part of the ambitious civil servant in his play. The story gave Gogol an excellent opportunity of expressing his contempt for the ruling hierarchy of Petersburg, and, at the same time, of revealing the tragedy of the little man caught in the toils of selfish, hypocritical and ambitious bureaucrats.

'Damn it [Poprishchin writes in his entry of November the 13th], it's always either a Court Chamberlain or a General. The Court Chamberlains and Generals get everything that is best in the world. You find some modest competence, you are about to grasp it in your hand and—a court chamberlain or general snatches it away from you. Damn it all! I wish I could be a General myself: not in order to marry and so on, no, I'd like to be a general just to see how they [i.e. his chief and his chief's daughter] would dance attendance on me, scrape and bow and play the hypocrite, and then tell them I don't care a damn for either of them.'

Between the ravings of Poprishchin, who listens to the conversations of dogs and reads their letters, Gogol managed to slip in a number of unpalatable truths which might otherwise have been blue-pencilled by the censor. Such, for instance, is Poprishchin's cry in his entry of November the 12th: 'Give me a human being! I want to see a human being; I demand food—food that would nourish and regale my soul!' which might well have been Gogol's own despairing challenge to the Russian ruling classes. Not that the censors could be so easily hoodwinked. In December 1834 Gogol wrote to Pushkin: 'Yesterday I met with an unpleasant obstruction from the censorship in connexion with *The Diary of a Madman*, but, thank God, things are a little better today; at least all I shall have to do is to cut out the best passages.'

Among the 'best passages' the censorship would not pass was the entry of October the 3rd which described the expectations of a decoration by Poprishchin's chief, with whose daughter the lowly civil servant had fallen in love:

'He is a very strange man [the girl's lapdog Meji writes to her friend Fidèle]. He is silent most of the time. He rarely utters a word; but a week ago he kept saying to himself: "Shall I get it or not?" He'd take a piece of paper in one hand, close the other, and say: "Shall I get it or not?" Once he even turned to me with the question: "What do you think, Meji? Shall I get it or not?" I couldn't understand what he meant, sniffed at his boot and went away. Then, *ma chère*, a week later papa arrived looking very pleased with himself. All morning gentlemen in uniform came to see him and congratulated him upon something. He was very happy at table and kept telling funny stories. I have never seen him so happy before. And after dinner he lifted me up to his neck and said: "Look what I've got, Meji!" I saw some kind of ribbon. I sniffed at it but could not discover any smell at all, however much I tried. At last, when no one was looking, I licked it: a bit salty, I thought.'

The censors also demanded the excision of the following passage in the entry Marchoctober 86, describing the mercenary ambitions of some high-placed officials: 'There they are,' Poprishchin writes, 'these people in high places, there they all are, the gentlemen who are ingratiating themselves with the court circles and go on repeating that they are patriots: it's government contracts they are after, these patriots, government contracts! They would sell their fathers and mothers for money, these ambitious gentlemen would. They would sell their Christ, they would!'

Gogol devotes considerable space in his story to the political events in Spain and the struggle for succession which followed the death of Ferdinand VII in 1830, as well as to the July revolution in France in that year. 'I've been reading the *Bee*', Poprishchin writes in his entry of October the 4th. 'What a stupid people the French are! What *do* they want? Good Lord, I'd take them all and give them a good thrashing!' Originally he finished his story with the remark: 'The French King has a boil under his nose' (the Russian word *shishka*, a boil, is also used colloquially for 'trouble', and the sentence could therefore also mean: 'The French King is in a devil of a mess', a reference to the abdication of Charles X in August 1830). But the abdication of a king after a revolution being a rather dangerous subject, Gogol altered it to: 'The Bey of Algiers has a boil under his nose', a reference to the deposition by the French in 1830 of the last Bey of Algiers,

Hussein Pasha. Towards the end of the story Poprishchin imagines himself to be Ferdinand VIII, King of Spain. 'Today', he writes in his entry of the 43rd of April 2000, 'is a day of the greatest solemnity. Spain has a King. That King am I.' And he ends his entry with a statement that might have been written by Gogol himself when he was a clerk in one of the ministries: 'Haven't been to the office. . . . To hell with it! No, my dear friends, you won't lure me there now; I'm not going to copy your disgusting papers!'

There are several references to England in the story. For instance, in the entry of 'January of the same year which happened after February', Gogol sums up the international situation in one short sentence: 'When England takes snuff, France sneezes.'

Arabesques was not a success. 'Please', Gogol wrote to Pogodin on the 23rd of March 1835 (O.S.), 'put in an announcement in the *Moscow News* about *Arabesques* to the effect that now people everywhere are talking about *Arabesques*, that this book has aroused general interest, that it is selling like hot cakes (N.B. till now I haven't had a farthing's profit from it), and so on.' Neither did *Mirgorod*, the volume of four stories (*The Old-World Landowners*, *Taras Bulba*, *Viy*, and *The Story of the Quarrel between Ivan Ivanovich and Ivan Nikiforovich*), which he published at the same time as *Arabesques*, bring him in any money.

Mirgorod inaugurated Gogol's correspondence with Stepan Shevyryov, who was to become his literary executor, but whom he actually met only at the end of 1838 in Rome. 'I am sending you my *Mirgorod*', Gogol wrote to Shevyryov on the 10th of March 1835 (O.S.). 'Please express your opinion of it in the *Moscow Observer*. I've also heard that you wish to say something about *Arabesques* . . . I have been very fond of you', Gogol went on, 'ever since you began editing the *Moscow Herald*, which I began reading while I was still at school, and your ideas suggested many things to me which even now have not quite developed. . . . I'd like to ask you earnestly for your friendship. You will acquire a friend to whom everything can be said to his face and who is ready to do all he possibly can to hear the truth. . . .'

Gogol gave *Mirgorod* the subtitle: 'Stories which are a continuation of the *Evenings on a Farm near Dikanka*', and, in a way, such a subtitle was justified, since all the stories in the volume deal with Ukrainian life. But though two of the stories, namely the historical novel *Taras Bulba* and the fantastic tale *Viy*, still fell short of artistic excellence and, indeed, were thoroughly revised later, *Mirgorod* undoubtedly shows a tremendous advance in Gogol's development as a creative writer. He was never again to write anything so deeply moving as *The Old-World Landowners*, nor anything conceived on so grand a scale as *Taras Bulba*. Again, *The Old-World Landowners* and *The Story of the Quarrel between Ivan Ivanovich and Ivan Nikiforovich* show Gogol as having attained that complete integration of idea and character which is the hallmark of creative genius.

The Story of the Quarrel between Ivan Ivanovich and Ivan Nikiforovich was written at the beginning of 1833 and published for the first time in an almanac in 1834. On the 7th of April 1833 (O.S.), Pushkin noted in his diary: 'Yesterday Gogol read me his tale of the quarrel between Ivan Ivanovich and Ivan Nikiforovich. Very original and very funny.' Gogol got the idea for the story from the interminable lawsuits brought by the landowners of his district (Mirgorod is a district town near Vassilevka) against each other and, particularly, from his grandfather's lawsuit against one of his neighbours. A similar story, *Two Ivans or The Passion for Litigation*, had been written by Vassily Narezhny, another Ukrainian author writing in Russian, in 1825, though Narezhny's story lacks the vehemence of Gogol's social criticism, let alone its humour and depth of characterization, being in essence simply a didactic, sentimental tale ending in the reconciliation of the two litigants. The last word about Gogol's story was said by Belinsky in his first analysis of Gogol's works in the article on *Russian Short Stories and the Short Stories of Mr. Gogol*, published in September 1835, in the *Telescope*, which he was editing at the time. 'Really,' Belinsky wrote, 'to make us take the liveliest interest in the quarrel between Ivan Ivanovich and Ivan Nikiforovich, to make us shake with laughter at the stupidities, worthlessness and feeble-mindedness of these living travesties of humanity is an amazing feat, but to make us afterwards feel genuine pity for these idiots, to make us take leave of them with a sort of deeply melancholy feeling, to make us exclaim with him, "It's a tedious world, gentlemen!"—that is real divine art which is called creative; that is the true expression of an artistic talent for whom where there is life there is also poetry!'

The plot of *Taras Bulba*, one of the most famous historical novels in Russian literature, does not differ very greatly from that of other popular historical novels of the period. An article published in the *Moscow Herald* in 1828 gives the following 'recipe' for an historical novel:

'The author takes a few historical personages, clothes them in traditional costumes and involves them in some sort of a plot. It is preferable to choose the fall and the razing of castles and cities. This is a very good choice, for, to begin with, during the description of a siege a great deal of martial noise and thunder can be introduced; secondly, one can bring on the scene two lovers, one of whom must belong to the besieging forces and the other to the besieged, so as to increase the interest of the reader. Among the historical characters there must be a fictitious one possessed of supernatural powers, a sorcerer or a gipsy or best of all a Jew. These Jews are extremely fashionable; they derive their origin from Shakespeare's Shylock and Walter Scott's Isaac. He must be omniscient and be able to untie all the knots of the plot. ... As for the form of the story, it is best to divide it into chapters and have each chapter begin with a description of a morning or a night or a storm, etc. And the more florid the style the better.'

In *Taras Bulba*, too, there is the siege of a fortified city, two lovers—Taras's younger son Andry and the daughter of the governor of the besieged fortress—belonging to the two hostile forces, and the ubiquitous and omniscient Jew Jankel, who gets Taras out of all sorts of dangerous scrapes. The first version of the story, too, is full of melodramatic phrases which Gogol eliminated in its final version, the text of which had been expanded from nine to twelve chapters. Gogol worked for six years on the text of *Taras Bulba* and its final version shows his less tolerant attitude towards religion and his naïve belief in the innate virtues of the 'Russian soul', a myth which he more than anyone else was responsible for creating. 'Let us drink', Taras addresses his comrades-in-arms, 'first of all to the holy orthodox faith, to the time when it will at last spread all over the world and everywhere there will be only one holy faith', and he follows up this toast in his long speech on 'comradeship' by the extravagant claim that 'to love as a Russian heart can love, to love not with your heart or with your mind but with all that God has given you, with everything you have—ah! no one else can love like that!'

Gogol's painstaking method of work is recorded by Nikolai Berg, a poet and translator who was for a time a contributor to the Slavophil periodical *Moskvityanin*. 'Once', Berg, who met Gogol in Moscow in 1848, writes, 'Gogol told us how he usually wrote his works and which method of writing he considered best. "At first", Gogol said, "you ought to jot down in a notebook everything as it occurs to you, however bad and watery it may be, but absolutely *everything*, and then forget all about it. After a month or two or even longer (you'll know when yourself), take your notebook out and read it over again: you will see that a great deal in it isn't as it should be, that a great deal of it is superfluous and that something is missing. Make your corrections and observations in the margin and put it away again. When you come to read it again, make new notes in the margin, and if there's no room left there, take a piece of paper and paste it in at the side. When the page is all covered, copy it out in your own hand. While doing this, new ideas, cuts, additions and emendations of style will occur to you by themselves. Among the words you have already written new words will suddenly appear, words which simply have to be there, but which for some reason did not come to you at once. Then, again, put it away. Go on a journey, enjoy yourself, do nothing or write something else. When the right time comes, you will remember your notebook: take it out, read it over again, correct it in the same way, and when it is all filled again, copy it out in your own hand. You will notice as you do so that together with the improvement in your style and the greater polish of your sentences, your hand seems to have become stronger; you write the letters more firmly and more resolutely. This, in my opinion," said Gogol, "must be done at least *eight* times. Someone may find that he could do it in fewer times, and someone else in more times. I do it eight times. Only after being copied out for the eighth time, and always in my own hand, is my work completely and artistically finished. Any further corrections and revisions are quite likely to spoil it; this is what is known among artists as *overdrawing*. Of course," Gogol concluded, "you cannot always follow such rules. I am talking of the ideal. Sometimes you let something out of your hands sooner. A man, after all, is a man and not a machine".'

Viy is the only fantastic story in *Mirgorod*. Gogol began writing it in 1833, and in a footnote to the story explains that it is based on a folk legend and that he had written it just as he heard it. So far, however, Russian scholars have failed to trace a single folk-lore story which bears any resemblance to *Viy*. While certain elements in the story are close to a number of fairy-tales and legends, and the description of the Kiev theological college where Gogol's father and grandfather had received their education closely resembles certain details in Narezhny's story *The Divinity Student*, published in 1824, most of the material of the story is original. The main theme of *Viy*, as has already been remarked, is closely connected with Gogol's neurosis, and that is why the fantastic elements in it are so vivid and terrifying. But Gogol's humour, too, is given full play in the description of the everyday life of the divinity students and, particularly, in the person of its hero, the 'philosopher' Khoma Brut.

Gogol wrote two other famous stories before he left Russia in 1836. One of them, *The Nose*, he wrote specially for the *Moscow Observer* at the request of Pogodin, but it was sent back to him because in the view of his Moscow friends it was too 'sordid'. It was published in *The Contemporary* with the following note by Pushkin: 'N. V. Gogol would not agree for a long time to the publication of this joke; but we found so much that was surprising, fantastic, hilarious and original in it that we persuaded him to permit us to share with the public the pleasure which his manuscript gave us.' The 'joke' was, of course, the fact that the hero of the story, Major Kovalyov, loses his 'nose', but this fantastic element of the story gave Gogol the opportunity he had first exploited in his *Diary of a Madman* of writing a bitingly satirical exposure of the stupidity of officialdom, and of the snobbery, self-complacency and indifference of the higher classes of Russian society. 'If', Gogol wrote to Pogodin on the 18th of March 1835 (O.S.), 'the stupid censorship should object to the fact that the "nose" pays a visit to the Kazan Cathedral, I might take him to a Catholic church. But I can't believe it has lost its senses to such an extent.' But Gogol's fears were justified: the censorship did object to the scene in the Kazan Cathedral and Gogol had to send his 'nose' to the Shopping Arcade instead.

Gogol's other story—*The Carriage*, a satire on provincial life, was written in the autumn of 1835 and published in the first issue of *The Contemporary* for 1836. This story, too, fell foul of the censorship, which cut out several sentences considered derogatory to the honour of the army, such as 'the uniforms of the General, the Colonel, and even the Major were entirely unbuttoned, so that their noble braces of silk material were just visible, but all the other officers, conscious of the respect due to superior rank, had their uniforms done up except for the last three buttons'.

Gogol always shut himself up in his room to write his stories and, according to one of his friends, he seemed to go through a curious series of physical jerks before starting work. 'He waved his arms about,' his friend, who watched him through the key-hole of his room, records, 'planted his fists on his hips, went through all sorts of contortions, and clutched at his hair, ruffling it wildly and pulling most extraordinary faces. That was why', his friend concludes, 'he never went up to his desk without first locking the door of his study and leaving the strictest orders to his servant not to let anyone come near it.'

¶ 2

So far it was only among his closest friends that Gogol's genius was fully, or at least sufficiently, appreciated to make him feel that he would no longer be 'buried in obscurity'. The Petersburg press, that is, *The Northern Bee* and *The Library for Reading* continued to attack his works as 'sordid', but, as Annenkov observes in his *Marvellous Decade*, Gogol was 'not so much upset and embarrassed by the violent attacks of Bulgarin and Senkovsky, as by the general coolness of the Petersburg public and even of his friends. He was a solitary figure', Annenkov declares, 'and he did not know where to turn or how to escape from this situation. His Moscow acquaintances and well-wishers expressed in their periodical (the *Moscow Observer*) their sympathy for his creative talents in a very reserved and hesitant manner, revealing their real views only in private and in their correspondence.' It was at this critical stage in his career that Belinsky, who had first met Gogol at Aksakov's house in May 1835, came to his rescue with his long article *Russian Short Stories and the Short Stories of Mr. Gogol*, in which he uncompromisingly declared that Gogol was 'the head of Russian literature' and 'occupies the place vacated by Pushkin'. This article made a tremendous impression on the twenty-six-year-old Gogol. 'I had the opportunity', writes Annenkov, 'of seeing the effect of this article on Gogol. At that time he had not yet arrived at the conviction that Belinsky's criticism had wickedly misinterpreted all his literary aims and intentions, and he fully agreed with Belinsky's remark that "there is in all Gogol's stories a feeling of profound sadness, a feeling of profound pity for the conditions under which Russians have to live", and was pleased with the article; indeed, he was more than pleased, he was overjoyed with the article. . . .' Gogol seemed particularly impressed with the passage in the article defining the qualities of true creative art, and on one occasion, when Annenkov discussed it with him, he read out to him the following passage from it: 'The characters of the artist are still a secret to everyone, he has not yet taken the pen in his hand, but already he can count the folds of their clothes, the wrinkles on their faces furrowed by passion or grief, and already he knows them better than his father, brother and friend, better than his mother, sister and sweetheart; he knows, too, what they will say and do, he sees the whole skein of events which will entwine and tie them together. . . .' 'That is absolutely true', Gogol observed.

A few months earlier, Gogol had taken his mother severely to task for calling him a genius (Maria Ivanovna's enthusiasm where her Nikosha was concerned knew no bounds; she even went so far as to ascribe to him all the most recent inventions and discoveries). 'You let yourself be carried away too much by your dreams', he wrote to her on the 2nd of April 1835 (O.S.). 'Speaking of my work, you call me a genius. . . . Please, mother, never call me that again, particularly in conversation. . . . I know many intelligent people who pay no attention whatever to literature, and I respect them no less for that. Literature is not at all a matter of intelligence, but of feeling—just like music and painting. I have, for instance, no ear for music, but no one despises me because of that. I don't know anything about mathematics and if I began talking about it, everyone would laugh at me. If only you knew how unpleasant it is to hear your parents talking continuously about their children and praising them. . . . And one more thing', Gogol concludes, 'please, my dear, intelligent mother, don't ever express an opinion on literature. For instance, you ascribe to me the works of an author who has absolutely nothing

in common with me, who is generally regarded with contempt
even by ordinary readers, and yet in spite of my denials, you
pay no attention to them. . . . I can't help feeling annoyed when
I see an intelligent lady like you, endowed with true nobility of
soul, compromise herself and fail to realize how much subtlety
and a special flair for literature, which is rare even among
literary men, one has to possess to be able to pass a true judgment.'

Gogol might well have resented his mother's extravagant
opinions about him, which made him look ridiculous among the
neighbouring country squires and their ladies, but he certainly
did not consider Belinsky's opinion of him extravagant, though at
the time it quite probably made him look somewhat ridiculous in
the Petersburg literary circles. It may have also introduced a
certain ambiguity into his relations with Pushkin and quite
certainly increased his resentment at having his articles unceremoniously cut and corrected by the poet. At the time Belinsky's article appeared, he had already begun work on *Dead
Souls*. 'I have begun writing *Dead Souls*', he wrote to Pushkin on
the 7th of October 1835 (O.S.). 'The subject has already expanded into a very long novel and I think it's going to be very
funny. But now I have got stuck in the third chapter. I am looking for a slanderer with whom I might get well acquainted.
In this novel I should like to show the whole of Russia, even if it
is only from one side.' But though he does not acknowledge it in
his *Author's Confession*, it was most certainly Belinsky's first
article that made him feel the need of writing a great work that
would do full justice to his genius. 'Pushkin', he wrote in his
Author's Confession, 'thought that the subject of *Dead Souls* was
particularly good for me because it would enable me to travel
all over Russia with my hero and create a great number of the
most diverse characters. I began writing it without forming any
definite plan in my head. I simply thought that the droll project
which Chichikov attempts to carry out would naturally lead
me to the invention of all sorts of characters; that my bent for
laughter would of itself create a large number of funny episodes,
which I intended to intersperse with moving ones. But [and this,
surely, was the result of Belinsky's article] at every step I stopped
myself with the question: Why? What is it for? What should
such and such a scene or character express? You will ask what

is one to do when such questions occur to one. Get rid of them? I tried, but I found it impossible to get rid of them. . . . I saw clearly that I could no longer write without a clearly defined plan, that I must first of all explain to myself the purpose of my work, its absolute usefulness and necessity, as a result of which the author himself would be filled with a genuine and powerful love for his work. . . .'

It was this feeling that first gave him the idea of leaving Russia so as to consider in solitude and away from his friends how best to write a creative work that would conform to his now publicly acknowledged position as 'the head of Russian literature'. But his journey abroad still seemed only a remote eventuality. For the time being he stopped working on his long novel and devoted himself to playwriting.

¶ 3

It was in 1835, while preparing his lectures on Anglo-Saxon England, that Gogol attempted to write his historical play, *King Alfred*. Alfred is portrayed as the ideal ruler who curbs the lust for power of his nobles and fosters the spread of learning. 'A king', he tells his nobles, expressing Gogol's own conception of a monarch, 'must command everything and everybody and rule as he thinks fit.'

Gogol wrote only a rough draft of the first act and two scenes of the second act of the play. The first act opens with a crowd scene of Anglo-Saxons awaiting the return of King Alfred from 'a pilgrimage to Rome'. The people are dissatisfied with the nobles who rob them of their land and press them into servitude. King Alfred arrives and is acclaimed as the deliverer of his people. He calls a council of his nobles and accuses them of ruining their country. The act ends with the arrival of the Danes, who sack London. In the second act the Danes attack the Anglo-Saxon forces, which are put to flight but, rallied by Alfred, defeat the Danes. A true Christian king, Alfred is merciful to his defeated enemies. He concludes a peace treaty with the Danes, who swear by their gods never to raid England again.

This fragment is the only extant example of Gogol's attempt to write an historical play, a genre he could never master.

Gogol finished his first comedy, *Marriage, an Utterly Incredible Affair in Two Acts*, in the spring of 1835, having completely re-written it from a version of a play he wrote two years earlier under the title *Suitors*. In the first version the action took place not in Petersburg, but in the country, and the chief character of the play was not a civil servant but a sprightly countrywoman who owns a large estate and goes to a fair in search of a husband. The full original text of the play has not been preserved, but it would seem that Gogol had conceived it as a broad farce, the countrywoman being so eager not to lose any of her suitors that in the end she loses them all. The hero of the new version, Podkolyosin, seems to be a dramatic elaboration of Shponka, and as such contains certain important autobiographical features, but the action moves on a light comic plane. It is Gogol's only attempt to portray a Petersburg middle-class environment, the bride-to-be being the heiress of a reputedly rich merchant. Gogol first read *Marriage* at Pogodin's in August 1835, on his return from Vassilevka to Petersburg. Pogodin left this description of the reading: 'Gogol read as no other man could read. It was the height of marvellous perfection. Shchepkin read certain things beautifully, Sadovsky [a leading actor of the Moscow Maly Theatre], Pissemsky, Ostrovsky read comic things beautifully, but they all have to give pride of place to Gogol. I'll say more: however excellently certain roles of his comedies were performed, they never made the same impression on me as his reading. When he reached the scene of the love declaration of the hero and heroine of the play—in what church were you last Sunday? What flower do you like best?—interrupted by three pauses, he expressed the silence so eloquently that you could read his thoughts on his face and in his eyes, so that all his listeners literally shook with laughter and could not recover for a long time. But Gogol did not seem to notice the effect he had produced. He kept silent and merely rolled his eyes.'

Gogol again revised the play in the spring of 1836, and once more for inclusion in his collected works in 1842, when it was published for the first time. Its first performance in Petersburg was on the 9th of December 1842, and in Moscow on the 5th of February 1843 (O.S.). In Petersburg it was a failure: its un-conventional plot and the absence of love interest damned it in the eyes of the spectators. 'I have just come from the theatre', Belinsky wrote to Vassily Botkin, the distinguished critic and close friend of Turgenev's, 'where *Marriage* was a flop and was booed off the stage. It was horribly acted. Sosnitsky [one of the chief actors of the Alexandrinsky Theatre, on whose benefit night the play was performed and who played Podkolyosin's friend Kochkaryov] did not even know his lines. . . . Now Gogol's enemies are triumphant.' In Moscow the play was better acted, but even there it was not a success.

On the 7th of October 1835 Gogol asked Pushkin to give him a subject for a comedy. 'My hand is itching to write a comedy', he wrote to Pushkin. 'If I don't, I shall be wasting my time. . . . I swear it will be funnier than the devil! For God's sake, my brain and stomach are both crying out for food!'

Two years earlier Pushkin had gone to Uralsk to collect material for his history of the peasant rising under Pugachov. On the way he stopped at Nizhny Novgorod, where he was very courteously received and excellently treated by the Governor of the province. From there he went straight to Orenburg where he stayed with the commander-in-chief, Count Perovsky, an old friend of his. One morning he was awakened by the loud laughter of the Count, who came into his room with a letter in his hand. The letter was from the Nizhny Novgorod Governor who warned the Count to be very careful what he said to Pushkin as he suspected the poet had been sent on a secret mission to report on any shortcomings in the Orenburg administration. It was this incident that Pushkin told Gogol in reply to his letter.

Gogol began writing his five-act comedy, *The Government Inspector*, in October and finished it on December the 4th, that is, in under two months. He read the play at Zhukovsky's on the 18th of January 1836 (O.S.), and it was apparently thanks to Zhukovsky and Pushkin, who had asked Alexandra Smirnov to intercede on Gogol's behalf with Nicholas I, that the play was passed by the censorship and was first performed at the Alexandrinsky Theatre in Petersburg on April the 19th. Nicholas I was present at the performance and was observed to be highly amused and laughing heartily. He is said to have remarked after the performance: 'Everyone has caught it, but I have caught it more than anyone.'

Gogol was present at the rehearsals of the play, but he seemed unable to do much to put over his ideas to the actors. One of them left this picture of Gogol during one of the rehearsals: 'Gogol was very nervous and quite obviously upset. He looked ludicrous in his gold-rimmed glasses, with his long, bird-like nose, screwed-up eyes and tightly pursed lips. . . . He looked like a caricature of a man.'

'Having made the acquaintance of our theatrical directors here', Gogol wrote to Shchepkin on the 29th of April 1836 (O.S.), 'I feel so disgusted with the theatre that the very thought of the unpleasantness that is in store for me at the Moscow theatre is enough to stop me from going to Moscow. . . . [It was performed for the first time in Moscow on the 25th of May 1836 (O.S.), without Gogol's participation.] In addition to the dirty tricks the administration of the theatre has played on me, I understand that the director Gedeonov, influenced by some petty personal dislike of some of the chief actors in my play, has decided to give the main parts to other actors after the fourth performance. . . . The effect it produced was great and noisy. Everyone is against me. Elderly and respectable civil servants are shouting that, having dared to speak like that about civil servants, I hold nothing sacred. The policemen are against me, the merchants are against me, the literary clique is against me. They abuse me and go to see my play; all the tickets for the fourth performance are sold out. But for the intercession of the Emperor, my play would never have been put on, and there are already people who are trying to get it banned. Now I realize what it means to be a comic writer. The least sign of truth and not one man but all classes of the population rise up against you. I can imagine what would have happened if I had taken for the subject of the play something from Petersburg life, which I know much better now than life in the provinces. It is grievous to see people whom you love with a brotherly love attacking you. . . .'

He was even more outspoken to Pogodin. In two letters to him on May the 10th and 15th, about a month before his journey abroad, he wrote: 'A modern writer, a comic writer, a writer of a comedy of manners, must be as far away from his country as possible. The prophet is without honour in his own country. . . . Everyone is against him. "He's an incendiary! He's a rebel!" Who says that? It is said by men occupying high offices of State, men of high rank, men of experience . . . men who are considered educated and whom the world, at least the Russian world, calls educated. Scoundrels are put on the stage and everyone is attacking me for putting them there. Let the scoundrels be angry; but those are angry whom I never took to be scoundrels. I am saddened by this sign of a profound, stubborn ignorance which pervades all our classes. . . . To say of a rogue that he is a rogue is considered to be undermining the foundations of the State; to say something that is true to life means to defame a whole class of people and arm others in defence of it. Just consider the position of the poor author who loves his country and his countrymen dearly. Would it be any consolation to him if you told him that there were a few people who understood him and who regarded him differently?'

Gogol's distress at the way his play was misinterpreted, for in his view it was not a political but merely a moral exposure of the evils that were endemic in Russia in those days, was more than justified. Annenkov, who was present at the première of the play, declares in his reminiscences that Gogol's 'fussiness' at the rehearsals, which seemed so strange to his friends and, as some of them thought, almost indecent, was justified by the appallingly bad performance given by the actors. 'Gogol', Annenkov writes, 'was in agony the whole of that evening. . . . [Gogol shared a box with Zhukovsky, Prince Vyazemsky, the poet, and Count Mikhail Vyelgorsky, a talented cellist and composer, who also did a great deal to obtain the Emperor's permission for the public performances of the play.] Even after the first act everyone in the audience looked perplexed (it was a select audience in every sense of the word), as though no one could make up his mind what to make of what he had just seen on the stage. And yet there were certain features and scenes in this "farce" which were so true to life that once or twice, especially in those places which did not seem to contradict their preconceived idea of comedy, there were outbursts of laughter. Something quite different happened in the fourth act: laughter could still be heard occasionally from one end of the auditorium to the other, but it was a sort of timid laughter, which stopped as soon as it began; there was hardly any applause at all; but the intentness with which the audience followed the development of the action of the play, and sometimes the dead silence, showed that what was going on on the stage was making a profound impression on the spectators. At the end of the act, the former bewilderment grew into general indignation which found full expression during the fifth act. Some people called for the author at the end of the play because they thought he had written a comic masterpiece, others because some of the scenes showed talent, but most people because it made them laugh. The general opinion of the select members of the audience, however, found expression in the phrase: "This is impossible, it is a libel, a farce."'

After the performance, Gogol arrived at Prokopovich's in an irritable mood. Prokopovich offered him a copy of *The Government Inspector*, which had just been published, with the words: 'Feast your eyes on your child.' Gogol flung the book on the floor, went up to the table, and said wistfully: 'If only one or two people had abused it I should not have minded, but all, all . . .'

Nikitenko, a more conservative witness of the 'public indignation' Gogol's great comedy had aroused, wrote in his diary: 'Gogol's comedy has caused a sensation. It is being constantly performed—almost every second day. I was present at the third performance. The Empress, the heir to the throne [the future Alexander II], and the Grand Duchesses were also there. The comedy amused them very much. The Emperor ordered his ministers to go and see *The Government Inspector*. In front of me sat Count Chernyshov and Count Kankrin. The first expressed his satisfaction; the second merely said: "It wasn't worth while coming to see this stupid farce." Many people think the Government should not have given its approval to a play in which it is so cruelly censured. I saw Gogol yesterday. He has the air of a great man who is suffering from a feeling of wounded pride. However, Gogol really did a great thing. The impression made by his comedy adds a great deal to the impressions of the existing order of things which are accumulating in the minds of people.'

What were Gogol's own views of the drama and the aims of dramatists? In March and April, that is, at the time *The Government Inspector* was being rehearsed, Gogol was preparing an article, published posthumously, on *The Petersburg Stage in 1835-36*. (Part of it he later incorporated in his article, *Petersburg Notes for 1836*, published in *The Contemporary* at the beginning of 1837.)

He begins his article with an examination of the nature of the romantic movement and its influence on the emergence of a new kind of drama on the European stage. The romantic movement, he declares, was nothing but an attempt to grapple more closely with the problems of modern society, from which the writers of the neo-classical school had completely cut themselves off by their desire to imitate the ancient writers. The transition to this movement was, as a rule, made by 'daring and desperate men, who organize rebellions in society'. They see forms that are not characteristic of modern life and rules which do not correspond to prevailing manners and habits, and they stop at nothing in their efforts to overcome all obstacles. They know no limits, they break down everything without thinking and in their desire to correct what is wrong, they do as much harm as good. As a rule, they are the first to go under in the chaos they have themselves created. But out of this chaos a great creative writer emerges, who erects a new edifice and by his wise and comprehensive judgment embraces both the old and the new. Many writers have amazed their readers by their 'romantic boldness' and stunned them by their 'new vocabulary'. But as soon as a great talent emerges from their midst he transforms, with the inspired calmness of the artist, a romantic work into a classical one, or, better still, into a clear, precise and sublime work of art. 'This', Gogol declares, 'was what Walter Scott did, and if Byron had possessed as much calm and speculative intelligence he would have done the same to a colossal extent.'

The public, Gogol argues, was quite right in being dissatisfied with the neo-classical drama. 'Even Molière who, if he had been alive now, would have done away with the present rambling type of play, even Molière himself', Gogol writes, 'is felt to be long-winded and boring on the stage. If his plays are skilfully devised, they are devised in accordance with the old dramatic laws and on one and the same pattern; the action of the play is too decorous, and composed without regard to the age in which he lived and to which many of his characters belong. There is not a single event of his time which he treated in the same way as Shakespeare did.' Modern drama, Gogol thought, must reflect the problems of modern society and expose 'the springs that bring it into motion', and to do that, he added, one must possess great talent. . . . 'When the whole world danced to the tune of Byron's lyre, that was not absurd. But today the Dumas and the Ducanges have become the world's lawgivers!' His advice to the Russian playwright was, therefore, 'to take a good look at the living man of our far-flung country—see how many good people we have, but also how many weeds which make life unbearable for the good and which no law can control. On the stage with them! Let the whole nation see them! Let it have a good laugh at them! Oh, laughter is a great thing! Man fears nothing so much as laughter. It does not deprive a culprit of his life or property; but it fetters his powers, and, afraid of laughter, man will refrain from doing what no power in the world would have been able to restrain him from doing.' This rather idealistic conception of laughter as a moral force Gogol, as will be seen, modified considerably later on, but at the time when he was writing *The Government Inspector* he firmly believed in it. 'The theatre', he declared in his article, 'is a great school and its aim is profound: it teaches a living and useful lesson all at once to a whole crowd of people . . . and shows up the absurdity of man's habits and vices or the sublimity of his good qualities and lofty feelings. . . .'

In his second article, written after the performance of *The Government Inspector* when he had realized that, far from destroying evil, laughter can produce an explosion against the author who has shown it up, Gogol tried to explain this unforeseen and unpleasant result by the fact that his audiences were not used to seeing living characters on the stage. 'We have grown so used to the insipid French plays', he wrote, 'that if an author shows us a living character, we can't help suspecting that he is becoming personal. . . . If, for instance, one were to say that in a certain town a certain Court Councillor is a little too fond of the bottle, all Court Councillors would take it as a personal offence . . . as though one man could disgrace a whole class of people. . . . It is a pity. It really is high time we learnt that only a true portrayal of character, cast in a truly national form, is of any real use.'

But the portrayal of a character in a play depends perhaps as much on the actor as on the playwright. This Gogol realized very well as is evident from the letter he wrote to Pushkin on the 25th of May 1836 (O.S.). (It was first published in 1841 in *Moskvityanin*, and, in the same year, in the second edition of *The Government Inspector*.) In this letter Gogol includes a number of valuable hints to producers of his masterpiece.

'I was disgusted with my own play [he comments on the performance of *The Government Inspector*] just as though it were not

I who had written it. The chief part was ruined. Dyur [the actor who took the part of Khlestakov] had no idea what Khlestakov was like. Khlestakov in his interpretation had become . . . something like a naughty boy in a French farce. He became simply an ordinary stage liar—a colourless character which has been appearing in the same costume for the last two hundred years. Is it really impossible to see from the part itself what Khlestakov is like? Or have I fallen a prey to blind pride and were my powers to master this character so weak that not a shadow or hint remained in it for the actor? And yet it seemed perfectly clear to me. Khlestakov is not cheating at all; he is not a professional liar; he forgets himself that he is lying and almost believes what he says. He lets himself go, he is in high spirits, he sees that everything is going well, that he is listened to—and for that reason alone he speaks quite frankly, smoothly, unconstrainedly, and while telling lies he reveals himself in them as he really is. Our actors, on the whole, don't know how to tell lies. They imagine that to lie means simply to talk nonsense. To lie means to tell lies in a tone that is so near to truth, so natural, so naïve, that one could only tell the truth that way; and it is in that that the whole comic element of a lie consists. . . . Khlestakov [Gogol goes on] does not lie at all wildly or in a boastfully theatrical way; he lies with feeling; you can see the pleasure he derives from it in his eyes. This, in fact, is the best and most poetic moment of his life—almost a kind of inspiration. . . . In Khlestakov, nothing should be sharply defined. To all appearances, he does not differ from other young men. Indeed, he carries himself well, sometimes he even speaks with authority, and only when presence of mind or character is required does his mean and trivial nature come to light. . . . What, in the last analysis, *is* Khlestakov? A young man, a civil servant, a worthless fellow, as they say, but one who has many qualities possessed by people whom the world does not call worthless. To show these qualities in such people would be unjust on the part of the writer, for by doing so he would make a laughing-stock of them. Rather, let everyone find a part of himself in that role, and at the same time not be afraid to look about him lest someone should point the finger of scorn at him and call him by his right name. In short, this character must be the type of many things one finds in different . . . people, but which have here been concentrated in one character, as often happens in real life. Everyone becomes a

Khlestakov for a moment or for several moments, but quite naturally he does not wish to acknowledge it; indeed, he even likes to have a good laugh at it, but only, of course, when he notices it in someone else and not in himself. A dashing Guards officer will sometimes appear as a Khlestakov, a statesman will sometimes appear as a Khlestakov, and one of our own literary crowd, sinners that we are, will sometimes appear as a Khlestakov. In a word, it is seldom indeed that a man will not be a Khlestakov once in his life, the only difference being that afterwards he will turn round so cleverly that he will not seem to have been a Khlestakov at all.'

After declaring himself satisfied with the performance of Sosnitsky, who played the mayor, Gogol turns to the two comic characters in his play, the two gossipy landowners, Bobchinsky and Dobchinsky, which were also acted very badly.

'Even before the beginning of the performance [Gogol writes], when I saw them in their costumes, I gasped with horror. These two men, who are essentially tidy and neat, rather stout, with carefully smoothed hair, were got up in ungainly high grey wigs, tousled, untidy, with enormous shirt-fronts sticking out of their breeches. On the stage they looked so unnatural and affected that it was simply unbearable. Generally speaking, the costumes were bad and made the actors look like caricatures. I had had a feeling it would be like that and asked to have one of the rehearsals in costume; but I was told that it was quite unnecessary and uncustomary and that the actors knew their business. Seeing that they paid no attention to what I said, I left them alone. . . .

'During the performance [Gogol continues], I noticed that the beginning of Act IV was rather cold; it seemed to me as though the movement of the play, hitherto smooth, was interrupted at this point and was dragging along lazily. I admit that during the reading of the play a knowledgeable and experienced actor remarked to me that it was a mistake to make Khlestakov ask for a loan first, and that it would be better if the civil servants offered him one themselves. Respecting this rather perceptive remàrk, I did not, however, see any reason why Khlestakov, being Khlestakov, should not ask for it first. But the remark was made, which means, I said to myself, that I did this scene badly. And so it was, for now, during the performance, I saw clearly that the beginning of the fourth act was colourless and showed some signs of fatigue.

On returning home, I sat down at once to revise it. Now, I think, it is a little stronger, at least it is more natural and more to the point.

'One more word [Gogol goes on] about the last scene. It was a complete failure. The curtain comes down at a sort of confused moment and the play does not seem to be over. But that was not my fault. They refused to listen to me. I still maintain that the last scene will not be successful until it is understood that it is simply a mute scene, that it ought to represent a group turned to stone, that here the drama comes to an end and is replaced by dumb-show, that the curtain must not come down for two or three minutes, that all this ought to resemble the so-called *tableaux vivants*. But I was told that this would cramp the actors, that the scene would have to be produced by a choreographer, which is rather humiliating for an actor, etc., etc. Many more *etceteras* I saw written on their faces, and these were much more disagreeable than their words. In spite of these *etceteras*, I persist in my opinion and I say for the hundredth time: "No, this will not cramp the actors—this is not humiliating." I don't even mind if a choreographer designs and produces the group, provided he is capable of feeling the real position of each character. A man of talent can never be confined within prescribed limits, just as a river is not stopped by its granite banks; on the contrary, when it enters between them, it grows deeper and flows more swiftly. In a given pose, too, a sensitive actor can express everything. His face is free to express any emotion—it is only the grouping that is composed. And in this dumb-show there is infinite variety. The panic of each character is as different as his nature, and the extent of his fear depends on the extent of his transgressions. The mayor is struck dumb in a different way from his wife or daughter; the judge is scared in a different way, and so are the postmaster and the superintendent of schools, etc. Bobchinsky and Dobchinsky are struck dumb in a special way and turn to each other with a question frozen on their lips; only the guests are struck dumb in the same way, but they form the background of the scene, which must be painted with one stroke of the brush and in one and the same colour. In short, everyone has to carry on with his part in mime and, in spite of the fact that apparently he merely carries out the instructions of the choreographer, he can remain a great actor. But I have no more strength to plead or argue [Gogol concludes]. I am exhausted in body and soul. I swear no one knows or hears of my suffering. Let them do as they like; I am sick and tired of my play. I'd like to run away anywhere now, and my imminent journey, the steamship, the sea and other, far-away skies alone can refresh me. God alone knows how I long for them.'

¶ 4

The notices of *The Government Inspector* in the Petersburg press were, with the one exception of an article in *The Contemporary* by Prince Vyazemsky, highly critical, too. The play was attacked for its lack of love interest, as well as for its social criticism. Bulgarin in his *Northern Bee* argued that the whole theme of the play was highly improbable and practically a libel on the Russian government, while Senkovsky in his *Library for Reading* echoed Bulgarin's views and declared that 'administrative abuses exist all over the world' and that there was 'no sufficient reason to ascribe them only to Russia'. Gogol himself summarized Bulgarin's views in his defence of his play, written in the form of a dialogue under the title *After the Play*, which he first sketched out in April–May 1836, and thoroughly revised for the first edition of his collected works in 1842. The action of *After the Play* takes place in the foyer of the Alexandrinsky Theatre. The author of the play hides behind a column and listens to the opinions expressed by the spectators as they are leaving the theatre. The first opinion is expressed by a middle-aged civil servant.

A Middle-Aged Civil Servant (*coming out with hands out-spread*): This is goodness only knows what! Such a— Such a— It's— it's terrible! (*Goes out.*)
A Gentleman a Little Careless about Literature [Bulgarin] (*addressing another*): It's a translation, isn't it?
The Other: Good heavens, no. The action takes place in Russia. It's our customs and even our ranks.
A Gentleman a Little Careless about Literature: I seem to remember something of the kind in French, not altogether of the same kind, though.

Bulgarin, whom Gogol characterized in a letter to Danilevsky from Rome on the 13th of May 1838, as 'a man whom it is as revolting to thrash as to kiss', next appears in the guise of two literary gentlemen. In one scene he is addressed by A Nondescript Gentleman.

A Nondescript Gentleman: I am no judge of literary merit, sir, but the play has wit. Yes, sir, it's witty, witty.

A Literary Gentleman: Good heavens, what's so witty about it? What low people, what a low tone! Most trivial jokes. Why, it's obscene.

A Nondescript Gentleman: Well, sir, that's a different matter. I said I am no judge of literary merit. I only observed that the play was funny. I enjoyed it.

A Literary Gentleman: It's not funny at all. Good heavens, what's so funny about it and how could you have enjoyed it? A most improbable subject. Full of the most absurd and unlikely situations. No plot, no action, no understanding.

A Nondescript Gentleman: Of course, that may be. So far as literature is concerned, you're quite right. It may not be amusing from a literary point of view, but from any other point of view it is.

A Literary Gentleman: Is it? Good heavens, even from any point of view there's nothing amusing in it. What dialogue! Who talks like that in high society? Tell me yourself, do we talk like that?

A Nondescript Gentleman: That's true, sir. You're very clever to have noticed that. I thought so myself. There's no nobility in the dialogue. None of the characters seems to be able to conceal his low origin—that's true.

A Literary Gentleman: Well, there you are! And you're praising it.

A Nondescript Gentleman: Who's praising it? I'm not. I can see myself now that the play's rubbish. I'm afraid I'm no judge of literature.

(*Both go out.*)

Another Literary Gentleman (*comes in accompanied by several people whom he addresses, brandishing his arms*)*:* Believe me, I am an authority on this sort of thing: it's a disgusting play! A sordid, sordid play! Not a single life-like character, all carica-

tures! There's nothing like it in life. Believe me, there isn't.
I know, I'm a writer myself. . . . His play isn't a comedy even.
It's a farce, a farce, and a very unsuccessful farce. Compared
with it, the silliest comedy by Kotzebue is like Mont Blanc
before Pulkov Hill. I'll prove it to them, prove it to them
mathematically. It's simply his friends who have praised him
up to the skies and I shouldn't be in the least surprised if he
didn't think he was a Russian Shakespeare. It's always a man's
friends who give him big ideas about himself. Take Pushkin.
Why does the whole of Russia talk about him now? It's all
because of his friends: they shouted, shouted and now the
whole of Russia is shouting with them. (*Goes out with his
friends.*)

He is followed by two army officers, one of whom agrees with
him that Gogol's play is a farce. 'But', objects the other, 'didn't
you say that you had never laughed so much in your life?' But his
friend merely repeats Bulgarin's arguments, claiming that his
laughter had nothing to do with it. Gogol then brings on 'two art
lovers', one of whom, referring to Bulgarin's criticisms, declares
that only people 'who talk of drawing-rooms but are admitted no
further than the entrance hall' condemn the play as sordid. His
objection to the play is that it has no real plot.

Second Art Lover: Yes, that's true; if by plot we understand what
is generally understood by it, that is, love interest, then it has
no plot. But it seems to me it is time we stopped regarding this
particular kind of plot as important. All you have to do is to
look around you. Everything in the world has changed. The
important theme in a plot now is the desire to obtain a good
job, to eclipse your rival by your brilliant wit, to avenge yourself for being disregarded or laughed at. Does not rank, capital
or an advantageous marriage mean more today than love?
First Art Lover: That's all very well, but even then I can't see a
good plot in the play.

Gogol's reply to this sort of criticism, which he puts into the
mouth of the Second Art Lover, is that people are merely used to
the conventional type of play ending in marriage. A plot that
revolves round two characters, however, is no longer interesting;
its subject must be of vital concern to all the characters. 'In such

a play', he claims, 'everyone is a hero. . . . It is the idea, the thought behind the play that ought to govern its action. . . . At the beginning, comedy was the creation of a whole people. Such, at least, Aristophanes took it to be. It was much later that the love interest gained predominance in it, but how weak is such a plot even in the hands of the best playwrights, how insignificant are these stage lovers with their cardboard love!' It is the social element in comedy that the Second Art Lover, that is, Gogol himself, considers of the utmost importance. 'Can't comedy and tragedy', he argues, 'express the same lofty idea? Doesn't absolutely everything about a mean and dishonest person show us what an honest man ought to be like? Does not all this accumulation of base actions, all this miscarriage of law and justice, give us a clear idea what law, duty and justice require of us? . . . In the hands of a man of talent', he concludes, 'everything can serve as an instrument of the Beautiful, provided it is guided by the high ideal to serve the Beautiful.'

A third and a fourth art lover appear on the scene.

Fourth Art Lover: What can serve as an instrument of the Beautiful? What are you discussing?

First Art Lover: We are discussing comedy. We were all talking about comedy in general. No one has as yet said anything about the new comedy. What do you say?

Fourth Art Lover: What I say is that you can see that the playwright has talent, that he knows life, that his play is very amusing, true and taken from life but, on the whole, there seems to be something lacking in it. . . . It is strange that our writers of comedies can't do without the government. No comedy ends without it.

Third Art Lover: That's true. But on the other hand, it is quite natural. We all belong to the government, we almost all serve the government, and the interests of us all are connected with the government. It's therefore no wonder that this fact is reflected by our writers.

Fourth Art Lover: True enough, but in that case this connexion must be felt. The funny thing is that no play can possibly end without the interference of the government. It is sure to appear, just as Fate did in ancient tragedy.

Second Art Lover: Well, you see, this is therefore something that is natural to all our writers of comedies, and that represents the distinguishing character of our comedy. A sort of secret faith in our government is rooted deep in all our hearts. Well, there is nothing wrong in that: God grant that our government should always and everywhere live up to its calling to be the representative of Providence on earth, and that we should believe in it as the ancients believed in Nemesis which overtook the evildoers.

This identification of the government with Providence was, of course, one of Gogol's basic beliefs, indeed, almost an article of faith with him, and that is why it never occurred to him that by exposing the vices of the government officials he also exposed the viciousness of the régime of which they were an inseparable part. To the officials themselves, however, any sort of exposure was tantamount to an attack on the government itself, and that is why they never hesitated to express their hatred of Gogol's works, and this in the end became the official attitude of the government, too.

Gogol's defence against this attitude is summarized by the Very Modestly-Dressed Man, the first of his thoroughly 'good' characters which he was to draw so unconvincingly in the second part of *Dead Souls*. He is a provincial official and he refuses the offer by Mr. A. of an important post in Petersburg because he fears that some corrupt official might take over his humble post in the provinces. Laughter, the Modestly-Dressed Man declares, is the best way of exposing hypocrisy.

I confess [*he says*] I felt glad when I saw how absurd well-meaning words sound on the lips of a rogue, and how laughably absurd everyone from the gallery to the stalls thought the mask he put on. And after this there are people who say that one ought not to allow it to be put on the stage! I overheard a remark made, I believe, by a very respectable man who wondered what the common people would say if they saw that such terrible abuses exist among us.

Mr. A.: I confess that I, too, asked myself the question what the common people would say if they saw all this.

Very Modestly-Dressed Man: What the common people would say? (*Steps aside.*)

(*Two persons in drab peasants' coats pass by.*)

The Blue Coat (to the grey one): I dare say our governors were lively enough in the old days, but they all took fright when the Tsar's justice caught up with them.

(Both go out.)

Very Modestly-Dressed Man: That's what the common people will say. Did you hear?

Mr. A.: What?

Very Modestly-Dressed Man: I dare say our governors were lively enough in the old days, but they all took fright when the Tsar's justice caught up with them. Do you hear how a man's natural feelings never lead him astray? How true is the judgment of the simple person if it is not clouded over by theories and ideas taken out of books, but is based on an understanding of man's nature. Why, isn't it quite clear that after a performance like this the common people's faith in the government will increase? Yes, they need such performances. Let them dissociate the government from the bad servants of the government. Let them see that abuses do not originate with the government, but with those who do not understand its demands, those who do not want to give an account to the government. Let them see that their government is actuated by noble sentiments, that its unslumbering eye watches equally over everyone, that sooner or later it will catch up with the violators of the law, honour and sacred duty of man, that those whose conscience is not clear will pale before it. Yes, they ought to see these performances; believe me [Gogol, carried away by his specious argument, did not seem to realize that he was now ascribing to the Russian people an attitude of mind that was becoming more and more characteristic of his own attitude in the 'forties], even if they happened to be the victims of injustice and oppression themselves, they would come out comforted after such a performance, with firm faith in the unslumbering supreme law. . . . It's a good thing there isn't an honest man in the play [he concludes]. Man is vain: show him one good trait of character among many bad ones and he will leave the theatre feeling proud of himself. Yes, it is a good thing that only exceptions and vices are exhibited on the stage, for they are such a thorn in the flesh of every honest man that he is ashamed to confess that such things are possible.

Having thus driven the argument in defence of his play to its logical and at the same time absurd conclusion, Gogol turns to the question whether serious subjects should be discussed in a comedy. The argument for and against is carried on first by three men who leave the theatre together, and then by a young society lady and her husband.

The first man declares that vices and abuses are not a fit subject for comedy, the second replies that there are hundreds of light comedies and there is no reason why one or two serious comedies should not exist. 'I must say,' he goes on to voice Gogol's own predicament, 'I should not like to be in the author's shoes. How is he to please the public? If he chooses some trivial society subject everyone will say: "He writes nonsense, his play lacks a deep moral purpose"; if he chooses a subject which has some serious moral purpose they will say: "It's not his business, let him write nonsense."'

The young society lady enjoyed the play, finding that everything in it was true. She laughed—and again Gogol is speaking through her mouth—because the villainy and baseness exposed in the play would remain villainy and baseness however dressed up and wherever found.

Mr. N. (going up to the lady): A clever woman told me just now that she, too, had laughed, but the play had made her feel sad in spite of that.

Young Lady: I don't care what your clever woman felt. My nerves are not so sensitive, and I'm always glad to laugh at what is intrinsically funny. I know that some of us are ready to have a good laugh at a man's crooked nose, but haven't the courage to laugh at a man's crooked soul.

With this parting shot, Gogol winds up his argument against the detractors of his great play, though he carries it on for a few more pages, in which several more people make unflattering remarks about him as 'an utter ignoramus' who had been sacked from his job, and about his play as 'just an amusing fairy-tale'. He ends with a long monologue by the author of the play, in which he again considers the nature of laughter in *The Government Inspector*.

'I regret [he writes in reply to the many criticisms that there is not one positive character in his play] that no one has noticed the honest character in my play. This honest and noble character is—laughter. It is noble because it decided to appear in spite of the low esteem in which it is held in the world. . . . Laughter is more significant and more profound than people think. Not the laughter which is aroused by temporary irritation and a morbid and jaundiced disposition; nor that light laughter which serves for the idle amusement and entertainment of people, but the laughter which issues from man's serene nature . . . the laughter which deepens everything, draws attention to what might have passed unnoticed, and without whose penetrating force man would have been disheartened by life's trivialities and emptiness. . . . No, they are unjust who say that laughter arouses our indignation. It is only the dark aspects of life that arouse our indignation, but laughter is bright. . . . They are unjust who say that laughter makes no impression on those against whom it is directed and that a rogue will be the first to laugh at a rogue whom he sees exposed on the stage: the rogue of a later age will laugh, but the contemporary rogue will not have the nerve to laugh . . . for even he who is not afraid of anything in the world is afraid of ridicule. . . . The world says that what is amusing is low, and only that which is uttered in a stern voice is described as high. But, good Lord, how many people one meets daily, for whom there is nothing high in the world! Everything created by inspiration is just nonsense, just amusing fairy-tales to them: Shakespeare's works are just amusing fairy-tales; the sacred emotions of one's heart are just amusing fairy-tales. No, it is not my injured pride that makes me say that. I am not saying that because my weak and immature works have just been called amusing fairy-tales. . . . Centuries have passed, cities and peoples have vanished from the face of the earth . . . but the "amusing fairy-tales" are alive and are read today. . . . The world would have gone to sleep without such "fairy-tales", life would have grown shallow, and the souls of men would have been covered with slime and mildew. Amusing fairy-tales, indeed! Oh, may the names of those who listened sympathetically to these "amusing fairy-tales" remain for ever sacred to posterity; the wondrous hand of Providence was always stretched out over the heads of their creators. In times of trouble and persecutions all who were noblest among nations became their patrons: the crowned monarch sheltered them behind his imperial shield from the height of his unapproachable throne.

'Onward with a stout heart! [Gogol concludes]. And let not my soul be downcast by censure, but receive thankfully any indication of faults, without despairing even when denied the possession of high impulses and sacred love of humanity! The world is like a whirlpool: opinions and idle talk move about in it everlastingly, but time puts everything in its true perspective. Like husks, the false values fly off and, like hard seeds, the immutable truths remain. . . .'

It took Gogol some time to realize that there was a serious flaw in his argument that abuses could be rectified by exposing them on the stage. Nor did his attempt to exonerate the government from the misdeeds of its officials greatly impress those who were in close touch with government circles. It is true that three days after the première of *The Government Inspector* Gogol received a present of eight hundred roubles from the Emperor, but that was in appreciation of the copy of the play Gogol had presented to him: it was simply a matter of court protocol. Nicholas I, no doubt, approved Gogol's exposure of the bribery which was rampant in his Empire, but it is very doubtful whether he was intelligent enough to appreciate the full implications of the play; if he had, he would most certainly have shared the sentiments of those who wished to ban it.

Gogol, who ever since his last years at school had believed that he had a special mission to perform for the salvation of his countrymen, was fortified in this belief by the storm his play had raised. His faith in the moral influence of art now seemed to have been confirmed. His next work, *Dead Souls*, was to create an even greater sensation, and its moral influence in eradicating the evils from which his country suffered was to be greater still. A novel, after all, was accessible to a much wider public. And he knew that he could write such a masterpiece. 'I swear,' he declared in a letter to Zhukovsky three weeks after leaving Russia, 'I swear that I shall do something that no ordinary man could do. I feel a lion's strength in my soul and I can almost hear the transition from childhood, spent in school exercises, to manhood.' He wrote this at a time when, with the exception of *Dead Souls*, he had written most of his masterpieces. But so obsessed was he with the idea of his mission that these seemed only 'school exercises' to him. When, six years later, he saw how mistaken his belief in the immediate moral influence of art was, he not only tried to explain away *The Government Inspector* as a parable that had nothing to do with reality, but embarked on ten agonizing years of vain endeavour to find in his own moral regeneration the key to endowing art with the magic properties of converting villains into angels, a task that finally resulted in his tragic death.

Part Five

DEAD SOULS

¶ 1

Gogol left Petersburg by sea for Lübeck on the 18th of June 1836. He was seen off by Vyazemsky who gave him a number of letters of introduction to his friends abroad. He was accompanied on his journey by his old school friend Danilevsky and their mutual friend Ivan Zolotaryov, with whom he later travelled to Italy. He remained abroad for twelve years, returning to Russia only twice, in 1839–40 and in 1841–2, for a stay of eight months each time. In a letter to Zhukovsky from Hamburg on June the 28th, he reviewed his past literary work and sketched out his future plans. 'If we examine impartially and fairly what I have hitherto written,' he wrote, 'what does it all amount to? It seems to me as though I were turning over the pages of a schoolboy's notebook and see written on one of them laziness and carelessness and on another haste and impatience. . . . Only occasionally will you find a page which the teacher might commend, seeing in it the germ of a better future. It is high time', he went on, 'I did some decent work. Oh, what an inconceivably wonderful meaning all the events and circumstances of my life have had! How salutary were all my trials and tribulations. There was something elastic about them, and whenever I touched them I seemed to leap higher, at least I felt my resilience growing stronger within me. I can honestly say that I have never sacrificed my talent to the pleasures of the world. No amusement, no passion can for a moment take possession of my soul and divert me from my duty. For me there is no life outside my life. And my present withdrawal from my country has been decreed from above by the same great Providence which has sent me everything for my education. This', he declared, 'is the great turning point of my life. I know that many unpleasant shocks are in store for me, that I shall suffer poverty and privations, but I shall be away for a long time and will not return for anything in the world. I shall stay abroad as long as I can. And though my thoughts, my name and my works belong to Russia, I myself, my perishable body, will be away from it.' He had taken with him two thousand roubles which he hoped would last him till October when he expected to get another thousand roubles from the sales of *The Government Inspector*.

The reason for his determination to stay away from Russia as long as possible he explained in a letter to Pogodin from Geneva on September the 22nd. 'There is such a large number of vile faces in Russia', he wrote, 'that I could not bear to look at them. Even now I feel like spitting when I remember them.'

On his arrival in Lübeck Gogol parted from his two companions, who were going to Paris. He himself intended to consult a specialist in Aachen about his (mostly imaginary) illnesses. On the way there he stopped in Hamburg for a week to renew his acquaintance with the city he had visited five years before. In Hamburg he went to an open-air performance in a park and was very much amused by the German women who went on knitting during the whole of the performance. He also went to a ball, where he was surprised to see that most of the men were English. 'An Englishman', he wrote to his little sisters in Petersburg, 'is a rather tall man who always sits down jauntily on a chair, crossing his legs and turning his back on his lady.' He next visited Bremen where he went to see the famous wine caves, the old cathedral and a crypt in which for some reason human bodies were not subject to decay. There were fifteen bodies there, he told his sisters, and the Germans treated them without any respect, picking them up and throwing them down. He did not stay long in Aachen, where the specialist he consulted assured him that there was nothing the matter with him. He went by stage-coach to Cologne, from where he sent a sketch of the cathedral and a humorous drawing of a German innkeeper to his sisters. From Cologne he sailed down the Rhine to Mayence. 'The river Rhine', he wrote to his sisters on July the 26th, 'is a very remarkable thing in Germany. It is overhung by hills on both sides and strewn with towns. Our steamer sailed for two whole days and in the end I got tired of the unending views. . . . Before your portholes there pass, one after another, cities, hills, cliffs and ruins of old castles. Some of the castles are very picturesque and still very beautiful. All the hills are covered with vines. This is the country of the Rhine wines, of which there are hundreds of varieties, most of which are unknown in Russia. In Mayence I disembarked but did not stay there, though the city was worth a visit, and took coach for Frankfort.' Gogol found Frankfort a very noisy city, full of foreigners, but he liked the opera which, he told his sisters, was the best in Europe.

From Frankfort Gogol travelled to Baden-Baden, where he had intended to stay for only a few days, but meeting the family of his former pupil Maria Balabin there, he stayed for over three weeks. The Balabins introduced him to the family of Prince Nikolai Repnin-Volkonsky, with whom they were connected by marriage, and this was the beginning of Gogol's association abroad with a number of Russian aristocratic families which, in the view of several of his biographers, had a disastrous influence on his life. Gogol was undoubtedly flattered by the attentions of these grandees though when, many years later, he was taken to task by Pogodin for it, he denied it vehemently. In Baden-Baden he enjoyed himself immensely in the company of the Repnins and Balabins. 'Gogol', Princess Varvara Repnin records, 'was full of high spirits and amused us constantly. He came to see us every day and was treated like one of the family. He liked to talk to his former pupil Maria Balabin [he read *The Government Inspector* and *The Diary of a Madman* to her] and her mother [a highly educated and well-read Frenchwoman] whom he treats with great respect, never forgetting to kiss her hand.' The princess, noticing Gogol's fondness for sweets and dessert, used to prepare a special 'compote' for him herself, which he described in a letter to Maria Balabin from Lausanne as 'the field-marshal of compotes'.

From Baden-Baden Gogol travelled to Switzerland where he spent three months. He was little impressed by Basle, Berne and Lausanne, and though the mountains made a great impression on him at first, he soon lost interest in them. 'Mountains, mountains and mountains', he wrote to Prokopovich from Geneva on September the 27th. 'I am so sick and tired of them that if at this moment, I came across some mean, flat Russian landscape with a log cabin and grey skies, I'd admire its appearance as something new.' He stayed for a month in Geneva, but finally left it because of its 'stupid climate', the winds there being, he told Prokopovich, 'fiercer than in Petersburg—a regular Tobolsk'. He went to

Vevey where Dostoevsky, too, forty years later, was to take refuge from the fierce winds of Geneva. There he again met the Balabins, who were taking 'the grape cure'. He spent almost a month in Vevey, re-reading, as he wrote to Zhukovsky, the works of Molière, Shakespeare and Walter Scott, going for long walks in the mountains and visiting Verney.

'This morning [he wrote to Prokopovich on September the 27th] I paid a call on old Voltaire. The old man lived well. A long, beautiful avenue—a triple row of chestnut trees—leads to his house. The house, a two-storied building of grey stone, is still quite well preserved. I [the word has been burnt out] in the drawing-room where he dined and received visitors. Everything is just as it was when he lived there, the same pictures on the walls. From his drawing-room a door leads straight into his bed-room, which he used as his study. On the walls hang the portraits of his friends—Diderot, Frederick and Catherine. His bed was made up, the blanket was very old and almost falling to pieces, and I had a feeling that at any moment the door would open and an old man in the familiar wig and wide, open collar would walk in and ask, What do you want? The garden is very large and pretty. The old man knew how to cultivate it. A few avenues have intertwined to form an impenetrable vault, skilfully trimmed, while others are strung along irregularly. Along the whole length of one side of the garden is a wall of clipped trees in the shape of an archway, and through this archway another avenue can be seen leading to a wood and with a view of Mont Blanc. I heaved a sigh and scratched my name in Russian letters without knowing myself why I did so.'

All the time Gogol was stuffing himself voraciously, which no doubt accounted for his terrible attacks of indigestion in Paris afterwards. 'Gluttonous Europe', he wrote to Prokopovich, 'is pursuing me with her dinners. Oh, those dinners!'

In Vevey Gogol resumed his work on *Dead Souls*. After des- cribing to Zhukovsky (in a letter from Paris on November the 12th) his visit to the Castle of Chillon where he had scratched his name at the bottom of the last column in the dungeon, not daring to scratch it 'under the illustrious names of the creator and trans- lator of *The Prisoner of Chillon*' (Byron and Zhukovsky), Gogol went on: 'The autumn was beautiful in Vevey, almost like summer. It was very warm in my room, and I sat down to write

Dead Souls, which I had begun in Petersburg. I thoroughly revised everything I had written, thought over the whole plan of the novel more carefully, and now I am writing it calmly, almost like a chronicle. From then on Switzerland became more pleasing to me and her grey-lilac-azure-blue-pink mountains lighter and more airy. If I do this work as it ought to be done, then—oh, what an enormous, what an original subject! What a heterogeneous crowd! The whole of Russia will appear in it! It will be the first decent thing I have written, a thing which will make my name famous. Every morning after breakfast I added three more pages to my poem, and the laughter in those pages was enough to sweeten the solitary day for me.' But it soon grew cold and, sensitive to changes of weather as Gogol was, he became depressed and could not go on writing. This increased his depression and his doctor advised a change of place. He had intended to spend the winter in Italy, but a cholera epidemic was raging there and he went to Paris instead. He arrived in Paris at the beginning of November and stayed there till the end of February 1837. 'For the first time since we had parted', Danilevsky records, 'we met in Paris. He lived with me at first, then he took a room in a hotel, where he froze because his room had no stove, but only a fireplace. At last we found a warm flat at the corner of the Place de la Bourse and Rue Vivienne. Here Gogol spent most of his time writing *Dead Souls*. I did not interfere with him because he was always busy; but in the evenings we often went to the theatre.' To Zhukovsky Gogol wrote: 'It amuses me to think that I am writing *Dead Souls* in Paris. I am planning to write another Leviathan. A holy tremor passes over me when I think of it: I can already apprehend some of it—I shall taste divine moments—but —now I am all immersed in *Dead Souls*. Immensely great is my work, and its end is far off. New classes of the population and many more people will rise up against me, but I'm afraid it cannot be helped. It is my lot to be in conflict with my fellow countrymen. *Patience!* An invisible someone writes before me with a mighty sceptre. I know that my name after me will be luckier than I and that the descendants of these self-same countrymen of mine will perhaps murmur words of reconciliation to my shade with eyes full of tears.'

What 'leviathan' Gogol had in mind has remained a mystery, for he never referred to it again. But, then, it never occurred to him when he wrote this letter that the time would come when, far from wishing to arouse his countrymen's displeasure he would himself regard his writings, including the first part of *Dead Souls*, as the greatest mistake, if not indeed the most unforgivable sin, he had committed in his life.

To Pogodin, who was just then planning to publish a periodical and was asking Gogol for contributions, he wrote on November the 28th that he was so busy with his novel that he could not promise to send him anything. He told him the title of his novel but refused to say anything more about it except that the whole of Russia would appear there. 'All I see before me now', he declared, 'is stern posterity, pursuing me with the inexorable question, Where is that work of yours by which we can judge you? And to give an answer to it I am ready to condemn myself to a life of wandering and poverty, to profound and uninterrupted seclusion, which I now carry within myself everywhere, be it in Paris or the African desert. . . . I am writing to you nothing about Paris. Here everyone is interested in politics and I have eschewed politics. It is not the poet's business to intrude into the world's market-place. Like a silent monk he lives in the world without belonging to it and his pure, spotless soul speaks only to God.'

Gogol meant every word of it, as indeed he proved afterwards, but this sort of thing made his friends wince and doubt his sincerity. His life in Paris certainly did not resemble the life of a silent monk or a poet who spoke only to God. He still indulged in gargantuan meals which, because of the severe bouts of indigestion they caused him, he nicknamed 'burnt offerings'. In Paris he met many of his old Russian acquaintances, including Alexandra Smirnov and Alexander Turgenev, a distant relation of the novelist and a brother of the Decembrist Nikolai Turgenev. He visited the Louvre several times as well as the Jardin des Plantes where, he wrote to his mother, 'elephants, camels, ostriches and monkeys walk about just as if they were at home' and 'the cedars have trunks as thick as those you only find in fairy-tales. The whole of Paris', he concluded his letter, 'is now full of musicians, singers, artists and actors of every kind. The streets are all lit by gas. Many of them are made into arcades with glass roofs and they have marble floors which are so smooth that you could dance on them.' He enjoyed the Paris shows, especially the opera. 'The Italian opera', he wrote to Prokopovich on the

25th of January 1837, 'is simply marvellous. Grisi, Tambourini, Rubini, Lablache are such a wonderful quartet that one cannot help wondering how they all came together here.' He went to the Théâtre Français during the celebration of the two hundred and fifteenth anniversary of the birth of Molière. 'They were giving two plays,' he told Prokopovich, '*Tartuffe* and *le Malade imaginaire*, which were excellently performed, at least as compared with the way in which they are performed on our stage. Every year', he went on, 'the Théâtre Français celebrates the anniversary of Molière. There was something moving about it. At the end of the performance the curtain went up revealing a bust of Molière. All the actors, to the accompaniment of music, marched on to the stage in twos to crown the bust. A heap of wreaths piled up on his head. I was overcome by a strange sort of feeling. Does he hear all that, and where does he hear it?' He went three times to see the famous French dramatic actress Anne Boutet Mars who was then fifty-eight. In one play she acted a girl of eighteen, which struck him as a little comic at first, but her voice was still so fresh that when he closed his eyes he easily imagined her a girl of eighteen. He admired the simplicity and vitality of her acting. He also saw Talma's successor, Pierre Ligier, act Louis XI in Delavigne's play and thought that Delavigne could not have written the part as well as Ligier played it. He admired the interiors of the French theatres chiefly because one could see and hear everything to the last word. The Paris stage, he told Prokopovich, was all gold, heavy silk and velvet. 'The people of Paris,' he concluded, 'especially the supporters of the republican party, love dramas. They are a gloomy crowd and seldom applaud. The rest go to see farces—the middle classes in the Variété theatre or the Pathé Royale. The aristocracy, as always, pretend to be opera-mad and go to the Italian or the Grand opera where the *Huguenots* and *Robert le Diable* are still running and the orchestra beats the kettle-drums and cymbals with all its might; or sometimes to the Opéra Comique. . . .'

In this letter to Prokopovich, too, he expressed his contempt for all his previous writings, describing them as 'scribbles' he would like to forget. 'They appear before my eyes', he wrote, 'like stern accusers. My soul demands oblivion. And if a moth suddenly appeared and ate up all the copies of *The Government Inspector*, *Arabesques*, *Evenings* and all the rest of the rubbish with it, and not a single word were written or spoken about me by anyone for a long time, I would thank my stars for it. . . . Only fame after death (for which, alas, I've done nothing so far) is known to a true poet. Contemporary fame isn't worth a farthing.' He had just read Pushkin's story *The Captain's Daughter* and he thought it marvellous. Little did he dream that a month later (on February the 22nd) Pushkin would be dead. The news was a terrible blow to him. One evening Danilevsky met him in the street with Alexander Turgenev (one of Pushkin's close friends). Gogol took him aside and said: 'You know how much I love my mother, but even if I had lost her I wouldn't be so distressed as I am now: Pushkin no longer exists in this world.' To Pletnyov he wrote from Rome on March the 28th: 'Not a month, not a week passes without some new bereavement, but I could not receive any worse news [than the news of Pushkin's death]. All the joy of my life has disappeared together with him. I never undertook anything without his advice. I never wrote a single line without imagining him before me. . . . My present work was suggested by him. I owe it entirely to him. I can't go on. I have taken up my pen a few times, but it has dropped out of my hand. I am broken-hearted.' Two days later he wrote to Pogodin: 'You ask me to return to Russia. What for? To share the fate of poets in our country? . . . What am I to come back for? Haven't I seen the precious gathering of our educated ignoramuses? Or don't I know what our Councillors are like? You write that everyone was deeply moved by Pushkin's death. But what were these people prepared to do for him while he was alive? Haven't I been a witness to the bitter moments Pushkin had to experience? . . . Oh, when I remember our judges, our Maecenases, our learned and clever gentlemen, our noble aristocracy—my heart shudders at the very thought of it. . . . In a foreign land I'm ready to put up with anything, but in my own country—never! . . . I'm a homeless vagabond who is continuously tossed by the waves, and the only thing I can rely on is the anchor of my pride which a higher power has given me. I shall not lay down my head in my native land. . . .'

And of course it is quite true that Pushkin's death meant that another tie that bound him to Russia had been severed. Sergey Aksakov went even so far as to express the view that Pushkin's death was 'the only cause of the morbid manifestations of Gogol's

spirit, as a result of which he set himself all sorts of insoluble problems to which his genius . . . could find no satisfactory answer.'
This is certainly an extreme view. Gogol, as he himself acknowledged, had almost superhuman powers of resilience, and it took
a great many heavier blows than Pushkin's death to break his
spirit.

¶ 2

Gogol left Paris for Rome at the beginning of March 1837.
According to Danilevsky, the only reason why he stayed so long
in Paris was that he had met the Polish poet Adam Mickiewicz
there and was anxious to see him as often as possible. He travelled
to Rome with Ivan Zolotaryov by way of Marseilles, Genoa, Leg-
horn, Pisa and Florence. Italy was to become in more than one
sense his second home, and he took to her at once. 'What shall I
tell you of Italy?' he wrote to Prokopovich on March the 30th.
'She is beautiful. She strikes you less the first time than afterwards. Only by looking at her more and more closely does one see
and feel her secret fascination. There is a kind of silver radiance
in the sky and in the clouds. The sunshine spreads over a much
wider horizon. And the nights? They are lovely. The stars shine
more brightly than at home and they look larger than ours, like
planets. And the air? It is so pure that distant objects seem near.
There is no sign of mist.' To Danilevsky he wrote on April the
15th that he felt as though he had come to visit some old Ukrainian landowners. 'The same decrepit front doors with hundreds
of useless holes, which cover your clothes with chalk; ancient
candlesticks and lamps reminding you of the lamps in churches.
The dishes are all special ones, everything is old-fashioned.
Everywhere else I have seen things changing. Here everything
has stopped dead and goes no further. When I drove into Rome,
I couldn't at first make up my mind about it. It looked so small to
me. But the longer I am here, the bigger it appears to me, the
buildings are more enormous, the views are more beautiful, the
sky more lovely, and there are enough pictures, ruins and ancient
monuments to look at for a whole lifetime. You fall in love with
Rome slowly and gradually—but for as long as you live. . . .'

Rome's appeal to Gogol was not only aesthetic; he was attracted to it also because it was a political backwater, the Papal State being the only state in Europe in which history seemed to have stopped dead. So that, as Annenkov remarks in his reminiscences, 'sustained by the solitude of Rome, Gogol devoted himself entirely to his creative work and stopped reading anything or caring what was happening in the rest of Europe. He said himself that at certain periods one good book was sufficient to fill a man's whole life. In Rome he only re-read his favourite passages in Dante, Gnedich's translation of the *Iliad*, and Pushkin's poems. That was entirely on a level, as it were, with the city which, under the rule of Pope Gregory XVI, turned towards the past. That good-natured shepherd, who smiled so affectionately at his flock during his ceremonial processions, and who blessed it with so much love, knew how to nip in the bud the European ideas which took root in his diocese, and when he died they were still in a state of paralysis. The means which he employed to achieve this end no one of the resident foreigners cared to find out. . . . The desire of the population of Rome to share in the benefits of European civilization was alive in the hearts of many people even then. Gogol knew it, but it made him rather sad. I remember one day saying to him that I expected there were people in Rome who regarded it differently from us. He replied with a sigh: "Yes, my dear fellow, indeed there are." He was, I would go so far as to say, in love with his idea of Rome. . . .'

Gogol himself put it more succinctly in a letter he wrote to Maria Balabin in April 1838. 'If I were asked,' he declared, 'naturally not by some Emperor or King but by someone mightier than they, what I should have preferred to see before me —ancient Rome in its brilliant and terrible glory or present-day Rome with its ruins, I should unhesitatingly have said that I preferred the present-day Rome. It is beautiful by the very fact that one half of it belongs to the pagan and the other half to the Christian era—and between them they represent two of the greatest ideas in the world.'

From the very beginning Rome cast its spell on Gogol. He was gay and talkative, Zolotaryov, who shared a flat of three rooms with him at 17, via Isidore, records. He forgot all about his imaginary illnesses and, in spite of his earlier unhappy experiences, began gorging himself at every meal. His favourite dish, according to Zolotaryov, was goat's milk, which he boiled in a special way, adding rum to it (he always carried a flask of rum about with him). This dish he laughingly called 'Gogol-Mogol'. He resumed his work on *Dead Souls* and on the 3rd of June 1837, he asked Prokopovich to send him all his notebooks from Petersburg, as he was 'sitting down to work in good earnest'. Before beginning to write he would become thoughtful and exceedingly taciturn, pacing the room in silence for a long time and, when addressed, asking to be left alone. Then he would shut himself up in his 'den' and work there uninterruptedly for several days.

In Rome, Gogol made many friends both among the Russians and the Italians. One of his closest Italian friends was Cardinal Giuseppe Mezzofanti, a professor of Bologna university and a great linguist, who at their first meeting addressed Gogol in Russian. Gogol also met the Balabins and Repnins in Rome, and he became particularly friendly with Princess Zinaida Volkonsky, a relation of the Repnins. In the 'twenties Princess Volkonsky had had a literary *salon* in Moscow where Pushkin, Mickiewicz, Vyazemsky and other poets were frequent visitors. Secretly converted to Catholicism at the age of thirty-seven in 1829, she later settled in Rome, where she was known as Beata. Like most Catholic converts, she became a fanatical adherent of the Roman Church and tried to convert as many Russians as she could. She did her best to convert Gogol, too. At the beginning of 1838 she summoned two Polish priests to her aid. 'We had a long conversation with Gogol', one of the priests wrote to his ecclesiastical superior in Warsaw, 'and we liked him very much. He has a noble heart, and, besides, he is still young; if we succeed in influencing him more deeply later on, he won't be deaf to truth and will turn to it with all his heart. The princess [Zinaida Volkonsky] cherishes this hope, of which we, too, feel a little more confident.' Rumours that Gogol was about to be converted to Catholicism reached Maria Ivanovna in Vassilevka and she wrote at once asking him to deny them. 'You are quite right', Gogol wrote to her from Rome on the 22nd of December 1837, 'to deny the rumours that I am about to change the rites of my religion. For', he explained, and this explanation is interesting considering his later views on the supremacy of the Greek Orthodox Church, 'our religion is in no way different from the Catholic religion and there is, therefore, no need to change one for the other. Both are true. Both of them recognize one and the same Redeemer, one and the same Divine Wisdom, which once visited our earth and suffered extreme humiliation upon it in order to raise up our souls and direct them towards heaven. And this being so', he concludes, 'you should never doubt my religious feelings.' Gogol was a frequent visitor at Princess Volkonsky's villa Palazzo Poli, outside Rome, and could be seen lying for hours on the terrace, an old Roman aqueduct, with his back propped up against the ancient wall, gazing at the blue sky and the magnificent Roman campagna. It was at this villa that, at the end of 1838, Gogol gave a public reading of *The Government Inspector* in aid of a poor Ukrainian artist. This reading is described in his reminiscences by the Russian engraver Fyodor Iordan. Gogol's audience, which was composed of people belonging to the highest circles of Russian society (it took place during the visit of the Russian heir to the throne, the future Emperor Alexander II, to Rome), looked bored and did not bother to listen. 'He fed us with this dull rubbish in Petersburg', Iordan overheard some of them saying as they went out after the reading, 'and now he has brought it to Rome.'

Gogol had, naturally enough, made friends with the Russian colony of artists as soon as he arrived in Rome, but he became really intimate only with one of the most talented of them, Alexander Ivanov, 'a rather stout man', Annenkov describes him, 'with a handsome round beard, a pair of unusually intelligent, keen eyes, and a typical Slav face in which kindliness and serious, penetrating thought were, as it were, palpably expressed'. As for the rest of the Russian artists, Gogol had no patience with them. 'What a crowd!' he described them. 'What frightful bores, and each of them is absolutely convinced that he possesses great talent! . . . You know yourself what the Russian *pittori* do', he wrote to Danilevsky on the 13th of May 1838. 'From twelve o'clock to two, they are at *Lepre* [the famous restaurant in Rome where Gogol learnt how to cook macaroni], then at *Caffe Greco* [Gogol's haunt in the early 'forties], then on Monte Pincio, then at the *Del Buon Gusto*, then again at *Lepre*, and then they play billiards. In the winter they started Russian tea parties and card games, but fortunately these entertainments came to an end. Tea here is something horrible,' he concluded, 'something like a ghost that comes to frighten us.'

The inevitable result of Gogol's gormandizing in Rome was

that his digestion was giving him trouble again and, what was much worse, that his meagre resources were soon exhausted. To remedy the second and much more serious misfortune, Gogol asked Zhukovsky to forward a letter he had written to the Tsar asking for a grant similar to that received by the Russian artists in Rome 'or even one which is given to the deacons of our church here'. He begged Zhukovsky 'to find an opportunity to draw the Emperor's attention to *The Old-World Landowners* and *Taras Bulba*, two of my lucky stories which people of all tastes and temperaments seem to like'. It is doubtful whether Nicholas I actually read Gogol's two stories, but he did accede to his request and on the 30th of October 1837, Gogol wrote to Zhukovsky acknowledging the receipt of a grant of five thousand roubles, which he hoped would last him for at least sixteen months.

With the coming of the hot season Gogol began to feel more and more painfully the result of his prandial excesses and he decided to go to Baden-Baden for a cure.

He did not enjoy his journey across Northern Italy and Switzerland. 'I was sorry to leave Italy even for a month', he wrote to Varvara Balabin, his former pupil's mother, from Baden-Baden on July the 16th. 'And when, on reaching Northern Italy, I saw poplars instead of the cypresses and the dome-like Roman pines, I felt terribly depressed. The tall, slender poplars, which I would certainly have admired before, seemed banal to me. . . .' Baden-Baden, too, had lost all fascination for him. 'Here is my opinion', he wrote in the same letter: 'He who has been to Italy may say good-bye to other countries. He who has been in heaven will not wish to return to earth. It seems to me I shall not be able to enjoy a beautiful view anywhere else now. The mountains which seemed blue to me before Italy, now look grey. There is no air, none of that transparent air of Italy. The sun does not love the earth and the people here as in Italy. . . . In short, compared to Italy, Europe is like an overcast day compared to a sunny day.'

In Baden-Baden Gogol met Alexandra Smirnov again and he spent a great deal of time with her. 'Gogol', Alexandra Smirnov writes in her reminiscences, 'was not taking the cure, but in the mornings he drank cold water in the Lichtenthal Alee. We met every morning, but he was often so absorbed in his thoughts that I could not make him hear me when I called, and he refused to go for walks with me, inventing all sorts of absurd excuses. All his life', she adds, 'he was very good at inventing absurd excuses.' One day in July he gave a reading of *Dead Souls* at Alexandra Smirnov's house, but a sudden thunderstorm so worked upon his nerves that he stopped at the beginning of the second chapter and went home. He refused to read any more of his novel, but read instead Zhukovsky's epic poem *Undine*, based on Lamotte-Fouqué's prose tale and published that year.

Gogol left Baden-Baden at the beginning of September 1837, intending to return to Rome, but he had to stay in Geneva for a month because of a cholera epidemic in Italy. 'In Geneva', he wrote to his mother from Milan on November the 24th, 'I was not bored, particularly as I was lucky enough to meet Danilevsky there and we spent the time quite agreeably together. All the same, I was glad to leave Switzerland as a prisoner is glad to leave his prison.' This time he went to Italy by way of the Simplon Pass and was suitably impressed by the magnificent scenery of the Alps. He spent a few days in Milan, visiting the cathedral, the art galleries and the theatre, and by the middle of October he was back in Rome. 'If only you knew', he wrote to Zhukovsky on October the 30th, 'how glad I was to leave Switzerland and fly to my darling Italy. She is mine! No one in the world will take her away from me. I was born here. Russia, Petersburg, the snows, the scoundrels, the Ministry, the Chair at the university, the theatre—it is all a bad dream! . . . Oh, Pushkin, Pushkin! What a beautiful dream I had the good fortune to have and how sad was my awakening. What kind of life would I have had after that in Petersburg? But, as though by design, the all-powerful hand of Providence flung me beneath the gleaming sky of Italy so that I should forget my grief, the people and everything, and feast on her magnificent beauty. . . . I am happy,' he concludes his letter, 'my soul is full of joy. I am working and am doing my best to finish my work as soon as possible. Life, life, a little more life! I haven't yet done anything to justify your touching faith in me, but perhaps the work I am doing now will be worthy of it.'

Gogol found a new flat on the top floor of 126, via Felice, which was to be his permanent residence in Rome. The next eight months he spent there were the happiest months of his life. His letters during that period are lighthearted and full of fun. 'There is no better fate than to die in Rome', he wrote to Pletnyov on the 2nd of November 1837. 'A man is a whole mile nearer to God here. . . . I have few acquaintances in Rome now (the Repnins are in Florence), but I was never so happy, so content with life.' He enjoyed the carnival and entered into the spirit of it with all the joy and abandon of a young man. He even bought himself a white hat, which completed his eccentric outfit of a blouse and ticking-cloth trousers he had bought in Hamburg.

His most lighthearted letters he wrote to his former pupil Maria Balabin, who had returned to Petersburg. He wrote his first letter to her on the 25th of March 1838 in Italian, the only Italian letter in the whole of his voluminous correspondence.

'Imagine [he wrote], I often seem to see you walking in the streets of Rome, holding Nibbi's guide-book in one hand and in the other some sacred antique you picked up in the road, dirty and black as a piece of coal, which requires at least the strength of Hercules to carry it. Perhaps you, too, conjure up my nose, long and like a bird's beak (oh, sweet hope!). But let us leave my nose in peace: it is a ticklish matter and, speaking of it, one might be left with one's nose out of joint. Everything in Rome [he went on] is as well as you left it. Your old friends, St. Peter's, Monte Pincio, Piazza Barberini and the Colosseum send you their regards. The goats and the sculptors are still taking walks along Strada Felice and everyone is sorry you have left. The Colosseum, especially, is heart-broken. That is why I am afraid to go near him, for he always asks me, Tell me, my dear little man (he always calls me that), what is my sweetheart Miss Maria doing now? She swore to love me always and yet she is silent and does not want to know me. Tell me, why is that? And I reply, I don't know, and he says, Tell me, why isn't she fond of me any more? And I reply, Because you are too old, Signor Colosseo! Hearing such words, he knits his brows and his forehead becomes stern and angry, and his cracks—those wrinkles of old age—appear gloomy and menacing to me then, so that I am overcome by fear and retire terrified.'

Maria Balabin had asked him to bow to the first abbot he met, and this is how Gogol carried out her request:

'I left my house and went in the direction of Monte Pincio [he wrote to her in April 1838] and at the Trinità church was about to go down the steps when, lo and behold, an abbot was mounting the steps from below. Remembering your commission, I took off my hat and gave him a very courteous bow. The abbot, it seems, was very touched by my civility and bowed to me even more courteously. I liked his face, which I thought full of nobility, so that I stopped involuntarily and looked at him. He came up to me and asked me very civilly whether he had the honour to know me, because he had the unfortunate habit of not being able to recognize people. Here I could not help laughing, and I told him that a young lady who had spent her happiest days in Rome had become so attached to it in her thoughts that she asked me to bow to what is most remarkable in Rome and, incidentally, to the first abbot I met, irrespective of his looks, provided only he wore socks which were stretched tight over his legs, and that I was glad it was he who had received my bow. We both laughed and said simultaneously that our acquaintance had begun in so strange a manner that we ought to continue it. I asked his name and—just fancy— he is a poet who writes quite good verse, he is very intelligent, and we are now friends. And so let me thank you for this pleasant acquaintance. . . . God, what a spring [he repeated the constant refrain in his letters during those happy months]! Do you know what spring is like among ancient ruins covered with ivy and wild flowers? How beautiful are the patches of blue sky between the tops of the trees with their fresh, almost golden foliage, and even the cypress trees, black as a raven's wing, and farther away—the deep blue and turquoise mountains of Frascati, Albana and Tivoli. What air! When you breathe it, it is just as though seven hundred angels flew into your nose. A wonderful spring! The whole of Rome is covered with roses; but sweeter still is the scent of the flowers which have just begun to bloom and whose name I have forgotten. We haven't got them in our country. I know you won't believe me, but I am often overcome by a mad desire to be turned into one enormous nose—to have nothing else, no eyes, no hands, no feet, except one huge nose with nostrils the size of large buckets so that I could inhale as much of the fragrance of spring as possible. . . .'

Inevitably, in a nature so precariously balanced as Gogol's, the intensity with which he imbibed the delights of spring in Rome was bound to produce a violent reaction. It came with the hot Italian summer, and it was all the more violent because his work on *Dead Souls* had come to a sudden stop. His inspiration, as had happened before, seemed to have left him and, as always, this drove him to extreme and quite absurd expedients to regain it.

He asked Danilevsky to buy or order a wig for him in Paris, not, he explained, for the same reason as in Petersburg (where he had shaved his head and worn a wig to make his hair grow), but 'to see whether it would help to open up the pores of my scalp and thus release my inspiration which is getting clogged'. His mental condition had an immediate effect on his state of health. 'My health is bad', he wrote to Vyazemsky on June the 25th. 'Every kind of work, even the lightest, makes my head heavy. Italy has prolonged my life, but she has not the power to eradicate my illness which has become part of my constitution. What', he asked and, as it turned out, prophetically, 'if I cannot finish my work? Oh, away with that terrible thought! It holds an inferno of suffering from which may the Lord save every mortal on earth.' Together with his despair there came the first indications of an arrogant attitude towards his friends, an assumption that he was set so far above them that he was justified in lecturing them and telling them what they ought to do and how they ought to live. In June, he received the news of the death of Danilevsky's mother, and in his letter to his old friend he expressed the hope that he would now finally 'walk with firm steps along the highway of life. Perhaps', he went on, 'this terrible blow, which the higher powers have thought fit to deal you, is meant for the revival of your soul. At all events, your faithful old friend, who has been inseparable from you since the days of your early youth and whom you may never see again, conjures you to think and act in accordance with this idea. These words of mine must be sacred to you and have the power of a last testament. Anyway, I want you to know that if I have to part from this world where I have enjoyed so many beautiful and divine moments, half of them with you, these will be my last words to you.'

He did not die, as he had genuinely persuaded himself (not for the first or last time) that he would, and he was to meet Danilevsky quite soon in Paris, but he could no longer endure to stay in one place. 'The open road', he wrote to Danilevsky in the same letter, 'is indispensable to me: it alone distracts me and suits my feeble organism. I shouldn't stay in one place so long.' He went to Naples, admired its view, the sea 'as blue', he wrote to his mother on July the 30th, 'as the sky', and the lilac and pink mountains with towns around them. He watched Vesuvius belching flames and smoke. He visited the famous blue grotto on Capri and admired the way the water in it seemed to be lighted up from beneath by a kind of blue flame. But he could not bring himself to like Naples. 'No,' he wrote to Danilevsky on August the 20th, 'Rome is better. Here it's close, dusty and dirty. Compared with Naples, Rome seems a second Paris. The cafés, shops and hairdressers in Rome are magnificent compared with those in Naples. You can't recognize the Italians here; one has to carry a stick to protect oneself from them—it's worse than in Russia.' He tried the local waters, but it was no use. 'Alas,' he wrote to Pogodin on August the 12th, 'my health is bad. And my proud plans— Oh, my friend, if only I could enjoy good health for four or five more years! . . . My haemorrhoidal illness has spread to my stomach. It's an intolerable illness. It exhausts me. It never leaves me in peace for a moment and interferes with my work. But I am carrying on with my work, and it will be finished, but my other plans— Oh, my friend, what great subjects there are! Have pity on me. . . .'

Gogol's diagnosis of his illness was no less fantastic than his most fantastic stories, but this time he had a good reason for making it sound as bad as possible, for he had a very 'prosaic' request to make to his friend: he wanted a loan of two thousand roubles, which he promised to repay within a year or a year and a half. He wanted the money immediately to send to Danilevsky, whose money had been stolen in Paris. The news of Gogol's illness and financial straits had reached Moscow, where he was said to be desperately ill and even imprisoned for debt. Pogodin, Aksakov and a few more of his Moscow friends and admirers clubbed together and sent him the two thousand roubles he had asked for. Gogol did not wait for the money to come from Russia, but, having received Danilevsky's appeal, borrowed it from Princess Varvara Repnin and decided to take it to Paris himself. This time the open road seems to have had its desired effect, for at an inn between Genzano and Albano he wrote a whole chapter of his novel at one sitting. This is how Gogol, as recorded by Berg, recounted this episode at Shevyryov's ten years later:

'This is the sort of thing that happened to me', Gogol said. 'I was travelling one July day between the little towns of Genzano and Albano. Halfway between those towns is a miserable inn standing on a little hill, with a billiard table in its main saloon, where people are constantly talking in different languages and the billiard balls never cease clicking. I stopped there. I was writing the first volume of *Dead Souls* at the time and never parted from my manuscript. I don't know why, but I felt like writing as soon as I entered the inn. I ordered a small table to be brought and sat down in a corner of the saloon. I took out my manuscript and, in spite of the noise made by the rolling balls, the indescribable din, the rushing about of the potboys, the smoke, the close atmosphere, I became completely lost to the world and wrote a whole chapter without stirring from my seat. I consider that chapter one of the most inspired in the whole novel', he concluded. 'I have seldom written with such inspiration.'

¶ 3

In Paris, where he arrived on the 19th of September 1838, Gogol went through one of the most violent emotional crises of his life. What caused this emotional upheaval is not clear. It may have been Gogol's state of mind at the time, his recurrent attacks of hypochondria which sapped his powers of resistance to what he later euphemistically described as 'the outpourings of my inmost feelings'; or his ingrained masochistic tendencies that made him admire and often fall under the influence of a man with a stronger will than his own; or, again, it may have been the not so uncommon experience of a man's getting himself suddenly emotionally involved with a person he had known a long time and for whom he had never felt so deeply before. Whatever the cause, there can be no doubt that during a period of six months Gogol showed all the symptoms of an unreasoning and violent attachment to his childhood friend Danilevsky. The difference between the letters he wrote to Danilevsky before and after his brief visit to Paris in September 1838, is so striking that there can be no doubt about that. What actually happened during the week Gogol stayed in Paris is impossible to say, but it can be surmised that it must have been as embarrassing to Danilevsky as it was painful to Gogol. Indeed, when it was all over the correspondence between Gogol and Danilevsky ceased, and for nearly two years they did not exchange a single letter.

On his way back to Rome, Gogol wrote Danilevsky two letters, one from Lyons and the other from Marseilles (which has not been preserved). His Lyons letter was written on September the 28th, and is full of love-lorn complaints. Paris, which he detested, had, now that Danilevsky was there, become 'that sun of splendour'; the restaurants he had been to with Danilevsky were 'temples'; the dinners they had there 'divine services', and the waiters—'high priests'. 'Good-bye, my darling,' he concludes his letter. 'I do not doubt that we shall meet each other many times again [they did not meet again till many years later]. I hope to get a reply to this when I reach Rome.'

But he found no letter from Danilevsky on his arrival in Rome on October the 15th. He waited another fortnight and still there was no word from Danilevsky. It was then that his reserve broke down completely and he wrote the following desperate letter to his friend:

Aren't you ashamed of yourself? Aren't you sorry at all? I expected to find a letter from you on reaching Rome. Don't you remember our promise to write to each other as often as possible? What has happened to this promise? I wrote to you from Lyons and Marseilles. Will you even now pretend that you have not received my letters? You know that I am passionately interested in what is happening to you now. I want, I have to know absolutely everything; even the boredom you feel, even the most unimportant and trivial events of your life in Paris could supply you with a subject for a letter, for you should realize that you are writing to *me*. So that your dinner, your breakfast, your indigestion, diarrhoea and constipation, the Italian opera, Montmartre, and Philippe, not the Philippe who caught *la liberté* of the French nation by the moustache, but the Philippe who appears with a large silver coffee pot, which is, no doubt, *più dimandato da noi che le belle putte* [more desirable to us than pretty wenches], all this you can put in a letter, so that you needn't go very far for a subject. But I do not demand long letters. All I ask for is a short note, but please see that I get one often. That would remind me that you still exist, that you are still close to me, that you are walking arm in arm with me, though invisibly. Please, I beg you, I implore you, I pray to you, I conjure you. At the same moment, in the same magnificent temple where you offer up a double sacrifice to the gods, as soon as you have had your coffee or, at any rate, after the *Courier Français*, but before you pick up the billiard cue, take a pen or pencil and quickly scribble a note to me, and then, after three or four games, go out and post it. I assure you, you will yourself feel happy and contented afterwards. Your stomach will digest your food properly. Rubini will sing better. Grisi will be a thousand times more attractive. Just try and do it. I've not yet recovered my senses in Rome. There seems to be a sort of film over my eyes which prevents me from seeing her in that miraculous splendour in which she appeared to me when I entered her for a second time. Perhaps that is why I haven't yet adapted myself to life in Rome. . . . My thoughts are still fixed on Montmartre and the Boulevard des Italiens. Here I have met a few of my acquaintances, who have not, however, helped me to slip into my former rut in which I should have jogged along slowly or—anyhow—somehow or other.

I embrace you a million times and am waiting impatiently for your explanation.

Your G.

But another six weeks passed and Danilevsky still did not write. Gogol seems to have made an attempt to accept the inevitable. At the beginning of December, after complaining in a short note that he had received 'not a word, not a syllable—nothing', he added the surmise that 'perhaps' Danilevsky found it 'difficult' to write, and expressed the hope that they might meet again in Russia next winter. But, again, his 'inmost feelings' got the better of him and on December the 28th, three months after his parting from Danilevsky, he dashed off another despairing letter.

Aren't you ashamed [he wrote] not to write to me? Do you really find it so difficult to write one line, just one line, so that I should at least know that you are alive? I never expected this of you. Three letters and not one reply. But never mind, I forgive you this time, too. Only admit that you are wrong. If you have one drop of love, admit that you are wrong, and get a pen and paper at once and write to me two or three words, no more, to show that you are still alive. You can't imagine how worried I have been about you all this time. Who knows, perhaps this letter will be as unsuccessful as the three previous ones. Perhaps you're no longer in Paris, but somewhere else, in Brussels or some other town in Europe. I'd have written to you about many things, but . . . I didn't want to waste words and feelings without knowing whether anyone would hear them. . . . I am awaiting impatiently your reply. One word, one syllable, but in your hand and as quickly as possible.

For the first time I feel angry with you.

N. G.

Danilevsky was in Paris all right, and at last he took pity on Gogol and replied to his letter. Or did he reply merely because he had run out of money again? At any rate, he seems to have asked Gogol for more money.

'Thank God [Gogol wrote in reply on December the 31st], I've got your letter at last. Well, at least you are alive. I am very sorry to hear you are in difficulties. God knows how readily and gladly I would have helped you, and how happy this would have made me, but, alas, what can I do? I can at least share what I have with you; I am sending you a banker's bill for a hundred francs, which I have kept a long time. I never touched it, as though knowing what a delightful purpose it would serve.'

He had just received the two thousand roubles from Pogodin and he promised to send Danilevsky another two hundred francs shortly. After complaining of his feelings having become blunted and of his loss of appetite, he went on:

'Now, if I were rich I'd like—what would I like?—I'd like to spend the rest of my life with you, to offer up the same sacrifices in the same temple, to have a game of billiards sometimes after tea as—remember?—we used to have not so long ago. I tried to play billiards here, but somehow I did not enjoy it and gave it up. I don't want to play with anyone but you. I feel that you would have filled my days which seem so empty now. But why despair? Haven't we said good-bye for ever to each other many times and yet met again and thanked God? Perhaps we shall meet again one day, and live together again. . . . Well, good-bye [he concludes]. I kiss you hundreds of times. . . .'

After he got Danilevsky's letter acknowledging the receipt of the money, Gogol wrote complaining sadly that he thought more often of Danilevsky than Danilevsky thought of him. 'Your letter', he writes, 'begins thus: It is four or five days since I received your letter and the money, etc. I don't act like that: I have made it a rule always to write to you on the same day I receive your letter, whatever I might be doing at the time. . . . You and I are approaching (alas, how awful!) that time of life', he went on, 'when our vivid impressions sink deeper to the bottom and when our powers are weakening and becoming numb and we, alas, are often unable to rouse them as easily as before, when they used to rise to the surface by themselves. We ought to be constantly afraid lest the hard covering which envelops us should become harder and grow, finally, so thick that we would really not be able to break through it. Let us at least abandon ourselves to the lyrical outpourings of our inmost feelings which are being constantly chased away by their mortal enemies—our vulgar pastimes, our preoccupations with our dinner, our fatal thirty years [both Gogol and Danilevsky were approaching their thirtieth birthdays], an odious stomach and all the nastiness of a stale and addled mind. . . .'

A week later Gogol, stung to jealousy by Danilevsky's mention in his letter of a certain Klothilde, demanded that Danilevsky should change his 'sensual' life for a 'spiritual' one. 'It is high time', he wrote, 'you got rid of the devil who sits in your stomach and incites you to indulge in lechery. . . .' His desire to possess some part of Danilevsky made him wish to have at least his stick. 'You made me a present of it', he wrote three weeks later on the 7th of March 1839, 'and I don't know why I didn't take it with me.' On April the 2nd he got it. 'I went into my room', he wrote to Danilevsky on that date, 'and saw your stick lying on the table. That was a wonderful surprise. It seemed to me as though I saw a part of you. . . .'

The stick seems to have been the last manifestation of this brief and turbulent affair. In his last four letters to Danilevsky from Rome, Gogol reverts to his usual affectionate tone. All he wanted, he wrote on April the 14th to Danilevsky, was to forget: 'to forget my suffering, to forget my past, to forget my age and my youth, to forget my memories, to forget my present trivial mode of life. But', he goes on, 'if there is a place in the world where suffering, grief, bereavements and one's own impotence can be forgotten, it is only in Rome. What would have happened to me if I were in any other place? Here the parting from one's nearest and dearest, which is so hard, is less terrible.'

Several circumstances during the first six months of 1839 combined to make it easier for Gogol to forget. Between December the 19th and February the 17th Zhukovsky, who had accompanied the Russian heir to the throne on his official visit to Italy, spent most of his time with Gogol sightseeing, climbing to the dome of Saint Peter's and sketching. 'He is still as kind and as fond of me as ever', Gogol wrote to Danilevsky on December the 31st. 'He came to me like a heavenly messenger, like the butterfly he described which flew into the prisoner's cell, though Rome can hardly be called a dungeon, however great your grief. . . . I have been spending more time holding a brush than a pen in my hand . . . I live,' he went on, 'as you no doubt know, in the same house and the same street, Via Felice, No. 126. I see the same familiar faces round me, the same German artists with their narrow, reddish little beards and the same goats, also with narrow beards; I hear the same conversations and my neighbours talk about the same things as they poke their heads out of their windows. The Annunziatas, Rosas, Nannas and others utter the same squeals and shrieks in their woollen dressing-gowns and worn shoes. Winter in Rome is cold as never before; there is frost in the morning, but it runs away when the sun comes out as darkness does from light. However, I've got used to the cold weather and do not even bring a stove into my room. The sun warms it. Now the carnival has started. It is noisy and gay. Our "his Highness" is highly satisfied and, driving through the streets with his suite, throws basketfuls and bagfuls of flour at the people and at everything that meets his eye. . . .'

On the 8th of March 1839, Pogodin arrived in Rome (Shevyryov had arrived earlier and his first meeting with Gogol took place during this visit), and took a room next door to Gogol's on the third floor, up the steep staircase, from which one could catch a glimpse of the dirty, stone-paved garden hemmed in by high, grey-stone walls. Pogodin's impressions of Rome were quite different from Gogol's. All he saw was the squalor of the city. 'There is no other city as dirty as Rome', he wrote in the diary of his voyage abroad. 'Here everything is done in the street. When I first came to see him, Gogol emptied a huge vase of slops out of the window.' Gogol showed him round Rome, 'dragging him', as Pogodin put it, first to Saint Peter's, and finishing up with a visit to Ivanov's studio. Pogodin stayed in Rome till April the 18th, when he and Shevyryov left for Paris, Gogol accompanying them as far as Civita-Vecchia.

But it was not Zhukovsky, nor Pogodin, nor Shevyryov who helped to take Gogol out of himself and get rid of the obsession that darkened his mind. It was a twenty-three-year-old consumptive boy whom he nursed in his last illness, and watched slowly passing away with so calm a fortitude that it made him realize his own unpardonable weakness. The boy was Count Joseph Vyelgorsky, the son of Count Mikhail Vyelgorsky, and Gogol met him for the first time on the 20th of December 1838. He was working on a history of Russian literature and this at once created a close bond between him and Gogol. At the beginning of May it was becoming clear that 'poor, gentle, noble-minded Joseph', as Gogol described him in a letter to Pogodin, was dying. 'There is no life in Russia for fine people like him', Gogol added. 'Only swine seem to prosper there.' Gogol now spent all his time at the Vyelgorsky villa—a small house with a tower, built inside the ancient Roman walls and surrounded by vines and flower gardens, with fine views of the Roman viaducts and mountains on one side and of the Colosseum and Saint Peter's on the other. 'I am now spending sleepless nights at the bedside of my dying friend, Joseph Vyelgorsky,' Gogol wrote to Maria Balabin on the 30th of May 1839. 'You have no doubt heard of him, perhaps even seen him occasionally; but you do not know his beautiful soul nor his beautiful feelings nor his strong, rather too unbending character for such a young man, nor the extraordinary soundness of his mind; and all this is the prey of inexorable death; and he will not be saved by his youth nor by his right to life which, without a doubt, would have been beautiful and useful! I clutch eagerly at every minute of his life. His smile or his momentary air of cheerfulness is a whole epoch for me, a great event in my monotonously passing day. . . . My poor Joseph, the only fair and truly noble one of your Petersburg young men, and he . . . I swear, inexplicably strange is the fate of everything good in our Russia! No sooner does it appear than death lays its cold hand upon it—pitiless, inexorable death! I do not believe in anything now, and if I come across anything beautiful, I at once close my eyes and try not to look at it. It reeks of the grave. "It only lasts a brief moment", a voice whispers dully in my ear. "It is only given us so that it should fill us with everlasting pangs of regret, so that our spirit should be profoundly and sorely afflicted . . .'"'

In his notebook, Gogol left a moving description of his feelings during the sleepless nights he spent at the bedside of his dying young friend under the heading of *Nights at a Villa*. 'They were sweet and painful—those sleepless nights', he wrote. 'He sat in an armchair. I was beside him. Sleep dared not touch my eyes. It seemed instinctively and silently to respect the sanctity of this nocturnal vigil. It felt so good to sit beside him, to look at him. We had already been using the familiar *thou* for two nights when speaking to each other. How close he seemed to me after that! He sat there looking the same as ever: gentle, calm, resigned. Lord, how gladly, how cheerfully I'd have accepted his illness! And if my death could have restored his health, how readily I should have welcomed it!'

One night Gogol could not overcome his sleepiness and went home for a rest. But his sleep did not refresh him and he was tormented by remorse. But in the morning Joseph gave him the same angelic smile he always did. He shook his hand lovingly. 'Traitor,' he said to Gogol, 'you have let me down!' 'My angel,' Gogol cried, 'forgive me. I myself suffered like you. I was tormented all night. My rest brought me no relief. Forgive me.' The dying boy pressed his hand and Gogol felt rewarded for his sufferings during the night.

A few days before Vyelgorsky's death Gogol wrote to Pogodin: 'I am now very much occupied with my sick Vyelgorsky. I sit beside him at night and am constantly at his beck and call. These are sacred services of friendship and I must perform them now. But the remarkable thing is that I feel no fatigue. My health has not deteriorated at all. My face doesn't show any signs of exhaustion. I am even told that I look better. Sweet and sad are my present moments. . . .'

Vyelgorsky died on May the 21st. Shortly before his death Gogol rushed out to get a priest to administer extreme unction and himself read the prayer for the dying over him. Before he died, however, a bizarre scene occurred. Princess Zinaida Volkonsky burst into his room with a Catholic priest and, bending over the dying man, whispered to the priest: 'Now is the time to convert him to Catholicism.' But the priest refused. Then the Princess bent over the dying man again, whispered something over him and then said: 'I saw the soul which came out of his body, and it was a Catholic soul!'

'A few days ago', Gogol wrote to Danilevsky on June the 5th, 'I buried my friend, whom fate had given me at a time of my life when friends are not given. I am speaking of my Joseph Vyelgorsky. We have long been attached to each other, we have long respected each other, but became real, inseparable and true friends, alas, only during his illness. You cannot imagine what a noble, high-minded and child-like bright spirit he was. We often meet upstarts of intellect and talent, but intellect, talent and good taste combined with such sound principles and such a courageous and firm character, are things that occur rarely among people. And together with this firmness of character, this striving to be useful and generous, he possessed such virginally pure feelings. He was a man who would have adorned the reign of Alexander II. The rest of the people who surround him haven't a grain of talent. And the great and beautiful has to perish as all that is great and beautiful perishes in Russia. . . .'

¶ 4

Gogol left Rome at the beginning of June 1839, sailing with Count Mikhail Vyelgorsky for Marseilles to meet Countess Luisa Vyelgorsky, who was too late to see her son before his death.

It was during his voyage to Marseilles that Gogol met the French critic Sainte-Beuve on board ship. In his review of the first French translation of Gogol's stories by Louis Viardot with the assistance of Turgenev (published in the *Revue des deux mondes* in December 1845), Sainte-Beuve recalls this meeting with Gogol in the following passage:

'J'aurais un avantage pourtant que je réclame, c'était d'avoir rencontré autrefois, sur un bateau à vapeur, dans une traversée de Rome à Marseille, l'auteur en personne, et là j'avais pu, d'après sa conversation forte, précise et riche d'observations de moeurs prises sur le fait, saisir un avant-goût de ce que devaient contenir d'original et de réel ses oeuvres elles-mêmes. . . . C'est ainsi que M. Gogol me dit avoir trouvé à Rome un véritable poète, un poète populaire, appelé Belli, qui écrit des sonnets dans le langage transtéverin, mais des sonnets faisant suite et formant poème. Il m'en parla à fond et de manière à me convaincre du talent original et supérieur de ce Belli, qui est resté si parfaitement inconnu à tous les voyageurs.'

Gogol mentioned Giuseppe Gioacchino Belli in his letter to Maria Balabin from Rome in April 1838. 'I don't suppose', he wrote, 'you have read the sonnets of the modern Roman poet Belli, which one really ought to hear him read himself. There is such a lot of unexpected wit in these sonnets and they reflect so faithfully the life of the present-day trasteverines that I'm sure they would make you laugh and you'd forget all about your present worries and your wretched headaches.'

From Marseilles Gogol left for Marienbad, where he intended to take the waters. 'My health,' he wrote to Maria Balabin from Rome shortly before his departure, '*non vale un fico*, as the Italians say. It is worse than our present Russian literature. I shall spend the summer in Marienbad.' By then he had conceived a strong dislike for the Germans. 'How can you,' he wrote to Maria Balabin in the same letter, 'who have expressed such an admiration in your letter for Shakespeare, that profound, bright spirit who, like a mirror, reflects faithfully the whole enormous world and everything that goes to make up a man, how can you, reading him, think at the same time of the smoky German confusion! And can one say that every German is a Schiller? I agree that he is a Schiller, but only the Schiller whom you will find in my story *Nevsky Avenue*, if you ever have the patience to read it.' He reverted to the subject of Germany and the Germans in his letter of the 5th of September 1839, to Maria Balabin from Vienna, where he had arrived on August the 24th, and where he stayed for a fortnight. In reply to Maria Balabin's objections to his views of the Germans, Gogol, remembering no doubt his own juvenile poem *Hans Kuechelgarten*, wrote:

'When I had read your letter and folded it, I hung my head and a feeling of sadness stole into my heart. I remembered the beautiful years of my irrecoverable youth and, I am ashamed to say, I nearly burst into tears. That was the time when my powers were still fresh and my impulses were as pure as the sound produced by a true bow. Those were the poetic years of my life. In those days I loved the Germans, not knowing them, or perhaps mixing up scholarship, German philosophy and literature with the Germans. Be that as it may, but German poetry carried me away in those years, far, far away beyond the distant horizons, and I liked its complete remoteness from life and the things that really mattered. For in those days I used to look much more disdainfully upon the ordinary and everyday things of life. I still love those Germans whom I saw in my imagination at that time. But [he went on, thinking of his state of mind just then] let us drop the subject. I dislike awakening the rusty chords in my heart. All I can say is that it is hard to find oneself an old man at an age that still belongs to youth. It is awful to discover ashes instead of flowers deep inside you and to become aware of the helplessness of your enthusiasm. Collect in one crowd all the unhappy people in the world, choose the unhappiest among them and you will find that he will be happy compared with him whom fate has doomed to such a state of mind. . . . Now [he concluded his confession] I esteem nothing higher in the whole world than nature. People, cities, nations and their interrelationships and everything that destroys, excites and wearies men have vanished from my sight. Nature alone I see and live by. That is why I am so partial to her: she is my only wealth. He who has experienced deep spiritual losses will understand me. . . .'

On his way to Marienbad, Gogol stopped at Hanau where he met Nikolai Yazykov, a poet he had greatly admired, and who was to become one of his closest friends. 'Gogol', Yazykov, who was stricken with paralysis, wrote to a friend on the 1st of July 1839, 'came to see me yesterday on his way to Marienbad. I found him a jolly companion. I liked him very much. He knows Rome like the back of his hand. I expect he must have written a lot in Rome.'

There Yazykov was mistaken. Except for revising *The Government Inspector* and some of the scenes of his unfinished comedy *Vladimir Third Class*, Gogol had not written a great deal in Rome. Most of his work on *Dead Souls* he did in 1837 and the first half of 1838.

In Marienbad Gogol took the cure and went for long walks with Pogodin, with whom he shared a room, and a rich Petersburg businessman, Dmitry Benardaki, from whom he tried to find out as much as he could about the cases of embezzlement that were tried in the courts. Most of his time, however, he spent in reading

Ukrainian folk-songs, for he was planning to write a Ukrainian historical play. 'If I don't succeed in writing it', he wrote to Shevyryov on August the 25th, 'I shall be a great fool. Whether it is the Ukrainian songs that have suggested it to me, or whether the past has become real to me by some power of clairvoyance, the fact remains that I seem to understand a great deal of it, which happens but rarely to me now.' But his work on the play was not proceeding as quickly as he had hoped. 'The work which I began', he wrote to Shevyryov on September the 10th, 'is not progressing, though I can't help feeling that it could be an excellent thing. Or has one to work at a play, as I used to work in the past, in the sight of the stage, in the awful dark hole where the faces and eyes of the spectators gaze at you from all sides? We shall see.'

Gogol had arranged to go back to Russia with Pogodin to take his sisters from the Patriotic Institute where they had finished their course of studies and, as he told Shevyryov in the same letter, he put his trust in the open road where he used to think out all his subjects.

In Moscow, where he arrived on the 26th of September 1839 (O.S.), Gogol stayed at Pogodin's house. He was given a large room on the top floor under the iron roof which helped to keep it warm. He loved to play with Pogodin's children. 'Every morning', Pogodin's son Dmitry records, 'my sister and I used to go up to Gogol's room, knock on the door and ask him if he wanted anything. In spite of the heat in the room, we always found him wearing a woollen sweater. "Remember, no noise," he used to say to us, carrying on with his usual work, such as knitting a scarf or skull-cap or writing something on tiny bits of paper in a very small hand. These bits of paper he sometimes read to himself in an undertone, tore them up as though in anger, or threw them on the floor and made us pick them up and put them together on the table according to his instructions. He would pat us on the head when he was pleased with us and seize us by the ears and show us out of the room when he wished to be left alone.' He did not leave his room till dinner, and at dinner he was very cheerful and cracked jokes. A peculiar habit of his at dinner was the rolling of bread pellets which he threw at the people sitting round the table (a habit he seems to have acquired as a child), or, if he disliked some drink, putting them into the decanter. (He did it at the Aksakovs too, but they were too polite and well-bred to take any notice.) After dinner, he went up to his room where he shut himself up till seven o'clock. After seven, he would come down and start walking through all the rooms of the house. Two large decanters of cold water were placed in the two drawing-rooms at either side of the house, and every ten minutes Gogol would pour himself out a glass and drink it. 'Gogol', Dmitri Pogodin writes, 'used to walk so fast and with such abrupt steps that the stearin candles (oil lamps were not even heard of in those days) would gutter and my grandmother would shout to the maid, "Grusha, Grusha, fetch me a warm scarf, the 'Talian (so she called Gogol) has let loose a storm again!" "Don't be cross, old lady," Gogol would say to her good-humouredly, "let me finish the decanter of water and I'll stop." And, indeed, having finished the second decanter of water, he would go back to his room upstairs. When walking,' Dmitri Pogodin continues, 'Gogol always cocked his head on one side. Of all his clothes, he paid particular attention to his waistcoats: he always wore velvet waistcoats and only of two colours: blue and red. His fame', he concludes, 'wearied him and when people who came specially to see him found him in my father's study, he used to withdraw into his shell like a snail.'

The Aksakovs were still in the country when Gogol arrived in Moscow. The news of his arrival was brought to them by Shchepkin and the enthusiastic twenty-two-year-old Konstantin let out such a yell that his cousin, Maria Kartashevsky, promptly fainted. The Aksakovs returned to Moscow on October the 1st, and the next day Gogol dined with them. Gogol had changed so much that Aksakov barely recognized him. 'There was no trace of the former closely-shaven and, except for his quiff, closely cropped little dandy in his fashionable dress-coat', Sergey Aksakov writes in his reminiscences. 'His beautiful, thick fair hair reached almost to his shoulders; his handsome moustache and imperial completed the change. All the features of his face had assumed quite a different aspect; his eyes, especially when he spoke, were good-humoured and gay, but when he was silent or fell into thought they immediately assumed a serious expression. Instead of a dress-coat, which he put on only on formal occasions, he wore a frock-coat. His figure looked much more impressive in a frock-coat.'

Gogol's visit to Moscow did not pass off without a public scandal. Gogol had not seen a performance of *The Government*

Inspector on the Moscow stage, and it was decided to give a special performance of it in his honour. It took place on October the 17th. The theatre was packed with Moscow notabilities; the entire literary world, including Belinsky, was there. Gogol sat, or rather lay down (so anxious was he not to be seen) in a box in the stalls with Yelisaveta Chertkov, the wife of a well-known historian and archaeologist, whom he had met in Rome. At the end of Act III the audience suddenly rose and, turning towards Mrs. Chertkov's box, began calling for the author. Konstantin Aksakov, almost mad with excitement, shouted and clapped louder than anyone. At these frantic cries, Gogol sank lower and lower in his chair, and then almost crept out of the box. After a time the curtain rose and an actor came out to announce that the author was not in the theatre. Sergey Aksakov, who had been watching Gogol in his box and had seen him beat a hasty retreat, rushed out after him and overtook him near the entrance of the theatre. He asked him to go back and take the call, but Gogol refused and ran away. 'The audience', Aksakov writes in his reminiscences, 'was incensed, taking Gogol's action as a personal offence, and ascribing it to the author's immense vanity and pride.' Next morning, Gogol wrote a letter to Mikhail Zagoskin, whom he addressed as 'a member of that enlightened circle which constitutes the honour and pride of Moscow', explaining that at any other time such a wonderful reception from a Moscow audience would have made him shed 'streams of grateful tears', but that 'a few minutes before the performance' he had received such alarming news from home that 'when the unanimous thunder of applause, so flattering to an author', reached his ears, his heart contracted and he felt too weak to face the audience. 'I looked with a sort of contempt at my inglorious fame,' he wrote, 'and thought: now I am enjoying it while my nearest and dearest, for whom I'd gladly give the best moments of my life, are facing so terrible a calamity—and my heart turned over! Amid the shouts and clapping, I could not help hearing their cries of distress. I had not the strength to bear it. I vanished from the theatre. . . .' Feeling that he was rather putting it on, Gogol added: 'The public may not believe my words and . . . even laugh at me. Well, let it add contempt to the hatred which many of my fellow-countrymen feel for me, but I swear I shall never forget those spontaneous expressions of its favour and cordiality.'

This letter is typical of Gogol when driven into a tight corner by his own folly, for it was stage-fright and his fear of 'the awful dark hole' and nothing else that drove him out of the theatre. Far from receiving any bad news from home, he was so anxious that his mother should not know that he was in Moscow (he did not want her to come before he had brought his sisters back from Petersburg) that he headed the two letters he wrote to her 'Trieste' and 'Vienna', and even went so far as to counterfeit Austrian stamps on the envelopes. Fortunately, he showed Pogodin his letter to Zagoskin, and Pogodin realized that it would make Gogol's position even more ridiculous and sent it to Aksakov for his opinion. Both advised Gogol not to send it, and he agreed.

¶ 5

Gogol left Moscow for Petersburg on the 26th of October 1839 (O.S.), travelling with Sergey Aksakov, his son Mikhail who was to enter a military college, and his daughter Vera. 'This journey', Aksakov writes in his reminiscences, 'was so pleasant and gay that I still remember it with pleasure. Gogol was so amiable and kept cracking such amusing jokes that we held our sides with laughter. . . . He spoke with enthusiasm about his life in Italy, about painting (which he loved and for which he had a decided talent), about art in general and comedy in particular. . . . For the greater part of the journey, however, he read some book, which he either hid under his seat or put away in the bag he always took with him when we stopped at an inn. In this huge bag he kept his toilet articles: some sort of oil which he used to apply to his hair, moustache and beard, several hair brushes, scissors, tweezers and nail brushes and, finally, a few books. My fourteen-year-old Misha [who sat next to Gogol in a partitioned off part of the carriage] always showed us by signs what Gogol was doing, whether he was reading or drowsing. He even peeped to see what Gogol was reading: it was Shakespeare in a French translation [Gogol was reading Shakespeare to get a few hints for the Ukrainian historical play he was writing at the time].'

On October the 30th, Gogol and his companions arrived in

Petersburg, where Gogol at first stayed at Pletnyov's. His financial position was desperate. He had to raise two thousand roubles to buy clothes for his sisters, pay for their lessons, their fares to Moscow, etc., and his hopes that the Empress—the patron of the Patriotic Institute—might make them a present of the money fell through because the Empress was ill and Zhukovsky, who had promised to intercede with her, could not do so. To make matters worse, he had lost his wallet with all the money he had in the world, and an advertisement he put in the police journal about it had had no result. In desperation, he turned to Aksakov, who immediately offered to lend him the money (Aksakov himself had to borrow it from Benardaki, 'the only man in Petersburg', Aksakov declared, 'who called Gogol a genius and considered acquaintance with him a great honour.'). Aksakov made his offer with such delicacy and with so genuine a conviction that it was Gogol who was doing him a favour by accepting the money that, he writes, 'Gogol's face not only brightened, but looked positively radiant. Instead of an answer, he thanked God for having met me and my family, held out his hands to me, pressed mine warmly and looked at me as he did a few months before his death, when he left Abramtsevo [Aksakov's estate] for Moscow. I think that even then he had a presentiment that he was parting from me for ever. . . .' Gogol relaxed to such an extent that, though he hated to discuss his literary plans with anyone, he told Aksakov that in addition to the work Pushkin had bequeathed him, that is, *Dead Souls*, the completion of which he considered to be 'the task of my life', he had also been working on an historical tragedy of which he had everything ready to the last detail, even to the clothes worn by the characters, and that he thought it would be his best work and that it would only take him two months to get it finished.

What amazed and grieved Aksakov was that among the high officials in Petersburg there was not one who appreciated Gogol's genius. He could not find even one who had read all his works. Aksakov, though, had his revenge on two privy councillors whose views of Gogol were so outrageous that, in a letter to his wife, he called them 'calibans in the understanding of art'. Unable to listen to their talk any longer, he proposed that they should have a game of cards and, Aksakov writes, 'it was with malicious joy that I took their money at the end of the game'.

In Petersburg Gogol read the first four chapters of *Dead Souls* at Prokopovich's. Though little impressed by the laughter of his audience, Annenkov, who was present at the reading, records, he was genuinely pleased by the delight he saw on their faces. After the reading Annenkov took him, as usual wrapped up to the eyes in his fur coat, to the Winter Palace where he had been living in Zhukovsky's flat since November the 15th.

It was at Zhukovsky's that Aksakov caught a glimpse of Gogol while engaged in writing. Zhukovsky took him to Gogol's room and, as he opened the door, Aksakov nearly cried out in surprise. 'Before me', he writes, 'stood Gogol in the following fantastic costume: instead of boots he wore long Russian woollen stockings reaching above his knees; instead of a frock-coat he wore a velvet spencer over his flannel vest; his neck was wrapped round with a large multi-coloured scarf, and on his head was a crimson, gold-embroidered head-dress such as is worn by Russian peasant women. Gogol was standing at his desk writing and he was so absorbed in his work that he gazed unseeingly at us a long time, but was not at all embarrassed by his odd costume. . . .'

At last, on December the 17th, after long delays, Gogol with his two sisters and the Aksakovs left Petersburg for Moscow. His sisters, 'little savages', as Aksakov described them, drove Gogol to distraction. 'Knowing and understanding nothing', Aksakov writes, 'they were afraid of everything and shrieked and cried, especially at night. . . . Besides, they kept quarrelling with each other like children. All this made Gogol despair of their future. Poor Vera had a great deal of trouble with them and I was surprised at her patience. I don't know what Gogol would have done without her. They would have driven him out of his mind. It was pitiful and amusing to watch Gogol: he did not know what to do with them, all his efforts and admonitions were inept, out of place, ill-timed and absolutely useless, and in this predicament the writer of genius was more absurd than any ordinary man. . . . At the inns, during dinner or breakfast, tea or coffee, we did not hear a single joke from Gogol. He and Vera were constantly busy with the "patriotic" young ladies, who disliked everything because it was not like what they had been used to at their "institute". Poor Gogol. He was a real martyr. . . .'

In Moscow Gogol went back to live at Pogodin's, his sisters staying in a large room opposite his. He spent his last roubles on two black silk dresses for them, but he had as a last resort to engage a priest ostensibly to impart 'the great truths of Christianity' to them, though in fact to stop them from bickering with one another. He was beginning to long for the quiet time he had had in Rome. 'Oh, Rome, oh, Rome,' he wrote to Zhukovsky on the 11th of January 1840 (O.S.), 'if only I could get there now, how refreshed in spirit I should be!' But he had no money left. Zhukovsky had been negotiating with the Petersburg publisher and bookseller Smirdin for the publication of a collected edition of his works, but Gogol refused to accept Smirdin's offer of six thousand roubles. 'I told you', he wrote to Zhukovsky on January the 4th, 'that I couldn't see any advantage in publishing an edition of my works now. What if all the copies of *The Government Inspector* and *Mirgorod* have been sold, there are still lots of unsold copies of *Arabesques* and *Evenings on a Farm*. Apart from *The Government Inspector* they are not in great demand and the best proof of it is the ridiculous offer made by Smirdin. But such is my luck: the booksellers have always taken advantage of my straitened circumstances. If I wait another year till my novel is finished I shall have four thousand readers eager to buy it and then there will again be a great demand for those of my works which are now forgotten. ... And so', he concludes, 'I have decided not to sell my works but find the means which would enable me to delay, if not to stop, my run of bad luck for at least a year, and return as soon as possible to Rome, where my crushed spirits will revive as they did last winter and spring, sit down to work and finish my novel in one year. But how am I to get the money? This is what I have thought of: let my friends club together and lend me four thousand roubles for one year. I give you my word to repay the whole sum with interest within one year. This will enable me somehow or other to get out of my present difficulties and give me back to myself. ...'

Zhukovsky preferred to lend him the four thousand roubles himself, and in his reply Gogol thanked him as his 'deliverer' and promised to do his utmost to repay them. 'Rome is mine!' he exclaimed ecstatically.

But Rome was not his yet. He had first to do something about his sisters, whom he did not want to send home. 'In Vassilevka', he wrote to his mother from Rome on the 12th of March 1839, 'they will not find husbands, but may lose what they have acquired from their education. . . . Just think what kind of society they will find at home. What company will they be able to keep there? And don't forget that they have such different characters that they were constantly quarrelling even at the institute, and what will happen when they live under one roof? . . . You say you know of a young man in the neighbourhood with an annual income of two hundred thousand, who might marry Annette. That is a delusion. It's better not to think of it. I, too, know many young men with even larger incomes, but that doesn't mean that they would marry Annette. You may be sure that if you had a carriage of your own and, as you say, the means of dressing decently and driving out decently, it would not be of the slightest help. Marriages are arranged among equals and one has to be a real fool or a very original man indeed to go against the wishes of one's parents, against one's own interests and one's own social position and choose a poor and unknown girl for his wife, or else the girl has to be a paragon of beauty, perfection and intelligence herself, which can hardly be said of Annette, though she is a kind-hearted girl and may well become a good wife. . . .'

Gogol's own plan, however, was no less fantastic than his mother's. He wanted his sisters, the eighteen-year-old Anna and the sixteen-year-old Yelisaveta, to stay in Moscow and earn a living doing French translations. 'For the time being,' he wrote to Pogodin, 'they will translate and work for your future journal *Moskvityanin* and for me. I want to accustom them to a hard-working and active life.' In Moscow he tried to introduce them into literary circles, and made them translate 'together with some students' (as he wrote to Shchepkin from Vienna on August the 10th) one of Shakespeare's plays for Shchepkin's benefit night. But they were utterly unfit either by inclination or knowledge for any literary work.

Gogol went to see the Aksakovs almost every day and dined with them three times a week. 'He came to us for a rest from his creative labours,' Aksakov writes, 'to talk nonsense, to crack jokes and to have a game of billiards, which he played very badly. But Konstantin sometimes managed to draw him into serious conversation on art. . . .' Every Saturday he prepared his favourite dish of macaroni. Standing before a huge bowl, he would roll up his sleeves, put in the macaroni, previously half-cooked for him, add a big lump of butter and begin stirring it quickly and regularly

186

with two sauce spoons. Then he added salt, pepper and grated Parmesan cheese and went on mixing it for a long time. 'It was impossible to watch Gogol without laughing', Aksakov observes. 'He was so absorbed in his work that it seemed to be his favourite occupation and I could not help reflecting that if fate had not made him a great writer he would certainly have become a culinary artist.' As soon as the macaroni was ready, that is to say, as soon as the cheese had become one sticky mass, Gogol put huge slabs of it on the plates of his hosts, who were too polite not to eat it, though it gave them indigestion afterwards. Gogol, however, ate it all with great relish, and to Aksakov's surprise suffered no ill effects afterwards.

Gogol gave several readings of the first chapters of *Dead Souls* at the Aksakov's and one at Kireyevsky's. Panayev, who had been invited by Aksakov to one of these readings on the 8th of March 1840 (O.S.), has left an amusing description of it in his reminiscences. Gogol, who was supposed to read something from *Dead Souls*, arrived late as usual. He looked bored and seemed hardly able to force himself to exchange the usual courtesies with the large company who were all agog to hear him read his masterpiece. Konstantin Aksakov was beside himself with excitement. He watched Gogol's every look and every movement, while Gogol, who could not help noticing the veneration he inspired, tried to cover up his gratification by a show of outward indifference. After dinner he retired to Aksakov's study where he sprawled on the sofa and pretended to go to sleep. Immediately everybody in the room fell silent. Panayev, Shchepkin, and the Aksakovs tiptoed out of the room while Konstantin, hardly daring to breathe, kept pacing up and down in front of the door as though on sentry-go and at the slightest movement waved his arms and hissed in an excited whisper:

'Shh—shh—Nikolai Vassilyevich is dozing!'

At dinner, Gogol never mentioned his promise to read and no one dared to remind him of it. While Gogol was dozing, everyone was wondering whether he was going to read or not. At last Gogol yawned loudly. Konstantin peeped through the keyhole and, seeing that Gogol had opened his eyes, went into the room.

'I'm afraid I must have dropped off', said Gogol, yawning and peering at the people who were crowding in the doorway.

The ladies in the drawing-room, hearing that Gogol was awake, kept calling for Konstantin and asking him in a whisper whether Gogol was going to read, but the young man merely shrugged his shoulders in reply. At last Aksakov himself took the bull by the horns and addressed Gogol directly.

'I believe', he began cautiously, 'you've promised to read us something today, Nikolai Vassilyevich. You haven't forgotten, have you?'

Gogol made a wry face.

'Promised? Have I? Oh, yes! But I'm afraid I don't feel like reading today. I'm sure I shall read badly, and I'd be glad if you'd let me off this time.'

But Aksakov had by now learned how to handle Gogol's unaccountable tantrums, and after half an hour of tactful and highly diplomatic entreaty, Gogol relented.

'Well,' he said, stretching himself, 'all right, I will read you something. Only what?'

Shchepkin gave a start, and his cheeks began to shake. Konstantin beamed with delight. An excited whisper passed through the house: 'Gogol is going to read!'

Gogol got up from the sofa, looked balefully at Panayev, whom he did not know well (he disliked reading before strangers), and went into the drawing-room where the ladies had been waiting for hours. He walked up reluctantly to the large oval table in front of the sofa, sat down, glanced cursorily at the people in the room, said once more that he did not know what to read, that he had nothing that was really finished and—suddenly hiccoughed once, twice, three times.

The ladies exchanged glances, the men dared not move and looked, bewildered, at each other.

'What's the matter with me? I seem to have indigestion', said Gogol, and paused.

Mr. and Mrs. Aksakov looked embarrassed. They wondered if their dinner had given him indigestion.

'Yesterday's dinner', Gogol went on, 'has stuck in my throat —all those mushrooms and the fish-soup! You eat and eat and goodness only knows what you eat. . . .'

Gogol hiccoughed again, took a manuscript out of his back pocket and placed it before him on the table. 'Let's have a look at the *Northern Bee* and see what they've got there . . .' he went on, this time reading from his manuscript.

It was only then that his audience realized that his hiccoughing and the words he had spoken were merely the beginning of a monologue. It was, in fact, from one of the scenes of his unpublished play *Vladimir Third Class*, which he included two years later in the first collected edition of his works under the title of *Lawsuit*.

Gogol gave his last reading at the Aksakovs'—the sixth chapter of *Dead Souls*—on April the 17th, Easter Sunday. At the time he had been looking for a companion with whom he could share the expenses of his journey to Rome, and had even advertised for one in the *Moscow News Supplement*. A friend of the Aksakovs, Vassily Panov, who was present at the last reading, was so impressed by it that he decided to accompany Gogol to Italy. After the reading they all went to the Kremlin to hear the first stroke of the bell of Ivan the Great, and it was on their way back that Panov told Gogol of his decision, which Gogol gratefully accepted.

At Easter, Maria Ivanovna with her youngest daughter Olga arrived in Moscow. She looked so young that, according to Aksakov, she could be taken for Gogol's sister. Maria Ivanovna would not give up her plan of marrying Annette to a rich man and insisted on taking her back to Vassilevka. Gogol placed his younger sister Yelisaveta in the house of a rich Moscow woman, Praskovya Rayevsky, where she showed no desire to take up the literary career mapped out for her by Gogol and occupied herself entirely with domestic duties. She returned to Vassilevka in 1842, and nine years later married an army officer. Poor Annette never married and after her mother's death in 1868 left Vassilevka and went to live in Poltava.

Maria Ivanovna and her two daughters, Anna and Olga, left Moscow for Vassilevka on the 27th of April 1840 (O.S.), and on May the 9th, his name-day, Gogol gave a dinner to his Moscow friends in the large garden of Pogodin's house. Vyazemsky and Lermontov were present at this dinner. Lermontov read excerpts from his famous poem *Mtsyri*. Afterwards Gogol regaled his friends with punch, which he liked to prepare himself. The occasion was a great success, though Gogol looked very preoccupied most of the time.

Gogol left Moscow with Panov on May the 18th. Aksakov and his son Konstantin, as well as Shchepkin and Pogodin, accompanied them part of the way. On one of the hills overlooking

Moscow they all alighted and Gogol and Panov, Aksakov records, took leave of the ancient Russian capital and bowed low to her. Gogol was very cheerful and talkative. He repeated the promise he had given Aksakov at dinner the day before to return to Moscow in a year's time and bring with him the first part of *Dead Souls* ready for publication. 'This promise', Aksakov writes, 'he kept, but at the time we did not quite believe him. We did not like his going abroad and it seemed to us that he loved Italy too much. We could not understand Gogol's assertion that he had to retire to Rome in order to be able to write about Russia; it seemed to us that Gogol did not love Russia enough, that the Italian sky, the free life among all sorts of artists, the exotic nature of the climate, the romantic ruins of a glorious past, that all that put our climate and our life in the shade.' At the first stage they all had dinner and Gogol made punch 'for auld lang syne rather than because we liked to drink', Aksakov observes. After dinner they all sat down, according to the Russian custom, then offered up a prayer. 'Gogol', Aksakov writes, 'took leave of us, especially of Konstantin and me, very tenderly. He was deeply moved, but he did not want to show it.'

On their way back to Moscow Aksakov and Konstantin were surprised by what seemed to them a heavenly portent. The western sky became suddenly overcast with black clouds and a feeling of impending doom descended upon them. But half an hour later a strong north-westerly wind dispersed the ominous clouds and the sun shone again, filling their hearts with joy. 'This phenomenon', writes Aksakov, 'produced so deep an impression on Konstantin and me, especially on me, that for the rest of Gogol's life I was never depressed by the black clouds which not only obscured his way, but even threatened to cut off his life before he could finish his great work. Up to the last terrible news I was convinced that Gogol could not die before accomplishing the task assigned to him from above.'

An overcast sky followed by a burst of bright sunshine—portent or no—that was exactly what Gogol went through during his second short sojourn abroad.

¶ 6

The journey from Moscow to Vienna was uneventful, except that occasionally Gogol, that 'capricious egoist' (as Zhukovsky described him), and his companion got on each other's nerves and quarrelled about 'a dinner or the Russian language', as Panov wrote to Aksakov from Vienna on June the 23rd. But there were also times during the journey, especially after a good dinner or tea, when Gogol relaxed and sang folk-songs, danced the Cracovienne, recited Yazykov's poems and taught Panov Italian. They arrived in Warsaw on June the 7th and stayed there six days sightseeing, visiting the picture galleries and going to the theatre. From Warsaw Gogol wrote to Aksakov on June the 10th to ask him to send some official memoranda he wanted for *Dead Souls*. In his letter Gogol apologized for his absent-mindedness at their parting. 'I do not recognize partings,' he wrote, 'and that is why I do not regard them as seriously as others. For that reason', he concluded rather surprisingly, 'none of my friends can die, for they live with me always.' Vienna, Gogol wrote to Aksakov a month later, gave him a royal reception: for two weeks the best opera singers of Italy 'powerfully stirred, moved and administered beneficial shocks' to his feelings. 'Great are the mercies of God', he exclaimed. 'I shall revive yet!' And, indeed, after Panov's departure from Vienna on July the 11th, Gogol threw himself feverishly into work. With the help of some Russian students he translated and adapted for Shchepkin *L'ajo nell' imbarazzo* (A Tutor in a Predicament), a comedy by Giovanni Giraud. But most of his time he devoted to the writing of his Ukrainian historical play, which he hoped to finish in a few weeks. But the play refused to be written. His characters would not come to life and his failure drove him to despair and finally to a state of nervous exhaustion which resulted in serious illness. For the first but not the last time in his life he was haunted by the fear of death. This is how he described the onset and course of his illness in Vienna to Pogodin in a letter from Rome on the 17th of October 1840:

'I left Moscow feeling well and the road to Vienna along our open steppes at once wrought a miracle upon me. I felt more fresh and vigorous than I had ever felt before. To relieve my stomach of all sorts of old and unpleasant superfluities and remainders of Moscow dinners I began drinking Marienbad waters in Vienna. This time it helped me wonderfully. I began to feel a kind of youthful vitality and the main thing was that I began to feel that my nerves were getting stronger, and that I was emerging from that mental lethargy in which I had found myself in recent years, and I felt ideas stirring in my mind like an awakened swarm of bees; my imagination quickened. Oh, if only you knew what joy that was! The subject [of his historical play], which latterly I had been lazily turning over in my head without even daring to start work on it, unfolded before me in such grandeur that everything in me thrilled with delight. Oblivious to everything, I suddenly found myself in a world in which I had not been for a long time and sat down to work at once, forgetting that I ought not to do so while taking the waters, for it was just then that I needed complete rest. . . . This all happened in the heat of the summer, and my nervous reawakening was suddenly transformed into nervous irritation. Everything all at once rushed to my chest. I got frightened. I did not understand my condition myself. I gave up my work, thinking that all that was because of lack of exercise while taking the waters and because of my sedentary life. I began taking exercises and got worse. My nervous irritability increased terribly, the heaviness in my chest and the pressure, which I had never experienced before, became aggravated. Luckily, the doctors found that I haven't got consumption, that it was all due to a gastric disorder which interfered with my digestion and caused an unusual irritation of the nerves. This didn't make me feel better, for my treatment was very dangerous, since what could help my stomach had a destructive effect on my nerves and vice versa. In addition, I fell into a state of morbid dejection which is quite indescribable. I was reduced to such a condition that I simply did not know what to do with myself. I could not remain quietly for two minutes in bed, in a chair, or on my feet. Oh, it was terrible! It was the same state of blank despondency and dreadful unrest in which I saw poor Vyelgorsky during the last minutes of his life. And every day I was getting worse and worse. At last the doctor himself could not hold out any hope to me. Botkin [brother of the critic], a very nice fellow, was with me and I shall always be grateful to him for that. He did his best to keep up my spirits, but he told me himself afterwards that he had not expected me to recover. I knew my condition was desperate and, summoning all the strength I had, I hastily scribbled a will to make sure that at least my debts would be paid immediately after my death. But I was afraid to die among Germans. So I made arrangements to be put into a stage coach and taken to Italy. When I got to Trieste I felt better. The open road, my only medicine, this time, too, had its effect. I could already move about. The air, though at the time it was still unpleasantly hot, refreshed me. Oh, how I wished at that time to go on a long journey. I felt, I knew and I know that it would have completely restored my health. But I had no money to travel anywhere. How gladly would I have been a State messenger, a courier, even if I had had to travel by post-chaise in Russia, and I would not have hesitated to venture as far as Kamchatka, the farther the better. I swear I should have been well. But I had only to travel three days to reach Rome. There was little change of air, but even that had a good effect on me and I felt much better during my first days in Rome. At least I could already take a little walk, though I felt as tired afterwards as if I had walked ten miles. I can't understand how I have remained alive. My health is still very precarious and treatment and medicines only make it worse. Neither Rome nor the Italian sky, nothing that fascinated me so much before, has any influence on me now. . . . All I want is the open road, nothing but the open road, in rain or slush, through forests and steppes, to the end of the world. . . .'

In his letter to Pletnyov from Rome on October the 30th, Gogol hinted at the real cause of his illness. 'And yet', he writes, referring to his historical play, 'everything seemed to begin so well. I had started something I had never done before—and now from the clouds into the mire. . . . If I should find', he goes on, 'that I could write nothing more (and, of course, for me there could be nothing more terrible in the world), then everything would naturally be at an end. I have no desire to increase the world's population by my miserable figure. I wouldn't give a farthing for my life and wouldn't put up any fight for it. . . .'

How much Gogol's illnesses were due to purely mental causes can be seen from the following episode related by Annenkov. It happened in Rome in the summer of 1841. A young Russian architect, a friend of both Annenkov and Gogol, had died. Gogol refused to visit him during his illness or to go to his funeral. But the day before the funeral Annenkov met him on the steps of the Piazza d'Espagna. As soon as Gogol saw him, he rushed up to him with a look of the utmost despair on his face. 'Save me, for God's sake,' he cried. 'I don't know what's happening to me. I am dying. I nearly died of a nervous attack last night. Take me away somewhere at once!' So afraid was Gogol to die that he spent most nights on a sofa in Annenkov's room [Annenkov shared his flat with him] then went back to his own room, sat there on the sofa till daybreak and then disarranged his bed to make it appear to the charwoman who tidied his room that he had slept in it. This, Annenkov observes, may have been a direct result of his serious illness in Vienna.

How serious Gogol's nervous collapse was can be gathered from the letter Panov, who had joined Gogol in Venice, wrote to Aksakov from Rome on the 12th of January 1841. 'When we arrived in Rome,' he wrote, 'Gogol could not make up his mind whether to go back to his old flat or not, for he found it difficult even to walk up a little hill, and to walk up a few steps he had to stop twenty times, and his old flat was on a hill and on the third floor.'

By December the 10th, however, Gogol could write to Pogodin that he was well again. 'Be comforted,' he wrote, 'great and miraculous are God's mercies. I feel quite refreshed and I am busy with the revision and continuation of *Dead Souls*. I am even contemplating publishing the first volume next year, if only God's wondrous power, which has revived me, continues to sustain me.' He could not tell him, Gogol went on, what had been going on within him all that time, but then 'he who has been brought into the world to create something in the depth of his soul and to live and breathe with his creations must appear strange in many ways. . . . The fresh air', he concluded, 'and the pleasant chill of winter in Rome are having a life-giving effect on me. I am so calm that I'm not even worried about being penniless. I'm managing somehow by living on my debts. I don't care a straw about anything now. If I go on feeling like this till the spring or summer I may be able to prepare something for publication in addition to *Dead Souls*. But the summer, the summer . . . I simply must take to the open road. . . . I don't know how I am going to do it. But—God is merciful.'

But already the realization of a return of his creative powers had filled him with renewed confidence in his mission and made him less reluctant to turn to his friends for help. 'I am now asking for assistance frankly and openly,' he wrote to Aksakov on the 5th of March 1841, from Rome, 'for I have a right to do so and feel it in my soul. Yes, my friend, I am profoundly happy. In spite of my sickly condition, which has again worsened a little, I experience divine moments. Something wonderful is going on inside me and my eyes are now continually overflowing with grateful tears. Here I see quite clearly God's holy will: such ideas are not humanly inspired; a man would never think of such a subject! Oh, if only I could count on three more years of such fresh moments! I am only asking for enough life to finish my work; I don't want an hour more. Now all I need is the open road and travel: they alone, as I have already explained, restore my health. I spent all my money several months ago. A loan has to be raised for me. Pogodin will tell you all about it. At the beginning of 1842 I shall repay it all, for the work I have got ready now [*Dead Souls*] and which, God willing, I shall publish at the end of the current year, will be enough to repay it. . . . Everything', he went on, 'was wonderfully and wisely contrived by a higher will: my arrival in Moscow and my present journey to Rome—everything was for the best. . . .' He was afraid to travel alone to Moscow in the autumn and he therefore asked Aksakov to send his sons Konstantin and Mikhail to Rome to fetch him. (Gogol did not know that Aksakov's youngest son had died on the day he wrote his letter.) 'What I need', he explained, 'is a tranquil and happy frame of mind; now I have to be looked after and cherished . . . not for myself—no! They [i.e. Aksakov's sons] will not be performing a useless task. They will bring an earthenware vessel with them. Of course, this vessel is now all cracked, it is rather old and on its last legs, but it holds a treasure and has to be cared for. . . .'

It was Pogodin who lent Gogol the money (four thousand roubles, half of which Gogol received in May) and, being now the editor of *Moskvityanin* (the first number of which came out in January 1841), he was naturally anxious to get something from Gogol for it. At first, however, he was unwilling to ask Gogol himself for a contribution to his journal. Instead, he seems to have approached Aksakov to ask Gogol for it. Gogol's reaction to such a request was a violent refusal. 'You write to ask me to send something to Pogodin's journal', he wrote to Aksakov on March the 13th. 'If you knew how painful, how fatal such a request is to me—into what an agony of mind it has plunged me! Just now to tear my mind away even for a moment from my sacred work is a tragedy. . . . I swear it is a sin, a great sin, an unforgivable sin, to distract me. . . . I'm dead now to everything trivial and am I to commit the unforgivable crime of writing some contemptible, vulgar, journalistic trash? . . . Embrace Pogodin, and tell him that I am grieved not to be able to be of any help to his journal, but that if he has an ounce of love for his country he must not demand any contributions from me. . . .'

Pogodin, too, was a great patriot, as one might have expected a good Slavophil to be, but he could not appreciate Gogol's reason for refusing to contribute to such a highly patriotic journal as *Moskvityanin*. Hence the misunderstandings that later on arose between him and Gogol in Moscow, and which resulted in a violent quarrel. Meanwhile, Gogol did promise to send Pogodin something (he may have had in mind his famous story *The Overcoat*, on which he had been working since 1839), but preoccupied as he was with finishing the first part of *Dead Souls*, he never sent it.

¶ 7

An excellent account of Gogol's life in Rome in the summer of 1841 was left by Annenkov, who spent two months copying the first part of *Dead Souls* at Gogol's dictation. Annenkov was twenty-eight at the time. He arrived in Rome on April the 26th and at once went to see Gogol. In the hall he was met by the landlord, who told him that his celebrated lodger was out of town and had left no address. Even when he returned, he added, he would go to bed at once and receive no visitors. While Annenkov, who knew very well that the landlord was merely repeating Gogol's instructions, was expostulating with him, a door suddenly opened and a familiar long-nosed face poked out.

'Why,' Gogol said reproachfully to his landlord, 'don't you know this is Jules from Petersburg? He must be let in. Good morning,' he addressed Annenkov in Russian, 'why didn't you come in time for the carnival?'

Annenkov followed Gogol into his room, furnished with a narrow bed, a large round table, a tall bureau, two chairs piled high with books, linen and clothes, a bookcase and a small cane sofa. Its mosaic floor was bare, except for two small rugs by the bed and the bureau. Its two large windows had venetian blinds. There was not a single ornament in the room, except for a night-lamp of ancient design, which Gogol lighted instead of candles at night. After getting Annenkov to tell him all the latest Petersburg news, Gogol showed him round Rome, 'doing it', Annenkov remarks, 'with as much pleasure as if he were discovering it himself'. At Easter they went in the evening to watch the illumination of the dome of Saint Peter's. On that night Gogol arranged that Annenkov should take the room next to his and spend an hour each day copying the first part of *Dead Souls*. In the evenings Gogol usually played boston with Annenkov and Ivanov, inventing new rules every time they started a game. At the beginning of summer Gogol spent the mornings cutting out and sewing muslin and cambric scarves for himself. Annenkov often found him standing at the table with a pair of scissors in his hands, pondering over the design of his scarves.

Gogol got up very early and at once set to work. On his bureau was a decanter of cold water which he drank in the course of the morning. He then adjourned to *Del buon gusto*, where Annenkov found him after breakfast with his face flushed and his eyes shining brightly: he could not stand the heat and often complained about a curious peculiarity of his: 'I am burning,' he used to say, 'but I never perspire.' After coffee they parted till the appointed hour when Annenkov had to copy *Dead Souls*. Before they sat down to work Gogol closed the venetian blinds, then, laying his manuscript on the table, he began to dictate slowly and solemnly, with such feeling and expressiveness that, Annenkov writes, 'the chapters of the first part of *Dead Souls* acquired a special vividness in my memory'. Sometimes the braying of a donkey in the street below, followed by a blow and a shrill woman's voice shouting, '*Ecco, ladrone*' (Take that, you brigand!) would interrupt Gogol's dictation. He would then pause and say with a smile, 'Grown soft, the scoundrel has!' and then go on dictating in the same tone as before. Sometimes the dictation would be interrupted by a discussion of some point of grammar or spelling, or by Annenkov who would burst out laughing. 'Try not to laugh, Jules,' Gogol would say with a serious mien, but sometimes he could not refrain from laughing himself, especially after dictating the blisteringly satirical 'Tale of Captain Kopeikin' in the tenth chapter of the novel.

'Well, what do you think of the story of Captain Kopeikin?' he kept asking, laughing heartily.

'But', Annenkov remarked, 'do you think it will ever be published?'

'Nonsense,' Gogol replied confidently, little dreaming that it would be the first thing the censorship would refuse to pass, 'of course it will!'

What Annenkov remembered best, however, was the feeling of elation with which Gogol dictated the sixth chapter of the novel, describing Chichikov's visit to the miser Plyushkin. Gogol got up from his chair and, raising his hand, accompanied his dictation with a 'proud, imperious' gesture. 'At the end of this remarkable chapter', Annenkov writes, 'I was so excited that, putting the pen down on the table, I said frankly: "I think, Nikolai Vassilyevich, this chapter is a real work of genius!" Gogol gripped the manuscript in his hand and said in a thin, hardly audible voice: "Believe me, the others are no worse." But raising his voice at the same moment he went on: "Do you realize we've still lots of time before dinner: come, let's have a look at the Gardens of Sallust, which you haven't yet seen, and we may as well knock at the door of Villa Ludovisi!" From the beaming look on his face and his proposal', Annenkov declares, 'one could see that the impression made on me by his dictation gave him great pleasure. This showed itself even more when we went out into the street. Gogol had taken an umbrella in case of rain, and as soon as we turned to the left of the Barberini Palace into a deserted lane, he burst into a gay Ukrainian song and then broke into a dance and began twirling the umbrella over his head with such abandon that in two minutes it flew off, leaving only the handle in his hand. He picked it up quickly and went on with his dance. It was in this way that he expressed the gratified feelings of an artist. Gogol was celebrating peace with himself, and even at the time', Annenkov concludes, 'I was not mistaken about the meaning of this stormy transport of gaiety which reminded me of the Gogol I had known in the old days.'

But it may well be that Gogol's dance was also an outward expression of his inward conviction that the great transformation in the second part of *Dead Souls* was, as he wrote to Aksakov on the 28th of December 1840, going to be 'something colossal'. In the second part, as he hinted at the end of the first part, 'some people will perhaps catch the sound of other, hitherto untouched, chords and get a glimpse of the untold riches of the Russian soul, of a man endowed with divine valour, or of a lovely Russian girl . . . with all the wondrous beauty of a woman's soul filled with generous instincts and self-sacrifice. And confronted with them, all the virtuous men of foreign lands will seem as dead as a dead book before the living word! And Russian movements will arise—and everyone will see how deeply that which merely skims over the surface of the nature of other nations has penetrated into the Slav nature. . . .'

Belinsky was dismayed by the sheer arrogance and unreality of Gogol's chauvinism. 'Gogol', he wrote in 1842, 'promises much, much too much, so much indeed that he could not possibly carry out his promise because such things do not exist in the world; we cannot help expressing our fear lest the first part, in which everything is comic, should remain a true tragedy, while the other two parts, where the tragic elements are to be given full play, should be comic, at least in the pathetic passages. . . .'

In fact, this arrogance of genius, which was soon to turn into what one Russian biographer called 'moral despotism', can be clearly perceived as early as 1841, when Gogol embarked on his long and tragic period of 'spiritual education'. Resuming his interrupted correspondence with Danilevsky, who had by that time returned to his estate and was still apparently at a loose end, Gogol advised him (in a letter from Rome on the 7th of August 1841), to reconcile himself to his position as a small landowner and try to make a success of it. 'You must do as I tell you', he wrote, 'for henceforth my words are invested with divine power, and woe to him who does not listen to them. . . .' Writing to Yazykov from Dresden on the 27th of September 1841, he again reiterated his belief in the divine power of his words: 'Oh,' he wrote to the poet, 'believe my words! . . . I cannot tell you any-

thing more than that you must believe my words. I myself dare
not disbelieve them.'

A year later this process of 'spiritual education' was already
clearly manifest. 'I can only tell you', he wrote to Zhukovsky from
Berlin on the 26th of June 1842, 'that every day and every hour
my soul is growing brighter and more solemn, that my journeys
and my absences and my withdrawal from the world were not
without purpose or significance, that during that time my
spiritual education was progressing invisibly, that I have become
a better man than the one imprinted on the memory of my
friends, that my heartfelt tears are shed more often and more
solemnly now, and that there dwells in my heart a profound faith
that the heavenly powers will help me to mount the ladder which
has been set aside for me, though I am still standing on its lowest
rungs. I have still a long way to travel, there is much work and
spiritual education still ahead of me! My soul must be purer than
the mountain snow and brighter than the sky, and only then will
I have the strength to begin my real work and my great career,
only then will the riddle of my existence be solved.'

This process of 'spiritual education' and self-analysis began in
1841 in Rome where, as Annenkov relates, he would spend hours
on the terrace of Princess Volkonsky's villa, gazing into the blue
Roman sky, or in the Tivoli, where he would sit down by some
waterfall and remain motionless for hours, gazing with flushed
cheeks at the dark foliage of the trees. These attacks of inner
contemplation occurred also when he looked, for the hundredth
time perhaps, at some monument of ancient Rome. 'That', he
used to say, 'was true religion, for otherwise its creator would not
have been imbued with such a feeling of beauty.' Art and religion
were beginning to mean the same thing to him. But in those days,
as Annenkov observes, there was no trace of Christian humility in
him. When Annenkov remarked to him that even cold-blooded
and practical Petersburg was shaken by Pushkin's death, he replied 'in a kind of arrogant and prophetic tone of voice': 'What's
so strange about that? A man can always be shaken. . . . You'll see
what will happen when——' he paused without finishing the sentence. 'Just wait!' he concluded.

They had to wait five years before Gogol's attempt 'to shake'
not only Petersburg but the whole of Russia misfired miserably
and brought him back to earth with a mighty thump.

¶ 8

In addition to *Dead Souls*, Gogol had by the end of 1841 finished *The Overcoat*. The genesis of this famous story goes back, according to Annenkov, to 1834. One day someone told a story in Gogol's presence about a poor civil servant, a passionate sportsman, who had stinted himself for years in order to save up enough money to buy a good shotgun. But on his first shooting expedition in the Gulf of Finland the gun, which he had placed carefully in the bow of his boat, was dragged by the thick reeds into the water. He took the loss of his gun so much to heart that he fell dangerously ill. He was saved from death by the generosity of his colleagues at the office who made a collection among themselves and bought him another gun. 'Everyone', Annenkov writes, 'laughed at the story, which was based on fact, except Gogol, who had listened to it pensively with a lowered head. This story was the germ of his wonderful story *The Overcoat*, the idea of which occurred to him that very evening.' Gogol began writing the story in 1839 and, as it seems from its original title of *The Civil Servant who Stole Overcoats*, he conceived it at first in a much lighter vein. In the final version the character of the inoffensive little civil servant is drawn with a compassion, simplicity, gentle humour and apparent casualness of style that makes the story one of the greatest achievements of Gogol's genius.

It was in Rome, too, that Gogol was working on the final version of *Taras Bulba* as well as on the final version of *The Portrait*, which he sent to Pletnyov on the 17th of March 1842 for publication in *The Contemporary*. He was also writing his novel *Annunziata*, only the beginning of which, published in the *Moskvityanin* in 1842 under the title *Rome, A Fragment*, has been preserved. 'The idea of the novel', Gogol wrote to Shevyryov on the 1st of September 1843, 'was not so bad. I tried to show the meaning of a nation that has outlived its day—and what a day it was!—in relation to other still living nations. Though of course it is impossible to come to any definite conclusion from the beginning [of the novel], yet it is easy to see that it deals with the impression made by the vortex of a new society on one for whom the present time almost does not exist. . . .' Gogol was replying to Belinsky's criticism that his views were no longer representative of the modern views of art and life. He argued that it was absurd to identify his own views with the views expressed by the hero of his novel, the Roman Prince. But the description of the prince as 'one for whom the present time almost does not exist' fitted Gogol more than his hero. Rome's influence on Gogol, as Annenkov points out, was becoming more and more perceptible in 1841 and found expression in his disgust with European civilization, his withdrawal within himself, his search for some firm foundation which would keep his spirit in a state of self-content. He was beginning to hate France intensely, and in *Rome* he quotes with evident approval Vittorio Alfieri's lines about the French:

> *Tutto fanno, nulla sanno,*
> *Tutto sanno, nulla fanno:*
> *Gira volta son Francesi,*
> *Piu gli pesi, men ti danno.*[1]

'The whole French nation', he writes in *Rome*, 'is a splendid vignette and not a picture by a great master.' He spoke with a good deal of sense, Annenkov states, about reformers who were unable to distinguish between those elements of national culture which no people could sacrifice without doing itself mortal harm, and those which it could give up without destroying itself as a people, but he would not recognize France's great contribution to European civilization. As an illustration Annenkov records this small but characteristic incident: 'Once at dinner, in the presence of Ivanov,' he writes, 'we were discussing a subject that always provoked a heated argument: we were talking about the emptiness (as Gogol called it) of the problems that were agitating the French in life, art and philosophy. Gogol spoke sharply, peremptorily, abruptly. Wishing to be fair, I pointed out to him certain facts whose importance for civilization were universally recognized. Gogol replied heatedly, which probably made me raise my voice, too; but the moment we felt that the atmosphere was becoming tense, we dropped the subject. We left the restaurant in silence, but after a few steps Gogol rushed up to a fruit-seller's stall and, returning with two oranges, offered me one. This orange touched me deeply; it became, as it were, a formula by which Gogol expressed his eagerness to effect a reconciliation.'

[1] They do everything, they know nothing; they know everything, they do nothing; the French are a giddy-minded people; the heavier the weight, the less they give you for it.

Gogol left Rome for Russia, where he intended to publish the first part of *Dead Souls*, at the beginning of August 1841. Before leaving, he composed a petition to the Russian heir to the throne for Ivanov, who was anxious for a renewal of his State grant. Gogol stopped at Frankfort to see Zhukovsky and ask him to put in a good word for Ivanov with his former pupil. He spent about a fortnight with Zhukovsky and it was during this visit that he destroyed his Ukrainian historical play (known by the curious title of *The Shaven Moustache*). Two years later Zhukovsky, who was living in Düsseldorf at the time, told Chizhov, Gogol's former colleague at Petersburg University, about this incident.

'Did you know', he said, 'that Gogol had written a tragedy? He read it to me in Frankfort. At first I listened, but it was so awfully dull that I couldn't keep it up and dozed off. When Gogol finished reading and asked me what I thought of it, I said: "I'm sorry, my dear fellow, but I couldn't help falling asleep." "Well," said Gogol, "if you felt like going to sleep, then I'd better burn it," and he threw it into the fire there and then. "And a good thing, too," I replied.'

From Frankfort Gogol went to Hanau to see Yazykov, at whose house he met the young Bakunin, the future founder of the anarchist movement, but at the time a fervent Hegelian and an admirer of everything German. That alone made Gogol detest him. He met him again in the train on the way to Dresden, and Bakunin's presence, as well as the wooden seats, he wrote to Yazykov, rather spoilt his enjoyment of the journey.

In Petersburg, where he spent five days, he seems to have enjoyed himself in spite of the bad weather. He went to see Alexandra Smirnov and, according to her, often dined at the Vyelgorskys', where he gorged himself and cooked his special dish of macaroni. By the middle of October he was in Moscow, and on the eighteenth paid his first visit to the Aksakovs. Aksakov found him greatly changed: he was thin and pale and 'a meek submissiveness to God's will could be heard in every word he uttered'. Nor, Aksakov remarks, was there any sign of his gastronomic excesses and his former 'puckishness'. Still, according to Vera Aksakov, who was twenty-two at the time, he did amuse them quite often. 'Gogol', she wrote to her younger brother Ivan, the future poet and Slavophil propagandist, 'often visits us but doesn't like us to tell anyone about it. He read daddikins the last chapters of the first volume of *Dead Souls*. Sometimes he is very amusing; one day he assured us very seriously that his boot is very like Professor Krylov [one of the Moscow censors]. He is very funny when he plays billiards; he plays very badly and keeps calling himself all sorts of names. . . .'

Immediately after his arrival in Moscow, Gogol sent his manuscript of *Dead Souls* to the Moscow censorship. To his great consternation the censors refused to pass it, but, as appears from the following letter he wrote to Pletnyov on the 7th of January 1842 (O.S.), the farcical aspect of it did not escape him:

'At first I sent it to the censor Snegiryov [a professor at Moscow University], who is a little more sensible than the rest [and] . . . he found it entirely unobjectionable both as regards the impression it might produce on the reader and its general purpose, and merely suggested one small alteration in the text and a change of two or three names, which I at once agreed to. This he told the other censors, too. Suddenly someone made him change his mind and he submitted the manuscript to the committee of censors for their decision. The committee received it as though they had all been warned against it and were quite ready to make fools of themselves, for all their objections were without exception farcical to the highest degree. As soon as the chairman of the committee, Golokhvastov [assistant chief of the Moscow Education Department], heard the title: Dead Souls, he cried in the voice of an ancient Roman: "No, I shall never permit that: a soul is immortal, there cannot be a mortal soul, the author is taking up arms against immortality!" It took some time to make the clever chairman understand that the book deals with serfs who have died but are still registered as living. But as soon as he and the other censors realized that dead serfs meant still-registered serfs there arose an even greater commotion. "No," shouted the chairman and after him half the other censors, "that certainly cannot be allowed even if the author changed the title to registered serfs, for that means an attack on the institution of serfdom." At last Snegiryov, seeing that things had gone too far, began to assure the censors that he had read the novel and that its plot was based on the amusing bewilderment of the sellers of the dead serfs and the cunning stratagems of their purchaser and the confusion such a strange purchase had caused, that it consisted of a number of fictitious characters and described the everyday life of a number of inhabitants of central Russia, in short, that it contained a series of quite unobjectionable scenes. But it was no use. "Chichikov's enterprise", they all began to cry, "is already a criminal offence." "But", my defender remarked, "the author does not justify him." "He may not justify him," they replied, "but he made him the hero of his novel, and others will take an example from him and start buying dead souls." That's the sort of thing they actually said, that's the sort of talk of these Asiatic censors, that is, old retired people who sit at home all the time. Now follow the opinions of the European censors, the younger ones who have been abroad. "Say what you will," said one of these, namely Krylov, "but two and a half roubles is a ridiculously low price to pay for a soul. It's an offence against decent human feelings, though of course the price is offered merely for a name written on a piece of paper, but still this name is a soul, a human soul, it lived, it existed. This must never be allowed to get to England or France or anywhere else for that matter. Why, after this no foreigner will ever come to our country." These were the main objections as a result of which they decided to ban my manuscript. I am not telling you of several small objections raised against it, such as: in one place it is said that a landowner ruined himself by redecorating his Moscow house in the modern style. "Why," one censor, Kachenovsky [professor of history at Moscow University] cried, "the Emperor himself is building a palace in Moscow!" This was followed by so extraordinary a discussion that it could not have occurred anywhere else in the world. There were other objections, which I am ashamed to repeat, and it all ended in the banning of the manuscript, though the committee had only read a few passages of it. This is the whole story. It is almost unbelievable. . . .'

Gogol therefore decided to send the manuscript of his masterpiece to Petersburg. 'My very existence is at stake', he wrote to Pletnyov, 'for they want to deprive me of my last crust of bread, which I have earned by seven years of hard work, self-sacrifice and withdrawal from the world and all its benefits.' As his messenger he chose Belinsky, who happened to be in Moscow at the time. He saw Belinsky in secret, and handed him the manuscript for delivery to his old friend Prince Odoyevsky, whom he asked to give it to Alexandra Smirnov for presentation to the Emperor. The news of Gogol's secret meeting with

Belinsky, however, soon leaked out and caused great consternation among his Slavophil friends, who regarded the Westerner
Belinsky as their enemy. 'We began to suspect', Aksakov writes
in his reminiscences, 'that Gogol had had dealings with Belinsky,
who had spent a short time in Moscow, in secret from us, because
by that time we could not bear Belinsky, who had gone to Petersburg and had become a contributor to *Home Annals* and showed
a bitter hostility to Moscow and to our entire Russian movement.'

The subsequent fate of Gogol's novel is described in the following letter Belinsky wrote to Shchepkin on the 14th of April
1842 (O.S.): 'On arriving in Petersburg, I was met by rumours of
anonymous leaflets received by the sergeants of the Guards regi-
ments. The government was alarmed and the censorship terror
was intensified. Uvarov ordered the censors not to pass novels in
which even one character belonging to the ruling class was presented in an unfavourable light. . . . Yet Odoyevsky gave the
manuscript to Count Vyelgorsky, who wanted to take it to
Uvarov; but just at that time the Grand Duchess was giving a
ball, and his excellency had no time to spare for such nonsense as
Gogol's manuscript. Then, luckily, Vyelgorsky changed his mind
and gave it to Nikitenko. . . . Having read it, Nikitenko told
Vyelgorsky that he would show certain passages to Uvarov. Fortunately, this manuscript did not fall into the hands of this
minister for the extinction of education in Russia. In Petersburg
the [political] weather changes a hundred times—and Nikitenko
refused to pass only certain phrases and the episode about Captain Kopeikin.'

In Moscow, meanwhile, Gogol was dismayed to learn that his
Petersburg friends intended to give his manuscript to Uvarov.
He therefore thought it more advisable to postpone the publication of *Dead Souls*. 'I am already beginning to see many faults in
it', he wrote to Pletnyov, 'and when I compare this part of it with
those which are to follow, I can see that a lot has to be toned
down and something has to be strengthened or deepened. . . .
Firm as a rock is my faith in a bright future, and an unknown
power tells me that I will be granted the strength to finish my
work. . . .' He also dashed off a letter to the Minister of Education
in which he pointed out that his entire fortune was invested in his
novel, and begged him not to ruin him by withdrawing his patronage, and another to the chairman of the Petersburg com-

mittee of censors, assuring him that he had written nothing against the government which had loaded him with benefits.

All this worry and excitement brought on another severe attack of nerves with all its accompanying dreadful symptoms. 'I was ill,' he wrote to Maria Balabin on the 17th of February 1842 (O.S.), 'very ill. . . . What really frightened me was my state of mind, which reminded me of my severe illness in Vienna, especially when I felt the same kind of terrible agitation coming on during which every image in my mind assumed a gigantic size, every insignificantly pleasant feeling being transformed into such overwhelming delight as no man could bear, and every gloomy feeling assuming the form of tormenting melancholy, and all this was followed by fainting fits and a state of complete torpor. And,' he concluded, 'on top of that, when my illness was unbearable anyway, I had to suffer all sorts of disagreeable scenes which even in health would have been difficult to bear.'

These 'disagreeable scenes' were caused by Pogodin, in whose house Gogol was again living during his stay in Moscow. At the time, Gogol owed Pogodin four thousand five hundred roubles and Pogodin naturally assumed that he would let him have some of his unpublished stories for the *Moskvityanin*. Gogol refused to part with them, fearing that their publication might injure the sales of the complete edition of his works which he was preparing. 'Pogodin', Aksakov writes, 'pestered and tormented Gogol, demanding articles for his journal and reproaching him for his ingratitude. Such a life became a torture to Gogol. . . . Now it is clear to me that Pogodin, whose nature was coarse, callous and clumsy and lacking in every feeling of delicacy, tact and tenderness, could not do otherwise when dealing with a nature so poetic, sensitive and tender as Gogol's. Pogodin always had good impulses and would do a favour even for a man who could not do the same for him; but as soon as he felt that the man he had helped was able to repay him, he took him by the scruff of the neck and said: "I helped you in your need and now you jolly well have to work for me!"' Aksakov warned Pogodin against treating Gogol harshly, but all the reply he got was: 'You warn me! Gogol will be angry! What am I—a scapegoat? Why, if I cut *The Government Inspector* into pieces and shoved each piece into some corner of my journal, Gogol would have no right to be angry with me!' There is, of course, no wrath like the wrath of an editor hungry for copy, and Gogol had in the end to give in and let Pogodin publish his fragment *Rome* in the *Moskvityanin*, but for five months, from January till the end of May when he left Moscow, he refused to speak to his 'soul-mate' and they communicated only by short notes. In one note at the beginning of April Pogodin accused Gogol of being 'as proud as the devil'. To which Gogol replied: 'Spare me your pride. Please do not worry me for at least a fortnight. Leave my soul in peace.' And this is the note Gogol sent to Pogodin in mid-April in reply to his insistent demands to let him publish a few chapters from *Dead Souls*: 'As regards *Dead Souls*, you are shameless, implacable, cruel, imprudent. If my tears, my lacerated soul and my convictions mean nothing to you, then at least for the sake of Christ, crucified for us, do what I ask you: have faith in me for at least another five or six months.' After leaving Moscow at the end of May 1842, Gogol did not write to Pogodin till the beginning of November 1843. 'I escaped from your house', he declared in this letter, 'as from a gloomy prison in which I had spent many years.' To which Pogodin, in the same laudable spirit of candour, replied: 'When you closed the door, I crossed myself and breathed freely as though a heavy load had been lifted from my shoulders.'

What Pogodin did not know, and what, indeed, he could not possibly have known, was that several years later, in his anxiety to save Russia, Gogol would not forget his misguided 'soul-mate', who of all his friends was most in need of salvation, and that in his great innocence he would deliver the most humiliating blow Pogodin had ever suffered in his life. In the meantime, however, Pogodin and his Slavophil friends took great care not to bring the present crisis to a head and make Gogol's stay in Pogodin's house impossible. They still hoped to enrol Gogol as a member of their movement and were greatly concerned lest, unaccountable as he was, he should go over to the camp of their enemies, particularly as they knew that Belinsky had been making overtures to him. Gogol, too, fearing publicity of any kind, was averse to an open break with Pogodin. And so he stayed on and celebrated his name-day on May the 9th, as he had the year before, in Pogodin's large garden; Pogodin was there, too, at Gogol's special request, though they did not speak. This, however, as Aksakov observes, could not be noticed in such a big crowd. Gogol's guests included the most eminent members of the Moscow literary and learned worlds. Maria Ivanovna, who arrived in Moscow on May the 9th to take leave of her son and to take her daughter Yelisaveta home, was also there. It was a fine spring day and Gogol joked and amused his guests. After dinner he made punch in the summer-house, and when the bluish flame of the burning rum and cham-pagne rose over the melted lumps of sugar on the grating, he repeated his old joke about its being Benkendorf (the head of the secret police, who wore a blue uniform), who had come to bring order into their stomachs, which provoked loud laughter among his guests. The dinner was a great success: even the nightingales, of which there were a few in the garden, joined in the jollification.

⁋ 9

Nikitenko passed *Dead Souls* for publication on the 9th of March 1842 (O.S.), but changed its title to *The Adventures of Chichikov or Dead Souls*, a sop to those who, as Gogol had found out in his dealings with the Moscow censors, thought its original title almost sacrilegious. Much more serious was Nikitenko's refusal to pass the Tale of Captain Kopeikin. Annenkov had been right after all and Gogol, who only received his manuscript back from the censors on April the 5th, was greatly upset by what he called 'the destruction of Kopeikin'. It was one of the best things in his 'epic poem', as he sub-titled *Dead Souls*, and, he told Pletnyov and Nikitenko in his letters of April the 10th, it had left a gap which he was unable to fill in. 'You, who have been endowed with aesthetic taste, can see yourself', he wrote to Nikitenko, 'that it is necessary not so much as a connecting link between the events of the novel as a means for distracting the reader, for changing one impression for another; anyone who is an artist in spirit will realize that it leaves a serious gap.' Gogol's explanation and flat-tery did not, however, have any effect, for he knew as well as Nikitenko that the objection of the censorship concerned the social criticism implied in the tale of Kopeikin. Gogol, therefore, drastically changed the story, throwing out everything that might be interpreted as an attack on the government, 'even', he wrote to Nikitenko, 'the Minister, even the words "his excellency"', and altering the character of the poor soldier who has been wounded in the wars and comes to Petersburg to obtain a pension but is arrested for his 'insolence' and sent back under a military escort to where he had come from. 'It is now clear', Gogol wrote to Nikitenko, 'that he himself is the cause of his troubles and not the lack of compassion in others. The chief of the ex-servicemen's Commission treats him as he deserves. In short, there is nothing left now which even the strictest censorship could consider in any way objectionable.' Gogol was so sure that, having put the whole blame for his misfortunes on the gallant captain and not on the authorities, he could get his new 'version' of Kopeikin's tale passed by the censorship that he sent his manuscript to the printers without waiting for a reply from Nikitenko. It was, of course, passed in due course, and the first part of *Dead Souls* was published on the 21st of May 1842 (O.S.).

There were to be two more parts to the novel, as Gogol points out at the end of the first part which, as he wrote to Danilevsky a fortnight before its publication, was only 'a pale introduction to the great epic poem which is taking shape in my mind and will finally solve the riddle of my existence'. To Zhukovsky he wrote on June the 26th: 'I have revised it thoroughly since the time I read the first chapters to you but for all that I cannot help feeling that it is quite insignificant when compared with the other parts which are to follow. It reminds me of the front steps of a palace of colossal dimensions hastily constructed by a provincial architect.'

The first part of the novel already contains vague hints of how Gogol hoped to solve the riddle of his existence or, in other words, how he hoped to fulfil his mission on earth. He felt that Russia was looking at him 'with eyes full of expectation' and that there was some 'mysterious connexion' between her and him. Brooding over the fate of his countrymen and of mankind in general, he was puzzled by man's perverse habit of straying from the road which lay wide open before him and which, if he followed it, would lead him to 'a magnificent palace fit for an emperor to live in'; instead he preferred to follow all sorts of will-o'-the-wisps to the abyss, and then asked himself in horror, Which is the right road? Which is the way out? Still more puzzling was the amazing way in which every new generation laughed at the mistakes of its forebears, and in the end followed a path that led it to the same abyss. He hoped, therefore, that by revealing the mysterious substance that lay buried deep in the Slav soul and by introducing 'colossal figures' and letting his novel follow a 'grandiose lyrical course' he would 'widen the horizon' and, by stopping the bolting 'troika' from rushing on no one knew whither, save Russia from the predicament in which she found herself. This hope itself was a will-o'-the-wisp which brought Gogol to the abyss into which he finally precipitated himself. At the time of the publication of *Dead Souls*, however, and up to the last moment, he believed in it, though fortunately it was too late to reshape the first part of the novel in accordance with his fantastic dream.

In the first part Gogol deals with the real and not an imaginary world, his characters are real people and not 'colossal figures' and that is why he felt obliged to anticipate the criticism that none of the characters of his masterpiece was 'virtuous'. At the beginning of the seventh chapter he draws a parallel between the romantic writer who disregards the seamy side of life and a writer like himself who has the temerity to put on show before the whole world 'the shocking morass of the trivial everyday things in which men's lives are entangled', and who is reviled by the critics, who do not seem to realize that even the seamy side of life can be the subject for a masterpiece (the famous phrase Gogol used was 'a pearl of creation'). He returns to it again in the last chapter of the novel. 'The time has at last come', he writes, 'to give a rest to the poor virtuous man, because the words "virtuous man" have become meaningless; because they have transformed the virtuous man into a horse and there is no writer who does not ride it, urging it on with a whip or anything else he can lay hold of; because they have starved to death the virtuous man, so that there is not a shred of virtue left in him, and what remains of him is just skin and bones and no body; because their appeal to the virtuous man is sheer hypocrisy; because they do not respect the virtuous man. It is high time', Gogol concludes, 'we harnessed the scoundrel. So let us harness the scoundrel!'

This attack on the contemporary novel naturally aroused the anger of the editors of the most popular periodicals, who were novelists themselves. Polevoy, Bulgarin and Senkovsky outdid themselves in vilifying *Dead Souls* as the work of a writer who had a grudge against Russia, whose novel was not only sordid, but also badly written and abounding in grammatical mistakes.

'*Dead Souls*', Polevoy wrote, 'is like a dirty inn—a slander on Russia. How much filth there is in this poem. And', he added rather surprisingly, 'we must admit that Gogol is a relation of Paul de Kock. He is a near relation of Dickens, but we can forgive Dickens his filth and deformity for his bright qualities, which we cannot find in Gogol. And did its author really think that *Dead Souls* contained a moral lesson? Can we really find the seeds of Chichikov in every Russian?' Bulgarin in *The Northern Bee* also found that all the characters of *Dead Souls* were fools and scoundrels, and Senkovsky in *The Library for Reading* accused Gogol of 'systematically humiliating the Russian people'. Both found the book sordid. 'Filth upon filth!' cried Senkovsky, while Bulgarin enumerated in detail all the 'indecent' words used by the characters in the novel. Nicholas I, incidentally, also objected to Gogol's outspoken vocabulary. 'Gogol', Alexandra Smirnov records him as saying, 'has a great deal of talent, but I can't forgive him for expressions and turns of speech which are too low and coarse.' Another line of attack concerned Gogol's mistakes in grammar, of which both Bulgarin and Senkovsky adduced many examples, the latter even distorting Gogol's text to prove his point. This fault even Belinsky had to admit. 'As a matter of fact', Belinsky wrote in *Home Annals* of July 1842, 'Gogol's language is not remarkable for absolute correctness and purity, and those who see no difference between grammar and style find him an easy prey; for they do not suspect that there is as immeasurable a distance between grammar and style as between the correct drawing of an ungifted academician and the living and original style of a great painter.' Which is, of course, quite true, except that it does not absolutely explain the undoubted incorrectness of Gogol's grammar, which Gogol himself admitted on many occasions. The difficulty of 'correcting' Gogol and, incidentally, the almost insurmountable difficulty of translating him, is that, if corrected, the rhythm of his sentences and periods and the consequent emotional impact of his writings on the reader is destroyed. Vladimir Dahl, the famous Russian lexicographer and author of many stories of peasant life which Gogol greatly admired, put this dilemma very well in a letter to Pogodin on the 1st of April 1842 (O.S.): 'Gogol', he wrote, 'is an extraordinary man! You are carried away by his stories, you swallow everything eagerly from beginning to end, you read him again and you don't notice what a queer, unnatural language he uses. You begin to analyse it minutely from the specialist's point of view and you realize that one should never talk and write like that. You try to correct it and you spoil it—not one word of it can be altered. What would happen if he really wrote Russian?'

The critics also poked fun at Gogol's description of his novel as an 'epic poem'. Belinsky himself was a little puzzled by it, and all he could think of was that Gogol used the word 'poem' in the sense of 'a work of art'. In that sense, he wrote, 'every imaginative work is a poem—an ode, a song, a tragedy or a comedy.' What Gogol himself meant by 'poem' becomes clear from the synopsis of the textbook of Russian literature he prepared in 1844–5. In it he defines a poet as a man who is capable of feeling the beauty of creation more than anyone else. 'The poet', he writes, 'can transmit his feelings to others in two ways, either from his own person, in which case his poetry is lyrical, or by portraying other people and making them express his ideas in action, in which case his poetry is dramatic and narrative. The third type of poetry, the so-called descriptive or didactic, can be found in both the other types, but is not by itself a way in which the poet transmits his impressions to the reader.' Gogol, therefore, used the words poetry and poet in their wider and original sense of any creative work or writer, whether in verse or prose. As for epic poetry, its hero, he declared, 'is a person who is constantly in close touch with a great many people and events, and round whom the age and the time in which he lived may be reconstructed', which, of course, is an exact description of Chichikov and the central place he occupies in Gogol's novel.

Of the critics favourable to Gogol, the first place must be given to Belinsky, who wrote a number of articles in *Home Annals* on every aspect of the novel, which confirmed him in his opinion that Gogol was 'a man of genius and the *first* writer of contemporary Russia'. It was true, he wrote, that Gogol often dealt with aspects of public life which in the hands of other writers would simply be intolerable alike to eye, nose and ear, but 'since Gogol does not copy reality but "raises it to a pearl of creation" and since his humour is calm, gentle and noble in spite of its force, toughness and depth, there is nothing low and trivial in his writings. He possesses the secret of genius of transmuting everything he touches into pure gold.' Another remarkable characteristic of *Dead Souls* observed by Belinsky is what he called Gogol's 'subjectivity', 'a subjectivity,' Belinsky explains, 'that does not permit him to pass by the world he depicts with apathetic indifference, but makes him pass the occurrences of the outer world through his *living* soul and in this way breathe a living soul into them. . . .'

These 'subjective' or 'lyrical' digressions which abound in *Dead Souls* are not simply comments or philosophic reflections or even attempts by the author to explain his characters to his reader; they differ from the novelist's usual method of conveying information in that their appeal is directed to the emotions rather than to reason, and it is this heavily charged emotional content, leavened by Gogol's inimitable humour, raising a laugh rather than a guffaw, that is responsible for the immediacy and freshness of their effect.

Two other favourable criticisms of *Dead Souls* appeared in the *Contemporary* and the *Moskvityanin*. The first was written by Pletnyov and the other by Shevyryov, and both were carefully objective. Shevyryov, in particular, damned the book with faint praise, expressing the hope that in the following two parts Gogol would depict positive characters rather than concentrate on 'the negative facets of Russian life'. The article that produced an uproar in Russian literary circles came from the pen of the twenty-five-year-old Konstantin Aksakov. It was entitled, innocently enough, *A Few Words on Gogol's Poem Chichikov's Adventures or Dead Souls*, but in it Konstantin Aksakov drew a rather ecstatic comparison between Gogol and Homer, which, Sergey Aksakov remarks, infuriated all the journalists and all Gogol's enemies and friends. Konstantin at first sent it to the *Moskvityanin*, but Shevyryov rejected it. He then published it himself as a brochure. Disregarding completely the social criticism of the novel, in which he followed the example of Pletnyov and Shevyryov, he went, however, further than they in claiming that Gogol's novel was 'the grandiose epic of the ancients' which had now again 'arisen before us in all its unfading beauty. This poem', he declared, 'embraces the whole of Russia and', he asked, 'does not perhaps the whole mystery of Russian life lie hidden in it?' This article provoked a violent reply, or rather two replies from Belinsky, who argued that far from being a Homeric epic, *Dead Souls* was of significance only to Russia (although in another article he quite rightly pointed out that one could find the same Chichikovs in England and in France). Gogol himself was far from pleased with Konstantin Aksakov's brochure which, as Sergey Aksakov admits, did Gogol a great deal of harm. 'I hope you won't be angry when I tell you', Gogol wrote to Konstantin Aksakov on the 24th of May 1843, 'that there is a great deal of inexcusable youthful enthusiasm in your article.'

But all this sound and fury happened long after Gogol had left Russia, returning for the last time only after his pilgrimage to Jerusalem six years later.

Part Six

THE BARREN YEARS

¶ I

With his departure from Moscow on the 23rd of May 1842 (O.S.), Gogol entered upon the last ten barren years of his life. But never before had he been so confident of success as he was just then. He intended to stay in Rome for the next two years, by which time he was certain to have finished *Dead Souls*. After that he planned to go to Jerusalem to offer up thanks at the Holy Sepulchre. His work had now assumed such gigantic proportions that he was waiting for a sign from heaven before embarking on it. This 'sign' he believed to have received before he left for Petersburg. On the very eve of his departure, Aksakov relates, he suddenly appeared at Aksakov's house looking absolutely radiant and with an icon in his hands.

'I was waiting all the time', Gogol said to Aksakov, 'for someone to bless me with an icon, but no one did so. At last [bishop] Innokenty blessed me. Now I can tell you where I am going—to the tomb of our Lord.'

Aksakov could only marvel at Gogol's simplicity: everyone, as he remarks in his reminiscences, received an icon from a bishop after a blessing. But to Gogol, who was waiting for his 'sign', this ordinary action by a bishop appeared almost in the nature of a miracle. 'Our meeting', he wrote to Bishop Innokenty on the day he left Moscow, 'was decreed by heaven. It is a pledge of our final meeting at the tomb of our Lord.'

At the time, while regarding the first part of *Dead Souls* as merely the front steps to the magnificent palace of his dreams, he was still convinced that it was, as he wrote to the bishop, 'not by any means useless'. In Petersburg he made his final preparations for the publication of the first edition of his collected works,

216

authorizing Prokopovich to supervise it. In Gastein, where he stayed with Yazykov from the beginning of July to the middle of September, he was working on the revision of *The Government Inspector* and of several other pieces, including his one-act comedy *The Gamblers*, a study of card-sharpers, the first draft of which, he told Prokopovich on September the 10th, he had written 'a long time ago'. In Rome, where he arrived with Yazykov on October the 9th, he revised *After the Play* and sent it to Prokopovich on October the 22nd. Then he settled down to write the second part of *Dead Souls*. 'I live a very solitary life with Gogol, who is working very hard', Yazykov wrote to his brother from Rome on the 16th of February 1843. 'I see him only at dinner at four o'clock in the afternoon. After dinner, we usually both have a nap and in the evening three Russian artists, including the famous painter Ivanov, usually come to see us. We talk for about two hours and at nine o'clock we all retire to bed.' But from the very beginning Gogol found the continuation of *Dead Souls* very hard going and his mood soon changed, so that towards the end of their stay in Rome there was no more talk in Yazykov's drawing-room in the evenings. 'One evening', Fyodor Chizhov, who lived in Rome at the time, writes in his reminiscences, 'we met as usual at Yazykov's. Ivanov dozed, his head propped up on his hands. Yazykov, looking very ill, sat silently in his armchair, his head dropping almost on to his chest. Gogol was lying down on a sofa and I half reclined on another. The silence continued for almost an hour. Gogol was the first to break it. "We'd make a lovely picture of Roman warriors sleeping at Christ's tomb", he said. And almost every time we were about to go home, Gogol would say, "Well, gentlemen, isn't it time we finished our noisy conversation?"'

Earlier, at the end of January 1843, Gogol's work was interrupted by the arrival in Rome of Alexandra Smirnov and her brother Arkady Rosset. In Moscow, as a preparation for writing the second part of *Dead Souls*, Gogol had begun to read the Gospels. As usual, he at once went to extremes. 'Have you ever felt a desire, a strong, irresistible desire, to read the Gospels?' he wrote to Maria Balabin on the 17th of February 1842 (O.S.). 'I don't mean the sort of desire that is indistinguishable from duty and that everyone assumes as a matter of course. No, a heartfelt desire, an impulse—but I'm afraid I have to leave my sentence unfinished. There are feelings one should not talk about and to say something about them means that one has already profaned them.' But in Petersburg, where he met Alexandra Smirnov again, Gogol found that he could talk to her about his heartfelt feelings without profaning them. 'To see you', he wrote to her from Rome on November the 29th, 'is a spiritual necessity for me.' Two and a half years later he was to describe her in a letter to Yazykov (on the 5th of June 1845) as 'the best of all Russian women I have known. . . . She was my true comforter', he declared, 'when scarcely anyone's words could comfort me. And, like twins, our souls were attuned to each other.' Gogol became so strongly attached to Alexandra Smirnov because she was the only person he ever met who was willing to submit to his moral authority. She was the only woman in his life, in so far as any woman could be said to have meant anything to him. She was born in the same year as Gogol and was still very attractive. She disliked her husband and was not particularly fond of her children. Her reputation as a 'siren' was not entirely undeserved, nor were the stories about her infidelities entirely without foundation. But her life had been a failure, society was looking askance at her and for a time she was even excluded from the court. She therefore turned to Gogol for spiritual comfort. Gogol had made all the arrangements for her stay in Rome and spent a whole week sightseeing with her and her brother, finishing his daily tour with Saint Peter's. 'You can never see enough of St. Peter's,' he used to say to her, 'though its façade is like a chest of drawers.' One day, when they visited the Colosseum, she asked him where he thought Nero used to sit.

'You ought to know', she said, 'whether he arrived on foot, in a chariot or on a litter.'

'Why are you pestering me about that scoundrel?' Gogol said angrily. 'You seem to imagine that I lived in Rome at that time or that I am an authority on the history of ancient Rome. I am not. The history has not yet been written in which a people or its outstanding personalities are vividly delineated. Only Muratori understood how to describe a people. In his history alone does one feel the life of the people and its connexion with the soil on which it lives. Bossuet's *Histoire universelle*', he went on, 'is excellently written, except that from the spiritual point of view it does not emphasize the freedom of man to whom the Creator has given the choice of good and evil. He was a zealous Catholic. I don't think Guizot's *Histoire des révolutions* is well written. It is written from both points of view, the feudal and the revolutionary. One should be able to find a middle way and write more clearly and vividly. I have always wanted to write a book on geography in which I could show how to write history. By the way,' he concluded, 'I will tell you that the villain Nero used to appear in his box at the Colosseum in a golden wreath, a red toga and gilt sandals. He was tall, very handsome and talented, and he sang and accompanied himself on a lyre. You saw his statue at the Vatican. It was sculpted from life.'

'In Rome', Alexandra Smirnov writes in her memoirs, 'Gogol was mostly silent. He usually walked at a distance from us, picked up pebbles, tore up the grass and waved his arms about, stumbling into trees and bushes. Sometimes he stretched himself out on the ground and cried, "Let's forget everything. Just look at the sky!" and gazed pensively but, somehow, dully at the cloudless vault of heaven. . . .'

Gogol did not stay two years in Rome. He went back with Yazykov to Gastein on the 1st of May 1843, first, because his work on *Dead Souls* had come to a standstill and, secondly, because Yazykov got tired of his company. 'Gogol', Yazykov wrote home from Rome on January the 9th, 'prides himself on his efficiency, but he makes a mess of everything. I feel cramped and cold, but Gogol walks about with a blue nose and assures me that it is very warm! He manages everything here because neither I nor my valet know Italian, and that is why everything here is topsy-turvy. He is constantly being deceived and robbed by the Italians, whom he respects and considers very honest. He throws money about like dirt, he fusses and bustles about and is absolutely convinced that he gets the better of everybody and buys everything cheaper than anybody else, and is terribly annoyed when he is even slightly contradicted.' Gogol never stayed with Yazykov again, but went rushing about from place to place, unable to settle down anywhere for long. 'Several times', as he admits himself in his *Author's Confession*, 'I sat down to write . . . and could produce nothing. My efforts almost always resulted in illness and suffering and, finally, in such attacks as made me give up my work for a long time.'

His illness followed the same pattern as during his unsuccessful attempt to write his historical play. His creative powers were deserting him. 'God', he wrote to Alexandra Smirnov several years later (on the 20th of April 1847), 'has deprived me for a time of the power and ability to create works of art in order that I should not arbitrarily invent things out of my own head, that I should not be tempted to idealize, but should keep to the essential truth', which to him now meant religious truth. He therefore concentrated his attention, as he declares in his *Author's Confession*, on 'the eternal laws which govern the actions of man and mankind in general'. He put it more clearly in a letter to Alexandra Smirnov from Frankfort on the 28th of December 1844. 'Ever since I left Russia', he wrote, 'a great change has been taking place in me. The *soul* is now my only concern and I can see all too clearly that if my soul does not strive to attain absolute perfection, all my abilities will become paralysed and I will not be able to use any part of my intellect for the benefit of my fellow-men, and without this spiritual education every work of mine, though perhaps significant for a time, will be essentially meaningless and futile.' More and more absorbed in himself, more than ever convinced in the messianic character of his work and that his 'mission' was bound up with the solution to 'the riddle of my existence', he persuaded himself that, as he put it in his *Author's Confession*, one could not talk and write of the highest feelings and emotions simply by relying on one's imagination: one had to possess a small grain of them oneself, one had, in short, to become a better man. He therefore came to the conclusion that he could not obtain the knowledge of the human heart he required for the completion of his novel unless he carried out a thorough analysis of his own heart first. By this 'inner knowledge of life', he explained to Danilevsky in a letter from Ems on the 20th of June 1843, he understood 'the sort of life in which a man no longer lives by his impressions, when he no longer seeks to taste the life he knows already but discerns through all this only one harbour and one shore—God, and in His name strives to make use of the talents He has given him and not to bury them in the ground, realizing that life was not given him for his own pleasures, that the duties it imposes upon him are much stricter, and that he will have to answer dearly if, absorbed deeply in himself, he questions himself and yet fails to discover what things are hidden deep inside him that may be useful and, indeed, indispensable to the world, and what his real place in it is, for there is no unnecessary link in the world.' This morbid introspection led him to a curious discovery of a way in which to know people. 'One has to live a long, long time', he wrote to Pogodin on the 2nd of November 1843, 'completely absorbed in oneself. For it is in yourself that you find a solution of everything. . . . This', he adds with immense confidence in his statements, completely disregarding the shifting foundations on which they rested, 'will be confirmed by many holy men who have taken the vow of silence and who are all unanimously of the opinion that, having lived such a life, they are able to read the most hidden thoughts in a man's face, however much he tries to conceal them. . . . Having tasted only a tiny bit of such a life', he concludes even more confidently, 'I can already see more clearly, my brains and my eyes have become sharper, and the best proof of this is that I can see my faults much sooner than I have done before, and I can discover them sooner than before. . . .'

¶ 2

Gogol had now embarked in good earnest on his 'spiritual education', which was to have such a disastrous effect on his writings. To begin with, he came to the conclusion that it imposed on him the task of looking for his faults and, since he could never be sure of spotting them himself and would have 'to answer dearly' for failing to spot them, he kept imploring his friends to point them out to him. 'Rebukes', he wrote to his mother on the 6th of April 1844, from Darmstadt (he was living with Zhukovsky in Frankfort, but had gone to Darmstadt, where there was a Russian church, for Easter), 'are good for the soul: the longer I live and the better I become, the more I crave rebukes. I'd give a lot to hear people abusing me. Even the most unjust abuse and insult is a present to me now, for it makes me examine myself anew and, having done so, I can see how much I am still wanting.' Secondly, having, as he thought, benefited so greatly from the discovery of his own faults, he was not chary of pointing out their faults to his friends, which resulted inevitably in the alienation of his closest friends in Russia. Even Aksakov, the mildest of men and one of

Gogol's greatest admirers, found it necessary to stop writing to him for a time. 'Please', he wrote to Shevyryov on the 3rd of October 1844, 'tell Gogol (when you write to him) that I shall not reply to his letters. It is time we left each other in peace.' Earlier that year, on February the 2nd, Gogol, who was avidly reading religious literature, was so excited by his 'discovery' of Thomas à Kempis's *Imitation of Christ* that he asked Shevyryov to buy copies of the book and send them to Pogodin, Aksakov, Yazykov and Alexandra Smirnov with a request 'to read a chapter of it a day' and then 'spend some time in meditation'. Aksakov was so outraged by Gogol's arrogance that he wrote to him: 'I read Thomas à Kempis before you were born.' To which Gogol, nothing abashed, replied that Aksakov's lack of Christian humility was obviously the work of the devil, adding a number of tips on how to deal with the enemy of mankind, a task that was really very simple, for all Aksakov had to do was to carry out his (Gogol's) advice in his letter to Shevyryov. Gogol went on to deny that he had become a mystic. All that had happened was that he could see many things much more clearly than before and call them by their right names. 'I simply call the devil the devil', he declared, 'and refuse to give him a splendid costume à la Byron, for I know that he wears a dress-coat made of . . . and that one has to . . . on his pride—that is all.'

But it was not all. For Gogol was becoming more and more obsessed by the idea that he would have to answer for all his sins, by which he meant the writings that had made him famous, and that his fits of depression and his agonies of mind were sent, as he wrote to Yazykov on the 15th of February 1844, to make him worthy of receiving what he asked for in his prayers. What he asked for, he told Yazykov on the 4th of November 1843, was inspiration, for, as he confessed to the same correspondent six months later, the writing of *Dead Souls* was proceeding 'very slowly' and 'not at all as I should like, and it is all due to my illnesses or to myself. . . . When I go forward, my work goes forward; when I stop, my work, too, stops.' But as quite obviously it was impossible to get so rare a thing as inspiration by simply praying for it one had to invent a special kind of prayer. How was it to be done? Gogol explained it at some length in his letter of November the 4th:

'A prayer [he wrote] is not a matter of words; it must be uttered with all the force of your soul; without that, it will never fly upwards. A prayer is ecstasy. If it attains the state of ecstasy, it asks for what God wishes to give us and not for what we wish ourselves. How is one to find out God's wishes? To do that one has to look at oneself with sensible eyes and find out which abilities given us at birth are higher and nobler than others, for it is with these abilities that we have mostly to work, and this work is what God wishes us to do, for otherwise they would not have been given to us. Thus, in asking for their awakening we are merely asking for something which is in accordance with His will. . . . This [Gogol goes on] is the sort of miracle that will happen: the first day you won't have an inkling of an idea in your head: you will simply be asking for inspiration. On the second or the third day you will not simply say: let me do it, but let me do it in *this* kind of spirit; on the fourth and the fifth—with *such* kind of force. Then other questions will arise in your mind: what impression will the work you write produce and of what use will it be? And your questions will immediately be followed by answers which come straight from God. The beauty of these answers will be such that your whole body will be filled with enthusiasm and at the end of another week or two you will find that everything you wanted has come to pass: the subject, its significance, its force, its deep inner meaning, in short, everything: all you have to do is to pick up your pen and write it down. . . .'

But however much Gogol might have been convinced in the efficacy of that kind of prayer, the fact remained that so far as *Dead Souls* was concerned it was of little use to him. He therefore went a step further and, by still further heightening the intensity of his prayer, made quite sure of the nervous breakdown which nearly cost him his life a year later.

'There is a way of praying [he explained to Yazykov on the 15th of February 1844] in difficult moments when physical or spiritual sufferings become unbearably agonizing. I have discovered it in times of great mental anguish, but I shall reveal it to you. If you find yourself in such a state, pray with weeping and sobbing. . . . There is no grief, there is no physical or mental illness that cannot be wept away. King David wept bitterly in his moments of great distress and received wonderful comfort from it. The prophets wept for days on end, craving to hear the voice of God in them, and it was only after a copious flood of tears that their souls were relieved, their eyes recovered their sight, and their ears heard the voice of God. . . . There are many mysteries we dare not even ask to have explained to us. . . . Often we ought not to ask to be delivered from misfortunes, but to be told their secret meaning . . . Who knows, perhaps the misfortunes which are visited upon us are meant to make us utter the cry that comes straight from our hearts and that, but for them, would never have been wrested from us. Perhaps the cry coming from your heart is destined to be the crucible of your poetry. . . .'

It was because even this method of praying was of no avail that Gogol began sending desperate letters to his friends to pray for him. But of all his Moscow friends none except Nadezhda Sheremetev, a very gentle and pious old lady with whom he had become very friendly during his last stay in Moscow and who treated him like a son, took him seriously. Even his own sisters, to whom he wrote long letters demanding that they should not only pray for him but obey him just as though he were their father confessor, were too terrified to write to him. 'Our brother', Yelisaveta wrote to Vera Aksakov on the 10th of December 1845 (O.S.) from Vassilevka, 'never tells us anything about himself. His letters are always full of admonitions and rebukes, so that every time he writes to Annette and me we are terrified to open his letter, and our forebodings hardly ever deceive us. Oh, he has completely changed now! Before, I enjoyed writing to him, but now we write to him very seldom and we find it very hard even when we do, for we have to weigh every word and he demands almost the impossible from us and says that we must write to him only about things that matter; and so we have to weigh every word to make sure it is not some nonsense, and our mother alone has been writing to him lately. Don't show my letter to anybody,' she concludes, 'for if my brother should get to know about it he is sure to start scolding us. Oh, those lectures of his! I'm sick and tired of them!'

The only people who were not sick and tired of his 'lectures' were the friends he met abroad, 'the few people', as he wrote in his *Author's Confession*, 'whose spiritual qualities made my own qualities look small', the people who, unlike his friends in Russia, never accused him, as he explained in a letter to Alexandra Smirnov on the 28th of December 1844, of lacking simplicity or being secretive and insincere. Many of Gogol's biographers blame these aristocratic friends of his for influencing his political views and, generally, for being responsible for his religious obsessions. It is quite true, of course, that they were all rabid supporters of the Tsarist autocracy who saw nothing wrong in the institution of serfdom. But so was Gogol. He, too, regarded the peasants, as he wrote to his mother in April 1843, 'as created to work for us and obey our orders'. The reason why he became so attached to his friends abroad was not because they shared his views, but because they seemed to submit to them. It was he who influenced them and not they him. Foremost among those friends was Alexandra Smirnov, with whom he became particularly intimate after spending four months with her in Nice (from the 19th of November 1843, to the 19th of March 1844). 'What a difference', Gogol wrote to her on the 28th of December 1844, 'between our acquaintance before and our acquaintance in Nice. Don't you think yourself that we have come to know each other only now and that we did not know each other at all before?'

In Nice, Gogol lived with the Vyelgorskys in rue de France near Alexandra Smirnov's villa. Every evening he went for long walks with her and the two daughters of Count Vyelgorsky, Sophia, who had two years earlier married the writer Vladimir Sollogub, and the twenty-year-old Anna, to whom, too, he became very much attached. It was the sunsets that he admired most. 'Two hours before setting', he wrote to Zhukovsky on December the 2nd, 'the sun begins to work miracles, painting the mountains in all sorts of colours. But it is with the nearest mountains, that is, the green ones that it performs the most amazing miracles. These green mountains become crimson.'

Gogol began Alexandra Smirnov's 'spiritual education' by reading to her passages from the writings of the Russian churchmen. He also made her learn by heart the psalms which, he wrote to Yazykov from Nice on February the 15th, 'are nothing else but the outpourings of a tender and deeply suffering soul, harassed and worried every minute and unable to find peace or refuge among men', a soul, in fact, that was in the same spiritual predicament as his. Alexandra found the learning by heart of the Psalms a rather difficult task, and every time she left out a word or sentence, Gogol would say in a reproachful tone of voice: 'Bad!' and tell her to repeat it. Gogol, in fact, was not quite satisfied with Alexandra's spiritual progress. 'Remember', he wrote to her on the 20th of April 1844, about a month after he had left

Nice, 'that we have found a common language only very recently; remember, too, that I had to exercise a great deal of patience to get even as far as that, for you kept obstructing me in every way, and in reply to a question which had anything to do with your inmost feelings and the circumstances connected with them you almost invariably replied: "What do you want to know that for? That's none of your business!" (And after that NB you wanted me to divine your soul, and find the appropriate medicines for it!) . . . You often', he went on expressing his annoyance with her, 'confided certain things to me as a great secret, and afterwards blurted them out to the first man you came across who knew how to worm the secret out of you and how to entertain you pleasantly. This', he concluded, 'is just a very little rebuke for you and I hope you will take it in good part, for I intend to administer much stronger rebukes to you in future. The time will come when your soul will be yearning for rebukes as for fresh water, for nothing but rebukes! Good-bye. . . . We shall have to talk about many, many things now; perhaps I shall really be able to be useful to you.'

Meanwhile all sorts of scandalous rumours about Gogol's relations with Alexandra Smirnov began to reach Moscow, and Nadezhda Sheremetev thought it her duty to warn Gogol about them. But Gogol did not think it necessary to justify himself. 'If you feel upset by any unpleasant rumours about me,' he wrote to Nadezhda Sheremetev on the 1st of January 1844, 'do as you have been doing till now: pray to God that all the bad things people say about me should not be true.' He did, however, think it wise to warn Alexandra Smirnov on her return to Russia. 'To begin with,' he wrote to her from Ostend on the 26th of August 1844, 'you will hear all sorts of rumours about yourself. These rumours are, perhaps, worse than you imagine . . . but do not be upset about them and be as gentle and serene as a dove.'

In Ostend, where he hoped to recover from his severe nervous attacks, Gogol spent about seven weeks from the end of July to the 15th of September 1844. It was there that his close friendship with Count Alexander Tolstoy began. Tolstoy was an unregenerate reactionary and religious fanatic, bigoted, narrowminded and uncompromising. Gogol was greatly impressed by the fact that he had been twice governor of a province. Tolstoy, he wrote to Yazykov on the 12th of November 1844, had reached the point 'where, without blowing people up or driving them away, he could do a great deal of real good, that is to say, bring peace where someone else would only sow dissensions and produce chaos.' Gogol's faith in Tolstoy's administrative genius which, by the way, the Count had not shown once during his two terms of office, was only clouded by the fact that, like himself, Tolstoy was a valetudinarian and spent all his time abroad consulting specialists. Curiously enough, it was Tolstoy's fanaticism and intolerance that worried Gogol. 'Take a vow of continence in *words*,' he besought Tolstoy in his letter of the 5th of March 1845, 'to wit: (1) speak more to *ladies* than to men; (2) in speaking to men, whatever the subject, try not to talk yourself but make them talk; and (3) do not get involved in any heated arguments and do not try to convert anyone to the Greek Orthodox faith.'

The only one of his friends abroad with whom Gogol discussed literary problems was Yazykov, whose violent political poems he hailed as coming straight from God. At the end of 1844 Yazykov wrote his poem *Earthquake*, in which he recounted the medieval legend of a small boy's prayer which saved Constantinople from destruction by an earthquake. Yazykov appealed to the Russians to take a lesson from this 'miracle' so that they too should be saved by prayer, a sentiment that naturally appealed to Gogol. 'What grandeur, simplicity and exquisite beauty of thought', Gogol commented in a letter to Yazykov on the 2nd of December 1844. 'I'm sure', he added naïvely, 'your poem has created a tremendous impression in Russia in spite of the diversity of opinions and tastes.' Gogol was even more enthusiastic about Yazykov's next poem *To Those Who Are Not of Us*, in which Yazykov launched a violent attack against the Westerners, particularly Belinsky, whom he described as 'the frivolous champion of dissolute thoughts and hopes'. 'God himself', Gogol wrote to Yazykov at the beginning of February 1845, 'suggested this beautiful and wonderful poem to you. Your soul was an organ and heavenly hands played on it.' And yet he was not sure. He had met Alexander Turgenev, head of the Department of Ecclesiastical Affairs, in Paris at the Vyelgorskys' and, far from being impressed by Yazykov's poem, Turgenev, who was a close friend of Zhukovsky's, was so outraged by 'the fanaticism of our patriots' (as he wrote to Zhukovsky on the 7th of February 1845) that even Gogol felt uneasy. 'Gogol', Turgenev wrote to Zhukovsky, 'does not entirely approve of the poem.' A month later Gogol warned Yazykov against the dangers of extremism and put in a plea for some kind of understanding between the Slavophils and the Westerners.

'Poetry [he wrote to Yazykov on the 5th of April 1845] ought to express violent anger against *the enemy of men* but not against *the men themselves*. And are those who are shortsighted really to blame for being shortsighted? And even if they are, are we justified in blinding them by a dazzling flood of light and then being angry with them because their feeble sight cannot stand it? Would it not be better to be a little more tolerant and let them examine and explore the things that stun them like thunder? Many of them are good people at heart, but now they have gone so far in their vehemence and stubbornness that to act differently would be to admit before the whole world that they have been behaving like fools. This, as you know yourself, is not so easy. . . . You know yourself [he went on to make what to the Slavophils would have seemed an outrageous admission] that not all their ideas are false and that, unfortunately, certain of their conclusions are not without foundation. Their mistake is that they tend to draw *general* conclusions from certain *isolated* facts, make exceptions into rules, mistake temporary diseases for chronic ones, see the *body* and not the *spirit* of everything and, drawing shortsighted analogies of what they see, dare to pronounce judgments upon the things that differ in spirit from everything with which they compare it. What ought to be done, therefore, is to campaign against these fallacies, examine them calmly and reveal their absurdity, but it must be done in such a way as to make it possible for them to withdraw from their difficult position without altogether losing face.'

Gogol had by that time resumed his correspondence with Sergey Aksakov, but his relations with Pogodin were still dogged by constant misunderstandings. On his return from Ostend he learnt that Pogodin had published Ivanov's portrait of him in *Moskvityanin* without his permission and this made him so angry that, although he had resumed his correspondence with Pogodin in November 1843, he did not write to him again for two years. A bigger insult, he wrote to Yazykov, Pogodin could not have thought of. The nature of this 'insult' he explained to Shevyryov on the 14th of December 1844. 'In that portrait', he wrote, 'I was painted just as I looked in my den a few years ago. I gave it to Pogodin as a friend because he had begged me for it, without suspecting that he was going to publish it. You can judge for yourself whether it is a good thing to display me before the world as a slovenly fellow in a dressing-gown, with tousled hair and moustache. Don't you know yourself what significance people ascribe to this sort of thing? I don't mind being exhibited as some debauched rake but, as you know very well, people will cut out my picture from the journal. Believe me, young people are stupid. Many of them have noble aspirations, but they are always eager to set up idols for themselves . . . and they will first of all imitate me in silly little things.'

It was Pletnyov who, in a letter to the literary historian J. K. Grot, declared that Gogol was 'as vain as Satan' and that 'his self-conceit and, so to speak, self-adoration throw an unpleasant light on his character', but even Pletnyov would hardly have thought it possible that Gogol would object to being 'exhibited' in a dressing-gown and with tousled hair for such a reason!

¶ 3

The first edition of Gogol's works was published in four volumes on the 26th of January 1843, but by the end of the year Gogol was still without funds and his position was becoming desperate. Earlier, on February the 28th, he again appealed to his Moscow and Petersburg friends to assume the responsibility for his financial affairs because otherwise he would not be able to finish *Dead Souls*. On September the 24th he wrote to Prokopovich demanding a full account of the sales of the books and the cost of publication. 'Now', he declared, 'I can see that I have acted unwisely in having published the edition in Petersburg. It means a loss of eight thousand roubles to me.' Prokopovich, who could read between the lines of Gogol's letters, took it to be an aspersion on his honesty and stopped writing to Gogol, letting Shevyryov disentangle the mess into which he had got himself. Pletnyov took Prokopovich's side and Gogol, anxious to show that he had never suspected Prokopovich of dishonesty, decided to donate his entire income from the edition to needy students. 'I am to blame for everything,' he wrote to Pletnyov in December 1844, 'and since the guilty one has to be punished, I am punishing myself by refusing to take the money due to me for all the sold copies of my books. . . . As every copeck of this money has been bought with dissatisfaction and insults to my friends, it would have weighed on my conscience. I have therefore decided to give all this money to the poor and deserving students in Petersburg and Moscow.' He repeated his decision almost in the same words to Shevyryov, adding that the money should be distributed anonymously. 'The account for it', he wrote, 'should be rendered to God, and therefore I want you to look upon the whole transaction as sacred and do all you can to make sure that every copeck of it is turned to good account. . . . My mind is made up. . . . However strange the whole thing may appear to you, you must remember that the wish of your friend must be *sacred*. . . .'

Gogol had not yet paid off the debts he owed his friends and he was penniless himself at the time, but he never went back on his quixotic decision, however much his friends, including Alexandra Smirnov, begged him to alter it. Only five thousand roubles were left over after covering the publication costs of the first edition of Gogol's collected works, of which three thousand roubles were distributed by Shevyryov during Gogol's lifetime, and two thousand after his death.

To help Gogol out of his predicament Zhukovsky and Alexandra Smirnov approached Nicholas I for another grant for him, and on the 27th of March 1845 he was granted a pension of one thousand roubles a year for three years 'in view of his ailing condition'. In his letter to Count Uvarov, acknowledging the official letter announcing this grant, Gogol went out of his way to emphasize his changed views and his anxiety to atone for his former writings. 'All I can tell you', he wrote to Uvarov at the end of April 1845, 'is that your letter saddened me. I am sad, first, because everything I have written till now is not worthy of attention: though I meant well, I expressed everything immaturely, badly, contemptibly . . . so that it is no wonder that the majority of people attach a bad rather than a good meaning to my works, and my countrymen do not derive any spiritual benefits from them. Secondly, I am sad because I have still not repaid the Emperor the debt I owe him for his former favours to me. I swear

I never intended to ask him for anything now: I have only been quietly preparing a work which I am sure will be of much greater use to my fellow-countrymen than my former scribblings, for which you, too, will thank me, if only I should be successful in finishing it conscientiously, for its subject is not alien to your own convictions.'

Gogol did not know, though he might have guessed, that Uvarov would immediately publicize his letter to show that Gogol had 'reformed'. The effect this produced was hardly in Gogol's favour. Even Nikitenko wrote in his diary on the 8th of May 1845: 'What a sad self-abasement on the part of Gogol! What a pity! It is just playing into Uvarov's and someone else's hands.' Who the 'someone else' was becomes clear from Belinsky's reference to this letter in his famous letter to Gogol after the publication of the *Selected Passages from Correspondence with my Friends*. 'Even before [your last book],' Belinsky wrote, 'your letter to Uvarov became known in Petersburg, the letter in which you expressed your concern about your works being given a wrong interpretation in Russia, and then declared your dissatisfaction with your earlier works, stating that you would be satisfied only when the Tsar was satisfied with them.'

The work Gogol mentioned in his letter to Uvarov was the *Selected Passages*. The first description of it is contained in his letter to Alexandra Smirnov on the 2nd of April 1845. 'It will be', Gogol wrote, 'a small work with an unsensational title, but important to many people.' It is evident, therefore, that however much the majority of Gogol's readers shared Belinsky's and Nikitenko's feeling of disgust at Gogol's letter to Uvarov, it expressed Gogol's firmly-held opinion of his earlier works. This becomes quite clear from the new ending he devised for *The Government Inspector* in 1846 and tried unsuccessfully to foist on Shchepkin. The dramatis personae of this new finale to the play include the actors and actresses headed by Shchepkin as 'the first comic actor', and a few spectators. It begins with the crowning of Shchepkin with a laurel wreath (a scene cunningly devised by Gogol to appeal to Shchepkin's vanity as an actor, which he deleted in his revised version afterwards) and continues with a long discussion between the first comic actor and the spectators, the spectators arguing that the play is of no benefit whatever to society, and objecting in particular to the mayor's words: 'What are you laughing at? You're laughing at yourselves!' as an unpardonable sign of disrespect to the audience. The first comic actor then explains that the whole play is an allegory and ought not to be taken literally:

'Observe closely the town which is shown in the play [Gogol makes the first comic actor address his "fellow-countrymen"]. Everyone without exception agrees that no such town exists in Russia: it is inconceivable that our civil servants should all be such monsters: two or three at least are honest, but here there isn't one who is. In short, such a town does not exist. That's right, isn't it? Well, but what if this town is simply our spiritual town and is to be found in every one of us? . . . The playwright's business is to show that our life, which we regard as a comedy, should not end as tragically as the comedy we have just performed. Say what you like, but the government inspector who is waiting for us at the entrance to our grave is terrifying. Don't you know who this government inspector is? Why pretend? This government inspector is our awakened conscience which will force us to have a good look at ourselves. From this government inspector nothing will be hidden, because he is sent by the express order of the Almighty and his arrival will be announced at a time when there is no turning back. . . . In the same way as we laugh at the vileness of others, let us laugh magnanimously at our own vileness, whatever form it takes in us! . . . Do not let us show any resentment if some angry mayor or, to put it more fairly, the evil spirit himself who whispered the words in his ears, says to us: "What are you laughing at? You are laughing at yourselves!" We shall say to him proudly: "Yes, we are laughing at ourselves, because we have become aware of our noble Russian blood, because we hear God's command to be better than other people!" . . .'

In the space of only a few years Gogol had travelled far from his conception of laughter in *After the Play* as a means of making people realize more clearly the evils to which they are so used that they never notice them. He had now exchanged his vocation of artist for that of preacher, but instead of impressing his congregation he merely bored them. Aksakov expressed the views of the overwhelming majority of Gogol's admirers in his letter to Shevyryov in which he demanded that the final scene of *The Government Inspector* (as well as the *Selected Passages*) should not be published. 'It is from beginning to end', he wrote, 'a lie and an utter absurdity, and if it is published it will make Gogol the laughing-stock of the whole of Russia.'

But the artist in Gogol did not give up his place to the preacher without a struggle. His work on *Dead Souls* may have assumed vast and unmanageable proportions, but he still thought of it as a work of art first and foremost. 'My friend,' he wrote to Alexandra Smirnov on the 25th of July 1845, that is, after he had destroyed the second volume of the novel, 'I do not like my works that have been written or published till now, especially *Dead Souls*. But you would not be fair if you condemned their author for them. . . . The subject of *Dead Souls* has nothing to do with the description of Russian provincial life or of a few revolting landowners. It is for the time being a secret which must suddenly and to the amazement of everyone (for none of my readers has yet guessed it) be revealed in the following volumes, if it pleases God to prolong my life and bless my future work. I repeat, it is a secret and so far the key to it is only in the soul of the author. . . .'

It was to remain a secret, and by the beginning of January 1845 his inability to reveal it nearly drove him into a state of nervous collapse. 'Kopp [the German doctor who attended Gogol] and Zhukovsky', he wrote to Yazykov on January the 15th, 'are sending me away from Frankfort, saying that it is the only remedy for me. My nervous restlessness and all sorts of other symptoms of a complete breakdown frighten me. I am about to go away, but I don't know myself where. I have no desire at all to travel.' Even the open road had by then lost all its magic for him. He went to Paris to stay with Tolstoy, but, he wrote to Zhukovsky on January the 12th, 'in Paris I have gone to pieces again. It is foggy and I am feeling quite breathless. My time passes purposelessly and I cannot settle down to anything. I would be glad to be able to do half during the long morning of what I did in Frankfort during a short morning.' To Yazykov he wrote on the same day: 'About Paris I can only tell you that I have not seen Paris at all. I never liked it before, and I like it even less now.' He told Alexandra Smirnov a fortnight later that he had been to the Russian church almost daily and was 'deemed worthy to savour sweet and heavenly moments'. He spent all his time studying the Greek and Latin texts of the mass with the help of a Russian scholar, and it was in Paris that he conceived the idea of writing his *Meditations on the Divine Liturgy.* He left Paris for Frankfort on March the 1st. He was planning to go to Italy in the winter after undergoing a cure in a German spa in the summer, and then without any further delay to leave for Jerusalem. At the beginning of March he wrote to Alexandra Smirnov: 'Every nerve in my body is shaking. I always feel cold and can't get warm. I need hardly say that I am as thin as a rake, feel dreadfully weak and am very much afraid that I may die before my journey to the promised land.' But he went on writing his novel. 'I tortured myself,' he wrote to Alexandra Smirnov on April the 2nd, 'forced myself to write, suffered agonies seeing my impotence, and have several times brought on an attack of illness by such compulsion, but I couldn't do anything and everything I wrote was forced and bad. And many, many times I was thrown into agony, almost despair, because of it. God', he cried in anguish, 'seems to have taken away for a long time my ability to create works of my *present* and not my *past* self.' His final and complete breakdown came at the beginning of summer. 'I want to tell you', he wrote to Pletnyov at the end of May, 'that I am very ill and God alone can cure me.' One night he was seized by the fear of approaching death and he dashed off the following note to the Russian priest in Frankfort: 'Come at once to administer extreme unction to me. I am dying.' At the end of May he went to Homburg for a cure, but his health still did not improve. 'I feel worse and worse every hour', he wrote to Alexandra Smirnov on June the 4th. 'The Homburg waters do not improve my health, and this is perhaps due to the fact that I live here in complete and dangerous seclusion. Every mental work I do increases my hypochondria and every other work is no work and, therefore, also increases my hypochondria. I am in a state of complete physical prostration.' To Yazykov he wrote a few days later: 'I repeat, my illness is very serious and only a miracle of God can save me. My strength is gone . . . I know very well', he added, 'that I have greatly injured myself by forcing myself to write when my soul was not ready for it and when I should have submitted to God's will.' At last he did what he should have done long before: at the end of June he burnt all he had written of the second volume of *Dead Souls*.

Why did he burn it? In the fourth letter to various persons apropos *Dead Souls* published in his *Selected Passages* he declares that it was burnt 'because it was necessary', because in it, he adds, he had failed 'to show the way to the Beautiful'. In his *Author's Confession*, however, he claims that he did it because many of its passages were 'too attractive' and its heroes 'too tempting'. Neither of these reasons rings true. He burnt it because of what he had earlier called its 'chaotic state' and because it offended his artistic sensibilities, which he had never lost. After he had burnt it, the crisis was over. 'When', he writes in his *Selected Passages*, 'the flames had consumed the last pages of it, it suddenly arose in my mind, purified and bright, like a phoenix out of the fire, and I realized in what a disorderly state was that which I had thought to be well-done and well-shaped. . . . I burn when it is necessary to burn and I'm sure I'm doing right, for I never do anything without a prayer', he concludes, for now he was rapidly approaching the state of mind in which he was convinced that he had God's sanction for everything he did.

His condition began to improve, though at first he ascribed it to the cold water cure he underwent together with Count Alexander Tolstoy at Priesnitz's establishment in Greffenberg in August and September 1845. By autumn he was fit enough to undertake a journey to Rome, where his recovery continued. 'I am again in Rome', he wrote to Alexandra Smirnov on October the 24th. 'The long journey helped me again. The eternal St. Peter's is once more before me; the Colosseum, Monte Pincio and all our old friends are with me again. God is merciful and my spirits will revive and my strength will be restored to me.'

His strength was restored to him, but his nerves, which now he himself admitted (in a letter to Aksakov on October the 29th) were the real cause of his illness, were to plague him again, for *Dead Souls* was still unfinished and the magnificent palace of which only 'the front steps' had been built was still only a splendid vision—a secret the key to which was buried deep in his tortured soul. The riddle of his existence was still unsolved. His final attempt to solve it ended in failure and—this time—in death. But that was still far in the future. At present another fantastic dream occupied his mind to the exclusion of everything else. And it, too, was destined to be shattered.

¶ 4

The burning of the second volume of *Dead Souls* did not mean the destruction of everything Gogol had written during the three years since his departure from Russia; for during those years he had been writing voluminous letters to all his friends, letters which he carefully edited, copied and preserved. Between 1842 and 1848, that is, during his last sojourn abroad, his correspondence ran to over three hundred and fifty thousand words, as compared with the ninety thousand words of the first part of *Dead Souls*. His nervous breakdown and his recovery, which he regarded as a miracle, could not but be interpreted by him as a sign from heaven. But what did it portend? Surely it could only mean that, as he put it in his introduction to his *Selected Passages*, 'an artist whose work has, by the will of God, become the work of the spirit, cannot engage in any other work; he can neither allow himself to be idle, nor can he occupy his thoughts with anything else, however much he tries to force them.' What, then, was he to do? How was he to carry out his mission to save Russia? 'Russia,' he wrote towards the end of the first part of *Dead Souls*, 'what do you want from me? What is the secret bond between us? Why do you look like that and why are your eyes fixed upon me with such eager anticipation?' Gogol was certainly sincere in addressing those questions to Russia, and now he as sincerely believed that he had got the answer to them. He had not been writing the letters to his friends in vain, because those to whom they were written found in them, as he declared in the introduction to the *Selected Passages*, 'more that is useful to man than in any of my works'. Indeed, some of them found much more in them than that. 'I dreamt', Alexandra Smirnov wrote to Gogol on her return to Russia, 'that I had received a letter from you which burnt with a bright light. The paper and the letters seemed to be transformed. I told this dream at the Vyelgorskys', and they were all amazed. May it be like that, may you be transformed in body and soul, and may we see with our own eyes the transformation of your *Dead Souls* into a life-giving source of love and strength for our own dead souls!'

Gogol began working on the second volume of *Dead Souls* in Rome in January 1846, but soon he was completely absorbed in quite another kind of work. 'Having gone over what I have written to different persons lately', he wrote to Yazykov on April the 22nd from Rome, 'those, especially, who were in need of and demanded spiritual help, I realized that a book could be made of it which would be useful to many people engaged in different occupations. . . . I shall try to publish it, adding something about literature.' And a little earlier he wrote to Count Alexander Tolstoy to ask the Russian priest in Paris to offer up special prayers for the success of his work 'which is becoming more and more needful at the present time, and which I should like to be as speedily and sensibly finished as possible, and done in the name of God. . . .'

What was Gogol like during his work on the *Selected Passages*? Two descriptions of him have been left by Count Fyodor Tolstoy, Vice-President of the Russian Academy of Sciences, and Annenkov. Count Fyodor Tolstoy met Gogol in Rome in February 1846, at the house of Countess Sophia Apraksin, sister of Count Alexander Tolstoy. 'I went to dinner at Sophia Apraksin's', Fyodor Tolstoy wrote in his diary on the 17th of February 1846, 'where I met Gogol, whom I had not yet seen. At first I did not recognize him. He looked younger and better, but I expect that was because he was much tidier than when he used to visit me in Petersburg. In spite of his illness his complexion is good and fresh and he is not at all thin. His doctor tells me that he worries about his health and thinks that his illness is incurable. . . . At the Apraksins' they like him very much and treat him as a friend of the family, though he has become a sanctimonious bigot and a great friend of Countess Apraksin's brother, who is the most bigoted person I've met. In the aristocratic houses he visits, Gogol plays the part of a man who is constantly absorbed in his own thoughts. Most of the time he never utters a word, just as at dinner today he hardly opened his mouth. The Apraksins have heard that he is a great Russian writer, and as Russians, though they scarcely know how to speak Russian, they feel that they have to show respect to a man who has distinguished himself in Russian literature. He promised to call, but somehow I don't think he will. . . .' Vera Aksakov adds the following malicious detail of Gogol's behaviour at the Apraksins': 'He always walks about with his eyes fixed on the ground, and when the Countess says to him, "Nikolai Vassilyevich, Nikolai Vassilyevich, how do you like the soup?" he replies, eating heartily, "Sophia Petrovna, think of your soul!"'

Annenkov met Gogol on passing through Paris in July, 1846. 'Gogol', he writes, 'looked older, but had acquired a special kind of beauty which can only be defined as the beauty of a thinking man. His face was pale and emaciated—but its general expression seemed to me somehow brighter and calmer than before. It was the face of a philosopher. It was framed, as of old, by thick long hair reaching to his shoulders, and within that frame Gogol's eyes, far from losing their lustre, seemed to me more than ever expressive and full of fire. . . . He told me that he was leaving for Ostend in a couple of days and asked me to accompany him to the Tuilleries gardens. On the way there he asked me whether there were any new literary talents in Russia, adding that he was only interested in new writers, as the old ones had already said all they had to say. He was very serious, and spoke slowly and in a soft voice, but did not seem to be very much interested in our conversation.'

A short time after, Annenkov met Gogol again in Bamberg. To Annenkov's surprised remark that he thought Gogol was in Ostend, Gogol replied that he was going there 'by way of Austria and the Danube'. He went with Annenkov to visit Bamberg cathedral, remarking, 'Perhaps you don't know it, but I am an expert on architecture.' After inspecting the cathedral Gogol assumed a very serious and solemn look: he was about to send the first letters of his *Selected Passages* from Schwalbach, and was, as usual, full of the importance of his new work and the tremendous results that he expected from its publication. He asked Annenkov to meet him in Naples, where he was going to reveal a great secret to him. Then he talked about the dangers of attempting to introduce European political ideas into Russia.

'For instance,' he said in a drawn-out voice full of strong conviction, 'in Russia people are now talking about the European political upheavals—the proletariat—they think they can turn our peasants into German farmers. What is it all for? How can you separate the peasant from the land? What sort of proletarian can you make of him? Why, our peasant cries with joy when he sees his land; some of them even fall down to the ground and kiss it as though it were their mistress. . . . That means something, doesn't it? One has to think it over very carefully.'

He was absolutely convinced, Annenkov points out, that Russia was a separate entity with its own laws and customs of which they had no idea in Europe. It was quite a different Gogol from the one Annenkov had left in Paris recently, and certainly quite different from the Gogol he had known in Rome. Gogol walked pensively at Annenkov's side, his eyes fixed on the ground and so immersed in his thoughts was he that he hardly noticed it when they arrived at the coach station.

'But what about your lunch?' asked Annenkov.

'Thank you for reminding me', said Gogol. 'Can you see a bakery or a pastrycook's anywhere?'

There was a pastrycook's quite near and Gogol chose ten sweet pies filled with apples, plums and jam, had them wrapped in paper and took them with him into the coach.

'Good-bye,' he said to Annenkov after sitting down sideways beside a middle-aged German. 'Remember what I told you. . . . Think of Naples.'

Then he put up the collar of his cloak, assumed a dead, stony expression of complete indifference which was calculated to deprive his fellow-traveller of any desire to engage him in conversation, and in this attitude of a statue, with his face half concealed and his eyes dead and expressionless, he gave Annenkov a farewell nod.

There can be no doubt whatever that Gogol really expected the publication of his *Selected Passages* to produce a spiritual revolution in Russia. 'Put everything aside', he wrote to Pletnyov on July the 30th from Schwalbach, enclosing the first batch of articles for his new book, 'and devote all your time to the publication of my book under the title *Selected Passages from Correspondence with my Friends.* . . . Get ready the paper for a second edition, which I believe will come out immediately after the first: this book will sell much better than any of my previous works because it is the only sensible book I've written so far.' At the same time he wrote to Nikitenko, whom he wanted to censor the book, assuring him that he was not worrying about the censorship at all, for, he explained, 'I am quite convinced of the harmlessness of my book, since while writing it I acted as its most severe censor myself.' He sent Pletnyov the rest of the thirty-two articles on August the 25th, September the 12th, and September the 26th, from Ostend, and on October the 16th from Frankfort. Writing to

Shevyryov from Frankfort on October the 5th, he repeated that he was convinced that it was his first 'sensible' book, which many people would find very useful, since 'what came out of the soul cannot but be of benefit to the soul'. To make quite sure that his book would be passed by the censorship he wrote to Alexandra Smirnov, who was living in Kaluga at the time, her husband having been appointed Governor of the province, to leave everything and go to Petersburg. 'The time is coming', he wrote, 'when the cause of my long silence and the secret of my inner life have to be explained, though only partly, to the world. My friend,' he went on, 'if God is merciful I could gather a rich harvest to the glory of His sacred name.' Five days later, on October the 20th, he wrote to Pletnyov from Frankfort: 'For God's sake do all you can and take all the necessary steps for the early publication of my book. It is necessary for the general good. . . . My heart tells me so and God's extraordinary mercy granted me the powers to accomplish this work when I did not even dare to think of it, when I did not even dare to expect the freshness of spirit I needed for it; and suddenly I was given it all: suddenly my severest ailments ceased. . . . This is simply a miracle of God. My friend, I did it all in the name of God. . . .' To Alexandra Smirnov he wrote on November the 9th from Florence: 'You must go to Petersburg. You are needed there as much for me as for yourself. When I was writing my book, I took up my pen to the glory of His holy name and that was why every obstacle was removed from my path. . . . My book', he concluded, 'was undertaken for the sole purpose of arousing reverence for everything our Church and our Government have decreed for us by law.' He was so certain that nothing could prevent the publication of his book that he gave Pletnyov detailed instructions to send copies of it to every member of the royal family, including the children. In Naples, where he arrived on November the 19th, he still had no news from Pletnyov about the publication of his book. But he did not worry. 'My soul', he wrote in identical words to Zhukovsky and Tolstoy on November the 24th, 'looks calmly to the future. Everything will be all right.' Then the first blow fell. Pletnyov wrote to say that the censorship had refused to pass three of the articles which Gogol considered to be of the utmost importance, including the article addressed to *A Man in High Office*, in which he outlined his ideas on the duties of a statesman. He at once

wrote back to Pletnyov demanding that he should submit the
censored articles to the Emperor. He followed this up by a letter
to Countess Luisa Vyelgorsky, a strait-laced aristocratic lady
who enjoyed great influence at court but who had very little
respect for literature or for Gogol, enclosing a letter to Nicholas I
and asking her to hand it over to the Emperor herself. 'I am
publishing this book', he wrote to her, 'in the firm belief that
just at this time it will be useful to Russia, for I am sure that if I
did not say what has to be said now, nobody would say it. . . . I
wrote those letters not without first uttering a prayer, and they
were written in a spirit of love for the Emperor and for everything
good in Russia. The censorship refuses to pass just those letters
which I consider more important than the rest. These letters
contain something the Emperor must read himself. . . .'

Nicholas I had visited Rome in January, 1847, to negotiate a
concordat with the Holy See, and Gogol, as he wrote to Zhukovsky on February the 6th, merely 'admired his beautiful figure'.
He found that the Emperor's face was 'more spiritual than ever
before'. He did not present himself before the Emperor because,
he wrote to Alexandra Smirnov on January the 27th, 'not having
done anything to deserve his favour' he did not want 'to remind
him of my existence'. What is so astonishing is not Gogol's
fantastic notions about Nicholas the First's 'spiritual face' and
'beautiful figure', nor his idea, in which he firmly believed and
which, incidentally, was quite true, that he had done nothing to
deserve the Emperor's favour, as his utter divorce from reality
which made him think that the Emperor, too, would benefit
from reading his book.

The *Selected Passages* were, in the meantime, published with
the excisions demanded by the censors. But Gogol, still believing
that the book would be reprinted immediately, repeated his
demand that the censored articles should be placed before the
Emperor; and so sure was he of the Emperor's approval that in
his second letter to Countess Luisa Vyelgorsky on January the
25th, he asked that an honour should be conferred on the censor
who passed the second edition of his book. Five days later he
asked Alexandra Smirnov to offer up a special prayer 'that the
Emperor should carry out my request and especially that God
should restore calm to my soul, which I shall find it very difficult to preserve now because my ailments have again begun

to plague me'. The news of Yazykov's death in Moscow on January the 7th increased his despair. He imagined that some evil power had been responsible for the excisions in his book. 'A sort of demonic insurrection has been organized to prevent its appearance', he wrote to Alexander Tolstoy on February the 6th. 'Certain mysterious parties of Europeans and Asiatics have united to confuse and perplex the censor.' He had worked himself up into such a state of excitement that he could not sleep and grew weak and, as he wrote to Anna Vyelgorsky on February the 6th, could scarcely raise his arms. 'Be a witness to my spiritual weakness and my inability to bear this blow', he wrote to Alexandra Smirnov on February the 22nd. 'Everything other people find it difficult to bear', he went on, 'I can bear with God's help, but I cannot bear the pain inflicted upon me by the censor's knife, which unfeelingly cuts off whole pages written with the best intentions in the world. . . . It is as though a mother's favourite child had been murdered before her eyes—so painful is this censorship murder to me. . . .'

But soon the news of the general disgust his book had produced in Russia began to reach him and the cuts made by the censor no longer seemed to be of any importance. He awoke as though after some dreadful dream, he wrote to Zhukovsky on the 6th of March 1847, 'feeling like a naughty schoolboy who has realized that he had gone too far. I have shown myself to be such a Khlestakov in my book that I haven't the heart to open it. . . . The appearance of my book', he summed up, 'came like some slap in the face: a slap in the face for the public, a slap in the face for my friends and, last but not least, a most violent slap in the face for me. . . .'

§ 5

The *Selected Passages from Correspondence with my Friends* consists of thirty-two articles, most of which were actually based on letters written by Gogol to the small circle of his intimate friends, including Alexander Tolstoy, Zhukovsky, Alexandra Smirnov and the Vyelgorskys. It begins with a long introduction in which

Gogol declares that, having been seriously ill and at the point of death, he had made a will in which he asked some of his friends to publish a few of his letters 'to atone for the uselessness of everything' he had hitherto written. 'My heart tells me', he wrote, 'that my book is needed and can be useful . . . and I therefore request my fellow-countrymen to read it several times. . . . I ask those who can afford to buy it to buy several copies and distribute them among those who cannot afford to buy it.' He promised that after defraying the costs of his own pilgrimage to Palestine, he would devote the rest of the money he received from the book to helping poor pilgrims. He then asked forgiveness from all his fellow-countrymen for having brought distress to many by his 'thoughtless and immature works', which had appeared 'in an imperfect state and misled almost everybody as to their real meaning'. He also asked everyone's forgiveness for all the personal insults he had inflicted on people 'since my childhood', and for any disrespect he might have shown to his literary colleagues, and he added, 'those who find it difficult to forgive I would like to remind that they are Christians'. In conclusion, he asked everyone in Russia to pray for him, promising to pray for them all at the Holy Sepulchre.

For his first article, he published the will he had made (so he alleged) during his severe illness in June, 1845, part of which is addressed to his mother and sisters, to whom he left the income from his books on condition that they gave half of it to the poor, specifying, however, that only those should benefit under his will who expressed 'a sincere wish to change their way of life and become better men'. He also asked his mother and sisters to re-read carefully all the letters he had sent them during the past three years, as 'a great deal will be better understood after my death'. Their house should be converted into a place of refuge for pilgrims rather than a landowner's country-house, so that everyone arriving there should be welcomed as a friend and none should leave without being comforted. 'If, however, the traveller is of low origin,' he adds characteristically, 'and it is inconvenient for some reason to find room for him in the house, he should be taken to the house of a well-to-do peasant who is known for his exemplary life and could help his brother with good advice.' He next gave orders that his body should not be buried until decomposition had set in, that no monument should be erected for him and that no one should mourn for him, 'since, even if a man died whom Russia really needs, no one ought to sink into despondency on account of it'. Finally, he referred to his portrait which Pogodin had published without his consent and asked all those of his readers who had a copy of it to destroy it, 'particularly as it is a very bad likeness of me. . . . This will of mine', he concludes, 'must be published immediately after my death in all the newspapers and journals, so that no one should be innocently guilty towards me and thereby incur a rebuke upon his soul.'

His second article on 'A Woman's Place in High Society' contains the astonishing assertion that the prevalence of bribery and corruption among the Russian civil servants is due 'either to the extravagance of their wives, who are eager to shine in society and demand money from their husbands for that purpose, or to the emptiness of their domestic life'. He advises the society woman not to shun the world, for 'it is not for nothing that God has commanded everyone to remain where He has placed him', and to remember that her duty was 'to bring your smile to the sufferer and a voice in which a man can hear his sister who has flown down to him from heaven—and nothing more'.

In his third letter, addressed to Count Alexander Tolstoy, Gogol explains his peculiar idea of the meaning of illnesses. 'Oh,' he writes, 'how much we need illnesses! Of the numberless benefits I have already derived from them I will mention only one to you: whatever I may be now, I'm still much better than I was before. But for these illnesses I should have believed myself to be what I ought to be, not to mention the fact that good health, which invariably arouses in a Russian the desire to show off before his friends, would have made me do all sorts of silly things. Besides, during the fresh moments which the mercy of heaven grants to me, and even in the midst of my suffering, ideas sometimes occur to me which are incomparably better than any of my former ideas, and I can see myself that everything that appears from my pen now will be of much greater importance than anything I have written till now.' He based this article on two letters he wrote to Yazykov on the 4th of November 1843, and the 15th of February 1844, in one of which he declared illness to be like a battle. 'The fight against it', he wrote, 'must be conducted in the same way as the fight against the devil . . . who cannot be conquered until you have offered up a fervent prayer to God. The same thing applies to illness.'

The fourth letter, on the Significance of Words, is remarkable for Gogol's attack on Pogodin, which is entirely in tune with his ideas of the beneficial effects of 'rebukes'. 'As for our friend P . . .', Gogol writes, 'he has been in a hurry all his life, hastening to share everything with his readers and let them know everything he himself has gleaned, without bothering whether the idea has matured in his head sufficiently to be accessible to everyone; in short, he has displayed himself before his readers in all his untidiness. And what has been the result? Have his readers noticed the noble and beautiful passions which coruscate so often in him? Have they accepted from him the things he wished to share with them? No, all they have noticed in him is his slovenliness and untidiness, which one notices first of all, and they have received nothing from him. For thirty years he has toiled and moiled like an ant, always in a hurry to hand over to everyone whatever he has found might help to promote Russian education and enlightenment. And not one man has thanked him for it; I have never met a single grateful young man who would acknowledge his indebtedness to him for any new idea or any beautiful craving to do good. On the contrary, I have myself had to argue and put up a fight for the purity of his intentions and the sincerity of his words even with people who, I should have thought, should have understood him. I could not convince anybody because he managed so to conceal himself from everybody that it was quite impossible to show him as he really is. . . .' And to make quite sure that Pogodin knew what he thought of him, Gogol had the following inscription written on Pogodin's presentation copy of the *Selected Passages*: 'To Pogodin, whose soul is untidy and dishevelled, who notices nothing, who keeps insulting everybody at every step without realizing it; to the doubting Thomas who measures people with a shortsighted and coarse yardstick, is this book presented in memory of his sins by a man as sinful as he and in many respects untidier than he.'

The fifth letter, like the tenth, thirteenth, fourteenth, fifteenth and thirty-first, deals with a literary subject, and in these six articles Gogol showed his usual perspicacity and good sense, which alone made the rumour that he had gone mad sound silly. In the fifth article, On the Reading of Russian Poets before an

Audience, he stresses the fact that skilful reading alone could make a poem intelligible. 'To read a lyric poem as it ought to be read', he writes, 'is not at all easy: to do it one has first to study the poem thoroughly; one has to share with the poet the lofty feelings he experienced when composing his poem; one has to feel every word of his with one's heart and soul—and only then step forward to read it. The reader must not work himself up into a passion; on the contrary, he must be very calm, for only then will his voice be imbued with tremendous strength, a sign of truly inspired feeling. This will be communicated to the audience and will produce a miracle: even those who have never before been moved by poetry will be deeply moved.'

The sixth letter, On Helping the Poor, expatiates on the theme he had already touched on in his will. The seventh letter On the *Odyssey* translated by Zhukovsky, which he had published in the *Contemporary* a year earlier, once again reveals the exaggerated importance Gogol ascribed to the works of his close friends. He was sure, he declared, that the *Odyssey* would influence the 'modern spirit' of Russian society, especially at a time when 'by the inscrutable will of Providence one hears everywhere a distressing murmur of discontent'. And he concludes by expressing the hope that the *Odyssey* would help to spread across Russia the patriarchal spirit of ancient times which was 'so deeply embedded in the Russian nature'.

The eighth and ninth letters are devoted to the Russian Church and clergy. Gogol regarded the Greek Orthodox Church as the only effective safeguard of the 'patriarchal' system of society in which he so firmly believed. 'With all its profound dogmas and rites', he declares, 'it seems to have been sent straight from heaven for the Russian people, for it alone is capable of solving all bewildering problems and producing a miracle in the sight of the whole of Europe, compelling every class of society to keep within its legal bounds, giving strength to Russia and astonishing the whole world by the perfect harmony of the self-same organism it has feared so much till now.'

In the tenth letter, On the Lyricism of the Russian Poets, Gogol pays a special tribute to Zhukovsky for restraining him while all his other friends always hurried him. 'How many silly things', he adds naïvely, 'would I have written if I had listened to my other friends.' Afterwards Zhukovsky was sorry he had let

Gogol publish his *Selected Passages*. 'Our severe critics', Zhukov-sky wrote to Gogol, 'have given you a good hiding, and, I confess, I blame myself for having done nothing to protect you from their blows, the more painful because you deserved them. . . . When you read your articles to me I was interested in your personality, but when, instead of the author, I had a dead book before me, much that I had thought so attractive and original before appeared strange and indecent to me.'

The eleventh letter, On Controversies, Gogol devoted to the violent polemic that was going on at the time between the Slavophils, headed by Pogodin, Shevyryov, the Kireyevsky brothers, and especially Konstantin Aksakov, and the Westerners, headed by Belinsky. Although in spirit close to the Slavophils, Gogol resisted all their blandishments to join them. He had already hinted to Konstantin Aksakov that he did not approve of his exotic clothes or of his attempt to persuade the Moscow ladies to wear *sarafans*. He was even more outspoken about it to Shevyryov. 'I was disturbed by your news of Konstantin Aksakov', he wrote to Shevyryov on the 20th of November 1845. 'His beard, his peasant's smock, etc. . . . He is simply playing the fool, and yet this folly had to happen. This man suffers from a superabundance of strength, physical as well as moral; both have accumulated in him and find no proper outlet. Both physically and morally he has remained a *virgin*. . . . Abstinence from all the diversions of life and the flesh have made him concentrate all his energies upon the spirit. He had, therefore, to become a fanatic. I have thought so from the very first.'

Gogol's views on the Slavophils and Westerners were, on the whole, exceedingly sensible and, compared with Dostoevsky's violent hatreds, extremely fair. He thought that the passionate controversies about 'our European and Slav principles' only showed that 'we are beginning to wake up but have not yet completely woken up' and that it was no wonder therefore that a great deal of nonsense was being said on both sides. The Slavophils and the Westerners seemed to him to be only caricatures of what they wished to be. They spoke of two different aspects of the same thing without realizing that they were not contradicting one another. 'One', he wrote, 'has walked up too near to the building, so that he sees only part of it, while the other has walked off too far, so that he can see the whole façade but cannot distinguish its separate parts.' His advice to the Slavophils was, therefore, to come a little nearer and to the Westerners to walk back a little farther. But he knew that they would not do so because both of them were possessed of the spirit of pride, each of them being convinced that only he was right. Still, he thought there was more arrogance on the part of the Slavophils who were 'boasters every one of them, imagining that they have discovered America'. But what really infuriated the Slavophils and, especially, Konstantin Aksakov was Gogol's defence of Peter the Great's reforms which, hating European civilization as they did, they abominated. Gogol, on the other hand, declared that Peter the Great 'opened our eyes by the introduction of European civilization and by giving us all the means and tools to carry on with our work'.

Letter twelve—The Christian Goes Forward—is largely a disquisition on intelligence and wisdom, the latter coming only from Christ. Letter thirteen deals with the works of the Russian eighteenth-century poet and historian Nikolai Karamzin, and in the fourteenth, on the One-Sided View of the Theatre and, generally, on One-sidedness, Gogol launches a violent attack on Count Alexander Tolstoy's puritanical views of the stage as a sink of iniquity.

'One-sided people [Gogol writes], who are fanatics as well, are a real menace to society; woe to the country in which such people obtain any kind of power. They know nothing of Christian humility and have no doubts about themselves; they are convinced that everyone is wrong and they alone are right. My friend [he addresses Tolstoy], take care—for you are now in this perilous position. It is a good thing you are out of office now, otherwise you, who I know are capable of occupying the most difficult and responsible posts, would have been the cause of more disorder and evil than the most incapable of officials. . . . Don't [he goes on] be like those sanctimonious persons who desire to destroy everything in the world, seeing only the devil's work in it. . . . Shakespeare, Sheridan, Molière, Goethe, Schiller, Beaumarchais and even Lessing, Regnard and other minor playwrights of the past century have produced nothing that would arouse disrespect for higher things. One ought to put on the stage all the most perfect dramatic works of all centuries and all nations. One must perform them more and more often, repeating the same play over and over again. And it can be done. One can make all their plays fresh, new and interesting to everybody, provided one knows how to put them on the stage. . . . Take any play, however familiar, and produce it as it should be produced and the public will run to see it. Molière will be a novelty to it and Shakespeare will be more enticing than the latest farce. . . .'

The fifteenth letter deals with Subjects for a Lyric Poet and is addressed to Yazykov. In it Gogol emphasizes his complete renunciation of his great masterpieces in favour of his belief in the efficacy of 'a lyrical appeal' to man. 'You can make no impression with a satirical work', he declares, refusing even to acknowledge the revolutionary reaction produced by *The Government Inspector*. 'Oh,' he exclaims, 'if only you could tell your readers what my Plyushkin will have to say when I come to the third part of *Dead Souls*!' Gogol intended to reform even Plyushkin by the magic of a 'lyrical', that is, a deeply felt, appeal to his better nature, and make him distribute his wealth among the poor. 'Hold up to scorn', he declares, appealing to Yazykov, but actually revealing his plan for the second and third parts of his novel 'the extortioner and his cursed luxuries, as well as his disgusting wife, who by her ostentatious ways and her finery has ruined both herself and her husband . . . so that all should run from them as from the plague. Glorify, in a solemn dithyramb, the humble hard-working man who, to the honour of the exalted Russian race, can be found even among the most unscrupulous officials. . . . Exalt in a hymn the giant who only springs from Russian soil and, awakening from his shameful slumber, suddenly becomes a different being: renouncing in the sight of all his abominations and most odious vices, he becomes the foremost champion of goodness. Show how this gigantic work is accomplished in a truly Russian soul; but show it in such a way as to arouse involuntarily in everyone his own Russian spirit, so that everyone, even those belonging to the coarse lower orders, should cry with one voice: "That's a fine fellow!" and feel that they, too, could become fine fellows like him. Go down on your knees before God and beseech Him to grant you anger and love!'

In his sixteenth letter on Advice there is a passage which might have been written today. 'Many among us,' Gogol writes, 'especially among the young, have begun boasting excessively of their Russian superiority without thinking of deepening and developing it within themselves, but merely anxious to parade it and say to Europe: "Look, foreigners, we're better than you!" This boastfulness is the root of all evil. It annoys others and harms the boaster. The best thing can be made to look cheap if you keep trumpeting it abroad and bragging about it. And in Russia we boast before ever accomplishing anything! We boast about our future! If you ask me, it is much better to feel depressed and dejected for a time than to have too high an opinion of oneself.'

The seventeenth letter on Enlightenment is addressed to Zhukovsky, whom he assures that in Moscow he would be treated 'like a patriarch', and that the young men there would receive his 'aged words' like 'pieces of gold'. Enlightenment itself Gogol regarded as coming only from the Greek Orthodox Church. 'The Western Church', he writes (and Dostoevsky only enlarged on the subject in the same vein), 'has only pushed people away from Christ, whereas the Eastern Church gives full freedom to man's heart and soul.'

The eighteenth letter is entitled 'Four Letters to Different People apropos of *Dead Souls*'. In it, Gogol tries to justify himself for having written the first part of his novel, and complains about the readers who disregarded his appeal to them in the introduction to the second edition of *Dead Souls* to send him advice and information for the remaining two parts. He repeats his assertion that all his latest works are 'the history of my own soul'. The reason why *Dead Souls* 'frightened Russia so much and produced such a sensation', he declares, was not because it revealed her 'wounds and internal diseases', but because its readers were frightened by the vulgarity it disclosed. When he read the first chapters of the novel to Pushkin the poet grew gloomier and gloomier and at last cried, 'Good Lord, how sad is our Russia!' Pushkin, Gogol adds, who knew Russia so well, did not notice that it was all 'a caricature and my own invention'. Since then he had been thinking only of how 'to soften the painful impression which *Dead Souls* has produced'. He himself had got rid of many of his bad habits by giving them to his heroes. He had laughed them to scorn and made others laugh at them. And he advised his readers to retire to their rooms for a few minutes and examine their past life in order to test the truth of his words. 'You will then understand', he declares, 'why I have not before now chosen any virtuous men for my heroes. You cannot invent them out of your head. For until you become like them yourself, until you acquire a few good qualities by your perseverance and strength of character, everything you produce by your pen will be nothing but carrion and you will be as far from the truth as earth is from heaven. Neither', he concludes truthfully enough, as the sorcerer in *The Terrible Vengeance*, the 'philosopher' Khoma Brut in *Viy* and the artist Piscaryov in *Nevsky Avenue* can prove, 'have I invented nightmares: the nightmares oppressed my own soul and what was in my soul came out of it.'

His next two letters, the nineteenth, on One Must Love Russia, and the twentieth, on One Must Travel All Over Russia, are addressed to Count Alexander Tolstoy. The first begins with the rather startling statement that Tolstoy has no love for God. Gogol goes on to advise the Count to acquire this love, without which he cannot hope for salvation, by loving his brethren, which, in turn, he can only do by loving Russia. 'You don't really love Russia', he tells the ex-governor of two provinces and the future Procurator of the Holy Synod. 'All you can do is to be irritated by the rumours of the evil things that take place in Russia. . . . And without loving your brethren you cannot love God, and without loving God you will never achieve salvation.' It seems, however, that there was still some hope for the pious Count. All he had to do to know Russia, Gogol declared in his second letter, was to travel all over the country (advice Gogol himself did not follow, declaring in one of his letters that all one could discover by travelling all over Russia was how inefficient stage-coach stations were and how corrupt the station masters).

His twenty-first letter, What is a Governor's Wife, Gogol devoted to a discussion of the duties of a provincial governor's wife. It is addressed to Alexandra Smirnov, whose husband's appointment as Governor of the province of Kaluga gave Gogol the chance of putting to the test his ideas of government by moral suasion. 'Be comforted,' he wrote to Alexandra Smirnov on the 11th of September 1845, 'your future is bright. It will begin in Kaluga.' This 'bright future' was to be a direct consequence of the detailed instructions for ruling her husband's province which he had given her in a long letter six weeks earlier, a letter the best comment on which was made by Turgenev in the words he put into the mouth of Bazarov in *Fathers and Sons*: 'Ever since I arrived here I have felt rotten, just as though I had been reading Gogol's letters to the wife of the Kaluga Governor.'

Gogol began his famous letter by assuring Alexandra Smirnov that her influence in the province was considerably more significant than the influence of her husband or even the Governor-General. This influence she was to exercise through the wives of the civil servants by converting these ladies to Gogol's extraordinary views on the primary causes of corruption in the administrative organs of the Russian Empire. One of the chief causes of bribery being, as Gogol had already explained elsewhere in his *Selected Passages*, the extravagance of the wives of the civil servants, all Alexandra Smirnov had to do was to dress simply, for then all the ladies in Kaluga would immediately follow her example and the evil of bribery would be scotched. She was, further, to stop all visits which, again, would make the other ladies stop visiting each other and thus put an end to gossip. She should, on the other hand, cultivate the acquaintance of the more intelligent women, persuade them to care for their souls, and make them give her detailed accounts of their good deeds. She might also call to her aid the priests, who in their sermons and in the confessional were to deal with the more recalcitrant spirits. Having converted the wives, she was to address herself to their husbands. She should find out all their unsavoury secrets and, to gain their confidence, she might even 'pay a call on them now and again and be nice to their wives and children'. Having discovered 'all the hidden springs' of the administration, she could nip in the bud many seemingly incorrigible evils by these 'quiet, gentle and beneficently Christian' methods. 'Look upon the whole town', Gogol writes in his letter, 'as a doctor looks upon a hospital. . . . Don't you think', he goes on, 'that I would be able to help your incurables? Have you forgotten that I can pray and that, having prayed, my prayer can reach God Himself?'

Alexandra Smirnov had not forgotten it. She tried to carry out Gogol's instructions faithfully and soon found herself the centre of malicious intrigues, so that in the end she had to give up her attempt to convert Kaluga to the Kingdom of Heaven according to Gogol's prescription. She had a nervous breakdown which conveniently absolved her from the sin of disobeying the orders of her spiritual mentor. By the time she had recovered, the storm had broken over Gogol's head and all his admirable precepts went by the board.

His letter on What is a Governor's Wife was followed by his

even more amazing twenty-second letter on A Russian Land-owner.

'Take up your duties of landowner [Gogol writes] as you ought to in the real and legal sense of the word. To begin with, get all your peasants together and explain to them what you are and what they are, that you are their landowner because you were born a landowner, that you will have to answer to God if you give up this calling for another, and that everyone has to serve God in the station in which he has been placed. . . . So they, too, having been born under your authority, must obey this authority, be-cause there is no authority which is not from God. And you must show them this in the Bible, so that they should all see it. Then tell them that you are not making them work because you want money to spend on your pleasures; and to prove it to them take out a bundle of notes and burn it before their eyes, and do it in a way that would really convince them that you set no store by money, but that you make them work because God has com-manded man to earn his bread by hard work and sweat [Gogol never hesitated to misinterpret the text of the Bible if it suited his purpose]. Confirm it all by the words of the Holy Writ; point with your finger to the very words, make every one of them cross himself beforehand and kiss the book in which it is written. . . . Those of your peasants who are scoundrels and drunkards you must order to show the same kind of respect to the good peasants as they show to your bailiff, your agent, the priest and even your-self. So that when they see an exemplary peasant in the distance, they should at once take off their caps and make way for him. . . . Don't beat a peasant [Gogol goes on with his good advice]; to box his ears does not require a great deal of talent; the district police officer, the assessor and even the bailiff can do that; the peasant is used to it and will only scratch the back of his neck. . . . To teach a peasant to read, to enable him to read the stupid books which the European humanitarians issue for the common people is absolute nonsense. The peasant has no time for it any-way. After such hard work he won't be interested in books, and on returning home he will fall asleep and sleep like a log. . . . If [Gogol concludes his advice to the landowner] you work dili-gently for a year you will become as rich as Croesus, contrary to the opinions of the shortsighted people who think that the inter-ests of the landowners and the peasants are poles apart. . . .'

After describing in his twenty-third letter, on The History Painter Ivanov, his friend's work on his large picture of the Epiphany, and appealing for financial assistance for Ivanov, Gogol in his twenty-fourth letter discusses a wife's duties to her husband. This letter is based on two letters he wrote to Alexandra Smirnov and Sophia Sollogub on the 24th of September 1844. Gogol was very fond of Sophia, whose husband was a typical man-about-town who, as Gogol put it in his letter to Alexandra Smirnov, 'does not appreciate the treasure he possesses'. Gogol, therefore, tried to suggest all sorts of ways which would make Sophia's life happier. His letters show his tender solicitude for the twenty-four-year-old girl and contain a great deal of sensible advice such as, for instance, that husband and wife should have different occupations, should not share the same rooms, should not see each other too often and, if annoyed with each other, should vent their anger when alone in their rooms. But in his letter on What a Wife Should Be to her Husband Gogol, unfortunately, abandoned his tone of tender solicitude for one of aggressive lecturing on a subject he knew nothing about. 'Far from being blessed', he tells the wife, 'your position is dangerous. Pray to God to give you strength. You can get anything you like from God if you pray to Him.' He then goes on to advise her to divide her housekeeping money into seven equal parts, one for the rent, water and fuel, another for food and the cook's wages, a third for the carriage, a fourth for her clothes, a fifth for pocket money, a sixth for unforeseen expenses, and the seventh 'for God, that is, for the church and the poor. . . .' She has further to get a special expense book for each and to make up her accounts at the end of every month. He finally advises her to find out all about the nature of her husband's work, for 'every man', he concludes, perhaps not so astonishingly, since he had in mind Count Vladimir Sollogub, 'is a good-for-nothing villain, and everything has become so topsy-turvy now that a wife has to order her husband to be her lord and master. . . .'

His twenty-fifth letter, on Village Justice, is no less amazing than his letter to the landowner. In it he tells the landowner to be his own judge over the peasants. 'Try every man', he goes on, 'by man's and God's judgement. . . . If you pass sentence in such a court it will be God who authorizes you. . . . Justice', he goes on, 'could be administered in our country better than in all other countries, because of all nations only the Russian nation believes that there is no just man but that only God is just. Our people firmly believe in this idea. Armed with it even a simple and unintelligent man is clothed with authority by the common people and can put an end to quarrels. It is only we, men of a higher social position, who do not pay any attention to it because we have acquired ridiculous, gentlemanly European notions about justice. We argue only about who is right and who is wrong, but if we examine any lawsuit carefully, we cannot help coming to the conclusion that both parties are wrong.'

But Gogol was aware of what he called in his next—the twenty-sixth—letter 'The Horrors and Terrors in Russia'. He was merely obsessed with the idea that if everyone followed his advice and served 'not as he served in Russia but in another heavenly kingdom, the head of which is Christ Himself,' then 'in another ten years Europe will be coming to us for the purchase of wisdom.'

In the twenty-seventh letter, To A Short sighted Friend, he further elaborated this view. 'To our shame', he writes, 'the Europeans even to this day point out their great men to us while we sometimes have men who, though not great, are much more intelligent than the great men in Europe; but the latter at least have left something lasting behind them, while we do all sorts of things which, like dust, are blown off the face of the earth. Oh, how much we need a public slap in the face delivered before the whole world!' he concludes, little dreaming how soon he was to receive this slap and how disagreeable he would find it.

It was on his twenty-eighth letter, To a Man in High Office, that Gogol naïvely relied to bring about a change of heart in the rulers of Russia and that was why he was so distressed at the news that the censorship had refused to pass it. It contains the essence of his belief in man's regeneration through faith, but at the same time it is full of so many dangerous admissions and fantastic assumptions that the authorities considered it unfit for publication.

After declaring that Christian humility would see the high official through any difficulties and do away with the self-deception which is so common even among intelligent people, Gogol went on:

'I know very well that it is difficult to govern anywhere in Russia . . . which is full of all sorts of abuses. Indeed, bribery has become so rampant in our country that it is quite impossible to eradicate it. I know, too, that all sorts of illegal practices have become so generally accepted that the laws of the land have become a dead letter. . . . There is not a single man in our country who is not to some extent guilty, so that it is impossible to say at first who is more guilty than another—indeed, there are many people who, though innocent, are found guilty and many who, though guilty, are found innocent. . . . The whole thing [here again Gogol reveals the main idea of the second and third parts of *Dead Souls*] will take quite a different turn if you show a man what crimes he commits against himself and not against others. . . . This will shock him so much that he will get the necessary courage to become a different man, and only then will people realize how noble is our Russian race even in a rogue. . . . The more one examines the workings of our provincial government [Gogol goes on], the more one is astonished at the wisdom of those who are responsible for it: one can't help feeling that God Himself built it up invisibly by the hands of our Emperors. . . . Another great thing you must do is to make the nobility realize the true nature of their social position. . . . During the latest European social upheavals and disturbances, some of our malefactors tried to spread the rumour among the nobility that the government intended to weaken their powers and reduce them to insignificance. But, thank God, the time has passed when a few madcaps could throw a whole kingdom into confusion. . . . Should not the Emperor love the flower of his people? For in our country the nobility is the flower of our people, and not some alien estate. . . . Our nobility has no feeling of pride in any of the privileges of their class. . . . No one in our country [Gogol goes on naïvely] boasts about his family or ancient lineage except, perhaps, some Anglophils who have become infected during their travels in England. There is only one thing they allow themselves to boast about—and that is the feeling of the moral nobility which God alone endowed them with. Our aristocracy is, as it were, a vessel which contains the moral nobility that has to spread across the whole face of Russia to make it clear to all the other classes of the population why the highest class in the country is called the flower of the people. . . . If you explain to them [that is, the noblemen, among whom Gogol, of course, included himself] that all Russia is crying out for help and that she can only be helped by great acts of nobility which, in turn, can only be performed by those who are already noble by birth, you will see that their hearts will beat as one with yours. Having completed their service to the State [Gogol went on in utter disregard of reality], they will not demand any rewards or honours or indeed any privileges for themselves, but will be content with having shown their superior qualities. . . .

'Your second great task is so to educate the peasants entrusted to your care that they should become a model of their class for the whole of Europe, for now many people in Europe are earnestly thinking about the ancient patriarchal life which has disappeared everywhere except in Russia and, having experienced the feebleness of all their own institutions, are beginning to talk freely about the superiority of our peasant economy [i.e. serfdom].

'Absolute love [he concludes] must not belong to anyone on earth! It must be transmitted in accordance with rank, and every high official who notices that it is becoming concentrated upon him must at once transfer it to his superior, so that in this way it will reach its legitimate source [i.e. the Emperor] and our beloved Emperor will solemnly transfer it in the sight of all to God Himself.'

The last four letters: Whose Lot is Better, A Farewell Message, What is the Essence of our Poetry and What are its Characteristics, and Easter Sunday—do not add anything to what has already been discussed of Gogol's views, except that in the last letter he again expresses his unshakable conviction that if his ideas were carried out the whole of Russia would be as one man. 'My soul tells me that emphatically,' he declares, 'and this is not just an idea that has entered my head. Such ideas are not invented. It is God Himself who puts them into the heart of man.'

¶ 6

Only Pletnyov and Anna Vyelgorsky entirely approved of the *Selected Passages*. Anna wrote to Gogol: 'I recognize you completely in your letters; everything in them is simple and comprehensible to me. When I read them I seem to hear you talking to us as you used to do, and I enter into your feelings, see with your eyes and think with your thoughts.' Pletnyov wrote to Shevyryov on the 4th of January 1847 (O.S.): 'I and every member of my circle are in raptures over the beautiful world into which Gogol has himself passed and to which he carries his readers. And they wanted to brand this man as a madman! He is not, to be sure, at all like those who dared to slander his sacred teaching. They are not going to call themselves mad, are they? That is why they put all the blame on him!' Shevyryov himself was, of course, in full agreement with Gogol's ideas, but he objected to the 'ecstatic' way in which they were expressed, and he even accused Gogol of being like Princess Volkonsky. 'Your comparison of myself with Princess Volkonsky,' Gogol wrote to Shevyryov on the 11th of February 1847, 'as well as your discovery of symptoms of Catholicism in me did not strike me as true. As for Princess Volkonsky, I have not seen her for ages and I haven't probed into her soul . . . as for Catholicism, I can only tell you that I have come to Christ in a *protestant* rather than in a *Catholic* way. My analysis of man's soul was the reason for my coming to Christ, for I was first of all amazed at His human wisdom and His hitherto unheard-of knowledge of the soul. It was only afterwards that I worshipped Him.'

It was Aksakov who was infuriated with Gogol's book. Gogol assured him in his letter of the 20th of January 1847, that he was mistaken in suspecting any new trends in his ideas. 'From early youth', he wrote, 'I have followed the same path. I was only secretive because I was not stupid—that is all.' He had antici-pated that his book would be attacked from every direction but, he declared in the same letter, 'these attacks are very necessary to me now because they reveal me to myself and, at the same time, reveal you, that is, my readers, to me'. To this letter Aksakov replied: 'Alas, I can no longer deceive myself: you have sincerely thought that your calling is the announcement of high moral truths to men in the form of discourses and sermons, a specimen of which is contained in your book. You are grossly and pitifully mistaken. You are completely confused and muddled, you con-tradict yourself continually and, while thinking of serving God and humanity, you only insult God and humanity.'

Gogol's reply was characteristic: he merely observed that Aksakov had no right to rely on his own intelligence and infallibility to draw any conclusions about him or his book. Instead, he advised him to pray that God might save him [Gogol] from all temptations of self-deception.

But of all his friends it was Pogodin who, naturally enough, took exception to Gogol's book on personal grounds. 'Aksakov', Gogol wrote to Pogodin on the 4th of March 1847, 'has written to me that you are deeply offended by what I said about you in my book. He said that you even wept and then, having calmed down, wanted to write to me as follows: "My friend, Jesus Christ teaches us to turn the other cheek, but where does He teach us to administer a slap in the face in public?'. . . . You all interpreted my words as being written in anger or, what is even worse, as inspired by vindictiveness. But I felt neither anger nor vindictiveness.'

This explanation did not mollify Pogodin. He wrote six long letters to Gogol between March the 29th and July the 26th, in which he subjected Gogol's book to a merciless analysis. To begin with, he explained that he had published Gogol's portrait because he had assumed that it would please him as well as his readers. Gogol's demands in his book, which he declared to be both physically and morally impossible to carry out, he ascribed to a temporary mental aberration caused by illness. 'Christ says continually,' Pogodin wrote, '"do not preach", but you preach from the first line of your book to the last. Christ says, "Condemn not", and you seem to condemn everything; "turn the other cheek", but you seem to think that you have to strike the other fellow's cheek, and as hard as you can, too. . . . You say you have given your vices to the characters of *Dead Souls*, but isn't it clear that you are all too inexperienced in Christian life? . . . In the whole of your book you haven't said anything degrading about yourself—and everyone saw in it not humility but pride, which in fact it is: concealed pride, hidden even from yourself under an assumed cloak of humility. You *think* you are humble, but you are proud. I notice no heartfelt love in your book. . . . As for your advice,' Pogodin goes on in another letter, 'it shows an utter ignorance of the circumstances about which you presume to teach. . . . Everyone is most of all confounded by your incessant desire to play the part of an apostle, to lecture, whereas a real Christian usually begins with himself. . . . Everyone', he declared, remembering no doubt Gogol's 'axiom' about the stupidities of the Russian ruling class, 'is disgusted with you for wishing to curry favour with the aristocracy, for whom you show quite an extraordinary partiality; you see merit in mediocrity and, generally, all you do is flatter them, while all the evil lies there. . . . Renounce your reason,' he advised Gogol, 'it is taking you goodness only knows where.' But Pogodin knew perfectly well that, however just his criticism, Gogol would pay no attention to it. He therefore reserved to the last a letter he had received from Bishop Innokenty, who had blessed Gogol with an icon before he left for abroad. 'Incidentally,' he writes, 'I'd better copy out a letter I received from Innokenty in reply to my question about your book. I wanted to know his opinion as one who is outside your high society circles.' And what Innokenty said must really have distressed Gogol. 'Tell him', the bishop wrote, 'that I remember, love and respect him as before, that I am glad of the change in him, but that I would only like to ask him not to parade his piety: it loves the inner room. Still, I shouldn't like him to lapse into complete silence. His voice is needed, especially by our youth, but if he is immoderate they'll only laugh at him, and whatever he says will be wasted.'

Gogol at first intended to publish 'a little book' in which, as he wrote to Pletnyov on the 10th of June 1847, he would reply to the criticisms of his *Selected Passages* and explain how he had come to write it. This 'little book' was published posthumously by Shevyryov, who also gave it its title—*An Author's Confession*. Gogol began writing it in May 1847, and completed it before the end of the year. His chief argument was that the ideas he expressed in the *Selected Passages* had evolved naturally out of the ideas that had inspired *The Government Inspector* and the first part of *Dead Souls*. But to make this argument convincing he had to commit himself to statements that were demonstrably untrue. That was, no doubt, why he decided not to publish his 'confession' and contented himself with his replies to the various critics of his book. In his reply to Pogodin (on the 8th of July 1847), however, the only criticism Gogol took up was his alleged partiality for the aristocracy. He had made friends among the aristocracy, he wrote, not out of snobbery, but simply because he had met kind and loving hearts among them. The rest of the letter is one longwinded justification of his quarrel with Pogodin, for which, of course, he put the entire blame on the luckless professor. He did, however, ask Pogodin to forgive him for his attack in the *Selected Passages*. 'It was written', he explained, 'at a time when I was educating myself with rebukes, demanded rebukes from everyone and dealt out rebukes to everyone. I'm afraid I forgot that what was permissible in letters between friends must not be paraded in public, at least not without first making it absolutely clear in what spirit it should be taken.' He resented most of all Pogodin's advice to renounce his reason. 'My reason', he wrote, 'advised me to get on with my work . . . and not to publish anything before I reached the point where nothing in my writings would lead anyone into temptation. My reason told me to be secretive, to put up with everything and to answer no questions about what I was doing. But I did not listen to my reason, and the fruit of my disobedience was my last book. . . .'

On the 8th of July 1847 Gogol replied, as was to be expected, at much greater length to Bishop Innokenty's criticisms of his book. He now claimed that he had published it to enable him to take a look at himself 'as though in a mirror'. If he had not been in such a hurry to publish it, he would have destroyed it and so deprived himself of the opportunity of looking at himself in a mirror, which it was obviously God's wish that he should. He had no desire 'to parade his piety'. All he had wanted was to acquaint the world with some of his 'experiments' in 'spiritual education', but it all turned out 'so awkward and strange' that he was not surprised at 'the storm of misunderstandings' his book had aroused. Indeed, what had struck some people as 'arrogant pride' was merely 'childishness and the immaturity of youth' (Gogol was thirty-eight at the time of the publication of the *Selected Passages*). Besides, while writing it he could not find a father confessor who might have put him right on many things. 'My nature', he went on, 'is in many ways unlike other people's. I have always been secretive and I have yet to meet a man who is "a seer of the soul", for my works are so closely connected with my soul that no ordinary man would be able to understand them even if I could explain myself better. . . .'

Such a 'seer of the soul' Gogol found in Matvey Konstantinovsky, a Rzhev priest whom Count Alexander Tolstoy regarded as the final arbiter in religious matters. Father Matthew, a short stooping man with long fair hair, grey expressionless eyes and a big flat nose, was as great a fanatic as Count Tolstoy. He differed from Gogol's religious friends, however, in that he possessed a strong, domineering, masculine personality combined with a primitive and coarse mind, a combination that Gogol was completely unable to resist. Hell and damnation were his stock-in-trade, and since he regarded art as a sin against the Holy Ghost, all his efforts were directed towards compelling Gogol to renounce literature and enter a monastery. In this he did not succeed; but the struggle cost Gogol his life.

It was Gogol who started this disastrous relationship. He had asked Pletnyov to send two copies of his *Selected Passages* to Father Matthew, expecting, no doubt, to be highly commended for his book. He also wrote a letter to the priest in February 1847, in which he asked him to be absolutely frank in his criticisms. But Father Matthew's first communication to Gogol already revealed the points of difference between them. For the priest objected very strongly to Gogol's defence of the theatre and, characteristically, Gogol dared not defend his views against him as he did against Count Tolstoy. 'I did not write my article on the theatre', Gogol wrote to Father Matthew on the 9th of May 1847, 'in order to make people conceive a liking for it, but in order to keep them away from the corrupt side of the theatre, from all sorts of ballet dancers and the large number of plays which have been recently translated from the French. I wished to put them off that sort of thing by drawing their attention to better plays, but expressed it all in such an absurd and inexact way that I made you think that I was sending people to the theatre and not to the church.' But the priest was also offended by Gogol's 'refractory and arrogant' spirit, and in reply to that accusation from a man whose refractoriness and blind arrogance knew no limits, Gogol had meekly to confess that it was all due to the insufficiency of his spiritual education. As for Father Matthew's view that his book might be harmful, Gogol refused to believe it. 'Why should God punish me so dreadfully?' he wrote. But it also occurred to Gogol that the priest's fury might be due to his fear of his (Gogol's) influence on Alexander Tolstoy, and he therefore thought it necessary to assure Father Matthew that he had not seen the Count for a long time and that even when he lived with the Count he had never discussed his *Selected Passages* with him (which is patently untrue, but Gogol had to say something to avert the priest's wrath from himself). He concluded by begging Father

Matthew to pray for him and promised that Alexander Tolstoy, who longed to see him 'as a bird in a cage longs for its freedom', and whom he [Gogol] hoped to see in Paris before his departure for Russia, would tell the priest everything he himself could not put in his letter.

Gogol was also deeply hurt by Belinsky's review of his *Selected Passages* in the February number of the *Contemporary*, now owned by Nekrasov. Belinsky had, of course, to be very careful what he wrote about it. 'Nature', he said about this review, 'meant me to bark like a dog and howl like a jackal, but circumstances force me to miaow like a cat and wave my tail like a fox.' It was not, therefore, what Belinsky said so much as the derisively humorous way in which he dismissed the book that annoyed Gogol. 'I have read with sorrow your article about me in the *Contemporary*', Gogol wrote to Belinsky on the 20th of June 1847. 'I was grieved not because of your wish to humiliate me before the whole world, but because in your article I could hear the voice of a man who was angry with me. . . . For I cannot help being distressed (I say this in all sincerity) when even a spiteful man—and I considered you a kindly man—nurses a personal resentment against me.'

Belinsky, then in the last stages of consumption, was undergoing a cure at Salzbrunn. Not knowing his address, Gogol sent his letter to Prokopovich with a request to forward it to Belinsky. 'When I began reading Gogol's letter aloud,' Annenkov, who together with Ivan Turgenev was looking after Belinsky, writes in his *Marvellous Decade*, 'Belinsky listened to it quite apathetically and absent-mindedly, but after reading over the passage in which Gogol had addressed him personally he flushed and said, "Oh, he doesn't understand why people are angry with him, does he? I'll have to explain it to him. I'll write a reply to him." He understood Gogol's challenge', Annenkov adds.

Belinsky's famous letter to Gogol became one of the most powerful political manifestos against the Tsarist régime and it was certainly ironic that Gogol should have been responsible for it.

'You are only partly right,' Belinsky wrote, 'to see in my review an *angry* man: this epithet, however, is too weak to describe the state to which the reading of your book has reduced me.' He went on to point out that even people who were of the same opinion as Gogol had condemned his book, which was not surprising, for Gogol knew Russia only as an artist and not as a thinker 'whose part you have so unsuccessfully assumed in your fantastic book'. Gogol was used to looking at Russia from his 'beautiful afar' where he lived immersed in himself, with people of the same opinions as he, who were too weak to resist his influence. Russia saw her salvation not in mysticism, asceticism or pietism, Belinsky went on, but in the success of civilization, enlightenment and humanity. She did not want sermons ('she has heard enough of them!'), nor prayers ('she has uttered enough of them!'); what she wanted was the awakening in her people of a feeling of human dignity, what she wanted was rights and laws which conformed not to the teaching of the church, but to common sense and justice. Instead, she presented the terrible spectacle of a country where people traded in people, a 'country where there are no provisions for the safeguarding of a man's personal rights, honour or property, a country which does not even have a decent police force, but is composed entirely of huge bands of official thieves and robbers'. The most vital national problems of Russia, Belinsky contended, were concerned with the abolition of serfdom and corporal punishment and with the strict observance at least of those laws which were already in existence. 'And', he went on, 'at just such a time a great writer, who by his wonderful works of art has so powerfully assisted in Russia's self-realization and enabled her to look at herself as in a mirror, comes out with a book in which he teaches the barbarian landowner, in the name of Christ and the Church, to make more money out of his peasants! . . . If you were really filled to overflowing with Christ's truth and not with the devil's teachings', Belinsky wrote, 'you would have written to your landowner that his peasants are his brothers in Christ and, as a brother cannot be the slave of his brother, he has either to give him his freedom, or at least to make use of his labours to his own advantage. . . .' Such a book, Belinsky declared, could not be the result of a difficult inner process. 'You are either ill, in which case you'd better consult your doctors or—I dare not finish the sentence. Preacher of the lash,' Belinsky went on, 'apostle of ignorance, champion of obscurantism, panegyrist of Tartar customs—what are you doing? Look under your feet—you are standing at the edge of a precipice! That you are justifying such teaching by the teaching of the Greek Orthodox Church —that I can understand, for the Greek Orthodox Church has always been the supporter of the lash and the tool of despotism, but why did you have to drag in Christ? . . .' He went on to claim that by its nature the Russian people was 'profoundly atheistic'. As for Gogol's 'dithyramb' about the love of the Russian people for its royal house, it merely lowered him in the estimation of many people who shared his views. 'The hymns to the authorities', he remarked, hinting at Gogol's grant from the Tsar, 'are profitable to a pious author. . . .' Gogol's conversion might be sincere, but his idea of acquainting the Russian public with it was unfortunate. 'The times of simple piety', Belinsky wrote, 'have long passed for our society, too. It realizes already that it makes no difference where a man says his prayers, and that people who look for Christ in Jerusalem have never borne Him in their breasts or have lost Him. He who is capable of suffering at the sight of the sufferings of other people and he who cannot abide the oppression of any people bears Christ in his breast, and he has no need to go to Jerusalem. The humility you preach is, in the first place, not new, and secondly, smacks of terrible pride and the most shameful degradation of human dignity. . . . Your book does not convey true Christian teaching, but a morbid fear of death, hell and the devil. . . .' His last word to Gogol was: 'If you had the misfortune to renounce your great works with proud humility, you ought now to renounce your last book with sincere humility and expiate the grievous sin of its publication by new works which would remind us of your earlier ones.'

This time Gogol had got more than he asked for: Belinsky's letter made him very angry and he dashed off a furious and, at times, incoherent reply to him. Then he tore it up (the admissions he made in it were, in fact, politically dangerous), but kept the torn pieces, which were later pasted together by P. A. Kulish, his first biographer. How furious Gogol was can be gathered from his references to Belinsky as one who had not even finished his university course (Belinsky was expelled from Moscow University for writing a play in which he exposed the evils of serfdom) and who had never read 'the great works', i.e. the religious tracts Gogol had been avidly reading during the last few years, but 'a few modern brochures, written by over-excited people, which lead one astray from the right path'. Anger, Gogol declared, had clouded Belinsky's eyes and prevented him from seeing things in their true perspective. It was Belinsky and not he (Gogol) who was standing at the edge of a precipice. It was Belinsky who had crudely misinterpreted his book and his intentions, though, Gogol admitted, here and there flashes of truth did appear in Belinsky's letter from 'the enormous heap of sophisms and thoughtless enthusiasms of youth (Belinksy was thirty-six at the time and he died shortly afterwards). May the Lord', Gogol added piously, though not without a touch of malice, 'restore peace to your suffering and tormented soul!'

It is obvious that none of Belinsky's arguments, especially those dealing with the Emperor, the church and the position of the serfs, could have made any impression on Gogol. 'You characterized the words I addressed to the Emperor as a lie,' Gogol wrote, 'but I only reminded him of the sanctity of his position and of his exalted duties. . . . Who knows,' Gogol went on, using his favourite qualifying words with which he began all his unrealistic arguments and then conveniently forgot, 'perhaps it will occur to the Emperor to spend all his leisure time modestly and in solitude, far from his corrupting court. . . . And then everything will turn out well. Everyone will decide to abandon his mad way of life. The landowners will go back to their estates and busy themselves with their affairs. The civil servants will realize that it is not necessary to be rich and stop stealing. And the ambitious man, seeing that important posts are not rewarded with high salaries, will leave the civil service. . . .' It was this fantastic notion, therefore, that was at the back of Gogol's mind when he demanded that the Emperor should read the censored articles in his *Selected Passages*: he had really hoped that he could reform Nicholas I and in this way save Russia.

As for Belinsky's views of the church and the clergy, 'Who,' Gogol wrote, 'in your opinion, could interpret Christ's teachings better? Not, surely, our present-day communists and socialists who assert that He has commanded us to rob and take away the possessions of those who have made a fortune! . . . What made you think that I was singing the praises of our odious (as you call it) clergy? Not because I said that a priest of the Eastern Church must preach with deeds and not with words? Why this spirit of hatred? I have known many bad priests and I could tell you many amusing stories about them. But I have also met priests whose holiness of life and deeds I admired, and I saw that they were the creation of our Eastern and not the Western Church. So that I never thought of singing the praises of the priesthood which disgraced our church, but of the priesthood which exalted it. . . . And what am I to say to your remark that the Russian peasant is not religious? . . . What can one say when thousands of churches and monasteries speak eloquently about it? They have not been built by the donations of the rich, but by the poor man's mite. . . . No, Vissarion Grigoryevich, a man who has spent all his life writing articles in periodicals has no right to pass judgement upon the Russian people. . . . I have more right than you to speak about the Russian people, for at least it is unanimously agreed that my works show a knowledge of the nature of the Russian people, a fact which you confirmed yourself in your articles. And what can you show us as proof of your knowledge of human nature and the nature of the Russian people? . . .'

As for his defence of serfdom, Gogol merely repeated the argument used by its supporters, namely that all sorts of difficult problems had to be solved before the serfs could be freed, for one had to make sure that their 'freedom was not worse than slavery'. He did resent, however, Belinsky's calling him an 'apostle of ignorance'. Belinsky, he wrote, took his remark about literacy in its narrow, literal sense. 'I addressed those words', Gogol wrote, 'to a landowner whose peasants were tillers of the soil. . . . The idea I was putting forward in my book was that before educating the illiterates we must educate the literates. . . . The peasants are less corrupt than the whole of our literate population. . . .'

The one thing about which Gogol seemed to agree with Belinsky was that the Russian Government consisted of 'a gang of thieves', but, he contended, that was so because 'we are at daggers drawn with one another. . . . You say', he went on, 'that our salvation lies in European civilization, but you ought first to define what you mean by European civilization. There we have phalansteries and reds and all sorts of people who are ready to devour one another, and all their ideas are based on such destructive principles that every thinking man in Europe is scared to death and is asking himself involuntarily where is our civilization. European civilization has become a phantom which no one has yet seen, and if you try to get hold of it, it crumbles in your hands. And the same is true of progress. . . .' What, then, was Gogol's solution? 'The welfare of society', he told Belinsky, 'cannot be brought about either by disorders or by hot-heads. Society organizes itself.

Society is composed of single individuals and it is necessary that each individual should do his duty. Man should remember that he is not a beast, but a superior citizen of a superior heavenly citizenship. So long as he does not lead, in however small a way, the life of a heavenly citizen, his earthly citizenship will remain in a disordered state. . . .'

In conclusion, Gogol appealed to Belinsky to drop politics and return to literature. 'A man of letters', he wrote, 'exists for other things. He must serve art, which instils in the soul of the world the higher truths of reconciliation and not enmity, love for man and not bitterness and hatred. . . .'

But Gogol's anger was soon gone, and the letter he did write to Belinsky on the 10th of August 1847 was much more conciliatory in tone. 'I could not reply to your letter sooner', he wrote. 'I can honestly say that there was not a single sensitive feeling left in me that had not been deeply wounded even before I received your letter. . . . What can I say in reply to it? God knows, perhaps there is some truth even in what you have to say. I have received about fifty letters about my book, and every one of them is different, there are not two men who agree on the same subject. . . . So far it seems to me to be an undeniable truth that I don't know Russia at all, that many things have changed since I was there and that I shall have to study everything almost from the beginning. And the conclusion I have drawn from all this is that I must not publish anything until I return to Russia and see many things with my own eyes and feel them with my own hands. . . .' All the same, he thought that both Belinsky and he had carried their arguments too far. 'Just as I have overlooked many *modern* problems and many things that I should have taken into account,' he wrote, 'so have you overlooked others; just as I have *concentrated* too much upon myself, so have you *dispersed* yourself. Just as I have to learn a lot of what you know, so you have to learn even a small part of what I know and which you disregard. . . .'

In a letter to Annenkov on August the 12th, Gogol also assumed the sober tone of a man who had woken up after a nightmare. 'Having spent a long time upon my own inner education', he wrote, 'and, while engaged in this work, meeting one who knows the soul of man more than any of us [i.e. Christ], I quite naturally became for a time estranged from everything contemporary. As a result, there has now awakened in me the curiosity of a child and

I am eager to know what I did not know before. . . . There is neither irritation nor fanaticism in me. I cannot commit myself to anyone's side, for I see a grain of truth everywhere and a great deal of all sorts of exaggerations and lies. . . .'

Did Gogol honestly believe in his protestations? Did he really suffer a change of heart? There can be no doubt that he was not purposely deceiving either Belinsky or Annenkov. With a character so unstable as his these sudden confessions and regrets were inevitable after such a crisis. But neither can there be any doubt that he had not changed any of the views he expressed in his *Selected Passages*. 'My book', he wrote to Aksakov, before whom he felt no need for apologizing, on the 28th of August 1847, 'is the legitimate and correct result of my inner education. . . . Seeing that I would not be able to overcome the difficulties of my *Dead Souls* for some time, and being sincerely grieved about the lack of character and the absolute anarchy of our literature, I hastened to discuss the problems in which I was interested and which I preferred myself to develop or create in living images and characters. My rash and, according to you, *unfortunate* book was published. It covered me with disgrace, according to you. And, indeed, it was a disgrace for me, but I thank God for this disgrace and I thank Him for letting it appear in the world. For without it . . . I should not have realized many things I ought to know for my *Dead Souls*, and I should have known neither in what condition our society was, nor what images and characters it needed and what a creative artist had to select today for his subject.'

To Tolstoy he was more outspoken. Father Matthew's letter, he wrote to the Count on August the 14th, had 'a comfortingly calming' effect on him. 'An angelic soul can be felt in the lines of his letter.' And, characteristically, writing to Tolstoy a week later he expressed his annoyance at the Count's journey to England to consult a dentist. 'Forget your wretched teeth', he wrote, 'which would not be worth a farthing even if they were sound. The soul is better than teeth and anything else in the world.'

His work on the last two parts of *Dead Souls* acquired a still greater importance for Gogol after the failure of the *Selected Passages*. But here, too, he was tragically deceiving himself. The significant thing about the *Selected Passages*, as well as about all his voluminous correspondence of this period, is the total absence of humour. Humour was the corner-stone of his creative genius.

It acted as a stabilizing agent and prevented his sense of a personal 'mission' from destroying his art. Without humour, his touch with reality was severed. Without it, he got himself more and more entangled in a great lie.

¶ 7

Gogol kept putting off his pilgrimage to Jerusalem, the idea of which he believed to be divinely inspired, for five and a half years. All the time he was waiting for a further sign from heaven as an indication that the right time for the journey had arrived. 'I believe', he wrote to Zhukovsky on the 24th of November 1846 from Naples, 'that when the right time and hour come for me to embark, my desire [to leave for Palestine] will increase to such an extent that I shan't know myself how I get on deck or how I fly along like an insentient ship obedient to the sentient heavenly breezes.' But when he wrote this letter he did not expect the cold blast that was so soon to overtake him from Russia. Even before he realized the extent of the failure of his book, indeed, at the first signs of the difficulties it had encountered with the censorship, he was already thinking of postponing his journey. 'Even my trip to Jerusalem,' he wrote to Pletnyov on the 4th of December 1846, 'which my heart longs for so ardently, I am unable to undertake as soon as I should like because of those impediments and delays. But in all this I recognize the will of heaven; I feel that all this takes place by the grace of God not without some excellent design. I must become more worthy of such a journey. I must grow more mature in spirit by that time.' But the unanimous condemnation of his book so affected his health that he had to postpone his pilgrimage for another six months. He went to stay at Ems with Zhukovsky, where he met Alexey Khomyakov and his wife Yekaterina, whom he greatly admired, and then left for Ostend, where he again met the Khomyakovs as well as the Vyelgorskys. He wanted to go to England with the Khomyakovs, but was afraid of the sea passage. 'In my opinion', he wrote to Annenkov on September the 7th, 'it is absolutely necessary to visit England, not just in order to have a look at London, but to live in England and then choose for the object of your study not only the class of the proletarians, which has become so fashionable an occupation nowadays, but all the classes of the population without distinction. In spite of the monstrous juxtaposition of extremes so contrary to one another that if any of us were to speak of both in one breath one would think that the speaker wished to serve both God and the devil—in spite of that, you occasionally find in England such a sensible fusion between the highest conception of *citizenship* and the original idea of the *patriarchal* system that many of your ideas and, particularly, your idea of what constitutes the modern system of society, will seem false to you.'

It was from Ostend that Gogol wrote to Annenkov (on September the 7th) about his wish to meet Alexander Herzen. 'People of all parties', he wrote, 'speak of him as of a most honourable man. . . . Give me an idea of the young Turgenev, too,' he went on, 'for I want to know what sort of man he is. I know him a little as a writer [from the first stories of *A Diary of a Sportsman*, published in the *Contemporary*]. His talent is quite *remarkable* and promises a great deal for the future.' Of the next generation of great Russian writers, Gogol had also mentioned Dostoevsky in a letter to Anna Vyelgorsky a year earlier. Dostoevsky's first novel, *Poor Folk*, was published in January, 1846, and in May of that year Gogol expressed the following penetrating opinion of its author, whose life was to become so unaccountably bound up with his own two years later (Dostoevsky was arrested and sentenced to hard labour in a Siberian prison for reading Belinsky's letter to Gogol at a political meeting in Petersburg): 'The author of *Poor Folk* shows talent, the choice of his subject says much for his spiritual qualities, but one can also see that he is still young. He is too verbose and too little concentrated in himself: everything in his novel would have been much more powerful and vivid if it had been more compressed.'

Gogol returned to Naples in November 1847, and began making all the necessary preparations for his journey to Jerusalem: he asked his mother to stay in Vassilevka while he was in the Holy Land and offer up prayers for him daily; he sent the same request for prayers to all his close friends together with the following prayer he had composed specially for the occasion:

'O God, receive his prayer and grant him strength to pray at the tomb of our Redeemer for his own flesh and blood, for all the people of our country, for the reconciliation of all who dwell in it and are rebellious and contentious in spirit, so that their hearts shall be filled with love and thy kingdom be affirmed in our land. And esteem him worthy, O Lord, to rise from the holy tomb with renewed strength and return to his work with zeal and courage for the benefit of his country, that all hearts may yearn to glorify thy holy name.'

But as the day of his departure drew nearer he became more and more worried about the success of his pilgrimage. 'Before', he wrote to Shevyryov from Naples on the 2nd of December 1847, 'I was at least deceived about myself. I thought that I was just a little better than I am. . . . Now I am thinking: wouldn't my arrival and worship be a sacrilege? For if my trip had pleased God, my desire to go would have been stronger and everything would have drawn me there and I should not have minded the difficulties of the journey. But my heart is indifferent and unfeeling, and the thought of the difficulties frightens me. . . .' He sent a hundred roubles to Father Matthew, half of it to be distributed among the poor, twenty-five roubles to pay for three church services for his safe return to Russia and twenty-five roubles to cover the postage of the letters he begged the priest to write to him. He sent another hundred roubles to his sister Olga, half of which was to be given to the poor, and the other half used to defray the expenses of church services for his safe return. What he really hoped for from his pilgrimage was that, as he wrote to Father Matthew a week before he left for Palestine on the 12th of January 1848, if by the grace of God he were imbued with an understanding of truth and a knowledge of man's duties on earth, the 'good' characters in his novel would become so attractive and his 'bad' characters so unattractive that his readers would 'involuntarily' try to imitate the first and dislike anything they could find in themselves of the others. But to be able to do that he had to become better himself. And yet, he knew that his self-love was so 'boundless' and his capacity for sacrificing his earthly desires for heavenly ones so feeble that he was appalled at his own pride, and wondered why God had not wiped him off the face of the earth. He even began to doubt his faith in God, which is not perhaps surprising, seeing how firmly he believed in the efficacy of prayer and how futile his own prayers had turned out to be.

'It even seems to me [he wrote to Father Matthew] that I have no faith in God at all; I acknowledge Christ to be man-God only because my reason, and not my faith, tells me so. I was amazed at His immense wisdom and felt with a certain awe that no ordinary man could possess it; I was amazed at His profound knowledge of the human soul, feeling that only its Creator could know it so thoroughly. That is all, but I have no faith. I want to believe. And in spite of all this, I dare to go now and worship at the Holy Sepulchre. And what is more, I want to pray for everyone and everything that exists in our motherland. Oh, pray for me that God should not strike me down for my unworthiness but make me worthy to pray for it all! Tell me why, instead of praying for forgiveness of all my former sins, I want to pray for the salvation of Russia, that peace should reign in her instead of confusion, and love instead of hatred? Why am I thinking of that instead of weeping over my own sins? Why, too, do I want to pray that God should give me strength to expiate my former bad works? Oh, pray for me, my dear, good soul! Pray that God should save me from temptation and reveal His true will to me. Pray, pray hard for me, and may God help you to pray for me. . . .'

Gogol's journey began unpropitiously. He had to go to Malta to join his steamer for Smyrna where he was to meet his old school friend Bazili, the Russian Consul-General, who was to accompany him to Jerusalem. He suffered from seasickness and arrived in Malta on the 22nd of January 1848 in a state of complete collapse. 'Against all expectation', he wrote to Count Alexander Tolstoy, 'Malta lacks all the comforts one associates with the English: the locks on the doors are defective, the furniture is of Homeric simplicity and the language is quite incomprehensible. One hears almost no English. . . .' The prospect of a four days' sea voyage to Smyrna made him rush off a letter to Shevyryov with an urgent request to 'order' two or three church services for his safe journey 'in such places and churches where you see priests who pray more zealously than others'. He had to wait a week in Malta for his boat, but seems to have made his passage to Smyrna without much discomfort. He travelled to Jerusalem by way of Sidon, Tyre, Acre and Nazareth. On the way across the desert, he suffered great discomfort and annoyed Bazili by his constant complaints. Occasionally he would lose patience and begin shouting at Bazili, who felt that his authority with the Arabs escorting them was being undermined by such high-handed treatment. He tried to appeal to Gogol to moderate his language, but in the end had to speak sharply to him. This both restored his authority with the Arab guards and kept Gogol quiet for the rest of the journey.

In Jerusalem, where he arrived on the 15th of February 1848, Gogol's worst fears were realized. 'At the tomb of our Lord', he wrote to Father Matthew on February the 28th from Jerusalem, 'I prayed as much as I could with all my heart, which does not know how to pray. My prayer consisted only of one weak expression of thanks to God for having sent you, my priceless friend, to me. I needed your letters very much: they made me take a closer look at myself and examine my actions more severely. Accept once more my thanks from this place sanctified by the steps of Him who brought us redemption. I shall be wonderfully glad to embrace you in person in July or August. Don't forget me in your prayers.' He wrote only five short letters from Jerusalem, which shows how great was his disappointment with the results of his pilgrimage. The longest letter he wrote to Zhukovsky. 'Oh,' he declared in this letter, also written on February the 28th, 'may God help us, you and me, to gather all our strength to accomplish the works we have cherished in the depths of our souls for the benefit of our country, and may He inspire us with the light of reason of His holy gospels! I am not staying long here, being in a hurry to return to Russia with my old school-fellow Bazili with whom I arrived here and who, being our Consul-General in Syria, manages our affairs in Jerusalem. So you can rest assured on my account. If it is not against God's will, we shall meet in Moscow and live near one another. . . .' Next day, on February the 29th, he wrote a letter home in which he told his mother and sisters rather grumpily that he had only prayed for himself, having commissioned others, who knew how to pray better than he, to pray for them. He hoped to be back in Russia in June or July, when he would 'perhaps' put in an appearance at Vassilevka. 'And you', he concluded his short note, 'do not cease praying for me as before. I am reminding you of this because now I feel more than ever the impotence of my own prayers.' On the same day he wrote also to Nadezhda Sheremetev, thanking her for her prayers and asking her to pray for his safe return to Russia. His last short letter from Jerusalem, written on March the 1st, the day of his departure, he addressed to Bazili's wife, informing her of their safe arrival and his pleasure at the prospect of seeing her and her children again shortly.

The only descriptions of Gogol's experiences in Palestine are to be found in two of his letters to Zhukovsky and in an account of his impressions of the Dead Sea related by Alexandra Smirnov's half-brother, Leo Arnoldi, in his reminiscences.

'I can scarcely believe that I have been in Jerusalem [Gogol wrote to Zhukovsky in his first letter from Beirut on April the 6th, a few hours before his departure for Constantinople]. And yet I was there all right; I fasted and received the Sacrament at the Holy Sepulchre. The liturgy was conducted at the gravestone itself. How striking it all was! You know already that the small cave in which the gravestone is placed is about the height of a man; you can enter it only by bending very low, and there is just room enough in it for three worshippers. It is entered by a small hall, a little round room almost of the same size, with a small table in the middle covered with a stone (on which sat the angel who announced the resurrection). This little hall has been converted into an altar. I stood alone in it; before me was only the priest conducting the service. The deacon who called the people to prayers was behind me, behind the wall of the sepulchre. I heard his voice only faintly. The voices of the people and of the choir who chanted the responses were even fainter. The combined singing of the Russian worshippers intoning "The Lord have mercy upon us" barely reached my ears, just as though it were coming from a different place. All this was so strange! I can't remember whether I prayed or not. I believe I was only glad to have found a place so suited for prayer and so conducive to prayer. But I had really no time to pray. So it now seems to me. The liturgy, I thought, was over so quickly that even the most winged prayers could not overtake it. I had scarcely time to come to myself when I found myself before the chalice carried out by the priest from the cave for administering the Sacrament to me, unworthy as I am. These are all my impressions from Jerusalem. . . .'

A much more detailed description of his impressions of Palestine is contained in Gogol's letter from Moscow on the 28th of February 1850 (O.S.), in reply to Zhukovsky's request for local colour for his poem *The Wandering Jew*.

'. . . My friend [Gogol wrote] you ask me to describe to you

Palestine with all its local colour. . . . Do you realize what a difficult task you have set me? What can I say that others have not said already? What colours, what features am I to depict when everything has already been told many times over and drawn again and again in all its smallest detail? And of what use are these poor descriptions when every event in the Scriptures already awakens in the mind of a Christian scenes which bring the *past* much closer than all the barren, dead prospects that can be seen today? What, for instance, can today convey the places along which lay the Redeemer's sorrowful way to the Cross, which are now all gathered under one roof of a church, so that the Holy Sepulchre, Gogotha, the place where the Redeemer was shown to the people by Pilate, the high-priest's house where he was taken, and the place where the life-giving Cross was discovered, are all now to be found in one and the same spot? What can all these places, which we are used to measure in long distances, do but lead the curious observer astray, unless, indeed, they had long before been graven on his heart and are constantly present in his mind's eye in the light of his blazing faith? What can the present view of Judea with its monotonous mountains, which look like endless grey waves of a storm-tossed sea, say to a poet-painter? All this, no doubt, was picturesque in the days of our Redeemer, when the whole of Judea was a garden and every Jew sat in the shade of the tree he had planted; but today when you very seldom see five or six olive trees growing on a mountainside, trees whose foliage is as grey and dusty as the rocks of the mountains themselves, with only a thin layer of moss and here and there bits of grass showing green along that bare and uneven expanse of rocks; when after some five or six hours' journey you catch sight of some Arab hut clinging precariously to a hill-side, a hut which is more like an earthenware pot, a small stove, or the lair of some animal than a human dwelling, how are you to recognize in such a country the land flowing with milk and honey? Imagine amid such a wasteland Jerusalem, Bethlehem and all the eastern towns, which look like some loosely piled-up heaps of bricks and stones; imagine the river Jordan, a thin stream amid a bare mountainous landscape, with only here and there a few little willow shrubs; imagine, too, amid such a wasteland, the Valley of Jehoshaphat at the foot of Jerusalem, with a few rocks and grottoes believed to be the tombs of the Kings of Judah. What can these places say to you, if in your mind's eye you do not see the star shining over Bethlehem, the dove descending over the river Jordan from the opened heavens, the fearful day of the death on the Cross within the walls of Jerusalem, with the city shrouded in darkness and shaken by an earthquake, or the bright Easter morn, compared with whose brilliance everything, past and present, seems plunged in darkness?

'. . . My journey to Palestine was really undertaken by me so that I should find out by myself and, as it were, see with my own eyes how *hardened* my heart was. My friend, this hardness is great indeed! I have been vouchsafed to spend a night at the tomb of our Redeemer, I have been vouchsafed to partake of the Holy Sacrament, which was placed on the tomb itself instead of an altar, and in spite of it all I have not become better, and yet all earthly things should have been consumed within me and only the heavenly remained. What can my dull impressions convey to you? I saw that land as though in a dream. On rising before daybreak, we mounted our mules and horses and set off accompanied by our unmounted and mounted guides; our long procession passed in single file across the small desert, along the wet shore or through shallow seas, so that on the one side the waves washed over the hoofs of the horses, and on the other there stretched the sandy beach or the whitish rocks of the foothills sparsely covered with low-growing shrubs; at midday we came to a well, a water reservoir paved with slabs of rock, with two or three sycamores or olive trees providing a shade over it. There we camped for half an hour, and then set off on our journey again until the evening when we caught sight of five or six palm trees on the horizon, no longer blue, but coppery red from the setting sun, and at the same time a little town dimly discernible through the opalescent haze. It looked picturesque from the distance, but squalid at close quarters, either Tyre or Sidon. And so up to Jerusalem. I can still see Jerusalem itself as though in a dream, from the Mount of Olives, the only place from which it seems large and magnificent: as one goes up the mountain the city appears clearly as though on a raised platform, the small houses look big, the little whitewashed humps on their flat roofs look like numberless cupolas and, sharply outlined against the extraordinarily blue sky by their whiteness, they, together with the minarets, present a sort of shimmering view. I remember seeing on the Mount of Olives the imprint of the foot of the Ascended, miraculously pressed into the hard stone as though in soft wax, so that one could see the slightest dent of an extraordinarily well-formed foot. I also remember the view suddenly disclosed amid the monotonous grey eminences on the way out of Jerusalem. Seeing nothing but hills and hills before me, I never expected to see anything else, when suddenly from the top of one hill, in the distance, in the blue light, I caught sight of a huge semicircle of mountains. Strange mountains: they looked like the sides of a huge soup-plate protruding at a sharp angle. The bottom of this plate was the Dead Sea. Its sides were of a bluish-red colour, and its bottom was bluish-green. I have never seen such strange mountains. They had no peaks, their tops merging in one straight line forming everywhere a gigantic shore rising to the same height above the sea. You could see neither declivities nor slopes on them; they all seemed to consist of a countless number of facets which glowed in all sorts of colours through the general bluish-red haze. This volcanic ridge—a piled-up heap of barren stones —shone with indescribable beauty in the distance. My sleepy soul has not carried away any other particularly striking views. Somewhere in Samaria I picked a wild flower, somewhere in Galilee another; in Nazareth, overtaken by rain, I spent two days, forgetful that I was in Nazareth, just as though I had been at a coach station in Russia. Everywhere and upon everything I could see only signs that all those now denuded countries, and Judea in particular (now the most barren one of all), had once indeed been lands flowing with milk and honey. All the mountains had terraces cut into them, the traces of the vineyards that had once been there, and even today all you have to do is to throw a handful of earth on those bare rocks for hundreds of plants and flowers to appear on them: how much moisture, necessary for vegetation, is contained in those barren rocks! But not one of the present inhabitants does anything, for regarding themselves as nomads, they just wander from place to place in this God-stricken country. Only in Jaffa did we see a small number of trees weighed down with fruits, and we could not help being amazed at their large size.'

It was Alexandra Smirnov who asked Gogol, during one of his visits to the hotel where she stayed in Moscow in 1849 (she was living in Kaluga at the time) to tell her and her half-brother Arnoldi something about his journey to Jerusalem. Gogol refused to enlarge on his experiences in Palestine. 'All I can tell you', he said, 'is that nature there is not at all like what we are used to seeing here; nevertheless, it strikes you by its breadth and grandeur. And the Dead Sea is marvellous! When we left it, Bazili made me promise not to look back before he told me to. For four hours we continued our journey from the shore. We seemed to be travelling along a flat plain, and yet we were imperceptibly rising higher and higher. I got tired and angry, but I did keep my word and did not once look back. At last Bazili stopped and told me to look back along the road which we had just travelled. I gasped with surprise! The plain, rising gradually, stretched for several miles. There was not a single tree or shrub to be seen. At the foot of the plain, or rather, mountain, I could see the Dead Sea, and beyond it straight ahead to the right and left again the wide plain, rising higher and higher on all sides. I can't tell you how beautiful the Dead Sea was at sunset. Its waters are not blue or green or azure, but violet. From that distance the irregularity of its shore could not be seen; it was perfectly oval and looked like a huge cup filled with a sort of violet liquid.'

Gogol's pilgrimage to Jerusalem was a failure. 'Never before', he wrote to Father Matthew on the 21st of April 1848 (O.S.), from Odessa, where he spent a fortnight in quarantine because of a cholera epidemic, 'have I been so little satisfied with the state of my heart as I was in Jerusalem and after Jerusalem.' His faith in the mercy of God was being overshadowed more and more by his fear of the devil. The dread of the Last Judgement, which he had experienced as a child, was coming back and gaining a firmer hold on him. Hence his growing dependence on the fanatical Father Matthew. But he never gave up the struggle. He went on writing *Dead Souls* and he went on fighting against Father Matthew's obscurantist views on literature. But it was an unequal fight, and he succumbed in the end.

¶ 8

The revolution of 1848 and the growing revolutionary movement in Rome, which made Gogol choose Naples for his residence during his last years in Italy, made no impression on his faith in the ultimate reformation of man in accordance with the views he was going to promulgate in the last two parts of *Dead Souls*. 'What does it matter to us', he wrote to Zhukovsky on the 15th of June 1848 (O.S.), 'whether our words have any influence or not or whether people listen to us or not? The important thing is that we should remain true to our ideal of beauty to the end of our days and that we should incessantly sing a hymn to it even at the moment when the world is toppling over and everything on earth is being destroyed. To die with a song on his lips is perhaps as inescapable a duty for a poet as to die with his weapons in his hands is for a soldier.' Nor did Gogol approve of the growing reactionary movement in Russia. A year later, after the arrest of Dostoevsky and his friends, to which he refers cautiously in the second part of *Dead Souls*, he wrote to Bazili from Moscow: 'Today one has to be very careful and intelligent even to say what is not very intelligent. We live in mad and disorderly times. I keep touching my head to make sure I haven't gone mad. The things that are being done are enough to make your head swim, especially when you see how the lawful authorities are doing their best to harm themselves and undermine their own position. Discords and differences of opinion are the order of the day. Only the preachers of destruction are united. Wherever it is a question of construction and organization there is dissension, indecision and precipitancy. And they have still not realized', he concludes ingenuously, 'that all they have to do is to call upon Him who alone is the builder of order.'

But if Gogol's fundamental outlook on life had not changed, the change his family found in him was staggering. 'How he has changed!' his sister Yelisaveta wrote in her diary on the 9th of May 1848 (O.S.), his name-day and the day on which he arrived in Vassilevka from Odessa. 'He has become so serious; nothing seems to cheer him up, and he is so cold and indifferent to us!' He spent his first morning at home shut up in his tiny study with its two icons over the bed and bureau. 'All morning', Yelisaveta records, 'we did not see our brother. How sad it is: we have not seen him for six years and he doesn't want to be with us.' On the following day they invited the peasants of the village to celebrate their master's return. There was dancing in the yard and everyone got drunk. That was too much for Gogol and next day he left for Poltava. He returned after a week, but was still 'cold and serious' and 'smiled very rarely'. Gogol was distressed by the disastrous state of affairs at home and his displeasure was increased by the appearance of a hawker whom his mother owed two hundred roubles for all sorts of trinkets she could never resist. He promptly gave the hawker all the money he possessed on condition that he never sold anything to his mother on credit again and left for Kiev, where he stayed with Alexander Danilevsky, who had got married in the meantime. He returned to Vassilevka a week later (on June the 3rd) and stayed there till August the 24th. He did some gardening, planted oak trees, made some designs for rugs, and tried to resume his work on *Dead Souls*.

'The thought of my work', he wrote to Nadezhda Sheremetev on May the 16th, 'does not leave me for a moment. I want to finish it as much as I did before, so that it shall have a good influence and so that many people shall come to their senses and turn to what ought to be eternal and immutable.' Five days after his return from Kiev he wrote to Pletnyov: 'I tried to resume writing, but either the heat tires me or I am still not ready for it. And yet I can't help feeling that the work which has been the subject of my thoughts for such a long time is more necessary now than ever before.' If, he wrote to Anna Vyelgorsky on June the 15th, he could, amid the shocking confusion of the times, manage to hold on to his peaceful literary profession and be a singer of peace in the midst of warfare, it would be a real miracle for which he dared not hope, but for which he still wished to pray. A fortnight later he fell ill. 'I am writing to you after having barely recovered from a debilitating attack of diarrhoea, which in three days has left me only a shadow of myself', he wrote to Pletnyov on the 7th of July 1848 (O.S.). 'Cholera is everywhere around here and I don't think it has ever spread so quickly before. . . . I am penniless. Please, send me some money, one hundred and fifty roubles will do. No one has any money around here, beginning with my family, who expect me to help them. We are threatened with a general famine. The harvest has not begun yet. Everything is burnt up and the peasants are not cutting the corn but tearing up single ears. . . .' Gogol had been out in the fields with his sister Olga and he watched the peasant women tearing the ears of corn out of the hard, burnt ground. But when they began complaining to him about the hard times, all he said was: 'It's a good thing you are suffering so much now, you'll be rewarded for it in the Kingdom of Heaven.'

Gogol left Vassilevka for Moscow on August the 24th. Two
days earlier Yelisaveta wrote in her diary: 'Today our brother
wanted to leave for Moscow, but thank God he has put it off till
Monday. Yesterday we all cried. We felt terribly depressed. I love
him very much, though he is very often horrid to us.' On August
the 24th she wrote: 'We got up very early. It is such a sad day:
our brother is leaving. I went to his room and helped him to pack.
At eight o'clock we went to church for Mass. We travelled to
Sorochintsy in two carriages: half the way Annette with my
brother, and the other half myself with him. In Sorochintsy I
begged him to stay till the next day. I got up early and went to see
him. He embraced me and kissed me affectionately. At nine
o'clock we took leave of him. He left with Danilevsky for his village and from there for Moscow. We all cried. . . .'

After a few days in Moscow, where he arrived on September
the 12th, Gogol left for Petersburg. There, at the house of a
friend of Prokopovich's, he arranged a meeting with a few young
writers, including Goncharov, Grigorovich and Nekrasov, chiefly
it would seem, in order to counteract the lamentable impression
created by his *Selected Passages*. According to Panayev, who was
present at this meeting, Gogol gave them to understand that his
unfortunate book had been written at a time when he was ill and
that he was sorry he had ever published it.

In Petersburg, Gogol saw a great deal of his twenty-five-year-
old friend Anna Vyelgorsky, to whom he made a proposal of
marriage two years later. On his return to Moscow he wrote her
a long letter (on the 29th of October 1848 (O.S.)) in which he
tried to convert her to his idea of a spiritual life which he and she
could share.

'About your health [he wrote], these are my instructions to
you: for God's sake do not remain sitting in the same place for
more than half an hour; do not bend over the table: your chest is
weak, you ought to know that. Try to go to bed not later than
eleven o'clock. Give up dancing altogether, especially wild
dances: they excite your blood but do not provide any of the
correct movements which the body requires. Besides [he added,
not realizing perhaps how much his words would hurt her],
dancing does not become you: your figure is not so light and
supple. You are not beautiful. Didn't you know that? You are
only beautiful when your face expresses some noble feeling; the

features of your face seem to be so arranged that they can only express spiritual nobility; as soon as you lose that expression you look ugly. Give up making social calls altogether. You can see society has not given you anything. You were looking for a kindred spirit in it, you thought of finding a man with whom you could go hand in hand through life, but all you found was pettiness and vulgarity. Give it up altogether. There are nasty things in society which cling to you like burs, however careful you may be. Something of it has already stuck to you; what it is I shan't tell you at present. God save you, too, from any hypocritical exchanges of social courtesies. Try to preserve the simplicity of a child—that is best of all.'

He went on to make several more laudable suggestions to her, such as that she should speak only to people from whom she could learn something useful, question Vladimir Dahl about the life of the peasants and Pletnyov about the Russian writers he knew, and talk to Alexandra Smirnov about Russia. In short, she should have dealings only with people who did not know society or whom society did not know.

Anna, Gogol thought, was capable of the kind of 'pure love' he saw in the 'spiritual' marriage of Count Alexander Tolstoy and his sanctimonious wife, who had forsworn the delights of the flesh. That was why Gogol proposed to her: the letters he wrote to her during 1849 make that abundantly clear. 'All I can tell you', he wrote to her on the 16th of April 1849 (O.S.), 'is that I am becoming more and more convinced that in this life we must not work for ourselves but for God. . . . Let us do all we can that our work shall be directed to the glorification of His name and that our whole life may be one incessant song of praise to Him. You like to draw—well, draw everything that can serve for the embellishment of God's temple and not of your rooms.'

Anna quite unconsciously encouraged Gogol in his belief in a 'spiritual' marriage. 'You, dear Nikolai Vassilyevich,' she wrote to him, 'have an aim in life which satisfies you entirely and occupies all your time. But what aim am I to choose?' But even she must have been surprised, if not shocked, by Gogol's proposal, which he forwarded through her brother-in-law, Alexey Venevitinov. Her parents, the Count and the Countess Vyelgorsky, were not only surprised by it: they could not understand how such a queer idea could have entered the head of a man of such intelligence, the idea, that is, that a man of such humble origin as Gogol should dream of marrying a high-born girl like their daughter. Gogol himself had so exaggerated his influence on Anna and was so obsessed with his idea of a spiritual marriage that the refusal came as a bitter blow to him.

'I feel I have to write to you at least a part of my confession [he wrote to her from Moscow in his last letter in the spring of 1850]. My spirit is crushed, and my condition is so painful, so painful that I cannot put it into words. It was even more painful because there was no one I could explain it to, no one I could ask for advice or sympathy. I could not confide it to my closest friend, for my relations with your family were involved in it, and everything that has any connexion with your family [he added, thinking no doubt of her brother Joseph he had nursed in his last illness in Rome] is sacred to me. You would be committing a sin if you continued to be angry with me for having surrounded you with clouds of misunderstanding. There was something strange about the whole thing, and I can't explain to you how it all happened. I think it happened because we don't know each other well enough and look upon many *very important* things lightly, at least more lightly than we ought to. You would have got to know me better if we had happened to live together somewhere, not idly, but engaged in some work. Why shouldn't you go to live on your estate near Moscow? You haven't seen your peasants for over twenty years. You don't think this matters, do you? Our peasants feed us, and we haven't any time to see them even once in twenty years! . . . We could have managed the estate together and looked after the peasants and cared for them and not for ourselves. . . . And if each of us had prayed ardently to God that He should help us to do our duty, our relationship would quite likely have become in a short time what it ought to be. Then both you and I would have realized quite clearly *what* I should be in relation to you. For [he added with despairing naïvety] I must be something to you: it is not for nothing that God brings people together in such an unusual way. Perhaps, so far as you are concerned, I ought to be like a faithful dog whose duty it is to guard his master's property. So, please, don't be angry. You see that though our relations have become difficult for a time because of some temporary resentment, they are not for all that such as to make you regard me as a stranger from whom you have to hide even what your offended heart would like to express in a moment of distress. May God protect you. Good-bye. Yours to the grave, N. Gogol.'

Gogol's plea was not answered. Anna subsequently married Prince Shakhovskoy. She survived Gogol by nine years, dying in 1861 at the age of thirty-eight.

¶ 9

On his return to Moscow on the 14th of October 1848 (O.S.), Gogol at first lived with Pogodin, with whom he had patched up his quarrel. On his birthday, November the 11th, Pogodin gave a party 'in Gogol's honour', to which he invited all the prominent personalities in Moscow. It was a very formal affair and all the guests wore white tie and tails. Pogodin and Shevyryov were very unpopular at the time. They were accused of having informed against the Russian Historical Society for publishing a translation of Giles Fletcher's *Of the Russe Common Wealth: or, Manner of Government by the Russe Emperour (commonly called the Emperour of Moscouia) with the Manners and Fashions of the People of that Countrey*, published in London in 1591. Queen Elizabeth suppressed the book by her former ambassador to Russia at the instigation of the London merchants, who feared lest their trade with Russia should be ruined because of Fletcher's irreverent references to Tsar Fyodor Ioannovich; Nicholas I, at the instigation of his two loyal historians Pogodin and Shevyryov, all but suppressed the Russian Historical Society and dismissed Professor Bodyansky from his post as secretary of the Society and from his Chair of Slavonic Languages at Moscow University for publishing the book two hundred and fifty years later. By giving the party, Pogodin wished to test the attitude of the Moscow literary world towards him. 'On November the 11th', Aksakov wrote to his son Ivan, 'Pogodin gave a party to which he invited everyone he could think of, particularly the decent people who had called him a scoundrel in public. Of all the decent people who understood Pogodin's intentions only one acted in accordance with his convictions: Samarin [a critic belonging to the

Slavophil camp and a great admirer of Alexandra Smirnov] sent him a note in which he declared that in view of the accusations made against him, he could not accept his invitation. . . . All honour to him! The rest came thronging into Pogodin's drawing-room like sheep. There were more than fifty of them! Pogodin could with a clear conscience say triumphantly to Gogol: "Here they all are, the people who call me a scoundrel! Even the sick have dragged themselves to my party from the remotest parts of Moscow!" It's horrible and disgusting!' Aksakov concludes. But Gogol did not seem to be impressed by Pogodin's triumph. 'Gogol', Pogodin noted in his diary, 'ruined my party. What a nuisance the man is!' Pogodin's real attitude towards Gogol can best be judged perhaps from the following entry in his diary on the 4th of May 1849, made after he had read some of his own stories to Gogol: 'Gogol listened carefully, but never uttered a word. Can it be that he feels vexed to be losing his pre-eminence as a writer? I shouldn't be surprised!'

By the end of December 1848 Gogol seems to have had enough of Pogodin (though as in former years he celebrated his fortieth name-day on the 9th of May 1849, by a party in Pogodin's garden), and he went to live with Alexander Tolstoy in his palatial house surrounded by a high stone wall. Gogol occupied two rooms on the ground floor, one of which—his study—was very large and comfortably furnished with two sofas, two tables, armchairs, a tall bureau at which Gogol, as usual, worked standing, and a large green carpet covering the whole of the floor. The stove against the wall opposite the entrance door was concealed by a green taffeta screen.

His work on the second part of *Dead Souls* was proceeding very slowly. He had to drag out each word as though with pincers, he complained to Professor Bodyansky. On the 24th of May 1849 (O.S.), he wrote to Pletnyov: 'I have worked myself up into such a state of irritation and excitement that no medical remedies and comforts have any effect upon me. I am again a prey to melancholy and hypochondria. . . .'

Fortunately, Alexandra Smirnov arrived in Moscow on June the 25th for a short visit and Gogol cheered up again. Alexandra and her half-brother Arnoldi visited Gogol on June the 27th and found his study in disorder. Gogol was reading an ancient treatise on botany. While he was talking to Alexandra, Arnoldi glanced

286

into a manuscript on one of the tables. He had only time to read the words 'Governor-General' when Gogol pounced upon him and took away his manuscript of *Dead Souls*.

Alexandra Smirnov soon left for Kaluga and on the 5th of July 1849 (O.S.), Gogol and Arnoldi followed her. Gogol travelled in Arnoldi's open carriage with his small suitcase and large briefcase containing the manuscript of *Dead Souls*, which he never let out of his sight, putting it beside him in the carriage and taking it with him into the inns they stopped at on the way. They left Moscow at five o'clock in the afternoon. Gogol was in an excellent mood. He continually took off his grey felt hat to mop his brow, divested himself of his green cloak, and was not even annoyed when next morning the axle of their carriage broke at the approach to Malo-Yaroslavets. There Arnoldi introduced him to a mayor of some district town, who happened to have stopped at the same inn. Gogol questioned him for a long time about the affairs of his town. He continued his researches into Russian provincial life during lunch at the inn, questioning the waiter minutely about his parents, his wages, the frequenters of the inn, the dishes they liked best, the sort of vodka the civil servants of the town drank, what their mayor was like, and so on. He seemed to be very satisfied with the waiter's replies and was in the same excellent mood for the rest of the journey, stopping the carriage and rushing into a field to pick some flower and telling Arnoldi to what genus it belonged, what its Latin name was, what the peasants called it, and what medicinal properties it possessed. Then he thrust it in front of him behind the coachman's box and five minutes later again stopped the carriage to pick another flower. Soon he had a whole bouquet of yellow, mauve and pink flowers.

At last they arrived at Smirnov's country house, where Gogol spent four days watching the haymakers and admiring the national dresses of the peasant women, visiting neighbouring villages, and in the evenings reading Zhukovsky's translation of the *Odyssey* to Alexandra Smirnov and her country guests. On the fifth day they all left for Kaluga, where he spent about a fortnight in the Governor's country residence. Gogol was given a room in a separate wing of the house. He loved the view from his windows, especially the pine forest and the river on whose steep bank the house was built.

In the morning he locked himself up in his room and worked

on his novel. Sometimes he would read a chapter or two from it
to Alexandra Smirnov, usually between twelve and two o'clock.
On one occasion Arnoldi was present at the reading. Gogol came
down only for dinner at three o'clock. On Sundays he appeared
in a pair of bright yellow nankeen trousers, a short, light-blue
waistcoat with gold buttons and a gold chain stretched across it,
and a dark-blue dress-coat with large gold buttons. He used to
say that everything ought to be different on a Sunday or a holy
day: the cream in the coffee must be extra thick, the dinner must
be extra good, and 'the expression of the faces must be specially
solemn'.

At table he made a point of talking to the invited officials and
was very polite to them. In the afternoons he liked to play with
Alexandra Smirnov's children: he used to paint posters for them
and go walking, fishing and mushroom-gathering with them. One
day he 'invented' a moon for them: he took out the bottom of a
round box, pasted paper over it, smeared it with oil and glued the
end of a candle inside it.

Gogol returned to Moscow on July the 29th. At the beginning
of August he read the first chapter of the second part of *Dead
Souls* at Shevyryov's and Aksakov's country houses near Moscow.
By that time all the eleven chapters had been drafted, but Gogol
thought that it would take him another year to get them ready for
publication. At the end of August Arnoldi met Gogol again at a
dinner party given by the civil governor of Moscow, Ivan Kapnist, the son of the playwright and one of Gogol's oldest friends.
This is the description Arnoldi gives in his reminiscences of the
attitude of the Russian high officials to Gogol:

'Dinner was served in a marquee in the grounds of the house.
Gogol was late and came into the marquee when all the guests had
already taken their places at the table. He was made to sit down
between two ladies, his great admirers. After dinner the gentlemen, as usual, sat down to play cards and the young people scat-
tered over the grounds. A group of people gathered round Gogol;
but he was silent, and, sprawling casually in a large armchair,
amused himself by picking his teeth. I sat at a table where three
senators and an army general were playing cards. One of the
senators, who wore an army uniform, kept casting indignant
glances at Gogol. "I can't bear to see that man", he said, addressing a fellow-senator in a frock-coat. "Look at him! What airs he

gives himself and how they all run after him! What attitudinizing, what *aplomb*!" And the four of them looked at Gogol with contempt and shrugged their shoulders. "Why," the senator in the army uniform resumed, "he is a real revolutionary. I am surprised he is received in decent houses. When I was a governor and his plays were performed at the theatre all the people in the stalls used to turn round and look at the Governor's box at every stupid joke and jeering remark against the authorities. I didn't know where to hide myself and at last I could not stand it any longer and banned his play. No one in my province dared even to think of *The Government Inspector* or of any of his other works. I have never been able to understand why the government lets him off scot-free: I'd have made it hot for him for his *Dead Souls,* and especially for his *Government Inspector*." The worthy senator's partners were entirely in agreement with him and only added: "Yes, he certainly is a dangerous man. We've known it for a long time."'

In September Gogol made a half-hearted attempt to gather material for his novel at first hand by undertaking a journey across several provinces of Central Russia. But, of course, what he wanted was *illumination* and not *facts*. Facts, which were indispensable to him when his creative powers were at their height, were a nuisance to him now: for they played havoc with his whole conception of his novel as a medium of salvation, but that he would not admit. His lame excuse for abandoning his journey was that unless he first gathered 'all sorts of information' he might travel all across Russia and, 'like the government inspectors', learn nothing. That was, at any rate, the excuse he gave to Sophia Sollogub in his letter of the 20th of October 1849 (O.S.). And he needed an excuse, for his novel was giving him trouble again. 'The brute Chichikov', he wrote to Zhukovsky in November, 'has only got to half of his journey, perhaps because a Russian hero has to be much wilier with the Russian people than a Greek with the Greeks [a reference to Zhukovsky's completion of his translation of the *Odyssey*]. Perhaps also because the author of *Dead Souls* has to be a much better man than the brute Chichikov.' And on December the 14th he complained to Zhukovsky about his 'aversion to writing'. 'What is it?' he went on. 'Old age or a temporary paralysis of my powers? I am either asleep or else sleepily awake. The sixteen months I spent in Russia have passed away like a dream and there was not a single event which would have refreshed me and after which, as after a cold douche, I should have felt that I was working soberly and accurately. My journey to Jerusalem seems to me now the only sensible thing I did. My work proceeds sluggishly. Trying not to waste a moment, I do not leave my desk or put down my pen, but I only write a few lines a day and time flies. Or am I really old at forty? Or does it mean that my *Dead Souls* ought not to appear in these dark days when, not having had time to come to its senses, society is still in a daze and is not in a condition to read a book as it should be read, that is, the right way up? . . .'

It was obvious that the slow progress of his work would inevitably end in another nervous breakdown. Gogol did his best to avoid it by frequent visits to his Moscow friends. On the 3rd of December 1849 (O.S.), he was present at a reading by Alexander Ostrovsky of his first play, *The Bankrupt*, at Pogodin's. He thought it a good play, but criticized the young playwright for not studying more carefully the 'immutable' laws of dramatic art, by which he meant Ostrovsky's failure to keep up the suspense of his audience by preparing it beforehand for the dramatic development of the last act. In his view, Ostrovsky should have ended the fourth act of his play by the arrest of the hero, the fraudulent bankrupt, before letting him appear in the last act as a prisoner. Gogol spent most of his free time at the Aksakovs' in the company of two of his Ukrainian friends, Professor Bodyansky, who had been reinstated in his post at the university, and Professor Maximovich, who was spending the winter in Moscow. The three of them sang Ukrainian folk-songs, one of Aksakov's daughters accompanying them on the piano. 'Gogol', Vera Aksakov wrote to her brother Ivan on the 15th of February 1850 (O.S.), 'sings with such abandon and with such innate sympathy, without of course being really able to sing, that he seems at that moment to be filled with the spirit of his people and expresses it in gestures, face and voice, while Maximovich stands in front of him stamping his feet and waving his arms. At first Bodyansky nearly broke into a dance, but he recollected himself and just went on singing.'

Gogol disliked large gatherings and was at his ease only among his closest friends. But even among them his gaiety was mostly assumed. 'Sollogub's report about my good health and high spirits', he wrote to Anna Vyelgorsky on the 30th of March 1849, 'is only partly true. He saw me as a guest and you can't look bored when visiting friends. One must willy-nilly at least appear to be gay.'

In February 1850 he fell ill again. 'My work has stopped,' he wrote to Anna Vyelgorsky on February the 11th, 'my nerves have gone to pieces and everything in me has gone to pieces. And I feel so awful that I don't know what to do with myself. . . . My wingless prayer falls lifelessly from my lips. . . .' To Alexandra Smirnov he wrote on the same day: 'I am sick, exhausted in spirit, I keep asking for prayers and consolation and can't find them anywhere. . . . My illness is accompanied by such restless excitement that not for a moment do my thoughts find rest, but, poor things, scurry about more restlessly than the patient himself.' He also dashed off a short note to Nadezhda Sheremetev, asking her 'to pray for me more fervently'. On February the 17th Aksakov wrote to his son Ivan that Gogol was feeling better, but he added: 'I was frightened by the suffering in his face which showed clearly the predominating influence of body over spirit.' On February the 28th Gogol was already sufficiently recovered to write his long letter with the description of Palestine to Zhukovsky, and Alexandra Smirnov's arrival in Moscow at the beginning of March completed his recovery.

Aksakov found that Alexandra Smirnov had changed greatly in the last three and a half years. 'She is an old woman', he wrote to his son Ivan on March the 3rd. 'It's simply terrible how she has changed. It is quite impossible to describe what Gogol looks like in her presence', he went on. 'He looks like that in the happy moments of creation. As there can be no question of his being in love with her, I can only explain it to myself by supposing that there exists complete agreement between them on all religious and moral questions. . . . My conversation with Alexandra Osipovna confirmed me in my belief. . . . She told me that she loved Gogol—Gogol and not the writer. I smiled and said that I loved him, too. When I said that thank God Gogol had not lost his talent and that he seemed to look sanely upon things, Mrs. Smirnov burst out laughing and, getting excited, blurted out to me that Gogol looked upon everything in the same way as in his letters, that without them he would never have written the second part of *Dead Souls*, that he had not gone back on a single word he had written in them and that he had decided to deceive me and everyone else in that respect. How accommodating is the faith of these people!' Aksakov comments bitterly. 'With it they are ready to commit any meanness. . . . They refuse to acknowledge the sanctity of other people's convictions. Tolerance has always been the foundation of my faith. . . . I am sorry I went to see her. She told me something about the further development of *Dead Souls* and I could not help feeling that the shadow of their false convictions lay over everything. She confided to me that Gogol would never present his manuscript to the Emperor. . . . No, he wanted to correct it again and again till every stupid, captious censor would pass it without making any difficulties. I said: What a pity, what a false idea!'

His forty-first birthday, on the 19th of March 1850 (O.S.), Gogol spent at the Aksakovs' with Bodyansky and Maximovich, all of them, as usual, singing Ukrainian folk-songs. On his name-day he gave his now traditional party in Pogodin's garden. His work on *Dead Souls* was still hanging fire and he decided to go on a journey again. 'Never before', he wrote to Father Matthew at the end of April 1850, 'have I felt my helplessness and infirmity so much. There is so much I want to say, but as soon as I pick up my pen it drops out of my hands. I am waiting, as I would for manna from heaven, for inspiration from above which would set all my powers in motion. God knows, I should not like to say anything that did not serve for the glorification of His holy name. I should like to show in living examples to my brethren living in darkness and playing with life as though it were a toy, that life is not a toy. And everything, it would seem, has been thought out and is ready but', he declared mournfully, not realizing that it was the artist in him rebelling against the moralist that was the cause of his inability to write, 'my pen does not obey me. I haven't got the necessary freshness for work. And (I don't mind telling you) this is the cause of my secret suffering. It is a sort of cross. . . .'

So far, he had only written four chapters of the second part of *Dead Souls* (he read the fourth chapter to the Aksakovs at the end of May), and he decided not to carry on with the novel until he had made a journey to the Greek islands, 'not', he wrote to Sophia Sollogub on May the 29th, 'for the sake of my health, but solely to make it possible for me to finish my work'. This was his last letter to Anna Vyelgorsky's sister, for after his luckless proposal to Anna the Vyelgorsky family broke off relations with him.

¶ 10

Gogol left Moscow with Maximovich on the 13th of June 1850 (O.S.), after dinner at the Aksakovs'. He was going first to Vassilevka, where he had invited Maximovich to stay with him for a fortnight. On June the 16th, after a visit to the Malo-Yaroslavets monastery, they arrived at Kaluga and had dinner at Alexandra Smirnov's. There Gogol met Alexey Tolstoy, the poet and playwright, who found a great change in him: before, Gogol had been very talkative and humorous, whereas now he was taciturn and full of his own importance. There was, Alexey Tolstoy observed, a dogmatic tone in his speech, just as though he wished to say, 'Listen to me carefully and don't miss a single word I say.'

Gogol and Maximovich next visited the famous Optina monastery where, Gogol wrote to Alexander Tolstoy on July the 10th, 'every monk seemed to me to be talking to heaven', and spent a day at Ivan Kireyevsky's estate at Dolbino. From Dolbino Gogol sent a letter to one of the monks at the Optina monastery asking him and the other monks to pray for him. 'My way is hard,' he wrote, 'and my work is such that without God's constant help I cannot write a single word, and without inspiration from above my powers are not only insignificant, they do not even exist.' He begged the monk to show his letter to the abbot so that he, too, should pray 'that God may consider me worthy to proclaim the glory of His name, steeped in sin though I am. He is strong and merciful and He can make even me, black as coal that I am, as white as snow, and raise me to that degree of purity which a writer who dares to talk of the beautiful and the sacred must achieve.'

Instead of saying his prayers during the journey, Gogol read the Bible in modern Greek as a preparation for his proposed trip to the Greek islands. At the coach stations he bought milk, skimmed off the cream and very skilfully made it into butter with the help of a wooden spoon. He also prepared his own coffee and between the stations picked wild flowers and got Maximovich to tell him their Latin names. He arrived in Vassilevka on July the 1st and stayed there till October the 17th.

To raise money for his proposed trip to the Greek islands Gogol drafted, at Alexandra Smirnov's suggestion, three letters, to

Count Perovsky, Minister of Internal Affairs, to the heir to the throne, and to Count Olsufyev, an aide-de-camp of Alexander and a friend of Zhukovsky's, in which he asked for a grant to enable him 'to spend three months on the islands of the Mediterranean or somewhere in the East not far from Russia'. In his letter to Perovsky he stressed the importance of his work. 'If, with God's help, I succeed in accomplishing everything as my soul desires,' he wrote, 'I shall perhaps be rendering a service to my country which is no less important than the services rendered by all honourable and honest men in other professions. . . . Before,' he explained, 'when all I wanted to show was what is worthy of ridicule in a Russian, what is insignificant and trivial and what constitutes only an excrescence on his body, I could write and publish my works more quickly; but now when I want to display the strong and healthy elements of our nature in such a way that even those who refuse to recognize them should become aware of them and be ashamed to have neglected the development of the great talents granted to the Russian people, I find it impossible to hurry with my work.' In addition, Gogol mentioned that he was contemplating writing a book on geography which would exhibit 'the characteristics and qualities of the Russian people so powerfully and paint every locality so vividly' that every reader 'would know what is peculiar to each part of Russia and it would never occur to him to introduce factories that are inappropriate for her and entrust them to foreign businessmen who think only of their own profits. This book', Gogol concludes, 'has long been the object of my thoughts and is maturing together with my present work and will perhaps be published simultaneously with it.'

Gogol did not send the letters, for he decided to give up the idea of going to the Greek islands and to raise the money he was so badly in need of by publishing a second edition of his collected works, including the second part of *Dead Souls*. He spent the winter in Odessa, where he arrived on October the 24th. He stayed at the house of his relative Andrey Troshchinsky. In Odessa he again met the Repnins, at whose house he usually dined, and made many more friends, especially among the actors of the local theatre. In Odessa, too, he worked very hard on the second volume of *Dead Souls*.

'Merciful God', he wrote to Zhukovsky on December the 16th, 'preserves me still and my powers are not weakening in spite of my poor health. My work is progressing at its old steady rate, and though it isn't finished yet, it is nearing the end. What's to be done? While a man is young he is a poet, even if he is not a writer; but when he grows to maturity, he must remember that he is a man even if he is a writer. And what is man? By the love of Christ who suffered for us he has been assigned a high purpose in life—to become higher than the angels of heaven. While a writer is young, he writes a lot and rapidly. His imagination pushes him on incessantly. He creates, he builds enchanting castles in Spain, and it is no wonder that there is no end to his writing and to his castles. But when pure truth has become his subject and his business is to reflect life clearly in the highest manifestations in which it ought to be, and can be, on earth, but in which it is so far found only in a few chosen spirits—in a case like that, imagination is of little use to the writer who has to take every little detail by storm. . . .' He worked only in the mornings, he told Pletnyov on the 25th of January 1851 (O.S.), and was already in bed by eleven at night. He drank a glass of cold water before breakfast, and one at night. The evenings he usually spent at a local restaurant in the congenial company of actors. He would arrive at five o'clock, dressed in a dark-brown frock-coat, a waistcoat of a dark, patterned material, black trousers, a cravat with some fantastic pattern or a black silk scarf, a brown cloak with a velvet collar or, on cold days, a raccoon fur-coat, a top hat and black gloves. Before his meal he drank a glass of vodka and in the course of it a glass of sherry. As the actors always had champagne at dinner, he too had a glass after dinner. He then regaled them with hot punch which he prepared himself, though he drank only a little of it. He certainly enjoyed their company. He liked to talk to them, telling them amusing stories and joining in their laughter. There was no sign of his supposed self-withdrawal or pride. Only on two occasions did he show displeasure at the questions the actors put to him: once when he was asked his opinion of the modern Russian writers, which he refused to give on the ground of his scanty knowledge of contemporary literature, expressing, however, his great admiration for Turgenev, and another time when he was asked why he had published his *Selected Passages*. 'It had to be done, gentlemen', Gogol replied in a tone of voice that put an end to any further questions. He was often to be seen at the theatre and, indeed, on one occasion took an active part in the rehearsals

of Molière's *l'École des femmes*, reading the play to the company
first, and after one of the rehearsals discussing it with each actor
individually. He also read Moliere's play, as well as Zhukovsky's
translation of the *Odyssey* and Pushkin's *Boris Godunov* at the
Repnins', and his own dramatic fragment *The Servants' Hall* to
the actors.

Gogol left Odessa on March the 27th for Vassilevka, where he
spent another two months with his family, making double doors
for their house himself, drawing up a plan for a new house and
tending the oak saplings he had planted the year before. He left
Vassilevka on May the 26th. On the way to Moscow he learnt of
the engagement of his sister Yelisaveta to an army captain by the
name of Bykov, and as usual the thought of an ordinary and not a
spiritual marriage displeased him. 'You are happy,' he wrote to
Yelisaveta from Poltava at the end of May 1851, 'but when I
think how hard you will find it to be a good wife, who must be all
obedience and heavenly meekness, I cannot help trembling for
you, especially when I consider that, unlike your sisters, you
never complied with my instructions. When I remember this I
cannot help being afraid and I cannot rejoice in your happiness
which I can't believe in. Oh, may God instruct and protect you.
All I can say to you is—pray to Him.' Yelisaveta, needless to say,
never took her brother very seriously and was little impressed by
his dark forebodings and even less by his peculiar ideas of a wife's
duties.

After his arrival in Moscow on the 5th of June 1851 (O.S.),
Gogol spent a few days at the Aksakovs' estate, Abramtsevo, and
then left with Arnoldi for Alexandra Smirnov's large country
house on the banks of the river Moskva with its French gardens
and English park with grottoes, ruins and ornamental bridges.
He was given two small rooms in one of the wings of the country
house. According to Arnoldi, he was quite unusually happy and
contented. He got up at five o'clock, washed and dressed without
the help of a servant, and then went for a walk in the park with
a prayer-book in his hand. At eight o'clock he returned for coffee
and afterwards shut himself up in his room and worked for three
hours. Before dinner he went for a bathe in the river with
Arnoldi. 'Gogol', Arnoldi writes in his reminiscences, 'used to
dance about most amusingly in the water, and did all sorts of
gymnastic exercises in it which, he claimed, were good for his

health.' After another walk in the park, Gogol and Arnoldi would go in to dinner and in the evening they would sometimes drive in open carriages to visit neighbours. Towards the end of his visit, cut short by Alexandra Smirnov's illness, he began to complain of the bad state of his nerves, his weak digestion and slow pulse.

In Moscow, where Alexandra Smirnov arrived for medical treatment, Gogol visited her every evening. At the end of July he read seven chapters of *Dead Souls* to Shevyryov at the latter's country house. On his return to Moscow he dashed off a letter to Shevyryov in which he begged him not to tell anyone about them and not to mention even the names of the characters. 'Something has happened,' he wrote. 'I am very glad that nobody except you knows anything about the last two chapters.' What had happened he did not say. Perhaps he was simply overcome by sudden doubts and was contemplating revising his novel again.

On September the 13th a Petersburg friend of Gogol's sent him an extract from Herzen's article *Du développement des idées révolutionnaires en Russie*, published in Paris. In it Herzen, referring to Gogol's *Selected Passages*, wrote: '*Gogol, l'idole des lecteurs russes, tomba tout-à-coup dans le plus profond mépris pour une brochure servile. . . . On ne pardonne pas en Russie à un renégat. . . .*' To be called a renegade by a man he admired was a severe blow to Gogol. Taking advantage of Turgenev's presence in Moscow, Gogol told Shchepkin that he would like to see him. A month earlier he had had a talk with Annenkov and had asked him to defend him before his friends, whose opinions he valued. Now he was going to ask Turgenev, a close friend of Herzen's, to do the same. When Turgenev, accompanied by Shchepkin, came to see him on the 20th of October 1851 (O.S.), Gogol complained bitterly about Herzen's article and tried to prove to Turgenev that he had never changed his views. He jumped up from the sofa and rushed into the next room, returning with a volume of his *Arabesques*, and read a passage in which he advocated the strictest obedience to the authorities. 'You see,' Gogol cried excitedly, 'I thought like that before and my convictions then were the same as now. Why, then, does he accuse me of being a renegade?' If he looked for sympathy from Turgenev, he did not get it. 'Shchepkin and I', Turgenev writes, 'were silent. At length, Gogol threw down the book and began talking about art and the theatre again. . . .'

On September the 22nd Gogol left Moscow for Vassilevka to attend his sister's wedding. Yelisaveta had written to him a month earlier to suggest that he might buy her a carriage as a wedding present. This request made Gogol angry. Quite apart from the fact that it showed how little his people at home realized in what straitened circumstances he lived ('I tell you', he wrote to Yelisaveta on July the 14th, 'that if I were to die today, there wouldn't be enough money to pay for my funeral'), he was infuriated by this further example of the improvidence of the Russian landowning class. 'If', he wrote to Maria Ivanovna on September the 2nd, 'the nobility do not give up their habits and all these so-called indispensable proprieties, their lot will be a most grievous and lamentable one.' He did, however, buy a second-hand carriage for his sister's wedding present and set off in it for Vassilevka. On the way he stopped at Optina monastery where one of those trivial incidents occurred which to Gogol was full of hidden forebodings and which certainly shows that Gogol's religious obsessions at the time amounted to a neurosis and justified to some extent the rumours current in Moscow that he was not in his right mind. What happened was that Father Makary, one of the holiest of the holy monks in the monastery, had bidden Gogol good-bye and, walking up with him to the monastery gates, said: 'For the last time, good-bye!' Gogol drove off, but on the way it suddenly occurred to him that the words 'for the last time' uttered by so holy a man, must be full of some dreadfully prophetic meaning. The thought filled him with dismay. Within a short time he had worked himself up into a state of nervous hysteria. He turned back, and wrote the following desperate letter to Father Makary (on September the 25th): 'Why, when you took leave of me, did you say: for the last time? Perhaps all this merely shows that my nerves are on edge, in which case I am very much afraid that a long journey might injure my health. I am a little frightened of falling ill on the way, especially as I would be tortured by the thought of leaving Moscow where my friends would help me to get over my attack of hypochondria.' He sent off the carriage he had bought for his sister Yelisaveta and himself returned to Moscow in a state of collapse. 'I had already left Moscow,' he wrote to his mother and sisters from Moscow on October the 3rd, 'but having got as far as Kaluga, I fell ill and had to return. My nerves had reached such a state of irritation from

all sorts of worries and agitations that the open road, always beneficial to me, has now become harmful.' Vera Aksakov wrote to her
cousin Maria Kartashevsky on October the 2nd: 'Gogol, who a
week ago left for Poltava, became ill on the way and has come
back. In Moscow he met daddikins and on the same day arrived
here [at Abramtsevo]. He has grown thin and has changed so
much that it is awful to see. What a morbid spirit and at a time
when his nerves are shattered, too! A trifle upsets him and brings
on a fit of dreadful melancholy.' On October the 15th, she wrote
to her father from Moscow: 'How morbid Gogol is! Yesterday he
grew suddenly excited and changed countenance, sent out for
soda water but there was not any to be found; then he suddenly
disappeared, came back after a little time, asked us to sing some
Ukrainian songs and cheered up again. However, he says he feels
quite well. On the advice of Dr. Inozemtsev, he is now rubbing
himself down every night with spirits of hartshorn and water.
Last night, I believe, he was put out because a candlestick fell
down and the candle broke. I think he got frightened.'

It is obvious that Gogol's depression had reached the point
where any shock or mental conflict might bring about a nervous
breakdown and undermine his will to live. Such a shock was to
occur with the arrival of Father Matthew in Moscow at the end of
January 1852. Turgenev, who had seen Gogol three times in
1851, was surprised at the way he had changed. He looked hag-
gard and thin and, Turgenev writes, 'a sort of hidden pain and
anguish, a sort of melancholy restlessness hovered over his shrewd
face'. Turgenev saw him for the first time at a performance of
The Government Inspector, where he sat in a box between two full-
bosomed ladies who screened him from the curious glances of the
audience. When Turgenev and Shchepkin came to see him a few
days later he met them with a cheerful look and, shaking Turgenev's hand, said, 'We should have met a long time ago.'
Turgenev looked at him more closely. His fair hair, which fell
straight from his temples, had still preserved its youthful tint, but
had grown perceptibly thin; his sloping, smooth white forehead
seemed to emanate intelligence. His small brown eyes occasionally sparkled with gaiety, but in general they looked tired; his
long pointed nose gave his face a cunning, fox-like expression;
and his small chin disappeared almost entirely inside his wide
black velvet cravat. An unfavourable impression was also made

on Turgenev by Gogol's full, soft lips under a clipped moustache. 'In their indefinite contours—so at least it seemed to me,' Turgenev writes, 'the dark sides of his character were reflected: when he spoke they opened up unpleasantly, revealing a row of bad teeth. There was something not exactly professorial but schoolmasterly, something that reminded one of teachers in provincial schools, in the movements of his body. "What a clever, queer and sick creature you are!" I thought involuntarily, looking at him.'

Like many other people who saw Gogol during the last months of his life, Turgenev could detect nothing about him to justify the rumours that he had gone out of his mind. Gogol embarked on a long dissertation on the meaning of literature and the vocation of the writer, and Turgenev was amazed at the remarkable conciseness and precision of his speech. He made a few very subtle and true remarks about the processes of creative work, and all of it in a language that was both original and imaginative. It was only when he began to speak of the censorship that Turgenev disagreed with him violently. Gogol almost extolled the censorship as a way of developing the writer's skill in defending his work as well as developing his patience and a great many other Christian virtues. 'These involved arguments', Turgenev writes, 'clearly showed the influence of those personages of high society to whom the greater part of the *Selected Passages* was dedicated.' But Turgenev was wrong: it was entirely Gogol's own idea. In justifying the Russian autocratic régime, he had quite naturally to find an excuse also for the censorship which was part and parcel of it, and he applied to it the principles of 'serpent-like wisdom' which he had always professed.

It was at Shchepkin's suggestion that Gogol arranged a reading of *The Government Inspector* for the actors of the Maly Theatre, with whose performance of the play a few days earlier he had been highly dissatisfied. The reading took place on the 5th of November 1851 (O.S.), a little over three months before his death. Turgenev, as well as Aksakov and Shevyryov, was present at it. Not all the actors turned up. They resented the fact, Turgenev remarks, that Gogol wanted to teach them their business. 'Gogol', Turgenev writes, 'was peeved by this lame response to his invitation. . . . His face assumed a gloomy and cold expression; his eyes narrowed suspiciously. On that day, he really did look ill.' Gogol began reading the first act in his usual inimitable way, but he soon lost interest: he hurried through the remaining acts, muttering under his breath, swallowing words and leaving out whole sentences. Turgenev thought that he had been angered by the sudden appearance of a young writer who had rushed into the room and, without uttering a word, sat down in a corner. But the young writer, Grigory Danilevsky, who was leaving for Petersburg in a few days, had been invited by Gogol, who wanted him to take some money for his fund for needy students to Pletnyov. Vera Aksakov was nearer the truth when she wrote to her cousin on November the 9th that the reason why Gogol had read so badly was that he had lost interest in his play.

¶ 11

During the last months of 1851 Gogol was working hard on the final chapters of the second part of *Dead Souls*. 'I am carrying on quietly with my work', he wrote to Zhukovsky on December the 20th. 'Sometimes I do not feel well, but sometimes God's mercy makes me feel fresh and strong and then my work proceeds much better, and my work is the same except that perhaps there is less youthful self-confidence and more consciousness of the fact that without a humble prayer nothing can be done.'

Unfortunately, Gogol destroyed the second part of *Dead Souls*, and the four first chapters and the fragment of one of the last chapters that were found after his death belong to an early draft of the novel so that no final judgement of the completed second part can be based on them. Still, certain general conclusions can be drawn from them. The first is that, like his *Selected Passages*, they are devoid of humour. Secondly, their positive characters, such as the idealized landowner Kostanjoglo and the idealized tax-farmer Murazov, are not living men at all, but merely pegs on which Gogol hangs the naïve ideas on the complex problems of his time he had already expressed in his *Selected Passages*. Chichikov appears in them as a pale reflection of what he was in the first part of the novel, and the Governor-General, who forgives Chichikov as well as his corrupt officials because injustice cannot be rooted out by punishment and the only way of restoring justice in Russia is to appeal to the inbred sense of honour in every Russian heart, is so fantastic a character that he could only have been created by a man who had lost all sense of reality. Even the gormandizer Petukh, the only solid character in the second part, lacks that vitalizing humour of Gogol's which would have brought him to life. Would Gogol, in the four years that separate these fragments from the completed version of the second part (if he did complete it), have been able so to alter his characters as to make them sufficiently credible, let alone so convincing as to bring about the conversion of his readers? The only indication we have of Gogol's own views is the reply he gave to Olga Aksakov, Sergey Aksakov's wife, when, only a short time before his death, she had asked him how soon he thought his book would be ready for publication. 'Not very soon', Gogol said, according to Vera Aksakov, who recorded it at the time in her diary. 'There is a great deal lacking in it and if I had to start it now, I'd have done it quite differently.' But he had gone too far to retreat now and if in the end he did destroy the second part of *Dead Souls* it was for quite a different reason.

During the last six months of his life Gogol was also busy correcting the proofs of the second edition of his collected works to which he intended to add several new essays, including his essay known as *Meditations on the Divine Liturgy* (the title is Kulish's). Gogol probably finished the first draft of the *Divine Liturgy* before his journey to Jerusalem. During the last years of his life he worked on its final revision, which, however, he never completed. It was found among his manuscripts after his death and consists of a brief preface and introduction, the description of two masses and their symbolic meaning based on 'the explanations given by the Fathers of the Church', and a short conclusion. As in everything he wrote during the last period of his life, Gogol's ideas on the influence of the liturgy on 'those who followed it attentively and repeated every word of it' were grotesquely exaggerated. Thus, his belief in a divine sanction for serfdom leads him to express the view (in the conclusion of his essay) that the effect of the liturgy on the soul of a serf or, as he put it, 'of a man who is subject to the power of another man', would be such as to make him 'obey his master just as willingly and lovingly as he would his Redeemer'.

On the 15th of January 1852 (O.S.), that is, about six weeks before Gogol's death, Alexey Tarasenkov, chief medical consultant of a Moscow hospital, who left a detailed account of Gogol's last illness, dined with Gogol at Alexander Tolstoy's and found him 'the picture of health'. The only peculiarity he noticed about Gogol was that he felt chilly though the temperature of the room was 65° F. Gogol paced up and down the large dining-room, rubbing his hands and hardly saying a word. Before dinner he drank a glass of absinthe and had a snack, both of which he obviously enjoyed. He looked more cheerful and stopped shivering. He ate his dinner with appetite. After dinner he sat down on a sofa and looked at an English illustrated magazine, although the people in the room were discussing religious subjects. It was only when Turgenev's play *The Provincial Lady*, which had been performed in Moscow for the first time a year earlier, was mentioned that he looked up and said: 'What sort of character is that? She's simply a flirt—that's all!'

So far as an experienced doctor could judge, therefore, there was nothing the matter with Gogol. And yet only a fortnight before a trivial incident had taken place which showed how easily Gogol's nerves could be upset. On New Year's Eve, on leaving his room to go upstairs, he met Alexander Tolstoy's German doctor, who wished him a happy new year in broken Russian, adding that he wished him not only a happy but also an *eternal* year. This curiously expressed wish so disturbed Gogol that he avoided meeting the doctor afterwards. But what really upset Gogol was the death on January the 26th of Khomyakov's wife Yekaterina, a sister of the late Yazykov. During her illness Gogol visited her often and her death was a great blow to him. He saw her in her coffin and said: 'Nothing can be more solemn than death.' He comforted her husband as much as he could, but did not go to her funeral on January the 29th. 'I conducted a requiem mass for her myself,' he told Aksakov, 'and mentioned those near to my heart who had passed away earlier and I felt better. But the moment of death is terrible.'

At the end of January Father Matthew arrived in Moscow specially to see Gogol. It was this visit that brought about the crisis which ended in Gogol's death. Father Matthew arrived for a purpose and Tolstoy could scarcely have been unaware of it. In fact, it was only a few weeks earlier that the Count had been to see

Father Matthew in Rzhev. What was the purpose of his visit at a time when Gogol was completing the second part of *Dead Souls*? Could it have been to induce Gogol to destroy the impious book by which he hoped to convert his countrymen, a function strictly reserved for the Church and, especially, for fanatical zealots like Father Matthew? The destruction by Gogol of the second part of his novel, which was so eagerly awaited by everybody, would have been a double triumph for Tolstoy and Father Matthew: it would have removed the last obstacle to Gogol's eternal salvation, namely his arrogant encroachment on the divine prerogatives of the Church, and—provided Gogol could be made to proclaim his conversion to their views by so dramatic a step—would also have confounded their political enemies, who used Gogol as their catspaw but whom Gogol, with true Christian charity of which they were incapable themselves, refused to give up as beyond redemption. What could be more natural than that Tolstoy should have gone to see Father Matthew in order to concert ways and means of bringing about this double *coup*? It is certainly strange that on his return from Rzhev, Tolstoy should never have mentioned Father Matthew's impending visit to Gogol. That he did not mention it becomes clear from the letter Gogol wrote to Father Matthew on the 28th of November 1851 (O.S.). 'Count A. P. Tolstoy', he wrote, 'has given me your regards and told me of his very pleasant and devout sojourn at your place. Thank you many, many times for keeping me in mind. The very thought that you are praying for me inspires me with the hope that God will deem me worthy of working much better than hitherto, infirm, lazy and feeble that I am. Your last two letters I carry about on me continually. Every time I re-read them I discover something in them I never noticed before, and each time I thank God who helped you to write them. Don't forget me in your prayers, kind soul. You know yourself how much I need them. And may God be with you to the last day of your earthly life until you are joined with Him in eternity. Yours gratefully, Nikolai Gogol.'

But Gogol's letter would only have strengthened Father Matthew's fanatical zeal; for Gogol was actually implying that his (Father Matthew's) prayers helped him to carry on with his godless work!

Father Matthew arrived in Moscow soon after Yekaterina Khomyakov's death—a nicely calculated moment for putting pressure on Gogol. He stayed at Alexander Tolstoy's house for over a week and during that time subjected Gogol to what can be best described as a religious third-degree. What happened between them can only be surmised, but there can be no doubt at all that he threatened Gogol with hell-fire and all the horrors of a doomed soul if Gogol did not carry out his demands. At one point Gogol is reported to have cried, 'Leave me alone, I can't bear it any more, it is too terrible!' But what neither Father Matthew nor Tolstoy realized was that, as Gogol must have told them many times, without literature life lost all meaning for him. Gogol, in fact, not only refused to comply with Father Matthew's demands, he seems to have gone so far as to insult him for making them. This becomes quite clear from the letter he sent to Father Matthew the day after the priest's departure from Moscow. 'I nearly wrote to you yesterday', Gogol declares in the last letter he wrote to Father Matthew on February the 6th, 'to ask you to forgive me for having insulted you. But suddenly God's grace visited me, too, cruel-hearted that I am, and my heart yearned to thank you warmly, very warmly. But why talk about it? I was only sorry I did not exchange fur coats with you. Yours would have warmed me better. Eternally grateful to you here and beyond the grave, Yours ever, Nikolai.'

But Father Matthew's threats brought Gogol face to face with a dilemma to which he could find no solution: his confidence in God's blessing on his work was undermined and the dread of eternal damnation oppressed his spirit. After the priest's departure he withdrew within himself more and more and spent all his time in prayer. At the beginning of Lent he refused to eat anything except a few spoonfuls of cabbage soup and, when offered something else, replied that his stomach was upset and that he was suffering from the same illness as his father who had died when he was Gogol's age. He refused all medical treatment, asserting that his father had died because of it. He took Holy Communion on Thursday, February the 7th. Before receiving the Sacrament, he prostrated himself and wept for a long time. He seemed to be extremely weak and could hardly stand on his feet. In spite of that he went to see the priest again that night and asked him to hold a service of thanksgiving, reproaching himself for having forgotten to do so in the morning. He refused to eat anything that day, and when he had eaten the wafer he called himself a glutton and was greatly distressed. In the hope of resolving the conflict in his mind he decided to seek the aid of Ivan Koreysha, a lunatic who enjoyed a great reputation as a 'seer' and whose incoherent mumblings his disciples twisted into divine messages. He took a sledge and drove to the lunatic asylum where the 'prophet' was confined. There he walked up and down before the gates for a long time, then he went into a field and stood in the wind and snow unable to make up his mind, but in the end his common sense prevailed over his superstitious fears and he drove back home. He had thought of another solution. On February the 10th he played his last card: he asked Tolstoy to send his manuscripts to the Moscow Metropolitan Filaret and let him decide whether he should burn any of them or not. This appeal to an ecclesiastical authority of whom Tolstoy did not approve (to a fanatic like the Count there was only one way to salvation) must have been interpreted by him as a challenge to the authority of Father Matthew, and he refused to have anything to do with it. Gogol could not very well send the manuscripts himself, for that would certainly have been interpreted as a direct defiance of Father Matthew. He was therefore left with no choice. On the same day, he wrote his last letter to his mother in which he told her that he was unable to sit down to work and asked her to pray for him. He hesitated for two more days, then on the night of February the 12th he decided to carry out Father Matthew's ultimatum. He prayed for a long time in his bedroom and at three o'clock in the morning he called his boy-servant Semyon and asked him if it was warm in the drawing-room.

'It's rather chilly, sir,' Semyon replied.

'Give me my cloak,' said Gogol, 'and let's go. I've something important to do.'

He crossed himself and then went into the drawing-room with a lighted candle in his hand, told the boy to open the flue of the stove as quietly as possible so as not to wake anyone in the house and hand him his briefcase from the cupboard. When the boy had handed him the briefcase, he took out a bundle of sheets tied round with a ribbon, put it into the stove and lighted it with the candle. Semyon, realizing what his master was doing, fell on his knees and besought him not to burn it.

'It's none of your business', Gogol replied, muttering a prayer. Meanwhile the fire went out, leaving only the corners of the manuscript charred. Noticing it, Gogol took it out of the stove, untied the ribbon and separated the pages to make sure that they would burn more easily. He then put it back into the stove, put the candle to it again, sat down on a chair and watched the work to which he had devoted ten years of his life burn to ashes. Then, crossing himself again, he returned to his bedroom, kissed Semyon, lay down on the sofa and wept. 'Some of it', he said after a moment's reflection, 'ought to have been burnt. As for the rest, they [Tolstoy and Father Matthew?] ought to have prayed for me. But when I recover from my illness I'll put it right again.'

He then sent his servant to fetch Tolstoy. 'Look what I have done', he said to the Count. 'I wanted to burn a few things I had long ago made up my mind to burn and I've gone and burnt everything. See how cunning the devil is! That's what he made me do! And there was a lot there that would have explained many things. It was the best I've ever done. From it everyone would have understood what was still obscure in my earlier works. I intended to send it to my friends before I died to do with as they thought fit. Now everything is lost!'

'This is a good sign', Tolstoy replied smoothly. 'Before, too, you used to burn everything and afterwards you did it much better. So that', he added, for of course Gogol's death would have spoilt his plan, 'you needn't think of dying now. You can remember it all, can't you?'

'Yes,' said Gogol, putting a hand to his head, 'I can, I can: it's all in my head.'

After that, he seemed to grow calmer and stopped weeping.

From that night on he grew steadily weaker. He shut himself up in his room, refusing to see anyone, and sat all day in his dressing-gown in an armchair, his feet resting on a stool. He did not speak to anyone and replied in monosyllables to the questions put to him. His replies, however, showed that he was in full possession of his faculties. To Khomyakov, who tried to cheer him up, he said: 'A man has to die and I'm going to die. I'm ready.' When, wishing to distract him, Tolstoy tried to talk to him about things in which he had shown an interest before, such as the finding of his mother's icon which had been mislaid, he replied with amazement: 'What are you saying? How can you talk to me of such things when I am preparing myself for such a fearful moment?'

It was during this time (between February the 13th and 18th) that Gogol made two wills, one addressed to his friends and another to his family. To his friends he wrote:

'Thank you very much, my friends. You have brought light into my life. I consider it my duty to say a few words of farewell to you. Do not be disturbed by any events that may take place around you. Let everyone of you carry on with his work, praying in solitude. Society will only improve when every individual man looks after his own affairs and lives like a Christian, serving God with the tools granted to him, and trying to exert a good influence on the small circle of people around him. Everything will adjust itself then, the right relations between people will be established by themselves . . . and mankind will march forward.'

The will addressed to his mother and sisters began: 'In the name of the Father, the Son and the Holy Ghost. I bequeath all the property I possess to my mother and sisters. I ask them to live in amity together in their village and remember that by devoting themselves to their peasants and to all people they are carrying out the words of their Saviour: Feed my sheep. . . . ' He further gave instructions to set free his old servant Yakim Nimchenko and his boy-servant Semyon 'after he has served Count Tolstoy for ten years'. He also repeated his request to his mother and sisters to re-read the letters he had written to them during the last three years because they would understand many things better after his death. In a codicil to his will, addressed to his sisters, he expressed the wish that they should convert their house into a convent and become nuns themselves. He hoped that one of them might even become an abbess. He finally asked them to devote half the income from his books to the building of a church. 'I should like', he concluded, 'to be buried, if not in the church, then in its precincts, and that requiems should be continually sung for me.'

He was now determined to die and refused all food and medical treatment. Tarasenkov, whom Tolstoy hurriedly summoned, visited him on February the 16th and was appalled to see a man whose wasted body he hardly recognized as belonging to the man who only a month before had looked 'the picture of health'. Gogol's face had lost all expression, his eyes looked dull and sunken, his cheeks were hollow, his voice was weak and he could move his tongue only with difficulty. He sat motionless in an armchair with his feet stretched out and stared vacantly before him, his head resting on the back of the armchair. When Tarasenkov went up to him, he raised his head a little, but could not hold it up for long. He let the doctor feel his pulse and examine his tongue. His pulse was weak, his tongue clear but dry, and his skin still preserved its natural warmth. He was not feverish and his refusal of food could not, Tarasenkov thought, be ascribed to loss of appetite. To reassure him, Tarasenkov pretended that his illness was not unusual and that it could be cured quickly with the aid of medicines. He insisted that if Gogol could not take solid foods, he should at least take more nourishing fluids such as milk, clear soup, etc. ' I've swallowed a pill as a last resort', Gogol said, 'but it had no effect. I suppose I ought to have taken a drink to wash it down.' Tarasenkov tried to explain to him that he needed fluids to keep his tongue and stomach moist and that they had to be nourishing to keep up his strength. But Gogol again dropped his head on his chest and the doctor left his room. He returned after a short while, however, and tried to impress Gogol by his sincerity. He spoke to him at length in an effort to convince him that patients had to carry out their doctors' orders, for if they did not they were committing a crime against themselves. But Gogol's face was as expressionless as before. He looked, Tarasenkov thought, like a man who had made up his mind once and for all and for whom all problems had been solved and all words were in vain. When the doctor stopped talking, Gogol said in a dull, lifeless voice, which, however, was full of determination: 'I know doctors are kind: they always wish one well.' Then he again dropped his head, but whether from weakness or as a sign of farewell Tarasenkov could not tell. As Gogol was being attended by his old friend Dr. Inozemtsev, medical etiquette prevented Tarasenkov from interfering with his colleague's treatment.

Meanwhile Gogol's strength was ebbing away, and though he was convinced that if he lay down in bed he would not rise from it again, he went to bed on Monday, February the 18th, and on the same day summoned a priest to administer extreme unction to him. On the same night he awoke suddenly and sent for the priest whom he told that he was not satisfied with his communion and wished to partake of the Sacrament again because he had dreamt that he was dead and heard 'voices' and already considered himself a dead man. The priest did his best to reassure him and tried to persuade him to take some light food which Gogol at first accepted but then refused again. Inozemtsev could do nothing with him. Gogol refused all medicines with the words, 'If God wishes me to live, I shall live.' Like his mother, he was now putting all the blame on God, and the 'voices' he heard were merely an expression of his subconscious desire for divine sanction for what was, in fact, his determination to commit suicide. On the same day he scribbled the following last words on a small piece of paper: 'Except ye become as little children ye shall not enter into the kingdom of heaven. Have mercy upon me, O Lord, sinner that I am! Forgive me, O Lord! Bind Satan again, I beseech thee, with the mysterious power of thy Cross! What am I to do to remember in my heart gratefully and for ever the lesson I have learnt? And terrible is the story of all the events in the Gospels!'

On the morning of Monday, February the 18th, Tarasenkov came to see Gogol again. He found his drawing-room filled with his friends, who stood about looking grief-stricken. Tarasenkov went into the bedroom and saw Gogol lying on a sofa in his dressing-gown and boots, with his face to the wall. In front of him hung an icon of the Virgin and in his hands he clasped a rosary. Tarasenkov took his hand to feel his pulse. 'Don't touch me!' Gogol murmured. But after a while he fell asleep and Tarasenkov felt his pulse: it was weak and rapid, his head and hands were cold, but his breathing was even and regular.

During the whole of Tuesday Gogol remained like that without talking or paying any attention to anyone. He seemed to be asleep most of the time, but occasionally he would wake up and ask for a glass of wine and water, each time holding up the glass to the light to make sure he had been given what he had asked for. In the evening they diluted his wine with soup. He was plainly losing his sense of taste, for all he remarked to his servant was, 'Why is it so muddy?' After that he was given only soup when he asked for a drink. At three o'clock on Wednesday, February the 20th, there was a consultation in Gogol's bedroom. His condition was unchanged, but his pulse was getting weaker. The doctors decided to use force. In spite of his protests, they subjected him to a thorough examination. When they pressed on his stomach, which had become so soft that they could feel his backbone, he began to scream, and he went on screaming during the whole of the examination. He refused to reply to their questions, only occasionally saying no without opening his eyes. At last he cried in despair: 'Leave me alone, for God's sake!' They decided to give him a hot bath and bleed him. When Tarasenkov, who had left not wishing to witness the patient's agonies, returned at six o'clock, Gogol had already been given his bath, seven big leeches hung from his nostrils and a cold compress was on his forehead. When he was being undressed and put in the bath he screamed that what they were doing was of no use, and when they put him back naked in bed he kept asking them to cover his back and shoulders. When they were applying the leeches, he kept repeating, 'Don't!' and after they had been applied, he kept saying, 'Take off the leeches! Take them away from my mouth!' But the doctors paid no attention to him and kept them on for a long time, pinning down his hands to prevent him from touching them. At seven o'clock more doctors arrived, ordered the application of more leeches as well as of mustard plasters to his legs and ice on his head, and forced him to swallow some medicine. They treated him like a lunatic, shouting at the top of their voices as if he were already dead. One of them kept turning him over and pouring some spirits on his head. 'Where are you in pain, Nikolai Vassilye-vich?' he kept asking. 'Tell me!' But Gogol only moaned and made no reply.

They left him in peace at last and went away. Tarasenkov stayed in Gogol's bedroom till midnight. Gogol's pulse was grow-ing steadily weaker and his breathing was becoming more and more laboured. Soon he stopped turning over and lay quietly on one side, but every time they removed or applied the mustard plasters, he cried out and moaned. Occasionally he said distinctly, 'Give me a drink!' but took no notice of what he was given. Later in the evening he was beginning to lose consciousness. Once he said, 'Give me the cask!' when he wanted to drink. He was given a glass of clear soup, but he was too weak to raise his head and had to be supported before he could drink it. Later he began mutter-ing something incoherently and repeated a few times, 'Give me! Give me! Come on, give me!' At eleven o'clock he cried in a loud voice: 'Quick, the ladder!' He tried to raise himself, but he had grown so weak that he could not hold up his head, which kept dropping like a newborn baby's. They tied a blister round his neck and put a nightshirt on him. He kept his eyes closed all the time, moaning incessantly. When they were putting him back in bed, he fainted. His pulse stopped beating, his breathing became stertorous, he opened his eyes, but they were lifeless. The fainting fit lasted a few minutes, and after it he no longer asked for a drink or turned over. He lay on his back with closed eyes, without uttering a sound. At twelve o'clock his feet began to grow cold. Tarasenkov placed a jug of hot water beside them and kept making him swallow some soup, which seemed to revive him. But his breathing soon became heavy and stertorous, his face grew thin, dark patches appeared under his eyes and his skin grew cold and clammy. Tarasenkov left hurriedly before his doctor arrived, not wishing, he writes, 'to have anything to do with the doctor-executioner who was convinced that he was saving a man's life'. The doctor, a professor of medicine at Moscow University, spent several hours at Gogol's bedside that night, giving him calomel and putting hot loaves of bread round his body, Gogol uttering piercing cries all the time. He died at eight o'clock in the morning on Thursday, February the 21st (O.S.), a month before his forty-third birthday.

Gogol's body was taken to the university chapel (he had been elected a Fellow of Moscow University in 1845), where he lay in state with a laurel wreath round his head and a bunch of immortelles in his hands. All night crowds passed through the church to pay their last respects to one of Russia's greatest writers. Tolstoy at first refused to have Gogol taken to the chapel of Moscow University, the majority of whose professors were 'liberals', and when his body was taken there he refused to pay the funeral expenses. Gogol was therefore buried at the university's expense. He had left nothing except his old clothes, including his blue dress-coat with gold buttons, six pairs of cotton and woollen socks, three handkerchiefs and five pairs of boots. His library consisted of two hundred and thirty-four books, eighty-four of which were translations, including works by Shakespeare, Byron, Fielding, Richardson and Walter Scott. The whole of Moscow turned out for his funeral on February the 25th. (After the service in the chapel there was a stampede of people trying to snatch a spray of immortelles from Gogol's hands.) His coffin was carried to the cemetery of the Danilov monastery by students of Moscow University. He was buried beside Yazykov.

The impression created by Gogol's death was so great throughout Russia that the Government immediately prohibited any mention of his name in the newspapers; Turgenev, who had managed to publish a short obituary notice of him in a Moscow newspaper, in which he spoke of Gogol as 'a great man', was arrested and exiled to his estate of Spasskoye. But Gogol's work was done and it was too late to do anything about it. Gogol himself could do nothing to counter the tremendous influence of his great works, however much he tried to delude himself into believing that the last two parts of *Dead Souls* would solve 'the riddle of his existence' by surpassing, in their moral influence, anything yet written. It was not his lack of education, as most of his 'educated' biographers maintain, that gave rise to this belief; it arose from his feeling of being 'different' and his conviction that, to quote a recurrent phrase in his correspondence, 'it was not for nothing' that that was so, that there was a divine purpose behind it; this conviction was mainly responsible for the idea, already vaguely present in his mind in his last years at school, that it was his transcendental mission to save Russia, an idea that was completely divorced from reality but that obsessed him to the exclusion of everything else—and that was the tragedy of his life.

BIBLIOGRAPHY

BIOGRAPHIES AND BIOGRAPHICAL STUDIES

ANNENSKAYA, A. N. *N. V. Gogol: Yevo zhizn' i literaturnaya deyatel'nost'* (N. V. Gogol: his Life and Literary Activity). Petersburg, 1891.

AVENTINO (pseud.). *Po sledam Gogolya v Rime* (On the Track of Gogol in Rome). Moscow, 1902.

GIPPIUS, V. V. *Gogol: materialy i issledovaniya* (Gogol: Materials and Studies). Moscow-Leningrad, 1936.

KULISH, P. A. *Neskol'ko chert dlya biografii N. V. Gogolya* (A Few Facts for a Biography of Gogol). Petersburg, 1852.

KULISH, P. A. *Opyt biografii Gogolya* (An Attempt at a Biography of Gogol). Petersburg, 1854.

KULISH, P. A. *Zapiski o zhizni N. V. Gogolya, sostavlenniye iz vospominanii yevo druzey i znakomykh i iz yevo sobstvennykh pisem* (Notes on Gogol's Life, compiled from the Reminiscences of his Friends and Acquaintances and from his own Letters). Petersburg, 1856.

LAVRIN, J. *Gogol.* London, Routledge & Sons, 1926.

MASHINSKY, S. *Gogol.* Moscow, 1951.

MASHINSKY, S. *Gogol i dyelo o vol'nodumstve: Literaturnoye nasledstvo* (Gogol and the Inquiry into Freethinking: Literary Heritage). Moscow, 1952.

MOSHIN, A. *Yasnaya Polyana i Vassilevka* (Yasnaya Polyana and Vassilevka). Petersburg, 1904.

SCHLOEZER, B. DE. *Gogol.* Paris, 1932.

SHENROK, V. *Materialy dlya biografii Gogolya* (Materials for a Biography of Gogol). Moscow, 1892–5–8.

SHENROK, V. *Uchenicheskiye gody Gogolya* (Gogol's School Years). Moscow, 1887–9.

SHIK, A. *Gogol v Nitse* (Gogol in Nice). Paris, 1946.

VLADIMIROV, P. V. *Iz uchenicheskikh lyet Gogolya* (From Gogol's School Years). Vladimir, 1890.

VODOVOZOV, N. V. *N. V. Gogol.* Moscow, 1945.

CRITICISMS AND STUDIES

BELINSKY, V. G. *Sochineniya* (Works). Moscow, 1948.

BELIY, A. *Masterstvo Gogolya: Issledovaniya* (The Workmanship of Gogol: A Study). Moscow, 1894.

BEREZINA, V. G. *Noviye danniye o stat'ye Gogolya 'O dvizhenii zhurnal'noy literatury v 1834 i 1835 godu'* (New Facts about Gogol's Article 'On the Activities of the Literary Journals in 1834 and 1835'). Leningrad University Press, 1954.

BOGOSLOVSKY, N. *N. V. Gogol o literature: izbranniye pis'ma i stat'i* (N. V. Gogol on Literature: Selected Articles and Letters). Moscow, 1952.

BRAZOL, B. L. *The Mighty Three: Pushkin—Gogol—Dostoievsky. A Critical Trilogy.* New York, 1934.

CHERNYSHEVSKY, N. G. *Polnoye Sobraniye Sochineniy* (Collected Works). Moscow, 1947.

CHUKOVSKY, K. *Gogol i Nekrasov* (Gogol and Nekrasov). Moscow, 1952.

FRIEDLAENDER, G. M. *Iz istorii rannevo tvorchestva Gogolya* (From the History of Gogol's Early Work). Leningrad University Press, 1954.

GIPPIUS, V. V. *Gogol.* Leningrad, 1924.

KASATKIN, A. A. *Gogol i prostiye lyudi Italii* (Gogol and the Common People of Italy). Leningrad University Press, 1954.

KHRAPCHENKO, M. B. *Tvorchestvo Gogolya* (Gogol's Creative Work). Moscow, 1954.

KOTLYAREVKSY, N. A. *N. V. Gogol, 1829–1842: ocherk iz istorii russkoy povesti i dramy* (N. V. Gogol, 1829–1842: A Sketch from the History of Russian Short Novel and Drama). Petersburg, 1903.

LAPITSKY, I. P. *Mysli Gogolya pri chtenii 'Povesti vremennykh lyet'* (Gogol's Thoughts on reading the Russian Chronicles). Leningrad University Press, 1954.

LAVRIN, J. *Nikolai Gogol (1809–1852): A Centenary Survey.* London, Sylvan Press, 1951.

LEGER, LOUIS. *Nicolas Gogol.* Paris, 1914.

MANDELSTAM, I. E. *O kharaktere Gogolevskovo stilya* (On the Character of Gogol's Style). Helsingfors, 1902.

MASHINSKY, S. *Gogol i revolyutsionniye demokraty* (Gogol and the Revolutionary Democrats). Moscow, 1953.

MEREZHKOVSKY, D. S. *Gogol i chort: issledovaniya* (Gogol and the Devil: A Study). Moscow, 1906.

MEREZHKOVSKY, D. S. *Lermontov—Gogol*. Petersburg, 1911.

MOCHULSKY, K. V. *Dukhovny put' Gogolya* (Gogol's Spiritual Path). Paris, 1934.

NABOKOV, V. V. *Nikolai Gogol*. New Direction Books, Norfolk, Conn., 1944; Editions Poetry, London, 1947.

OVSYANIKO-KULIKOVSKY, D. N. *N. V. Gogol*. Moscow, 1902.

POSPELOV, G. N. *Tvotchestvo N. V. Gogolya* (The Creative Work of N. V. Gogol). Moscow, 1953.

PREDTECHENSKY, A. V. *Proizvedeniya Gogolya kak istoricheski istochnik* (The Works of Gogol as an Historical Source). Leningrad University Press, 1954.

PRIIMA, F. Y. '*Slovo o polku Igoreve*' *v tvorchestve Gogolya* ('The Tale of the Host of Igor' in Gogol's Work). Leningrad University Press, 1954.

PUSHKIN, A. S. '*Vechera na khutore bliz Dikanki*', *izdatel'stvo vtoroye: Gogol v vospominaniyakh sovremennikov* (Review of 'Evenings on a Farm near Dikanka': Second Edition: Gogol in the Reminiscences of his Contemporaries). Moscow, 1952.

ROZANOV, V. *Legenda o velikom inkvizitore F. M. Dostoyevskovo: opyt kriticheskovo kommentariya: nyeskol'ko slov o Gogole* (Dostoevsky's Legend of the Grand Inquisitor: A Critical Essay: A Few Words on Gogol). Petersburg, 1894.

SAINTE-BEUVE, C. A. DE. *Nouvelles russes, par M. Nicolas Gogol, Traduction française publiée par M. Louis Viardot: Revue des deux mondes*. Paris, December, 1845.

SHEDOVA, N. Y. *Printsipy istoricheskoy stilisatsii v yazyke povesti N. V. Gogolya 'Taras Bul'ba: Materialy i issledovaniya po istorii russkovo literatunovo yazyka. Tom III.* (The Principles of Historical Stylization in the language of N. V. Gogol's Short Novel 'Taras Bulba': Materials and Studies in the History of the Russian Language. Vol. III). Moscow, 1953.

SMIRNOVA-CHILINA, E. S. *Poema N. V. Gogolya 'Myortviye dushi*' (N. V. Gogol's Poem 'Dead Souls'). Moscow, 1952.

SOROKIN, U. S. *Slovarny sostav 'Myortvykh dush' Gogolya* (The Vocabulary of Gogol's 'Dead Souls'). Leningrad University Press, 1954.

STEPANOV, A. N. *Gogol—publitsist* (Gogol the publicist). Leningrad University Press, 1954.

STEPANOV, N. L. *Velikiy russkiy pisatel' N. V. Gogol* (Great Russian Writer—N. V. Gogol). Moscow, 1952.

STEPANOV, N. L. *N. V. Gogol: Tvorcheski put'* (N. V. Gogol: The Creative Road). Moscow, 1955.

THIERS, FRANK. *Gogol und seine Buehnenwerke.* Berlin, 1922.

TRETYAKOVA, N. P. *Rabota Gogolya nad yazykomi stilem ' Tarasa Bul'by: Materialy i issledovaniya po istorii russkovo literaturnovo yazyka, Tom III* (Gogol's Work on the language and style of 'Taras Bulba': Materials and Studies of the Russian Literary Language, Vol. III). Moscow, 1953.

TYRNEVA, RAINA. *Nicolas Gogol—Ecrivain et moraliste.* Aix, 1901.

VERESAYEV, V. V. *Kak rabotal Gogol* (How Gogol Worked). Moscow, 1934.

VINOGRADOV, V. V. *Etyudy o stile Gogolya* (Studies on Gogol's Style). Leningrad, 1926.

VINOGRADOV, V. V. *Evolyutsiya russkovo natualizma: Gogol i Dostoyevsky* (The Evolution of Russian Naturalism: Gogol and Dostoevsky). Leningrad, 1929.

VINOGRADOV, V. V. *Yazyk Gogolya i yevo znacheniye v istorii russkovo yazyka: Materialy i issledovaniya po istorii russkovo literaturnovo yazyka* (Gogol's Language and its Significance in the History of the Russian Language: Materials and Studies on the History of the Russian Literary Language). Moscow, 1953.

YERMAKOV, I. D. *Ocherki po analizu tvorchestva N. V. Gogolya* (Sketches on the Analysis of Gogol's Creative Work). Moscow-Petrograd, 1923.

YERMILOV, V. *N. V. Gogol.* Moscow, 1952.

ZAPADOV, A. V. *Gogol o Derzhavine* (Gogol on Derzhavin). Leningrad University Press, 1954.

LETTERS

GIPPIUS, V. V. *Neizdanniye pis'ma: Gogol: Materialy i issledovaniya* (Unpublished Letters: Gogol: Materials and Researches). Moscow-Leningrad, 1936.

Gogol' v neizdannoy perepiske sovremennikov (1833–1853), Literaturnoye nasledstvo (Gogol in the Unpublished Correspondence of his Contemporaries, 1833–1853, Literary Heritage). Moscow, 1952.

BIBLIOGRAPHY

Neizdanniye pis'ma k Gogolyu: Literaturnoye nasledstvo (Unpublished Letters to Gogol: Literary Heritage). Moscow, 1952.

Pis'ma: Gogol: polnoye sobraniye sochinenii (Letters: Gogol: Complete Works). Vols. X to XIV. Moscow, 1952.

PUSHKIN, A. S. *Pis'mo k izdatelyu 'Literaturnykh pribavlyeniy' k 'Russkomu invalidu': Gogol' v vospominaniyakh sovremennikov* (Letter to the Editor of the 'Literary Supplement' to the 'Russian Pensioner': Gogol in the Reminiscences of his Contemporaries). Moscow, 1952.

SHENROK, V. I. *Pis'ma N. V. Gogolya* (Letters of N. V. Gogol). 4 Vols. Petersburg, 1902.

TURGENEV, I. *Pis'ma* (Letters). Moscow, 1949.

MISCELLANEOUS

BERKOV, V. *Gogol o muzyke* (Gogol on Music). Moscow, 1952.

DANILOV, S. S. *Ocherki po istorii russkovo dramaticheskovo teatra* (Sketches on the History of the Russian Dramatic Theatre). Moscow-Leningrad, 1938.

GEORGIEVSKY, G. P. *Rukopisi Gogolya. Katalog.* (Gogol's Manuscripts. Catalogue). Moscow, 1940.

GOZENPUD, A. *Gogol v muzyke: Literaturnoye nasledstvo* (Gogol in Music: Literary Heritage). Moscow, 1952.

HERZEN, A. I. *Dnevniki, memuary i stat'i.* (Diaries, Memoirs and Articles). Moscow, 1952.

POGODIN, M. P. *God v chuzhom krayu: dorozhny dnevnik* (A Year Abroad: A Travel Diary). Moscow, 1844.

STASOV, V. V. *Gogol v vospriyanii russkoy molodyozhi* (The Reaction of Russian Youth to Gogol). Moscow, 1952.

VARNEKE, B. V. *Gogol i teatr* (Gogol and the Theatre). Warsaw, 1909.

YAZYKOV, N. M. *Stikhotvoreniya* (Poems). Petersburg, 1858.

REMINISCENCES

AKSAKOV, S. T. *Istoriya moyevo znakomstva s Gogolem: Sochineniya S. T. Aksakova* (History of My Acquaintance with Gogol: S. T. Aksakov's Works). Moscow, 1890.

AKSAKOV, VERA. *Posledniye dni Gogolya* (Gogol's Last Days). Moscow, 1908.

ANNENKOV, P. V. *Literaturiye vospominaniya i perepiska, 1835–1885* (Literary Reminiscences and Letters, 1835–1885). Petersburg, 1892

ARNOLDI, L. I. *Moyo znakomstvo s Gogolem* (My Acquaintance with Gogol). Moscow, 1952.

BERG, N. V. *Vospominaniya o N. V. Gogolye* (Reminiscences of Gogol). Moscow, 1952.

BODYANSKY, O. M. *Dnevniki* (Diaries). Moscow, 1952.

BUSLAYEV, F. I. *Iz moyikh vospominanii* (From My Reminiscences). Moscow, 1952.

CHIZHOV, F. V. *Vstrechi s Gogolem* (Meetings with Gogol). Moscow, 1952.

DANILEVSKY, G. P. *Znakomstvo s Gogolem* (My Acquaintance with Gogol). Moscow, 1952.

GALAKHOV, A. D. *Iz Sorokovykh Godov* (From the 'Forties). Moscow, 1952.

GOLOVNYA, O. V. (*née* Gogol). *Iz semeynoy khroniki* (From My Family's History). Kiev, 1909.

GORLENKO, V. P. *Rasskaz Yakima Nimchenko o Gogolye* (Yakim Nimchenko's Account of Gogol). Moscow, 1952.

GROT, Y. K. *Vospominaniye o Goglye* (Memories of Gogol). Moscow, 1952.

IVANITSKY, N. I. *Gogol—adyunkt-professor* (Gogol as Assistant Professor). Moscow, 1952.

IORDAN, F. I. *Zapiski* (Diaries). Moscow, 1952.

LONGINOV, M. N. *Vospominaniye o Gogolye* (Reminiscences of Gogol). Moscow, 1952.

MOSHIN, A. *Vospominaniya o N. V. Gogolye yevo rodnoy sestry* (Reminiscences of Gogol by his Sister). Petersburg, 1909.

MUNDT, N. P. *Popytka Gogolya* (Gogol's Theatrical Venture). Moscow, 1952.

NIKITENKO, A. V. *Zapiski i dnevniki* (Notes and Diaries). Petersburg, 1905.

OBOLENSKY, D. A. *O pervom izdanii posmertnykh sochinenii Gogolya* (On the First Posthumous Edition of Gogol's Works). Moscow, 1952.

PANAYEV, I. I. *Literaturniye vospominaniya* (Literary Reminiscences). Leningrad, 1928.

PASHCHENKO, T. G. *Cherty iz zhizni Gogolya* (Facts from the Life of Gogol). Moscow, 1952.

POGODIN, D. M. *Prebyvaniye N. V. Gogolya v dome moyevo otsa* (Gogol's Sojourn in my Father's House). Moscow, 1952.

SHCHEPKIN, A. M. *Iz Rasskazov M. S. Shchepkina* (From the Stories of M. S. Shchepkin). Moscow, 1952.

SHCHEPKIN, M. A. *Vospominaniya o M. S. Shchepkine* (Reminiscences about M. S. Shchepkin). Moscow, 1952.

SMIRNOV, A. O. *Zapiski, dnevnik, vospominaniya, pis'ma* (Notes, Diary, Reminiscences, Letters). Moscow, 1929.

SMIRNOV, A. O. *Avtobiografiya (neizdanniye materialy)* (Autobiography—Unpublished Materials). Moscow, 1931.

SMIRNOV, A. O. *Vospominaniya o Gogolye* (Reminiscences of Gogol). Moscow, 1952.

SOLLOGUB, V. A. *Vospominaniya* (Reminiscences). Petersburg, 1887.

STOROZHENKO, A. P. *Vospominaniya* (Reminiscences). Moscow, 1952.

TARASENKOV, A. T. *Posledniye dni zhizni Gogolya* (The Last Days of Gogol's Life). Moscow, 1902.

TOLCHONOV, A. P. *Gogol v Odesse* (Gogol in Odessa). Odessa, 1902.

TURGENEV, I. S. *Gogol: Sochineniya* (Gogol: Works). Moscow, 1949.

WORKS

GOGOL, N. V. *Polnoye sobraniye sochinenii, desyatoye izdaniye, Red. N. S. Tikhonravov* (Complete Edition of Gogol's Works, Tenth Edition, Ed. N. S. Tikhonravov). Petersburg, 1889–96.

GOGOL, N. V. *Polnoye sobraniye sochinenii, Tom I–IX, Akademiya Nauk S.S.S.R.* (The Complete Works of Gogol, Vols. I–IX, U.S.S.R. Academy of Sciences). Moscow, 1952.

GOGOL, N. V. *Sobraniye sochinenii v shesti tomakh* (Collected Works in Six Volumes). Moscow, 1953.

INDEX